Global Nollywood

AFRICAN EXPRESSIVE CULTURES

Patrick McNaughton, editor

Global Nollywood

The Transnational Dimensions of an African Video Film Industry

EDITED BY **Matthias Krings**
AND **Onookome Okome**

INDIANA UNIVERSITY PRESS   *Bloomington & Indianapolis*

This book is a publication of

INDIANA UNIVERSITY PRESS
Office of Scholarly Publishing
Herman B Wells Library 350
1320 East 10th Street
Bloomington, Indiana 47405 USA

iupress.indiana.edu

Telephone orders 800-842-6796
Fax orders 812-855-7931

*Manufactured in the
United States of America*

*Library of Congress
Cataloging-in-Publication Data*

Global Nollywood : the transnational
dimensions of an African video film
industry / edited by Matthias Krings and
Onookome Okome.
    pages cm – (African expressive
cultures)
    Includes bibliographical references and
index.
    ISBN 978-0-253-00923-4 (cloth : alk.
paper) – ISBN 978-0-253-00935-7 (pbk.
: alk. paper) – ISBN 978-0-253-00942-5
(electronic book) 1. Motion picture
industry – Nigeria. 2. Video recordings
industry – Nigeria. I. Krings, Matthias,
[date], editor of compilation. II. Okome,
Onookome, editor of compilation.

    PN1993.5.N55G58 2013
    791.4309669 – dc23
2012051539

1 2 3 4 5   18 17 16 15 14 13

Contents

Preface and Acknowledgments

THE ORIGINAL INSPIRATION FOR THIS BOOK GOES BACK TO
the "African Film" conference that took place at the University of Illinois, Urbana-Champaign, in 2007. The conveners of this remarkable
conference, Mahir Şaul and Ralph A. Austen, had brought together not
only film scholars and social scientists but also – for the first time in such
scholarly meetings – researchers, critics, and even practitioners of the
two dominant and very different filmmaking practices of the African
continent: the Nollywood video film and art house cinema (of largely
Francophone provenance). Both of us took part in this conference and
also contributed to the collection of published essays titled *Viewing African Cinema in the Twenty-First Century* that came out of it. Inspired by
the success of this transdisciplinary approach, we convened our own
conference in May 2009 at the Johannes Gutenberg University in Mainz,
Germany. Focusing on the engagement of the Nigerian video film industry with the world beyond Nigeria, the "Nollywood and Beyond" conference expanded on yet another aspect – the de facto "pan-Africanism"
of Nigerian video film (to quote John McCall) and the emergence of its
audiences beyond the borders of Nigeria.

Encouraged by Indiana University Press to edit a collection of essays that focuses entirely on the diasporic dimension of Nollywood, we
decided to call in four additional contributors whose research proved
highly relevant to our topic. Thus, Jane Bryce, Alessandro Jedlowski, Sophie Samyn, and Giovanna Santanera provide us with fascinating chapters on the spread of Nollywood in Europe and the Caribbean. We are
also extremely happy that three brilliant essays, which were presented
at the "Nollywood and Beyond" conference by Lindsey Green-Simms,

John C. McCall, and Carmen McCain, and whose topics lay beyond the scope of the present volume, were published in 2012 in a special edition of the *Journal of African Cinemas,* edited by Jonathan Haynes.

For the generous financial support of our conference and the present book of essays, we express our gratitude to Johannes Gutenberg University in Mainz, especially the Research Center of Social and Cultural Studies at Mainz (SoCuM), the Center for Intercultural Studies (ZIS), the Department of Anthropology and African Studies, and the Friends of the University. We also owe thanks to the student assistants who helped organize the conference, namely, Andres Carvajal, Annalena Fetzner, Sandra Groß, Juliane Hebig, Janika Herz, Andrea Noll, and Elke Rössler.

We express our intellectual gratitude to those conference participants who are not represented in this volume, including Adedayo L. Abah, Gbemisola Adeoti, Maureen N. Eke, Till Förster, Lindsey Green-Simms, Biodun Jeyifo, Daniel Künzler, Brian Larkin, Carmen McCain, John C. McCall, Birgit Meyer, Sarah Nsigaye, Kayode Omoniyi Ogunfolabi, Kaia N. Shivers, Francoise Ugochukwu, and N. Frank Ukadike. Saartje Geerts screened her film *Nollywood Abroad,* a documentary about Nollywood-style filmmaking by Nigerian immigrants in Belgium. Discussions at the conference were also enriched by the presence of a delegation of the Nigerian Film Corporation, headed by its managing director, Afolabi S. K. Adesanya, and the president of the Directors Guild of Nigeria, Bond E. Emeruwa. We thank them both. We also extend our profuse thanks and gratitude to Dee Mortensen and Sarah Jacobi of Indiana University Press, who provided wonderful editorial support at the initial stages of this project, as did Pauline Bugler, Marie Brüggemann, and Annette Wenda during the final stages of our project.

Global Nollywood

Nollywood and Its Diaspora:
An Introduction

MATTHIAS KRINGS AND ONOOKOME OKOME

NOLLYWOOD, THE NIGERIAN VIDEO FILM INDUSTRY, HAS BECOME the most visible form of cultural machine on the African continent. It emerged before our very eyes, in our time. Beginning life in an uncharacteristic manner in Nigeria about twenty years ago, Nollywood has become a truly pan-African affair, as the essays in this volume show. Shot on video, edited on personal computers, and copied onto cassettes and discs, Nigerian video films travel the length and breadth of the continent connecting Africa, particularly Nigeria, to its diverse and far-flung diasporas elsewhere. Satellite television, the Internet, and piracy – at once Nollywood's boon and bane – facilitate the spread of its films across linguistic, cultural, and national boundaries. At the level of the individual spectator, Nollywood stirs the imagination, provoking its viewers to compare their own daily lives with what is presented on-screen as they explore the similarities and differences between the pro-filmic and the filmic world. The continent-wide influence of Nollywood, however, does not stop at this level. In Tanzania, Kenya, Uganda, and South Africa, for example, Nollywood has served as a model of film production and inspired the growth of local film industries, which in the case of Tanzania have already begun capturing a regional market. In these countries and elsewhere, Nigerian video films are appropriated and reworked into local forms of filmmaking and other cultural models of narrativization with local inflections that borrow and copy heavily from Nollywood. This diasporic influence of Nollywood – its spread across the continent and the fostering of localized versions of this mode of filmmaking – constitutes two dimensions of Nollywood's transnationality, which we focus on in this book. Our allusion to the concept of diaspora, which we find compelling in addressing the transnational in Nollywood, covers equally the use Nigerian and other African immigrants in Europe and the United States make of Nollywood – both as consumers of Nigerian video films and as producers of Nollywood-style films.

Although all this indicates that Nollywood has since become a de facto transnational practice in the broad sense of the word, if not a pan-African affair, calling Nollywood an "African popular cinema" is still provocative. At the least, this is how those studying Nollywood's *other*, the African auteur cinema, feel. The latter was the only cinema produced on the continent until Nollywood emerged. African celluloid filmmaking of this kind is centered in French-speaking West Africa and is identified by the biennial festival FESPACO (Festival Panafricain du Cinéma et de Télévision de Ouagadougou). Less commercially oriented than Nollywood, this tradition of filmmaking has been conceptualized by its practitioners and their scholarly proponents as a tool to decolonize the minds of African audiences. Often overtly political, it was, and still is, meant to counter the hegemonic Western gaze on Africa with emancipatory self-representational images. Nollywood challenges this older form of African cinema not only in terms of its far greater accessibility and therefore popularity with "the African masses" but especially through its representational regime, including lengthy depictions of witchcraft and magic, which in the eyes of Nollywood's critics constitutes a clear setback to the emancipatory politics of African auteur cinema. In two previously published essays, John McCall ("The Pan-Africanism We Have") and Onookome Okome ("Nollywood and Its Critics") have reflected on the tensions of this debate from the viewpoint of Nollywood studies. In this present volume, scholars and filmmakers Jyoti Mistry and Jordache A. Ellapen are cautious of our enthusiasm about Nollywood's popularity, questioning the political stakes in naming Nollywood African cinema. The main reference upon which this critical engagement draws comes from framing African cinema as part of postcolonial studies, which seek to reverse the Western hegemonic gaze of the continent.

Rather than reiterating the history and constitutive facts about Nollywood again, all of which has been documented in a number of publications and documentary films,[1] we wish to use the larger part of this introduction to focus on questions arising from Nollywood's pan-

African appeal and draw out some overall conclusions from the essays presented in this volume. Designating Nollywood "an African popular cinema" means taking into account the diversity and sometimes wholly contradictory perceptions of Nigerian video films in Africa and the African diaspora. Local contexts of consumption reveal that these films are full of modes of modernity, which Africans and people of African origin desire and copy, and contain forms of tradition that they find both frightening and contemptuous. Accounting for Nollywood's popularity thus also means discussing the nature of the controversy it stirs up. Why is Nollywood so popular in Nigeria and beyond, and why is it so controversial at the same time? What causes this odd sense of popularity and controversy? What significance does this have for the study of Nollywood, African cinema, and African culture more generally?

NOLLYWOOD'S APPEAL IN NIGERIA, AFRICA, AND BEYOND

As many observers have argued, accounting for Nollywood's appeal in Africa and beyond means examining the cultural affinity between what is represented on-screen and the immediate social world of Nollywood's African and other diasporic audiences. In a study about Nollywood viewership in Uganda, Monica Dipio argues, "Nigerian film is popular in the sense that it traverses the immediate culture in which it is set as people beyond the borders of the immediate community can identify with it" (53). The continental value of the Nollywood film, Dipio asserts, is that "the films are about the archetypal principles of good and evil" (ibid.), with which many African communities will readily identify. In a similar vein, Ngoloma Katsuva explains the popularity of Nigerian video films in the Democratic Republic of the Congo by referring to "the similarities between Nigerian culture and other black African culture" (96). The cultural proximity referred to in this and similar statements is, of course, subjectively relational. Measured against the reified culture of American films and television series broadcast by African TV stations, the culture on display in Nigerian video films may indeed look familiar to many viewers in Africa. Not surprisingly, therefore, across the continent Nigerian video films are first and foremost hailed for their Africanity, a point that Katrien Pype reports from Kinshasa in her contribution to this volume. This point is also commonly and tellingly expressed by audiences in Namibia, South Africa, Tanzania, and Barbados quoted in the contributions by Heike Becker, Claudia Böhme, and Jane Bryce, respectively. On the level of visual appearance, Africanity may refer to an all-African cast – something many viewers across the continent and its diasporas who are accustomed mainly to Western (and Eastern) movies experienced as a novelty. Barbadians, for example, cherish the voluptuous image of the female body depicted in Nigerian video films, one that values plumpness and thus differs from the Western concepts of beauty shown in Hollywood films (Bryce, this volume). A Ugandan viewer interviewed by Dipio adds that Nigerian video films are able to move their African viewers away "from struggling to fit into Western stereotypes of beauty as slimness" (67). In this way, this audience sees the Nigerian films as fostering the "acceptance of one's self, one's situations and circumstances, acceptance of one's body," as one of Heike Becker's South African interviewees concludes, and thus implicitly refers to what Hollywood movies lack for African audiences. Likewise, the settings of Nigerian video films, urban and rural, have a high degree of familiarity for many African viewers outside Nigeria.

Despite these superficial resemblances, however, there is also some difficulty in arguing for the cultural proximity between these films and their transnational African audiences, at least "in the sense of shared cultural heritage, shared cultural patrimony or devotion to a common store of values," as Moradewun Adejunmobi makes clear in her illuminating essay "Charting Nollywood's Appeal Locally & Globally." She argues instead that what matters is the films' "phenomenological proximity" and that they travel so well "because the conflicts they represent and the resolutions they offer are perceived to be experientially proximate for postcolonial subjects" (108–11). It is safe to say, therefore, that Nollywood matters to its audiences because it is concerned with contemporary topics that constitute the "thickness of which the African present is made," to quote Achille Mbembe (273).

But the culture of Nollywood films is loved not only for its perceived similarity to local cultural formations but equally for its alterity, so that copying patterns of behavior, fashion, and speech style from Nigerian video films becomes a playful means for individual viewers to distinguish themselves from the cultural patterns and social norms of their own societies. There are references across the continent to the fact that the aesthetics of Nigerian video films influence public culture elsewhere. Kenyan politicians have been spotted wearing Nigerian gowns (Ondego 116), Congolese seamstresses receive requests to sew dresses and skirts in Nigerian styles, new buildings in Kinshasa are inspired by architecture seen in Nigerian video films (Pype, this volume), names of Nigerian actors and film characters have become templates for nicknames in Kenya (Ondego 116), and South African students even consciously mimic the Nigerian English accent to set themselves apart from their fellow countrymen (Becker, this volume). It seems reasonable, then, to accept Becker's observation that the consumption of Nollywood films provides viewers in South Africa and Namibia "with the opportunity to claim, reinvent, and debate their Africanity." What this suggests is that the idea of Africanity that Nigerian video films elicit is never straightforward or always positive as a way of defining "Africanness." It all depends on the particular social context of consumption. Elsewhere, though, Nigerian video films are not cherished as much out of nostalgia for a lost "African" traditional past that seems to be specific to post-apartheid countries. Yet they certainly allow their viewers to imagine what it means to be modern in an African way. In that sense, Nigerian video films function similarly to Indian films for Muslim youths in northern Nigeria, as Brian Larkin argues in his essay "Indian Films and Nigerian Lovers." As Bollywood movies allowed their Muslim Hausa viewers to perceive a "parallel modernity" coming "without the political and ideological significance of that of the West" (407), Nollywood films offer their audiences in Nigeria and beyond a particular brand of "Afromodernity." As John Comaroff and Jean Comaroff, who coined this term, point out, Afromodernity is not "a response to European modernity, or a creature derived from it," but "a complex formation" that is "actively forged, in the ongoing present, from endogenous and exogenous elements of a variety of sorts" (202). The Afromodernity presented in Nigerian video films is forged equally out of a belief in magic and witchcraft, as of belief in Christian deliverance; out of village life and traditional custom, as of city life with all its modern items such as luxurious cars, fantastic mansions, and global technologies; out of opulent African attire, as of European designer clothes. Key to the Africa-wide appeal is the fact that the "vernacular modernity" (200) Nollywood forges is perceived as the same but different enough from African contemporary life elsewhere on the continent to allow for both identification and fascination prompted by alterity.

However, apart from such general observations, it is worth paying close attention to specific contexts of consumption, as several of the essays in this volume do. This reveals that Nollywood films may have different functions for specific audiences. A few examples will suffice to substantiate this point. Writing about Kinshasa, where charismatic Christianity permeates public culture and in particular its broadcast media, Katrien Pype discusses how pastors show Nigerian video films in churches and on their television channels. Interpreted by bilingual Evangelists, Nollywood films thus serve Congolese Christians as audiovisual parables. This is unlike the function they perform for young academics in Cape Town and Windhoek, which Heike Becker describes as triggering nostalgia for a lost African past, epitomized in Nollywood's depictions of village life, a sociocultural reality that these viewers have no actual experience of, but meets their yearnings "for a home of their own, as Africans, in the contemporary world." Regarding the diasporic Nigerian viewers in Italy, Giovanna Santanera's chapter focuses on Nollywood films serving as a means to reconnect to a cultural home in a more literal sense. For immigrant viewers who are new to Italy, the films provide a "map of experience" (Barber 5), a familiar, symbolic, and discursive order against which they measure themselves to cope with the "semantic void" of cultural dislocation.[2] Those who have lived in Italy for decades use Nigerian video films to critically reflect upon the culture of their former homeland, thus distancing themselves from certain cultural traits "while reaffirming the validity of others still considered appropriate in the new environment." And for the other diasporic viewers who no longer have any direct ties to this homeland, as is the case with Barbados in Bryce's example, the allure of Nollywood is somewhat different. Bryce's chapter speaks to a different kind of "semantic void," one that has been conditioned over three centuries of colonial history. Africa, the ancestral home of the majority of Barbadians, "remains a contested figure in the popular imagination, as often negative as it is nostalgic and heroic." Yet, as Bryce clarifies, in Barbados the transnational consumption of the world of the Nollywood film is experienced and culturally interpreted, not as a return to the "homeland," which is in this respect quixotic, but a symbolic return to a disputed past. According to a Nollywood fan quoted in a local newspaper, "We are accustomed to seeing Africans living in huts and dirt poor; but now we know that some also live in some really big houses with exquisite furniture." This quote is interesting because it shows a desire to see that past, which is connected to the cultural self-definition of the interviewee, as redeemable.

Other chapters of this book signpost the use of Nollywood as a trans-actional cultural anchor, that is, as a site where migrant subjects meet the homeland in different ways. Jonathan Haynes's chapter, which focuses on the genre of films shot partially or entirely in the diaspora, is inter-esting in this regard. Based on scripts that are often written by Nigerian expatriates, these films reflect diasporic life, diegetically and socially. Marketed both in the diaspora and in Nigeria, they have become a means to communicate the diasporic experience, including the hardship, which may be part of it, to those who stay behind. They also allow the filmmak-ers to address the tensions between the diasporic communities and Nige-rians back home. Claudia Hoffmann, who discusses three such films set in New York, argues that they are overtly critical of the deplorable state in the Nigerian homeland itself and the circumstances of immigrant life in America. They "are not primarily made to entertain, but made to inform and educate a Nigerian and African community from within." The Nigerian immigrant filmmakers that Sophie Samyn interviewed in the Netherlands, Belgium, and Germany express a similar intention.[3] Her contribution is even more direct in the way that Nollywood films are mobilized to create a diasporic Nollywood film culture with a clear cultural translation, which is at the heart of the transaction between both worlds. The filmmakers also told her of the desire to "celebrate Nigeria's popular culture," and even though the relationship with the homeland is problematic, they do create cultural bridges between the new home and the homeland. Since many of the diaspora films are also produced in conjunction with Nigerian producers who also bring Nigerian actors overseas, these productions actually establish contact between individu-als from Nigeria and Nigerian expatriates in more than just a symbolic sense. Face-to-face contact between Nollywood actors and their expa-triate fans also occurs during the road shows, galas, and premieres or-ganized by Nigerians living in Europe, which is briefly touched upon in Alessandro Jedlowski's chapter in this volume.

Though Nigerian video films have assumed a transnational existence, depending on the context, their accessibility in cultural and linguistic terms may still be limited, and the films therefore warrant one
form of mediation or the other. This is the case in Tanzania, where professional video narrators (re)mediate Nollywood films. These narrators
do live translations in Kiswahili so local audiences can follow the story.
Ad-libbing and adding observations with local inflections and personal
commentary to "spice up" the movies, they are adapting the stories to
a local hermeneutic framework (Krings, this volume). Since they also
sell their work on cassettes and discs with Kiswahili voice-over, they
are comparable to the Congolese dubbers Katrien Pype mentions in her
chapter. Over and above the translation and commentary, Kinshasa's
dubbers also insert a local praise genre of "name-dropping" into their
performances, thus weaving the films even deeper into the social world
of this city. Togolese pastor Luc Russel Adjaho, who runs his own television station, T V Zion, on which he broadcasts his highly original interpretations of Nigerian video films in Ewé, performs another similar
form of mediation through voice-over. Unlike his Tanzanian and Congolese colleagues, Adjaho is keen on teasing out a critical surplus value
for his audiences by inserting comparisons to local cultural phenomena
and even politics and political personae in his voice-over commentaries. One of the contributors to this volume, Babson Ajibade, recounts
his experiences of mediating Nigerian video films to European audiences. This experiment is to get European viewers, who are even further
removed from the culture of Nigerian video films, into the thick and
thin of Nollywood stories. During private screenings, he gave running
commentaries – thus performing more or less like his African counterparts – and then later embarked on a project of recutting these films for a
public screening. Surprisingly, with the recut versions of these films, the
European audiences had far fewer problems following the story. Taking
this into consideration, he argues that it is not so much a lack of cultural
knowledge that limits the accessibility of Nollywood films for European
audiences but their formal properties, which diverge from conventional
filmmaking standards.

In certain social contexts, Nollywood films have to be mediated
even more substantially to adapt their stories for audiences who might
oppose or be offended by some of the cultural content. A notable exam-

ple is the Christian imagery in some of these films. One way of achieving this is to embark on remakes, as exemplified by Muslim filmmakers
in northern Nigeria and Tanzania. In his contribution, Abdalla Uba
Adamu focuses on one such appropriation across cultural boundaries
within Nigeria – the Muslim Hausa remake of Tade Ogidan's *Dangerous
Twins* (one of the trailblazers of Nollywood's diaspora genre). Scrutiniz-
ing the producers' changes to the story, Adamu argues that the film is
not just remade but culturally "redirected" to make it more suitable for
a Muslim Hausa audience. While true remakes are rare in Tanzania,
where filmmakers adopt a technique of borrowing and mixing foreign
and local ideas, a cinematic phenomenon which Claudia Böhme refers
to as bricolage, local Muslim filmmakers no less exorcize the Christian
imagery of Nollywood films. Unlike Hausa remakes in which Christian
pastors are exchanged for Muslim clerics (Krings, "Muslim Martyrs"
195), traditional healers take over the former's part in Tanzanian horror
movies. In this genre, traditional healers fight epic battles with witches,
vampires, and other uncanny creatures. Böhme explains this difference
to the Nollywood template by referring to the high esteem in which
"tradition" is held in Tanzania, and by the fact that topics touching upon
Islam – such as depictions of Muslim clerics battling with demons – are
considered taboo. These two examples support the need for the cultural
adaptation of Nollywood films under certain conditions and point toward possible limitations of Nollywood's popularity. We will now turn
to the discussion of the controversy that Nigerian video films engender
as they travel.

CONTROVERSY

Critical debate about Nollywood film starts at home, where large segments of the Nigerian intelligentsia are up in arms over the movies'
popularity. "Some of the so-called movies that portray the African past
do no more than confirm the western concept of African primitivism,"
says John A. Afolabi as he mulls the images of Africa portrayed in Nollywood's epic genre (170). He sees *The Battle of Musanga* as a literal "confirmation of the jaundiced, Euro-centric views and European hegemonic
myths about the underdevelopment of Africans. It portrays the African
as underdeveloped, wild and beastly" (171). By and large, such criticism

targets the negative image Nigerian video films prompt about Nigeria and Nigerians and, *pars pro toto,* about Africa as a whole. Inscribed in this discussion is the anxiety that if watched by outsiders, especially Europeans and Americans (despite the fact that these are among Nollywood's most unlikely audiences; see Ajibade, this volume), these films will give a bad impression. Afolabi warns that the "impressions such films create about their countries of origin and the possible damage they could do are incalculable" (170). Even though Nigerian video films have provoked vociferous critiques in the homeland almost from the beginning, the criticism became particularly harsh when the films began to spread across the continent and beyond. In his essay "Nollywood and Its Critics," Onookome Okome has drawn attention to the anxiety this art form generates among Nigerian intellectuals who feel the need to correct the "erroneous and banal" images of the country Nollywood projects to the Nigerian public, to Africa, and to the world. For these critics "who seek to mediate popular Africa to the outside world and legislate the production of an 'authentic' culture and society in contemporary Africa," it is a matter of "mediating the unwanted mediator – Nollywood" (28). In what looks like the official position on this matter, the National Film and Video Censors Board of Nigeria in its six-year report (1994–2000) compiled a long list of what it calls "repellent subjects," including "fetishism," "the sale of women and women sell her [*sic*] virtue," "voodoism," "cultism," "witchcraft," "devilish spiritism," "homosexuality," "rituals and ritualistic killings," and "lesbianism" (107–11). Associating Nollywood with the display of these and similar cultural items, and based on this, critiquing it as a cultural machine of a dubious sort does not stop at Nigeria's borders; it is echoed among elites all over the continent. Olivier Barlet makes this point when he argues, "The mercantile sex and violence contained in the Nigerian videos that are exported and broadcast without carrying any warnings undermine the cultural values of the countries concerned" (126). Without doubt the "minor transnational practice," as Moradewun Adejunmobi has dubbed Nollywood filmmaking, has become a dominant regional force – not only in projecting its own particular version of Africa onto television screens from Cape Town to Kinshasa, and from Dar es Salaam to Dakar, but also by establishing a stylistic norm, an aesthetics, and a narrative format that local forms of cultural production have to cope with ("Nigerian Video Film" 10).

The example of the Democratic Republic of the Congo provides a telling tale of the mistrust and controversy that Nollywood has generated in the wake of its continent-wide circulation. Franck Baku Fuita and Godefroid Bwiti Lumisa report that "after a two-year period in which there was a flurry of broadcasting Nigerian video films, the Minister of Information and Media decided to call a halt" (107). He had been inundated with complaints from theater troupes who argued that Nollywood films, "which were better conceived and produced, and were packed with special effects," were the cause of the decline in theater patronage. In Ghana, whose own video film industry even precedes Nollywood, Nigerian video films posed a serious challenge to the survival of local film production. Quoting video filmmakers and spectators from Ghana, Birgit Meyer states that the local audiences preferred Nollywood films for reasons of both form and content (54). This only changed when Ghanaian filmmakers adopted Nollywood aesthetics (opulent costumes and sets and special effects) and narratives (witchcraft) and began producing films in vernacular languages. The Tanzanian situation is even more complex. While some of Dar es Salaam's video filmmakers consider Nollywood an African equivalent to the American dream factory and strive to model their own productions after this template – even hiring Nigerian directors and actors to act in their films (Krings, "Nollywood Goes East") – others articulate the need to emancipate "Bongo movies" from the Nigerian trailblazer and to develop a national film style in and of itself.[4] In this case, professional aspirations and elitist critique go hand in hand, and this is often remarked by the insertions of sensibilities of cultural nationalism. Claudia Böhme mentions a Tanzanian director who shouted at his film crew, "We don't copy the Nigerians!" thereby expressing exactly these concerns. As the examples from Congo, Ghana, and Tanzania show, it has become increasingly difficult for local cultural production, especially popular filmmaking, to thrive alongside Nollywood. It dictates tastes and trends, which filmmakers elsewhere on the continent cannot easily ignore. However, while these audiences crave Nollywood-like films in their local languages, intellectual critics-cum-protectors of national cultural identities accuse them of lacking creativity by copying from the Nigerians and of spoiling local mores by displaying moneymaking and witchcraft rituals.

Interestingly, the contribution by Jyoti Mistry and Jordache A. El-lapen hinges on the display of these cultural items in Nollywood films. The authors argue that the reiteration of these items in the narratives of Nigerian video films, without sponsoring a critical and ideological retake of them, will eventually prove a cinematic deficit, one that African cinema can ill afford at this point. The aim of the contribution therefore is to "open up the debate past the euphoria and celebration of Nollywood as a place of self-representation and its significance as an entrepreneurial endeavor that subverts conventional modes of exhibition and distribution," and "to reflect on the vital and productive contradictions that have enabled the development and evolution of video films as a site for significant cultural production on the African continent." They also argue that not only have South African video projects modeled on Nollywood been problematic for these reasons, but the suggestion that Nollywood films would redefine the theoretical canon of African cinema is at best provocative. The authors' ultimate aim is to problematize the transportability of the Nollywood model to other African cultural and political setups. Quoting from Third cinema theory as well as from African ideas of cinema's political role in the postcolonial project, Mistry and Ellapen tell us, "Rarely do Nollywood films consider revisionist colonial histories. Video film narratives are often informed by immediate social and cultural concerns facing the local community, and the inspirations for stories have a localized appeal." They conclude this by insisting that "the impotence of Nollywood might for now simply be the handicap that has been so emphatically outlined by numerous critics, and it is one of content, production value, and its ability to really function competitively on a global Market. Without truly interrogating its political substance, there is no space for Nollywood as a mode of cultural production to evolve." This position is similar to the stance taken by many self-nominated cultural mediators of Africa in answer to the question (see Okome, "Nollywood and Its Critics"). It is also similar to the position found in Olivier Barlet's article "Is the Nigerian Model Fit for Export?" Therein, he argues that Nollywood does not offer a politically conscious or empowering agenda. It seems to us that, following the argument that is rehashed in Mistry and Ellapen's chapter, the missing link is the avoidance of reading the cultural and artistic template in which the Nollywood film functions as art and that is undeniably popular culture. It means then that this position ignores, to a large extent, the place of the *popular* in this art form and instead wills it to be part of the larger discourse on postcolonial studies, one that is supported by the postcolonial establishment. Undoubtedly, Nollywood is produced in the atmosphere of the "postcolonial condition," but we also know that the very condition is experienced in manifold ways. We wish to argue here that the experience counts more than the condition itself.

Perhaps no other Nollywood film has garnered as much attention and controversy in Nigeria and abroad as Kingsley Ogoro's *Osuofia in London,* a film that has clearly established itself as an all-time Nollywood classic. Not only is this film a trailblazer of the diaspora genre (see Haynes, this volume), but for a long time it was the only Nigerian video film that *could* have attracted a non-African audience. The die-hard Nigerian-born Harvard culture critic Biodun Jeyifo is exceptionally enthusiastic about this film. He writes, "Built around the thin but original plotline of an inept and penniless village hunter who somehow gets to go to London where he inherits his late brother's vast wealth and fiancé, nearly every minute of this two-part film pulses with genuine humor and vitality" (18–19). But it is not just the story of this film that captivated this critic. He argues that the "London scenes are some of the best shot and edited scenes in Nollywood films" (19). Unlike Jeyifo, Bekeh Utietiang, a Washington-based expatriate, believes *Osuofia in London* "is unpatriotic to Africa." According to him, "Africans are presented in this movie as timid and uncivilized people who have no idea of what it means to use a rest room, a confirmation of what the West believe[s] already about Africans. . . . Osuofia is portrayed as a dumb idiot who would sign off every of his brother's property for a kiss from a white lady." In his opinion, therefore, the film is deliberately geared toward a Western audience and does a disservice to African identity politics. The contribution by Mistry and Ellapen and Okome's chapter elaborate on the film in this volume and are equally up front about the film's controversial aspects. In their review of *Osuofia in London,* Mistry and Ellapen are particularly taken aback by the stereotypes of differing female role expectations visible in the encounter between Osuofia and his late brother's British fiancée, Samantha. While Samantha is shocked to learn that Osuofia intends to "take over everything" – including her (thus acting in keeping with village custom) – he is even more perplexed when Samantha says that she does not know how to cook, and does not have to. Mistry and Ellapen read this as an indication for the film's positioning of "African tradition and culture against Western modernity" and as a suggestion of "the incommensurability of the two cultures." What they find even more problematic is that the narrative suggests marriage as the only solution for Samantha to siphon off Osuofia's wealth. To them, therefore, the film is "regressive" and fails to "empower women by subverting stereotypes." The critics' final statement is devastating when they say that the film's "images are vulgar and reflect an uncritical filmmaking practice." Interestingly, and this hints at Nollywood's controversial nature, Okome's reading of *Osuofia in London* is almost the opposite. To him the narrative is consciously designed as a "writeback" to the common European narrative of colonial conquest. It is Osuofia who conquers London, the epitome of the British Empire. His gaze is privileged, and the viewer questions British civilization from his perspective. According to Okome, Osuofia's "triumph is complete when out of desperation Samantha agrees to be his wife and to accompany him to 'Africa.' To conquer Samantha means conquering London and by extension the colonial past." Osuofia's conquest defies the picture of the simpleminded African that we are wont to come across in European texts such as Joseph Conrad's *Heart of Darkness* or, for that matter, Joyce Cary's *Mister Johnson*. Although he is also aware of the film's problematic gender matrix, Okome suggests that it has to be understood in terms of a "crazy comedy," a genre built on parody. He thus insists, "*Osuofia in London* offers a critical reading of the pro-filmic world from a postcolonial standpoint. Its semantic intention as parody is directed not only at itself and its social and cultural milieu but also at a larger historic community."[5]

AFRICAN CINEMA

High-low, elite-popular, art-business, political-entertaining, progressive-regressive, celluloid-video: these are some of the binary distinctions that have served to distinguish African auteur cinema from Nollywood filmmaking. These oppositions conflate the fact that the boundaries are not as strict as they appear to be at first glance. What tends to be overlooked, for example, is the fact that the older form of African cinema also

had a genre of popular films less interested in spreading political consciousness than in entertaining its audience (Diawara 141–43). We must
also note that some celluloid filmmakers of the first generation were
quite open to commercial adventures (Şaul 140). An independent filmmaker like the Nigerian Tunde Kelani, who works with the video format
and Nollywood-like marketing strategies, is as equally difficult to fit into
the picture as Cameroon-born auteur filmmaker Jean-Pierre Bekolo,
who is remembered for letting a character in his film *Aristotle's Plot* state:
"African films are shit!" One observer even attests the "spirited camp" of
Bekolo as an "undeniable affinity with the video products coming out of
Nigeria" (Şaul 153). And how do we accommodate Wanjiru Kinyanjui, an
auteur filmmaker, who embarked on two film-producing projects under
Riverwood conditions – the Kenyan equivalent of Nollywood?

Compared to the older form of African cinema, Nollywood films
may have technical flaws and very low production values, but their undeniable merits cannot be overemphasized, either. Since the early days
of African auteur filmmaking, part of the agenda was the search for a
proper African cinematic aesthetic, one that "encompassed both the
desire to 'contribute to universal art' and an effort to reach the local
audience" (Şaul 148). While the filmmakers succeeded with regards to
the former, they were less successful in terms of the latter. It is Nollywood's reliance on the small medium video that tackled the problem of
distribution often lamented in the discourse on African cinema, and it
is Nollywood that has reached African audiences across the continent.
Manthia Diawara recently confessed to being an "avid consumer of Nollywood videos" (185), and his appeal to African auteur filmmakers to give
the video medium a try, and learn from Nollywood how crucial stars
and distributors are to any popular cinema, shows how far the practice
and the discourse on Nollywood as an African cinema have come. "It is
to the merit of the cultural workers in Nollywood," writes Diawara, "to
have realized that stars and distributors are as important as 'auteurs,'
if not more so" (190). One other merit of Nollywood is the way it has
brought women into the broader picture of African filmmaking, both as
producers and as consumers. While women were almost absent from the
first and second generations of African auteur filmmakers, they do play
strong roles in Nollywood film production (as such characters as diverse
as Helen Ukpabio, Peace Anyiam-Fiberesima, and Stephanie Okereke

demonstrate). As it relies very much on the market, Nollywood has also solved the tricky problem of financing film production. While African auteur cinema largely depends on French or other European funding, and is thus bound to accommodate foreign cultural policies (at least to a certain extent), the ownership of Nollywood is African. According to Diawara, "Nollywood is African, and we cannot change it without changing the spectators," arguing, "What is good about Nollywood is therefore that it has revealed to us where the collective desires of a large portion of the African population reside" (185). This remark touches upon Nollywood's biggest merit, which is the fact that it is reaching the people, and this idea of "reaching" is not only due to the infrastructure, which is the medium employed and the innovative form of distribution, or the glamour of a star system, but much more due to the stories Nollywood projects and the way it does so. In other words, people across Africa and its diasporas are willing to pay to watch Nigerian video films, and this has a lot to do with the "extravagant aesthetics" (Larkin, *Signal and Noise*, 168) of this film form. To our mind, and contrary to Mistry and Ellapen's stance on this issue, the fact that Nollywood films are labeled "African films" and hailed for their "Africanity" by so many different people of African descent indicates that they must espouse something close to "a proper African aesthetic" and, if not "African" enough for some, at least one that is in tune with the postcolonial condition of the continent. These aesthetics are certainly different from the ones envisioned by the founding fathers of African cinema, but undeniably they seem to work well with popular audiences.

Nollywood films dramatize shocking transgressions of social norms. The main protagonists are driven by all sorts of human desires and thus share emotions most viewers are likely to have experienced themselves: the aspiration to get rich, envying other people's success, the longing for a beautiful man or woman. Unlike most viewers, Nollywood takes the human failings of villains to excess, as Adejunmobi observes ("Charting Nollywood's Appeal" 111). Men or women thus lust not just after anyone, but after their best friend's wife or husband. Others don't just aspire to become rich, but are willing to sacrifice family members to make this dream a reality. This manifestation of excess is equally recognizable in the level of cinematic imagery. Nollywood films revel in the display of luxurious cars, expensive clothes, large mansions, and opulent interiors.

These serve as indicators of success. But this success is tied to excess, the transgression of social norms, and the breakdown of morality. Similar to films with popular appeal from other film cultures, Nigerian video films demand narrative closure. Villains are thus punished and their victims avenged. "As is common in melodramatic narratives," Adejunmobi observes, "the wicked and immoral are always punished ... preferably experiencing a slow, painful and agonizing process of decline following a supernatural intervention" (112). Morality and social norms, threatened by transgression and excess during most of each film, are thus firmly in place again at the end of the film. It is important to note, however, that this cautionary pedagogy of Nollywood films is delivered not by any subtle means, but through what Brian Larkin has called an "aesthetics of outrage," which mobilizes the narrative of social transgression and excess to produce "continual shocks" and is "designed to provoke and affront the audience" (*Signal and Noise* 184). As Larkin argues, these aesthetics aim at physical stimulation. "The aesthetics of outrage force people to live the film so that external realities are intensified, vivified, and made sensate through the mediation of film narrative itself" (187). That this sense of cinematic affect is not limited to popular audiences, but is also experienced by the sophisticated connoisseur who is somewhat removed from the everyday life of the average Nollywood viewer can be gleaned from an interesting observation by Manthia Diawara after watching an unnamed Nollywood film on M-Net. Recounting a sequence that shows a man in bed with his secretary and whose wife is about to catch him in the act, he writes, "I was so manipulated and scared by the parallel editing and the fast pacing that I changed the channel just when she was about to open the bedroom door" (171). What becomes clear is that Diawara "lived the film," to quote Larkin once again. Although it is impossible to compare the differences between these aesthetics and that of African auteur cinema in any detail here, what should have become obvious is that Nollywood films address their viewers in a completely different manner and that they also expect different responses from them. Unlike auteur films, Nollywood films tend to reaffirm rather than question viewers' expectations (see Adejunmobi, "Charting Nollywood's Appeal" 113). With Nollywood films, the audience gets what it expects. Nothing is left open or to ponder, as the narratives require closure. "What is good about Nollywood is what's bad about it, and conversely what's bad about it makes possible the emergence of a vibrant and authentic African cinema" (Diawara 183).

A look at the critical discourse on African cinema clearly shows that Nollywood, as well as other popular cinemas that emerged before or after its inception (like those in Ghana and Tanzania, respectively), can no longer be excluded from the canon of African cinema in the field of film studies. It will find due scholarly attention, just as other popular cinemas have been accommodated in the disciplinary rubrics we call film studies. It is not only Manthia Diawara who has taken to the debate of Nigerian video film in a serious and sustained manner, including trips to the heart of its production in Lagos. Frank N. Ukadike, the other major expatriate scholar of African cinema, has equally documented his interest in several essays and proposes to devote a full-fledged study to Nollywood film. It looks as if Jonathan Haynes's call on scholars of film studies to bring their full arsenal of critical apparatus to the analysis of Nollywood films ("What Is to Be Done?") is beginning to yield its first positive results. Young and upcoming humanities scholars have begun to compare auteur and Nollywood films from specific perspectives. Stefan Sereda, for example, compares in his essay "Curses, Nightmares, and Realities" the differing forms of "cautionary pedagogy" in the two types of African cinemas by taking a close look at Ousmane Sembène's *Xala* and the Nigerian video film *Meet You in Hell*. In her essay "The Return of the Mercedes," Lindsey Green-Simms equally draws on *Xala,* comparing Sembène's signification of the luxury limousine with what is deployed by Kenneth Nnebue in *Living in Bondage.* Likewise, devoting scholarly attention to the critical study of even a single Nollywood film can be rewarding and yield rich results, as Okome's chapter on *Osuofia in London* (this volume) aptly demonstrates. And Haynes's contribution to this volume reveals that a methodological approach borrowed from genre theory makes it possible to map the constituting stylistic and narrative features of certain genres within the Nollywood tradition. A somewhat similar attempt is also found in Diawara's "narratological approach to Nollywood videos" (176–83). To add to this scholarly interest, the growing number of workshops and conferences dedicated to the study of Nollywood, some of which took place in Nigeria during the past few years, points to the fact that, finally, Nollywood is now considered worthy of serious academic attention in the country of its birth.

Outside academic discourse, the two African cinema practices – popular filmmaking à la Nollywood and African auteur cinema – hardly ever cross each other's path. Video parlors, which are still the most popular outlet for Nollywood film screenings across Africa, do not run African auteur films, and the film festivals of Ouagadougou, Carthage, Durban, and Zanzibar do not accept Nollywood films into their main competitions.[6] Nollywood filmmakers are proud to cater to the African masses and distinguish their products from "embassy films," as they call African auteur cinema (for the reason that it caters only to the niche audience of cultural programs run by embassies). However, this should not be mistaken as an indicator that Nollywood revels in some form of aesthetic and technological complacency as a film industry. This is not the case, as Alessandro Jedlowski's contribution to this volume indicates. Nigerian video filmmakers do have aspirations for the big screen.

In the recent past, beginning in 2006 with Jeta Amata's *The Amazing Grace,* a number of Nollywood films have been produced as international coproductions, most of them shot on 35mm film. Having a much bigger budget and higher production value than the average Nollywood video film, these films are shot with an international crew, often set in the diaspora and targeting mainly cinema audiences. Labeled the "New Nollywood," this trend goes hand in hand with the recent revival of a cinema-going culture – in Nigeria and elsewhere in Africa. It remains to be seen what implications this development has for African popular cinema in terms of aesthetics, stories, and accessibility. What is clear at the moment is that more can be expected of Africa's dream factory in the coming years.

NOTES

1. See Haynes, *Nigerian Video Films;* Haynes and Okome's earlier essay "Evolving Popular Media"; the special editions of *Postcolonial Text* and *Film International,* edited by Onookome Okome; John McCall's essay "Nollywood Confidential"; the volume *Nollywood: The Video Phenomenon in Nigeria,* edited by Pierre Barrot; and the two books of essays edited by Foluke Ogunleye, *African Video Film Today* and *Africa through the Eye of the Video Camera.* For documentary films, see *This Is Nollywood,* by Franco Sacchi; *Peace Mission,* by Dorothee Wenner; and *Nollywood Babylon,* by Ben Addelman and Samir Mallal.

2. Writing about the consumption of Nollywood films by subaltern economic immigrants from Zimbabwe, Zambia, Tanzania, and Ghana in Botswana, David

Kerr comes to a similar conclusion when he observes that "the interactive reception of the movies provided a discursive space to reflect upon cultural disjuncture, but at a relatively safe distance, through the simultaneously distant yet familiar culture of Nigeria" (75).

3. Similar statements are also made by John Osas Omoregie, whose filmmaking practice in Antwerp, Belgium, is at the heart of the documentary film *Nollywood Abroad*, by Saartje Geerts.

4. The label "Bongo movies" serves to distinguish the films. *Bongo* is a colloquial designation for Dar es Salaam, literally meaning "brain" – as it takes brains to survive in this bustling business metropolis. In extension *bongo* also stands for Tanzania as a whole.

5. A complementary interpretation of *Osuofia in London* has been brought forward by Matthew H. Brown in his essay "'Osuofia Don Enter Discourse,'" where he bases part of his argument on the fact that the voice-over narration at the beginning of the film is an appropriation and parody of similar sequences of Western docufiction genre films, in particular that of the much-criticized *The Gods Must Be Crazy*.

6. See Brown, "The Nollywood Difference," for the Durban International Film Festival of 2010; the Zanzibar International Film Festival of 2011, however, did screen some of Tanzania's popular Bongo movies, though only out of the competition in a separate section that had almost no audience attention (personal communication, Claudia Böhme).

WORKS CITED

Adejunmobi, Moradewun. "Charting Nollywood's Appeal Locally & Globally." *African Literature Today* 28 (2010): 106–21.

———. "Nigerian Video Film as Minor Transnational Practice." *Postcolonial Text* 3.2 (2007): n. pag. Web.

Afolabi, John A. "The African Video Film and Images of Africa." *Africa through the Eye of the Video Camera*. Ed. Foluke Ogunleye. Manzini, Swaziland: Academic Publishers, 2008. 166–75.

Barber, Karin. "Introduction." *Readings in African Popular Culture*. Ed. Karin Barber. Bloomington: Indiana University Press; Oxford: James Currey, 1997. 1–12.

Barlet, Olivier. "Is the Nigerian Model Fit for Export?" *Nollywood: The Video Phenomenon in Nigeria*. Ed. Pierre Barrot. Bloomington: Indiana University Press, 2008. 121–29.

Barrot, Pierre, ed. *Nollywood: The Video Phenomenon in Nigeria*. Bloomington: Indiana University Press, 2008.

Brown, Matthew H. "The Nollywood Difference: Finding Nigeria at the 31st Durban International Film Festival." *Journal of African Cinemas* 2.2 (2009): 187–93.

———. "'Osuofia Don Enter Discourse': Global Nollywood and African Identity Politics." *Ibadan Journal of Theatre Arts* 2.4 (2008): 57–72.

Comaroff, John L., and Jean Comaroff. "Criminal Justice, Cultural Justice: The Limits of Liberalism and the Pragmatics of Difference in the New South Africa." *American Ethnologist* 31.2 (2004): 188–204.

Diawara, Manthia. *African Cinema: Politics and Culture*. Bloomington: Indiana University Press, 1992.

———. *African Film: New Forms of Aesthetics and Politics*. Munich: Prestel, 2010.

Dipio, Monica. "Ugandan Viewership of Nigerian Movies." *Africa through the Eye of the Video Camera*. Ed. Foluke Ogun-

leye. Manzini, Swaziland: Academic
Publishers, 2008. 52–73.

Fuita, Franck Baku, and Godefroid Bwiti
Lumisa. "Kinshasa & Nollywood: Chas-
ing the Devil." *Nollywood: The Video
Phenomenon in Nigeria.* Ed. Pierre Bar-
rot. Bloomington: Indiana University
Press, 2008. 107–13.

Green-Simms, Lindsey. "The Return of
the Mercedes: From Ousmane Sem-
bene to Kenneth Nnebue." *Viewing
African Cinema in the Twenty-First Century: Art Films and the Nollywood Video
Revolution.* Ed. Mahir Şaul and Ralph A.
Austen. Athens: Ohio University Press,
2010. 209–24.

Haynes, Jonathan, ed. *Nigerian Video Films.*
Athens: Ohio University Press, 2000.

———. "What Is to Be Done? Film Stud-
ies and Nigerian and Ghanaian Video
Films." *Viewing African Cinema in the
Twenty-First Century: Art Films and
the Nollywood Video Revolution.* Ed.
Mahir Şaul and Ralph A. Austen.
Athens: Ohio University Press, 2010.
11–25.

Haynes, Jonathan, and Onookome
Okome. "Evolving Popular Media: Ni-
gerian Video Film." *Research in African
Literature* 29.3 (1998): 106–28.

Jeyifo, Biodun. "Will Nollywood Get Better? Did Hollywood and Bollywood Get
Better?" *West Africa Review* 12 (2008):
13–31.

Katsuva, Ngoloma. "Nigerian Home Video Films and the Congolese Audience:
A Similarity of Cultures." *African Video
Film Today.* Ed. Foluke Ogunleye. Manzini, Swaziland: Academic Publishers,
2003. 91–104.

Kerr, David. "The Reception of Nigerian
Video Drama in a Multicultural Female
Community in Botswana." *Journal of
African Cinemas* 3.1 (2011): 65–79.

Kinyanjui, Wanjiru. "Kenyan Videos: A
Director's Experience." *Africa through
the Eye of the Video Camera.* Ed. Foluke

Ogunleye. Manzini, Swaziland: Academic Publishers, 2008. 74–81.

Krings, Matthias. "Muslim Martyrs and
Pagan Vampires: Popular Video Films
and the Propagation of Religion in
Northern Nigeria." *Postscripts* 1.2–3
(2005): 183–205.

———. "Nollywood Goes East: The
Localization of Nigerian Video Films
in Tanzania." *Viewing African Cinema
in the Twenty-First Century: Art Films
and the Nollywood Video Revolution.*
Ed. Mahir Şaul and Ralph A. Austen.
Athens: Ohio University Press, 2010.
74–91.

Larkin, Brian. "Indian Films and Nigerian
Lovers: Media and the Creation of Parallel Modernities." *Africa* 67.3 (1997):
406–40.

———. *Signal and Noise: Media, Infrastructure, and Urban Culture in Nigeria.*
Durham, N.C.: Duke University Press,
2008.

Mbembe, Achille. "African Modes of Self-
Writing." *Public Culture* 14.1 (2002):
239–73.

McCall, John C. "Nollywood Confidential: The Unlikely Rise of Nigerian Video Film." *Transition* 95 (2004): 98–109.

———. "The Pan-Africanism We Have:
Nollywood's Invention of Africa." *Film
International* 5.4 (2007): 92–97.

Meyer, Birgit. "Ghanaian Popular Video
Movies between State Film Policies
and Nollywood." *Viewing African Cinema in the Twenty-First Century: Art
Films and the Nollywood Video Revolution.* Ed. Mahir Şaul and Ralph A.
Austen. Athens: Ohio University Press,
2010. 42–62.

National Film and Video Censors Board.
6-Year Report (1994–2000). Abuja, Nigeria: National Film and Video Censors
Board, 2000.

Ogunleye, Foluke, ed. *African Video Film
Today.* Manzini, Swaziland: Academic
Publishers, 2003.

————. *Africa through the Eye of the Video Camera.* Manzini, Swaziland: Academic Publishers, 2008.

Okome, Onookome. "Nollywood and Its Critics." *Viewing African Cinema in the Twenty-First Century: Art Films and the Nollywood Video Revolution.* Ed. Mahir Şaul and Ralph A. Austen. Athens: Ohio University Press, 2010. 26–41.

————, ed. Special issue, *Film International* 5.4 (2007).

————, ed. Special issue, *Postcolonial Text* 3.2 (2007).

Ondego, Ogova. "Kenya & Nollywood: A State of Dependence." *Nollywood: The Video Phenomenon in Nigeria.* Ed. Pierre Barrot. Bloomington: Indiana University Press, 2008. 114–20.

Şaul, Mahir. "Art, Politics, and Commerce in Francophone African Cinema." *Viewing African Cinema in the Twenty-First Century: Art Films and the Nollywood Video Revolution.* Ed. Mahir Şaul and Ralph A. Austen. Athens: Ohio University Press, 2010. 133–59.

Sereda, Stefan. "Curses, Nightmare, and Realities: Cautionary Pedagogy in FESPACO Films and Igbo Videos." *Viewing African Cinema in the Twenty-First Century: Art Films and the Nollywood Video Revolution.* Ed. Mahir Şaul and Ralph A. Austen. Athens: Ohio University Press, 2010. 194–208.

Utietiang, Bekeh. "Osuofia in London: A Philosophical Perspective." *Nigerians in America* (2005). Web.

FILMOGRAPHY

The Amazing Grace. Dir. Jeta Amata. Jeta Amata Concepts and Amazing Grace Films (Nigeria and UK). 2006.

Battle of Musanga, 1 and 2. Dir. Bolaji Dawodu. Gabosky and Chezkay Film (Nigeria). 1996.

Dangerous Twins. Dir. Tade Ogidan. OGD Pictures (Nigeria). 2003.

The Gods Must Be Crazy. Dir. Jamie Uys. C.A.T. (South Africa). 1980.

Living in Bondage. Dir. Chris Obi Rapu. NEK Video Links (Nigeria). 1992.

Meet You in Hell. Dir. Amayo Uzo-Philips. N. N. (Nigeria). 2005.

Nollywood Abroad: A Nigerian Movie Maker in Europe. Dir. Saartje Geerts. Associate Directors (Belgium). 2008.

Nollywood Babylon. Dir. Ben Addelman and Samir Mallal. AM Pictures (Canada). 2009.

Osuofia in London, 1 and 2. Dir. Kingsley Ogoro. Kingsley Ogoro Productions (Nigeria). 2003, 2004.

Peace Mission. Dir. Dorothee Wenner. Women Make Movies (Germany and the United States). 2008.

This Is Nollywood. Dir. Franco Sacchi. Eureka Film Productions et al. (United States). 2007.

Xala. Dir. Ousmane Sembène. Films Domireew (Senegal). 1975.

PART ONE

Mapping the Terrain

From Nollywood to Nollyworld: Processes of Transnationalization in the Nigerian Video Film Industry

ALESSANDRO JEDLOWSKI

IN THE PAST TEN TO FIFTEEN YEARS, THE NIGERIAN VIDEO industry has grown exponentially. According to a UNESCO report released in 2009, it is now the second-largest film industry in the world in terms of the sheer number of films produced. Nigerian video films travel all over the world, transforming Nollywood into a transnational and global phenomenon. Like the Indian film industry, the role played by diasporic audiences in the production, circulation, and consumption of Nigerian video films became progressively more influential in the past few years. In their 2005 collection of essays, Raminder Kaur and Ajay Sinha suggest that Bollywood is now considered a transnational industry, a "Bollyworld," as they dub it, in which local and transnational aesthetics and narratives and formal and informal modes of production and distribution find original interceptions. A look at the contemporary Nigerian video film industry reveals a similar process, even if it is still in its early stages.

Behind the rhetoric of Nollywood's UNESCO-sanctioned success, the reality of the phenomenon is complex and richly nuanced. After an initial decade of prosperity, the immense popularity of Nollywood began to waver. The market became saturated, generating a negative spiral, which brought the industry to a critical impasse. Paradoxically, the international recognition of Nollywood's success coincided with the worst crisis ever faced by the industry. This crisis hit the English video film–producing section, forcing it to experiment with new production and distribution strategies. The aim of this chapter is to analyze the role of the transnationalization processes within the broader context of the crisis.[1]

The Nigerian video film industry has long had a transnational dimension. Thanks to the informality of Nollywood's distribution networks, pirated copies of Nigerian videos have circulated throughout the
world since the mid-1990s. This informal transnationalism has played
an important role in making the industry recognized on the African
continent and on the global cinema stage. The main thesis explored in
this chapter is that once the domestic video market started to implode
under the strain of excessive informal practices and the lack of a formal
distribution network, an important section of the industry decided to
target the transnational audience generated by the global informal circulation of Nigerian videos.

The first section of the chapter, which draws on fieldwork I conducted in Lagos, identifies the causes of the production crisis that hit
the English–Igbo section of the video industry. These include the switch
from VHS to VCD technology, the emergence of new distribution channels (satellite television channels and Internet platforms), and the increasing demand for improved and diversified content among increasingly sophisticated domestic audiences.

The second section discusses the early transnationalism of Nigerian videos. They have long traveled the world via informal networks,
connecting diasporic communities to the different African homelands.
Although these networks of circulation did not have an influential role
in the development of the Nollywood economy precisely because of their
largely illicit nature, they have been the main vehicles for the transnational circulation of Nigerian videos. Producers and distributors today
see the transnational audience as a potentially lucrative market, and they
are trying to formalize the international circulation of Nigerian videos,
especially in places where Nollywood films are already popular.

The third section looks at two significant attempts to formalize these
transnational markets: the recent antipiracy campaign conducted by the
Filmmakers Association of Nigeria (FAN) in the United States and the
theatrical releasing system developed in Britain by a group of Nigerians
working at Odeon cinemas. These two examples are particularly useful
to understanding the key role of the Nigerian diaspora in the processes
of transnationalization of the video industry. They also highlight the
aesthetic and narrative transformations generated by transnationalization processes.

The fourth section analyzes recent films that reflect these changing conditions. The years 2009 and 2010 saw the birth of what might be called a "New Wave" in Nigerian cinema, characterized by higher budgets, improved production values, and transnational collaborations. Through a brief analysis of some of these recent releases, this section explains how processes of transnationalization in the Nigerian video industry's economy are transforming the aesthetic and narrative features of Nigerian cinema, opening up new directions for Nollywood's development.

BEYOND THE VIDEO BOOM: PRODUCTION
CRISIS AND EXCESS OF INFORMALITY

From an economic perspective, the Nigerian "video boom" is the result of two factors: the informality of the Nigerian economy and the adoption of digital technologies. These two factors are also the main drivers of the production crisis that has plagued the industry in the past few years. According to Jane Guyer, Nigeria has a commercial economy in which projections suggest that the largest part of the population will earn their money in the informal sector by 2020 and that "at least 60 percent of the currency, once issued, *never goes back through the banking system again. These two economies – that in which the formal financial institutions monitor the entire money issue every day, and that in which 60 percent of it is never monitored again in its entire life in circulation – coexist, interrelate, and reconstitute one another" (3). The video industry developed along the interfaces between these two economies. Its structure is rhizomatic, similar to most informal economies, and it relies upon unregulated interactions among many small segments. Whereas film industries elsewhere in the world tend to be organized around the activity of a few big production and distribution companies, the Nigerian video industry comprises a constellation of small enterprises, which disappear and reappear according to the economic conditions. There are no formal contracts or insurance arrangements. Transactions are based on systems of solidarity and (mis)trust. Furthermore, as Brian Larkin demonstrates, the video industry evolved from the infrastructures provided by media piracy, and thus its position between legality and illegality has always been fluctuating.

The flexibility of this system allowed the video industry to cope with a highly unstable and potentially risky economic environment. But the absence of regulation, the ineffective copyright regime, and the low barriers to entry exposed the industry to a high degree of imitation and to an exponential level of competition, resulting in extremely rapid growth for video production. In fact, in less than twenty years, the output of the video industry increased from a few films per year in the early 1990s to around fifteen hundred per year by the mid-2000s.[2] While this impressive growth attracted international bodies like UNESCO, it also brought the video economy to a point of inevitable saturation. Overwhelmed by the number of weekly video releases (in 2007 the average was five per day) and by the high level of repetition of plots and titles, the Nigerian audience progressively lost interest in the local entertainment industry.[3]

The specificity of the Nigerian technological environment intensified the crisis. The introduction of digital technology played a fundamental role in the video industry's evolution. Home video technologies (VHS and VCD) generated a straight-to-video distribution model that was resistant to the devastating effects of the structural adjustment programs on the Nigerian entertainment sector at the end of the 1980s (Haynes, "Nigerian Cinema"). Going straight to video allowed Nigerian cultural entrepreneurs to cut the unaffordable costs of celluloid production and bypass the problem of theatrical release in the context of collapsing cinema infrastructures. But this solution made the video industry particularly vulnerable to piracy. Unlike other high-piracy film industries – for instance, Bollywood and the Hong Kong film industry, which can rely on income from a regulated system of cinema screenings – the Nigerian video industry has no window of distribution other than the video format (in VHS, VCD, or DVD).[4]

Within this system of structural vulnerability, each shift from one technological format to another has its own consequences. Amaka Igwe, for instance, made this point clear when she told me in a recent interview that the switch from VHS to VCD technology created unexpected problems.[5] During the VHS era, producers tended to make between 100,000 and 150,000 copies per film. If a film flopped, they would recycle the unsold tapes for another release, thereby cutting their losses. When VCD was introduced, this was no longer possible. According to Amaka Igwe, "You couldn't invest on 100,000 copies because if you don't sell them, you are in trouble, so people started making just 5,000, 10,000 copies, but for a market of 150 million people, what is it to make 5,000 copies? And meanwhile, we didn't create a solid distribution. And a VCD, as soon as you buy it, you can put it in your computer and dump it, so piracy became a big problem." The small number of original copies available in the video market opened up unexpected opportunities for pirated products. In a context in which legitimate distribution could not reach the majority of the population, piracy filled the gap.

The introduction of the satellite channel Africa Magic in 2003 and rising Internet piracy sent sales of original Nollywood film copies plunging. This in turn led to increased audience engagement with Nigerian videos. But because a structured distribution policy was lacking, the industry was unable to transform this popularity into solid economic growth. When Africa Magic was introduced, industry practitioners were unable to agree on a collective response. This gave the channel a good bargaining position. Negotiations were conducted on an individual basis and in most cases resulted in very low acquisition prices for screening rights.[6] At the same time, the availability of a 24/7 pan-African Nollywood channel reduced the sale of original copies, especially among the expanding Nigerian middle class that enthusiastically bought into satellite television technology. The middle class accounted for the largest percentage of the industry's income, considering that the most important section of the Nollywood audience, that is, housewives and unemployed youth, rented movies from video clubs rather than buying original copies.

Whereas the introduction of Africa Magic progressively eroded the sale of original copies in Nigeria and in some other Anglophone African countries, the mushrooming growth of Internet sites offering free streaming of Nigerian videos eroded the economic potential of the diasporic market. Although Nigeria has one of the highest rates of Internet usage in Africa, the quality of the connection rarely allows people to access bandwidth-heavy content like video. Most Internet viewing of Nollywood films therefore occurs in the diaspora, with unauthorized sites eroding what used to be lucrative revenue streams. As Fred Jora emphasizes in a number of interviews with Nigerian video sellers in Europe, the impact of Internet streaming and satellite television has badly damaged their business, obliging them to cut the number of videos ordered weekly from Nigeria. Sunday Omobude, a Nigerian businessman who owns a video store in Amsterdam, for example, is reported to have cut his orders from 8,000 films a week to 1,500, while the Internet site onlinenigeria.com, which broadcasts Nigerian films for free, is reported to have up to 700,000 visitors in forty-five countries around the world (Jora). A report on an anti-cybercrime operation by Nigerian police said that in 2006, more than twenty-five websites broadcast Nigerian videos free of charge. According to the report, most of them were registered in Britain and the United States and were owned by Nigerians living abroad (Ezigbo).

The downside of Nollywood's excessive, informal infrastructure, the saturation of the market, and the increase of piracy together with the global economic crisis (which badly hit the Nigerian banking system) worsened during the political crisis preceding the death of former Nigerian president Umaru Yar'Adua. This pushed the industry to an economic impasse that arguably reached its nadir between 2008 and 2009.[7] At this point, many practitioners and analysts started believing that the industry was destined to die (Husseini; Njoku, "Nollywood Is Dying"). At this stage of its evolution, and partly because of the above-mentioned factors, the video market's value was on a small-figure scale. The amount of films produced had in fact become inversely proportional to the number of copies sold and the funds available for production. An extremely large number of videos were produced during the phase leading up to the production crisis. But each of them had progressively smaller budgets and fewer legal purchases. The industry thus imploded, with average budgets falling to 2 million naira (around US$15,000) and average legal sales dropping to between 10,000 and 20,000 copies. When output started to drop as well, this economy of small numbers became unsustainable. Before the crisis, the large number of videos released by each production company in a year compensated for the small number of copies sold. When output was reduced, profit levels dropped, and the business stopped being attractive for investors.

Within this context, the diasporic market seemed to offer a viable economic solution. In the interviews I conducted during my fieldwork in Lagos, many directors supported this position. Femi Odugbemi, a director and producer based in Lagos, for instance, suggested, "Every filmmaker from Nigeria must look at the diaspora audience very care-

fully because that is really where the market is." Lancelot Oduwa Imasuen, a very popular director, confirmed Odugbemi's point of view by
reiterating the point that the "diaspora must become an important window of distribution for Nigerian videos." Emem Isong, one of the most
successful Nigerian female producers in recent history, mentioned this
fact, too, revealing that she releases her films first in America and then
in Ghana and Nigeria simultaneously. She added, "Nigeria, at this point,
is the worst market we have."

This was not the first time that producers turned their attention to
foreign audiences. Diasporic and international markets had been targeted since the early stages of Nollywood's evolution. As Ayorinde reported, for instance, the Peckham market in South London was throughout the mid-1990s even "stronger than the Idumota and the Onitsha
market outlets" ("Video and Celluloid"). However, since the Nigerian
domestic market was still doing well, no real attempt was made to develop international distribution. The situation became different ten years
later – that is, in 2009.

PIRATE TRANSNATIONALISM: BUILDING THE
MARKET FOR A GLOBAL CULTURAL INDUSTRY

The Nigerian video industry developed not in a vacuum but within a
system of media transnationalism, which helped to shape it in profound
ways. On the one hand, informal, usually pirated networks of transnational circulation made transnational media products available on the
Nigerian market and contributed to the aesthetics and narratives of the
video industry. And on the other hand, media piracy and transnational
informal circulation made Nigerian videos travel all over Africa and the
world, transforming them into a pan-African and global form of popular
culture. Brian Larkin argued that in the late 1970s and early 1980s, the
combination of a number of elements (the suspension of the distribution of American films in Nigeria by the Motion Picture Association of
America in 1981, the evolution of digital technologies, and the effect of
the oil-boom economy on the consumption of media products) rapidly
pushed Nigeria into the global network of pirated goods. This provided
Nigerians with "a vast array of world media at a speed they could never
imagine, hooking them up to the accelerated circuit of global media

flows" (297). Until the early 1980s, Hollywood, Bollywood, and Hong Kong films were available in Nigeria only a very long time after their official release and as badly damaged celluloid copies. Complex networks of media piracy, which often came through the United Arab Emirates (Dubai, Abu Dhabi) or eastern Asian cities (Singapore, Kuala Lumpur), suddenly made them available to a larger audience in a much shorter time. The availability of these media products increasingly influenced the imaginations of video makers, who created a creole aesthetic formula in which local and transnational influences converged.

As forms of popular culture, Nigerian video films were thus intrinsically cosmopolitan, since their appearance on the Nigerian market and their aesthetic form were the result of extended networks of transnational circulation of (mainly pirated) media. Once the industry started to grow significantly, these same networks became responsible for the transnational circulation of domestically produced Nigerian videos, as well as imported (U.S., Indian, and Asian) content. As Karin Barber emphasizes, "Modern popular arts have the capacity to transcend geographical, ethnic, and even national boundaries. Located in the cities, the centers both of technological change and of the rapidly growing twentieth century transport networks, they are endowed with an unprecedented mobility" (15). In the case of Nigerian videos, this mobility quickly extended beyond the borders of Nigeria. In this process, the widespread communities of Nigerian expatriates often played an important role in introducing the videos in other sub-Saharan African countries as well as in Europe and the United States. Nigerian videos thus became very popular in places such as Ghana, Zambia, Uganda, Kenya, Tanzania, Congo, South Africa, and Namibia. They attracted a wide diasporic audience also in Europe, the United States, Canada, and the Caribbean, where, according to Philip Cartelli, "at least 80 percent of the music or videos being sold come from Nigeria" (112).

However, Nigerian producers and distributors rarely controlled the economy generated by this huge interest from the diasporic bloc. Nollywood films, on the contrary, traveled largely under the regime of piracy. An example from my fieldwork experience might be useful here to understand the complexity of Nigerian videos' transnational circulation networks. A couple of years ago, I was walking through one of the many markets in central Naples (Italy), close to the main train station, looking for some Nigerian videos to buy. Most of the African stands that I found in the market were run by Senegalese vendors and were selling copies of what I thought were Francophone videos. Most of the DVDs on the shelves were pirated copies, and at first glance it was hard to get an idea of their content. Thus, to satisfy my curiosity, I decided to buy a few of them. When I watched one of them at home, I realized that its content was not, as I had imagined, a copy of some Senegalese or Ivorian television series. Instead, it was a copy of a recent Nigerian hit dubbed in French. In this version of the film, Nigerian video trailers, which precede most movies, had been substituted by specific advertisements oriented toward diasporic audiences. In addition, before the film's original credits sequence, someone had included the logo of a Francophone production company with addresses and phone numbers in Paris and Piacenza, Italy. When I rang the number, the head of the production company, a young Ivorian who had moved to Italy a few years earlier and set up a production and distribution business using his previous experiences in television and theater in Abidjan, answered. It transpired that his company trades in both Ivorian and Nigerian media products in Europe. While chatting with him, I discovered that the film I bought in Naples was a copy of a copy of a copy. This biography of mobility was fascinating but difficult to retrace. The video was shot in Lagos around 2005. Probably only a few weeks later, a pirated copy was acquired by a television studio in Abidjan and dubbed by professional artists. The Ivorian producer based in Italy managed to access a copy of the dubbed version and replicated it, working in partnership with an Italian digital media company. The film was then sold in Italy, Switzerland, France, Belgium, and Germany. One of these "original" pirated copies ended up in the hands of some other entrepreneur, presumably Senegalese, who pirated it once again and put it on the market in Naples. This was the version I finally bought.

As this example shows, the informal and pirate circulation of Nigerian videos excluded original producers from enjoying the benefits of Nollywood's transnational success. Each stage of the circulation process, in fact, implied a partial reinvention or rebranding of the product, cutting the connection with its original producer. Even if extremely effective in boosting Nollywood's popularity abroad, this kind of transnationalism also deepened the production crisis the industry underwent during this period.

The transnationalism I have described above is "minor" and "from below" (Adejunmobi). It is grounded in practices that are "neither self-consciously resistant nor even loosely political in character" (Smith and Guarnizo 5), but it equally tends to be charged with oppositional potentialities. This is an implicit oppositionality – comparable to that which Ravi Sundaram underlines in his analysis of the electronic modernity of urban India – that is the expression of a survival strategy more than the manifestation of an explicit political choice. It is a phenomenon "that is everyday in its imaginary, pirate in its practice, and mobile in its innovation" (61). This pirate transnationalism, profoundly informal, unregulated, and segmented, problematically fluctuates between legality and illegality. Its networks are well developed and able to reach every corner of the globe. But for the industry to access the economic profit it expects to gain from the diasporic market, piracy has to be domesticated and this transnationalism formalized.

PATHS OF FORMALIZATION: THE DIASPORA AS A MARKET

Processes of formalization take a long time to develop, and pirate networks that distribute Nigerian videos all over the world are probably destined to play a central role in Nollywood's circulation in the future. But in the past few years, initiatives to formalize the Nollywood diasporic market have emerged, and these could have a significant impact on the industry's economy. My focus here is on two specific experiences: the Filmmakers Association of Nigeria campaign against piracy in the United States and the Nollywood premiere system developed at Odeon cinemas in Britain.

The United States–based Nigerian director and producer Tony Abulu along with Rabiu Mohammed, Bethels Agomuoh, and Caroline Okoli created the Filmmakers Association of Nigeria in the early 2000s in New York. At the time, Mohammed owned a small video shop in the Bronx and now owns Sangha Entertainment, one of the biggest United States–based distributors of African videos. Agomuoh was one of the first to sell Nigerian videos online, while Okoli is a Nigerian national with a background in management. Abulu got the idea for creating this association after releasing his first film, *Back to Africa*, in 1997. When the film was ready for release, Abulu realized that there was no viable distribution framework for this type of product in the United States. At that time, Nigerian video films were in fact circulating mostly through piracy and informal networks. From its inception, therefore, FAN's main objective was to establish a solid infrastructure to distribute Nigerian films in the United States. To do so, FAN first had to tackle the issue of piracy and organize a system of collecting copyright royalties on behalf of Nigerian filmmakers (Abulu). To achieve this, FAN sponsored a copyright conference in Washington in 2005 at which representatives of the video industry met a delegation from the U.S. Department of Justice, the International Intellectual Property Institute, the Public Interest Intellectual Property Advisors (PIIPA), and the African Artist Collaborative (ACC, a nonprofit institution created by Abulu himself). The most important outcome of this meeting was an agreement that PIIPA would provide free assistance to denounce and litigate copyright infringements in the country on behalf of Nigerian filmmakers who had registered the copyright of their films in the United States. As a result of the agreement, in the following years FAN encouraged Nigerian filmmakers to lodge such registrations in the United States through ACC.

As noted above, the diasporic market has suffered and continues to suffer deeply under Internet piracy, and particularly from Internet sites offering free streaming of Nigerian videos. With the support of U.S. antipiracy institutions, FAN started suing Internet pirates selling Nollywood films. Some of them reached some form of settlement and started to collaborate with FAN to distribute Nigerian videos legally.[8] However, following repeated complaints of pirated Nigerian films in Brooklyn, FAN put pressure on American police to act. In early November 2010, a large antipiracy raid was conducted, nine illegal video shops were investigated, and ten thousand pirated Nollywood videos were seized, marking a remarkable and highly visible success for FAN's antipiracy campaign.

In Britain, which is home to the second-largest group of Nigerians in the diaspora after the United States, most Nigerian videos were circulated through pirated networks. Even if in the early 1990s a number of marketers (Afelele and Sons, Alasco Videos, Bayowa) invested in the legal distribution of Yoruba videos in London (Ayorinde, "Video and Celluloid"), the years following the popular success of the videos further opened the market to piracy. The action undertaken by a number of Nigerians living in London in recent years has focused on taking Nollywood off the shelves and the pirate websites and bringing it into the cinemas. The introduction of scheduled movie premieres at Odeon cinemas was intended to progressively create a demand for the theatrical release of Nollywood films with a view to moving them into the mainstream cinema distribution network (Babatope). Since it began in 2006, this system has worked at achieving three main goals: encouraging diasporic Nigerian audiences to watch Nollywood films in the cinema, compiling economic data that could reflect the theatrical demand for Nollywood films and then convince mainstream cinema distributors to invest in them, and inducing Nigerian producers to upgrade the technical quality of their films to make them conform to cinema standards.

This theatrical exhibition system has precedents. Various cinema screenings of Nigerian films had been organized in Britain, as in the United States, since the early years of Nollywood, but they were not formally structured. In most cases, films were shown in privately rented screening rooms and conference venues or in neighborhood cinemas. With the introduction of the Odeon premieres (at Odeon Surrey Quay, near London Bridge, in the first three years, and in Odeon Greenwich during 2010), the premieres became a more sophisticated ritual, which mostly centered on the star system.[9] The premieres are designed as social events: journalists and media partners gather around a red-carpet area two hours before the screening begins, and fans line up near the entrance in anticipation of the stars' arrival. When the director and the actors arrive, tension rises, the atmosphere becomes glamorous, and people move in for a closer look. The aim is to create something that the audience can perceive as unique. As the experience of attending the premiere of Emem Isong's *Bursting Out* in October 2010 made me realize, it is a successful formula. That evening, the Odeon Greenwich was overcrowded, probably also because of the presence of superstar Genevieve Nnaji, who rarely attends public events, even in Nigeria. Two additional screening rooms had to be provided at the last minute to accommodate the Nollywood enthusiasts, and the celebrations went on until late at night.

Some of the films premiered during 2010 and entered mainstream distribution during 2011. The films selected are those that, according to some commentators, represent a new Nigerian cinema, or a "new Nolly-wood" (Ebere; Ekunno).[10] However, the debate around the definition of this new trend is still open. On the one hand, those who propose the term *new Nollywood* tend to emphasize a relation of continuity between the video-boom era and the new releases and argue that the emergence of this new trend is a direct consequence of the video phenomenon. On the other hand, those who prefer the term *new Nigerian cinema* under-line the specificity of this new trend and its distance from the defining aspects of the video phenomenon (low-budget production, straight-to-video modes of distribution, popular and populist narratives, and aesthetics). Personally, I prefer to define it as a "New Wave" in Nigerian cinema to underline the fact that although it emerged from the experi-ence of the video phenomenon, it is a trend whose defining aspects dif-fer from those of mainstream Nollywood releases. In fact, these films, which have high budgets and production values, are shot with an inter-national crew, are often set in the diaspora, and target mainly cinema audiences.

A NEW WAVE IN NIGERIAN CINEMA

Three films in particular can be seen as the avant-garde of the new wave: Jeta Amata's *The Amazing Grace* (2006), Kunle Afolayan's *Irapada* (2007), and Stephanie Okereke's *Through the Glass* (2007). These films repre-sent three different levels at which processes of transnationalization are transforming the video industry: modes of production, audiences, and settings.

Although it was not a big hit, Amata's historical film about slavery has to be considered here, as it was the result of an international copro-duction and targeted in particular international and diasporic markets. Amata's artistic biography is in itself an interesting example of the trans-national trajectories happening within the video industry. His career was boosted by his participation in the BBC documentary about the video phenomenon, *Nick Goes to Nollywood* (2004). During this project, he developed a strong friendship with Nick Moran, a British actor who played one of the main roles in *The Amazing Grace,* and Alicia Arce, the producer of both the BBC documentary and *The Amazing Grace.* This experience rapidly gave him a number of chances to develop his skills and to access international funding for his projects. *The Amazing Grace* was developed explicitly around the idea of pushing the video industry to a new level, improving technical standards (the film was shot in 35mm), and targeting international audiences through film festivals; it was presented at the Film Market during the Cannes Film Festival in 2006. This movie started a trend still followed by some new releases. Mamood Ali-Balogun's *Tango with Me* (2011) and Jeta Amata's *Black Gold* (2011), for instance, were both shot on celluloid and produced in Nigeria with an international crew. They both target international film festivals as a way of entering mainstream theatrical distribution.

Even if entirely Nigerian in terms of production, Kunle Afolayan's film *Irapada* represents the section of Nollywood that is trying to restructure the industry's economy from within, practicing an innovative funding strategy and developing formal modes of distribution that imply a new role for the diasporic market. *Irapada* is, in fact, one of the first films to have achieved mainstream release in Odeon cinemas in Britain in 2007, at a time when the premiere system described in the previous section was only beginning (Ayorinde, "Nollywood"). This film was also one of the first to be released on DVD only a few months after its theatrical release (and not, as usually happens, going straight to VCD at the same time as the theatrical release). It also managed to circulate in a number of international film festivals, anticipating the success of Afolayan's subsequent release, *The Figurine* (2009), and opening the way for a growing number of medium- or high-budget films shot in digital that intend to target local, pan-African, and diasporic audiences simultaneously, like Vivian Ejike's *Silent Scandal* (2009), Lancelot Oduwa Imasuen's *Home in Exile* (2010), and Teco Benson's *High Blood Pressure* (2010).

Stephanie Okereke's *Through the Glass* reflects another tendency within the framework produced by transnationalization processes. The film, a light comedy set in Los Angeles, was in fact shot in a diasporic context with a transnational crew. When released in Nigeria, this film earned more than 10 million naira (almost US$65,000) at the box office in three weeks, solely through theatrical release in a handful of Nigerian cinemas. It was the first theatrical success of its kind, and it clearly showed many industry practitioners that the revival of a cinema-going culture was a phenomenon to be taken seriously. Furthermore, through its diasporic setting, this film anticipates an important trend common to many of the recent high-quality releases. As I will discuss further below, the diaspora is the central plot in many of these films. Although diasporic settings are not new in the video industry (Ayorinde, "Video and Celluloid"; Haynes, "Africans Abroad" and this volume), their prominent role in the new wave testifies to the growing influence of the diaspora on the video industry as a site of production, a textual device, and a market.

According to Babatope, the list of films that have achieved mainstream release in British cinemas during 2011 and 2012 includes many that were shot in the diaspora. Lucky Ejim's *The Tenant* (2008), Chineze Anyeane's *Ije, the Journey* (2010), Lonzo Nnzekue's *Anchor Baby* (2010), and Obi Emelonye's *Mirror Boy* (2011), for instance, were all shot abroad with transnational casts and crews. They all premiered at Odeon in London, and most of them accessed theatrical distribution in Nigeria and, later, in England.

Within this list, the film *Ije* is particularly interesting. Shot in California and Nigeria's Plateau State, *Ije* is a thriller whose tension is built around the contrast between the illusion of the American Dream and the harsh realities of racism and sexism found in U.S. society. The film stars two extremely popular Nigerian actors, Genevieve Nnaji and Omotola Jalade-Ekeinde, with the rest of the cast mainly composed of African American and U.S. actors. The film was shot in 35mm with an international crew. The budget has never been disclosed, but it is likely that it could easily reach the record level (for a Nigerian film) of US$1 million. Once released in Nigeria, in July 2010, the film became the greatest box-office success since the reintroduction of cinema halls in Nigeria, more successful than mainstream Hollywood films like *Pirates of the Caribbean*. It made around 60 million naira (US$380,000) in three weeks of screening in just five cinemas in Nigeria: Silverbird, Ozone, and Genesis-Deluxe in Lagos; Silverbird in Abuja; and Genesis-Deluxe in Port Harcourt. If, as mentioned before, the box-office success of *Through the Glass* had brought the economic potential of theatrical release to the attention of Nigerian producers a few years earlier, the incredible success of *Ije* made them see it as more than simply potential. Furthermore, after its release in Nigeria, the film was successfully released in other African countries, and a Western distributor has negotiated to buy the rights for mainstream release in Europe and in the United States (Babatope).

As discussed throughout this chapter, while processes of transnational-ization have shaped Nollywood since the beginning, they are today as-suming a particularly influential role in the video industry. The economy of small numbers that characterized Nigerian video filmmaking in past years has probably ceased to be viable, and the pirate transnationalism that underwrote Nollywood's global success is today explicitly seen as a threat to the further expansion of the Nigerian video industry. Produc-ers are now interested in bigger numbers: high budgets, mainstream theatrical releases, and global audiences. Formalization became, thus, the strategy that most people consider the only one worth adopting. As long as the Nigerian economy maintains its high level of informality and plans to formalize the local industry continue to be ineffective, going transnational seems to be the only viable solution.[11]

What does this process mean in terms of the video industry's so-cial impact on local audiences? And what is going to change in terms of the popularity and accessibility of Nigerian videos? The success of the Nigerian video phenomenon has in fact been based on its capacity to in-terpret the dreams, fears, and expectations of its local popular audience. And the informality of Nollywood's specific modes of production and distribution has had a fundamental role in making videos accessible for the lowest classes of the Nigerian social pyramid. Even if the construc-tion of new theater halls throughout the country were under way, the transition to cinema would inevitably affect the popular accessibility of Nigerian films, transforming the very nature of the video phenomenon and its social impact.[12]

Moreover, what is going to happen to the aesthetics and narratives of Nigerian videos if producers start considering the Nigerian and world-wide African diasporas as their main audiences? What if the video era must die for cinema culture to be born again? The new wave described in the previous section has in fact shifted its focus from a local-popular to a transnational-elitist audience, an audience whose economic support might prove vital for the industry's survival, but whose tastes, interests, and social and cultural values probably differ profoundly from those of the popular audience that patronized the videos since the early days of the industry. This shift is provoking important aesthetic, narrative, and economic transformations that have to be taken into account by those who are analyzing the video phenomenon and its most recent developments. Nollywood has received much international scholarly attention in the past few years, and part of it has been attracted precisely by the features of the industry that are now seen as liabilities: the informality of its modes of production and distribution, the specificity and localism of its aesthetics, and the impact of straight-to-video distribution on the viewers' experience. What will the recent transformations represent for the industry as a whole? And how are they going to influence the way the video phenomenon is represented and discussed?

Nollywood revolutionized African screens in the past fifteen to twenty years, arguably because it was a commercially driven initiative in which no ideological project has counted more than the pragmatic and economic calculations made by the people who invested in it. The growing transnationalization of the industry appears to be commercially driven as well. It might be a phase, or it might be a solid development. It might mean the end of the video industry, but it could also represent a further revolution in the geography of media consumption on the continent and throughout the diaspora.

Going transnational and going back to the cinema are two movements on which a part of the industry is concentrating most of its efforts. Many are scared that this might turn the video industry away from its own audience. But this might equally not be the case. A question mark hangs over the industry's future. Important transformations are under way, and it is probably too early to make a coherent evaluation of their impact on the Nigerian mediascape.

The words of Moses Babatope, one of the distributors I interviewed during my research, can offer a conclusion that suggests a hopeful future for the industry, while recognizing the complexity of the present situation:

> I would say that Nollywood needs this phase, I don't think it would be permanent. . . . I hope I'm not being too optimistic, but I believe that this is a phase which the entire entertainment sector has to pass through, a process to filter off the negative elements that blocked the industry. I see a proliferation of cinema in the next three to four years, and there will be more affordable cinemas, as there are everywhere in the world. There are too many stories to tell, too much demand, to restrict the potential of the films, and hopefully this phase that we

are seeing is only a necessary phase that would bring us to a next step. We would be able to discover technologies that will help us combat piracy better . . . and I think that in three to four years we will have technologies in place, laws in place, that will make films again more accessible.

NOTES

1. This article is the result of research conducted mainly in Lagos. Therefore, the results presented here concern specifically the southern Nigerian section of the industry and particularly the English video film–producing section. I thank Ramon Lobato, Manuela Ribeiro Sanches, and the editors of this volume for their insightful comments, suggestions, and revisions.

2. Figures from the Nigerian Censors Board official website, http://www.nfvcb .gov.ng/statistics.php. Although the official statistics help to provide a general idea of the industry's tendencies, they are not completely reliable. In the early years of the Censors Board, only a very small percentage of video production passed through censorship. This explains the small number of films censored in 1994 (only three) at a time when the industry was already burgeoning. Even today, many films go straight to market without passing through the official channels. However, the Censors Board statistics are the only official figures in existence, and it is useful to consult them as a general reference.

3. According to the informal interviews I conducted with spectators of the films in Nigeria, many people had the feeling that the taste and the critical capacity of the audience were underestimated. The same feeling becomes evident when looking at the comments posted on Internet platforms dedicated to recent Nollywood releases.

4. By the terms *window* and *windowing,* the cinema industries indicate their control of circulation over time. In global film industries like Hollywood or Bollywood, a film is normally released in theaters, then after a while on DVD, then on pay TV, and finally on television stations.

5. VCD: video compact disc. According to Davis, "VCDs first caught on in Hong Kong when Japanese serial dramas, or *dorama,* were circulated in the mid-1990s" (166). Since then, thanks to their low manufacturing costs, versatility, and disposability, they have become extremely popular in most non-Western countries. They arrived in Nigeria around 1999–2000, apparently thanks to the initiative of a marketer who decided to pioneer in the business of selling Chinese VCD readers and consequently also invested in distributing Nigerian videos in this format (Ajirire).

6. The average price paid by M-Net is eight hundred to one thousand U.S. dollars for unlimited but not exclusive screening rights (Njoku, "We Are Not Responsible").

7. The number of English-language videos released in the past years evidences the crisis. In 2007 the Censors Board registered 682 English-language videos, in 2008 393, in 2009 244, and in the first ten months of 2010 only 114. These are figures from the Nigerian Film and Video Censors Board as reported in Oni (39).

8. The case of the Internet site http:// www.onlinenigeria.com is particularly interesting. It was in fact considered until recently the largest pirate online platform of Nigerian videos, with almost seven hundred thousand subscribers. After being publicly attacked by FAN, the owner of the

website, a Nigerian based in the United States, proposed to settle the matter and to use his successful platform for legal distribution (Abulu).

9. The Afro-Hollywood Awards, organized by a group of Nigerians in London since 1996, can be seen as the forerunner of star-centered-type events for the Nigerian diaspora in Britain. Since the first edition, in fact, the organizers brought many Nigerian stars to London and helped consolidate the ties between diasporic audiences and the Nigerian video industry.

10. In October 2010, the Virgo Foundation, created by London-based Nigerian actor Wale Ojo to promote Nigerian contemporary arts in Nigeria, organized the New Nigeria Cinema event at the British Film Institute in London. During this event, some of the new releases discussed in the next section were screened, and the emergence of a new wave in Nigerian cinema was discussed, promoted, and explicitly sanctioned. Interestingly, all the filmmakers attending the event were Nigerian diasporic filmmakers. The act

of sanctioning the existence of this new wave, thus, assumed a transnational dimension that emphasized the role of the diaspora in shaping the video industry's new developments.

11. The application of the new distribution framework introduced by the Nigerian Film and Video Censors Board in 2007 has hardly shown any result, nor has the Strategic Action Against Piracy enforced by the Nigerian Copyright Commission. For further discussion on this argument, see Jedlowski.

12. During the second part of my fieldwork in Lagos (December 2010–March 2011), I counted no fewer than seven different Nigerian companies investing in the construction of new cinemas – both multiplexes and neighborhood halls. However, as the general manager of the Ozone Cinemas told me, "Cinema is a business that might not expand as quickly as people tend to think" (Lee), because it takes more time to build the infrastructures and to generate the commercial demand than investors expect.

WORKS CITED

Abulu, Tony. Personal interview. Lagos, December 16, 2010.

Adejunmobi, Moradewum. "Nigerian Video Film as Minor Transnational Practice." *Postcolonial Text* 3.2 (2007): n. pag. Web.

Ajirire, Tosin. "How I Pioneered Video CD in Nigeria – Ken Hero." *National Concord*, July 15, 2000, 17.

Ayorinde, Steve. "Nollywood Leaps to London's Forefront." *Punch*, September 28, 2007. Web.

———. "Video and Celluloid . . . A Homeboy Shoots Up Abroad." *Guardian* (Nigeria), January 28, 1999, 47.

Babatope, Moses Olumuyiwa. Personal interview. London, November 16, 2010.

Barber, Karin. "Popular Arts in Africa." *African Studies Review* 30.3 (1987): 1–78.

Cartelli, Philip. "Nollywood Comes to the Caribbean." *Film International* 5.4 (2007): 112–14.

Davis, Darrel William. "Compact Generation: VCD Markets in Asia." *Historical Journal of Film, Radio, and Television* 23.2 (2003): 165–76.

Ebere, Reginald. "The New Nollywood." *National Daily*, March 12, 2011. Web.

Ekunno, Mike. "Nollywood and the New Cinema." *Next*, January 2, 2011. Web.

Ezigbo, Onyebuchi. "Anti-cyber Crime Operators Threaten Movie Pirates." *All Africa*, April 30, 2006. Web.

Guyer, Jane. *Marginal Gains: Monetary Transactions in Atlantic Africa.* Chicago: University of Chicago Press, 1997.

Haynes, Jonathan. "Africans Abroad: A Theme in Film and Video." *Africa e Mediterraneo* 45 (December 2003): 22–29.

———. "Nigerian Cinema: Structural Adjustment." *Research in African Literatures* 26.3 (1995): 97–119.

Husseini, Shaibu. "Nollywood 2008: Stuck in the Middle of Nowhere." *Guardian* (Nigeria), January 23, 2009, 24–25.

Igwe, Amaka. Personal interview. Lagos, January 25, 2010.

Imasuen, Lancelot Oduwa. Personal interview. Lagos, February 12, 2010.

Isong, Emem. Personal interview. Lagos, January 10, 2011.

Jedlowski, Alessandro. "Beyond the Video Boom: New Tendencies in the Nigerian Video Industry." Paper presented at ASAUK Writing Workshop, Birmingham (UK), April 16, 2010.

Jora, Fred. "The Big Rip-off: How Nollywood Films Are Shown on Net Free of Charge . . . Europe Based Stakeholders Cry Foul." *Vanguard,* October 27, 2007, 20.

Kaur, Raminder, and Ajay J. Sinha, eds. *Bollyworld: Popular Indian Cinema through a Transnational Lens.* New Delhi: Sage, 2005.

Larkin, Brian. "Degraded Images, Distorted Sounds: Nigerian Video and the Infrastructure of Piracy." *Public Culture* 16.2 (2004): 289–314.

Lee, Patrick. Personal interview. Lagos, February 17, 2011.

Njoku, Benjamin. "Nollywood Is Dying: Interview with Francis Onwochei." *Vanguard,* February 21, 2009, 36.

———. "We Are Not Responsible for Nollywood's Woes – Interview with Biola Alabi, M-Net MD." *Vanguard,* August 15, 2009, 26.

Odugbemi, Femi. Personal interview. Lagos, January 25, 2010.

Oni, Duro. "Lighting: Beyond Illumination." *Inaugural Lecture Series, 2010.* Lagos: Lagos University Press, 2010.

Smith, Michael P., and Luis E. Guarnizo. "The Locations of Transnationalism." *Transnationalism from Below.* Ed. Michael P. Smith and Luis E. Guarnizo. New Brunswick, N.J.: Transaction, 1998. 3–34.

Sundaram, Ravi. "Recycling Modernity: Pirate Electronic Cultures in India." *Third Text* 13.47 (1999): 59–65.

UNESCO Institute for Statistics. *Analysis of the UIS International Survey on Feature Film Statistics.* Montreal: UIS, April 2009. 1–15. Web.

FILMOGRAPHY

The Amazing Grace. Dir. Jeta Amata. Jeta Amata Concepts and Amazing Grace Films (Nigeria and UK). 2006.

Anchor Baby. Dir. Lonzo Nnzekue. Alpha Galore Films (Canada and Nigeria). 2010.

Back to Africa. Dir. Tunde Alabi. Bonag and Tony Abulu Film (Nigeria). 1997.

Black Gold. Dir. Jeta Amata. Jeta Amata Concepts et al. (Nigeria). 2011.

Bursting Out. Dir. Daniel Ademinokan and Desmond Elliot. Emem Isong Production (Nigeria). 2010.

The Figurine. Dir. Kunle Afolayan. Golden Effects (Nigeria). 2010.

High Blood Pressure. Dir. Teco Benson. Goodlife Production (Nigeria). 2010.

Home in Exile. Dir. Lancelot Oduwa Imasuen. Iceslides Films and Lancewealth Images (Nigeria). 2010.

Ije, the Journey. Dir. Chineze Anyeane. Xandria Productions (United States and Nigeria). 2010.

Irapada. Dir. Kunle Afolayan. Golden Effects (Nigeria). 2007.

Mirror Boy. Dir. Obi Emelonye. Nollywood Film Factory and OH Films (UK). 2011.

Nick Goes to Nollywood. Dir. Alicia Arce and Brenda Goldblatt. BBC (UK). 2004.

Pirates of the Caribbean: Dead Man's Chest. Dir. Gore Verbinski. Walt Disney Pictures (United States). 2006.

Silent Scandal. Dir. Tokunbo Falope. Vivian Ejike Production (Nigeria). 2009.

Tango with Me. Dir. Mamood Ali-Balogun. Brickwall Communication (Nigeria). 2011.

The Tenant. Dir. Onyekachi Ejim. Broken Manacles Entertainment (Canada). 2008.

Through the Glass. Dir. Stephanie Okereke. Next Page Production (United States and Nigeria). 2007.

TWO

Nollywood's Transportability: The Politics and Economics of Video Films as Cultural Products

JYOTI MISTRY AND JORDACHE A. ELLAPEN

THE OPPORTUNITY IS RIFE FOR A CRITICAL ENGAGEMENT WITH the central ideas espoused in contemporary writing on Nollywood as it relates to the broader historical and political concerns of African cinema and Third Cinemas as canonized through cinema and film studies. According to Larkin, both "form and industrial organization" of Nollywood filmmaking "represent a radical reworking of the basis of African cinema and visual culture" (173). The canon of African cinema when discussed in the context of Nollywood has easily been conflated with reference to a move from celluloid to video. Even though there are significant differences, broader philosophical and epistemic issues that have informed scholarship on African cinema appear to have eroded an ideological and aesthetic analysis of Nollywood. This chapter aims to open up the debate past the euphoria and celebration of Nollywood as a place of self-representation and its significance as an entrepreneurial endeavor that subverts conventional modes of exhibition and distribution. The intention of our analysis is to reflect on the vital and productive contradictions that have enabled the development and evolution of video films as a site for significant cultural production on the African continent. It is clear at the outset that the success of Nollywood marks a radical intervention to how video technologies can be mobilized to enable self-expression. However, the delimitations and implications in terms of how this informs content and aesthetic developments are less apparent.

Nollywood offers anthropology and popular culture studies invaluable analytical opportunities to address how new forms of representation emerge from postcolonial environments. The significance of Nollywood is its grassroots status, and that the people themselves create it represents at once a confluence of folkloric traditions and practices while also engaging with ideas of what might constitute African modernity as evidenced through narrative choices.

Nollywood video films stand to challenge and reconstitute the canonized theory of African cinema, and that they serve as inspiration to other African countries on account of their mode of production makes the study of these video films provocative. In South Africa, over the past ten years, there has been an emergence of grassroots video film industries that have strategically aligned themselves with Nollywood. Not only have they capitalized on the commercial success of the brand "Nollywood," but they have also positioned video filmmaking as the ideal manner in which film technology can be democratized in the postcolony.[1]

By exploring the emerging video film industries in South Africa, the issue of "transportability" comes to the fore not simply as a mode of production but also as it might relate to the historical concerns about the political and ideological influences of African cinema. These implications are informed by a complex matrix of competing and complementary forces: conditions of production, modes of distribution, content, and the pan-Africanism of Nollywood. In terms of distribution, we distinguish between "Market" and "market" appeals.[2] In the latter instance, copyright, formal economies, and trading structures are often subverted or violated.

By analyzing the interrelationships in this matrix, we propose to problematize the transportability of the Nollywood model that has attracted African film producers by positioning video filmmaking on the continent as the alternative to more institutionalized practices of filmmaking. In other words, in considering the conditions of production, we contrast the idea of institutional frameworks that enable and fund film production with the "looser" entrepreneurial mode of production emblematic of Nollywood. The success of Nollywood has been based on the entrepreneurial grassroots endeavors of producers, while more formal structures of filmmaking have conventionally been through state funding, broadcasters, coproductions, and other regulating funding bodies. The argument for these institutional frameworks (one aspect of the conditions of production) forms a vital part in determining content. It should be made clear that we do not deny the contribution of the entrepreneurial spirit that has made Nollywood successful, but rather wish to reflect on this specific aspect that creates an interesting conflation between the producers of content and their audiences. In addressing this omission of a critical distance between the audiences and filmmakers-producers, we intend to suggest reasons for the lack of reflexivity in content that arises from the dissolution of the more formal (institutional) relationship between content, producers, and consumers.

Under modes of distribution, we will consider how the contexts of viewing as described in the work of Brian Larkin and Onookome Okome perpetuate meanings and cultural constructs that do not necessarily enable a political agenda for social change. In this instance, the political emphasis of Third Cinema theorists and practitioners who saw the collectivizing experience of cinema as a vehicle for political and social development in the postcolony requires radical reassessment because of Nollywood's emergence as a cinema from the African continent. Phrased more directly, although anthropology and cultural studies have been quick to recognize the relevance of Nollywood films as a cultural product, Nollywood has not received similar attention from cinema and film studies, and its incorporation into the canon of African cinema has been delayed. There is an implicit tension between the politically progressive definitions of African cinema (derived from an alliance with Third Cinema) juxtaposed with the popular form of Nollywood films that may suggest an ideologically regressive politics.

In addressing the issue of content, we draw from the increasing literature that now offers a more critical position on narratives in Nigerian and Ghanaian video films; their representations of women, occult economies, and traditional customs and values; and the perpetuation of ethnic and gender (read: sexual as well) stereotypes. Under content, we interrogate the relationship between production conditions and content to examine how they are linked to each other.

In the final instance, the Nollywood model of low-budget, high-turnover films made by grassroots entrepreneurs for broad-based audiences (as opposed to niche audiences) is appealing to other African countries precisely because it offers alternatives that have not been possible in the past.[3] The remarkable shift in technology (digital cameras, editing software, and easier duplication) has created a fertile environment for video film productions that is immediate and can be produced by the consumers themselves.

NOLLYWOOD IN THE CONTEXT OF AFRICAN CINEMA

In his now canonical text *African Cinema,* Manthia Diawara tackles the complexity of defining an African cinema not just by addressing the issues of content but by recognizing that the modes of production and distribution are primary drivers in shaping the agenda of African cinema (viii).

What he refers to as "technological paternalism" (5) suggests that colonizers dominate by controlling technologies. The implication here for Diawara is that the medium of cinema itself and its infrastructural concomitants (film schools, distribution networks, and exhibition spaces) function to produce "knowledge" from within the colonizer's cultural structures. Both Diawara's *African Cinema* and Frank Ukadike's *Black African Cinema* suggest that the political agenda and the reflexivity of African self-expression are linked to an ideological agenda (harking back to orality, adaptation of classical and seminal African authors, and revisionist histories through cinema). Both authors link postcolonial African cinema to Frantz Fanon's national culture project and, by extension, to the political imperatives of a Third Cinema (accessible cinema that demystifies the production process and a cinema with the political imperatives of reclaiming a history from within the postcolonial experience).

Although we would attest that the historical moment of many Third Cinema debates might be revisited (consider Jim Pines and Paul Willemen), it offers an important way of considering the historical and political agenda informing the underpinnings of African cinema. The radical departure that Nollywood poses to the political and ideological debates in African cinema potentially challenges "the role of cinema" in the postcolony. In other words, "the role of cinema" as shaped by the ideas of Third Cinema and African cinema highlighted the political significance of cinema as a vehicle for reshaping history (revisionist histories), for creating social change, and for offering a greater alignment between the experiences of the masses and the images that were being represented but created from a position of critical reflection:

> Third Cinema is a cinema neither of nor for "the people," nor is it simply a matter of expressing opposition to imperialism or to bourgeois rule. It is a cinema made by intellectuals who, for political and artistic reasons at one and the same time, assume their responsibilities as socialist intellectuals and seek to

achieve through their work the production of social intelligibility. Moreover, remembering Edward Said's point about the need for criticism, their pursuit of the creative understanding of particular social realities takes the form of a criti-cal dialogue – hence the need for both lucidity and close contact with popular discourses and aspirations – with a people itself engaged in bringing about social change. Theirs is not an audience in the Hollywood or the televisual sense, where popularity is equated with consumer satisfaction and where pleasure is measured in terms of the units of local currency entered on the balance sheet. Theirs like Brecht's is a fighting notion of . . . an experimental cinema engaged in a constant process of research. And like Brecht, the Latin Americans reserve the right to resort to any formal device they deem necessary to achieve their goals, as is clear from their refusal to straitjacket themselves into a codified Third Cinema aesthetic. (Willemen 27)

We would like to suggest that the more recent Nollywood form de-tracts from the historically political, ideological, and aesthetic review of African cinema and instead might offer an alternative self-determinism that is perhaps about emerging (alternate) forms of representation that challenge previous notions of what constitutes contemporary African cinema. This quest for self-determinism beyond the "technological pa-ternalism" of (neo)colonial structures that inform funding and shape content choices is central to the vision of an African modernity that in turn is connected to alternate economic structures of trade and ex-change that have enabled the distribution of video films.

Diawara outlines three categories to describe African cinema: So-cial Realist Narratives (examples cited are *Le Mandat, Xala, Baara,* and *Finyé*), Colonial Confrontation (examples cited are *Sarraounia, Heritage Africa,* and *Camp de Thiaroye*), and Return to the Source (examples cited are *Yeelen* and *Wend Kuuni*) (140–66). Briefly, in the first category, "the filmmakers often use a traditional position to criticize and link certain forms of modernity to neo-colonialism and cultural imperialism. . . . The social realist movement draws from existing popular forms such as song and dance, the oral tradition (both literary and rumors), and popular theatre" (141). These similarities are maintained in contempo-rary Nollywood cinema. The second are "historical narratives . . . justi-fied by the need to bring out of the shadows, the role played by African people in shaping their own history. It is also the case that they want to film a liberation struggle to keep it forever in people's minds" (152). In a significantly rudimentary fashion, Nollywood relies on mythic or folkloric kinds of history to create narratives that have a contemporary interpretation. Rarely do Nollywood films consider revisionist colonial histories. Video film narratives are often informed by immediate social and cultural concerns facing the local community, and the inspirations for stories have a localized appeal. Consider the examples that follow later in this analysis: Kumaran Naidoo's films *Broken Promises* and *Run for Your Life* and Kingsley Ogoro's *Osuofia in London*. Finally, the third genre Diawara suggests is informed by a conscious polemic on the part of the filmmakers to reexamine African traditions by exploring cinematic aesthetics that speak to a political desire outside of colonial knowledges. This also criticizes a precolonial romanticism as Frantz Fanon warned about in *The Wretched of the Earth*, but nonetheless this category addresses the importance of reflexivity by filmmakers searching for an African idiosyncratic, visual language.

Achille Mbembe in his book *On the Postcolony* develops a framework for understanding aesthetics in the postcolony, which he refers to as the "aesthetics of vulgarity" (102). This construct offers a language to discuss why Nollywood has had to grapple with strong criticism of its content and production value (its idiosyncratic visual language). Nollywood consists of entrepreneurs who, although not formally trained filmmakers, have been successfully exploiting technological developments (digital filmmaking), which has created the context for a more accessible and democratic mode of production. Furthermore, these opportunistic creators of video films are not subordinate to any institutional frameworks (in this sense a *commandement*) but instead operate from within the postcolony as subjects who generate content.

> In the postcolony, the *commandement* seeks to institutionalize itself, to achieve legitimation and hegemony . . . in the form of a *fetish*. The signs, vocabulary, and narratives that the *commandement* produces are meant not merely to be symbols; they are officially invested with a surplus of meanings that are not negotiable and that one is officially forbidden to depart from or challenge. . . . We therefore need to examine: how the world of meanings thus produced is ordered; the types of institutions, the knowledges, norms, and practices structuring this new "common sense"; the light that the use of visual imagery and discourse throws on the nature of domination and subordination. (103)

This is important for how we might understand its implications for production conditions and the reflexive space necessary between filmmakers-producers and the subjects who consume the visual (the grotesque and obscene).[4] In this respect, the issue of transportability is one of a political climate and the implicit and explicit relationship between the *commandement* (the institutional frameworks through which content is produced) and the subjects who consume the content.

Onookome Okome draws from the work of Davis Hecht and Maliqalim Simone to address cultural and social formations as

> "invisible governance, a frame of elliptical efforts that maintain competing agendas and aspirations." . . . It is in this zone of social activities that the public is transformed into the active *audience.* The audience that I refer to is not constituted as an *a priori* category but by the semantics of the peculiar needs of the moment, which are always but loosely inspired by social and economic contingencies. In other words, the newly constituted audience exists, as it were, in a flexible geography of desire. . . . [I]t does not give up the aspiration of a social mobility that seek[s] to replace or even come to the same economic status as the political ruling class, which is perceived as the stumbling block to its common welfare.

The public here function as "subjects" in the absence of the *commandement* structure of production. Thus, there is no critical distance between the producers or drivers of content and the public. This critical distance is intrinsic to creating content that is not singularly about presentations of social conventions but about *representation,* the latter being the space for ideological and political engagement. In other words, the public are in effect the creators of content. Consider also Okome's reference to the ways in which news events and local incidents become the content for films, or the fact that local perception of political figures is perpetuated or reinforced through Nollywood films. Mbembe further argues that in the postcolony, "the emphasis should be on the logic of 'conviviality,' on the dynamics of domesticity and familiarity, inscribing the dominant and the dominated within the same episteme" (110).

This is perhaps one of the most convincing reasons for the immediate uptake of Nollywood as an analytical device in anthropology, because it often provides "unmediated" traces or symptoms of instantaneous concerns in the communities in which they are made and to whom they cater. Thus, "the dynamics of domesticity and familiarity" dismantles any hierarchical relationship between what is shown in the films and the audiences' experiences. It also counters the constant criticism that African cinema has faced regarding its literariness or symbolic specificity that has made itself elusive to mainstream (popular) African audiences.

In his article "The Emerging Video Film Industry in Nigeria: Challenges and Prospects," Patrick Ebewo not only challenges Nollywood's production values but also demands greater responsibility for the narrative representations. For Ebewo, the entrepreneurial measure of success forms only one quotient of its achievements. There is the suggestion that Nollywood should aspire to compete on a global Market in order to achieve this. He is in favor of improving the content on a representational level and in the production value: "Filmmakers should not delude themselves and settle for what is inferior. To deny the audience what is best because it cannot differentiate the classic from the pedestrian is a disservice to the community. . . . Attention should shift from commonplace, stereotypical themes to adaptation of classic literary works that are readily available in Africa" (55).

Brian Larkin suggests that the strongest criticism of Nollywood is from outside the epistemic conditions of production in Nollywood: "From the point of view of directors trained in film schools, [the video films] are vulgar, populist entertainment with none of the political or aesthetic skill of their celluloid cousin[s]" (178). However, the success of Nigerian video films is based on the fact that they have been able to engage "a popular African audience in a way that African cinema never has" (178). The levels of popularity achieved by these films in local communities suggest that this controversy is located among international audiences, critics, and mainly African academics. In the context of international or global communities, these films become antagonistic and lack reflexivity in their content that throws into relief the tensions between presentations of cultural mores versus their *representation*. When analyzing the role of the family in Nollywood films, Larkin evokes the term *grotesque*: "The grotesque here is harnessed to what I call aesthetics of outrage, a narrative based on continual shocks that transgress religious and social norms and are designed to provoke and affront the audience" (184).

The Nigerian video film *Osuofia in London* (2003), directed by Kingsley Ogoro, exemplifies this point. This comedy is about Osuofia, who learns through the village schoolteacher that his rich and successful brother from London has passed away and he has inherited his wealth. Osuofia has to travel to London from his African village to claim the inheritance. The director presents us with a familiar African story of a "country bumpkin" encountering the city and modernity for the first time. An important trope of this "genre" is the exploitation of the "country bumpkin" by the city-savvy inhabitants. When Osuofia lands in London, he is met by his brother's chauffeur and is driven to his mansion. Here he meets his brother's fiancée and immediately lays claim to her and to all his property and money. The encounter between the brother's fiancée and Osuofia is between different cultures and traditions, one that highlights the manner in which women have been positioned in different cultural contexts. Osuofia objectifies his brother's fiancée and expects her to play the role of the traditional African woman, predicated on a strict patriarchal hierarchy that positions her as subservient to her husband. At first she is outraged by his behavior, his ownership of her, and his extraordinary expectations. Osuofia is also visibly shocked when he discovers that she cannot perform the basic functions of a good (African) woman, one being to cook and serve his dietary needs. This film positions African tradition and culture against Western modernity and, by exploiting stereotypes of Africa and the West, suggests the incommensurability of the two cultures.

For an outside audience, these films highlight an unreflexive mode of filmmaking, one that does not consider the complex critical project of filmmaking practices, especially in the canonized tropes of African cinema and "its struggle against cultural imperialism" (Larkin 176). The film follows a familiar melodramatic trajectory when the brother's fiancée is convinced that the only way to scam Osuofia of the inheritance is by seducing him. At the end of the film, she agrees to marry him: for her this relationship is based on financial exploitation. Osuofia becomes her "patron," through whom she can live a life of wealth and financial security. To a global audience (outside of this specific cultural context), this narrative is regressive, as it does not empower women by subverting stereotypes but reinscribes stereotypes that are offensive and nonreflexive. Within the complex arena of representational politics, these images are vulgar and reflect an uncritical filmmaking practice (the absence of the *commandement*).

These films function within a cultural and traditional logic and claim an authenticity precisely because they are representational. Therefore, we argue that these films are "audacious" rather than singularly vulgar. The term *audacity* is mobilized, as it reflects the conflation of meaning in this context (evoking the rhetoric of culture and tradition) in the face of progressive politics; these films claim an authenticity by presenting cultural mores and tradition rather than taking on the responsibility of a reflexivity required through a *representational* practice. This emphasis on a representational practice may be aligned with the insistence Third Cinema has placed on the "relations between the signification and the social" (Willemen 8). Teshome Gabriel's seminal work on Third Cinema set a precedent in connecting cinemas in the developing world with an agenda of social and political liberation. His ideas served to challenge the perspective of cinema from a Westernized, privileged position of the viewer. Third Cinema was differentiated from first and second cinemas as a mode of creative expression that challenged colonial histories. In positing the role of Third Cinema as a liberating form in the postcolonial state, he proposed a cinematic form and practice that were free from hegemonic modes of production and their economic imperatives and put at the center of its practice cinema's ability to mobilize social and political change: "Gabriel, perhaps in accordance with the militaristic style of the early manifestos, gave his propositions a polemical edge and was explicit in granting preference to 'films with social relevance and innovative style and, above all, with political and ideological overtones.' These films contribute to a universal 'decolonization of the mind,' thus engendering the development of 'radical consciousness' which would in turn lead to 'a revolutionary transformation of society" (Guneratne 11).

TRANSPORTING NOLLYWOOD:
THE SOUTH AFRICAN CONTEXT

In September 2008, Cameroonian producer Leonard Ashu launched a video film movement called "Jollywood" with the screening of his first feature-length film, *Rainbow Love*. In 2004 Kumaran Naidoo, an Indian South African banker turned filmmaker, released his first video film, *Broken Promises,* under the banner of "Vollywood Productions."[5] Since the initial release of *Broken Promises,* Naidoo has produced and directed a sequel called *Broken Promises, 2* and has made a series of feature films called *Run for Your Life.* Naidoo's films were made specifically for the South African Indian audience, and their popularity and success (in terms of capturing a niche audience) are largely attributed to the narrative focus on local and community-based issues.

Ashu's and Naidoo's direct references to Nollywood, through the use of the labels Jollywood and Vollywood, are significant, as they highlight the desire to transport a filmmaking model that has achieved high levels of success as a popular form in Africa. The video films emerging from South Africa share an affinity with Nigerian video films in terms of production conditions and modes of distribution and how the content speaks to local and regional community concerns and their identities. Similar to Nigerian video films, the South African examples are mainly distributed through informal networks like cultural markets (for example, the Fordsburg market). The films are conceived and produced by individuals with no formal training in filmmaking, and the same person is usually involved in writing, directing, and editing the film. In several interviews, Naidoo claims that his films have achieved cult status not only among South African Indians but also in Pakistan, Canada, and Britain (Cordeur).

The narratives of *Broken Promises, 1 and 2* and the television series are broadly concerned with issues that are more specific to the South African Indian community, exploring themes like extended family relationships, culture and tradition versus modernity, and the dynamics of urban living. The feature films *Broken Promises, 1 and 2* are set in a predominantly Indian township in Durban called Chatsworth. The first feature film is about the intense relationship between a Hindi-speaking mother and her Tamil daughter-in-law. The relationship is problematic because the daughter-in-law speaks Tamil, and she has married into a Hindi-speaking family. The films draw on stereotypes and prejudices of Indianness that are historically associated with the Indian working classes. The humor is created from exploiting the accents and foibles of the Indian working classes and in many ways reproduces cultural and class stereotypes. The second feature film deals with the extended family and is compounded with the arrival of the mother's sister and her daughter.

In summary, Naidoo's films rely heavily on the codes and conventions of melodrama. As a genre, melodrama is characterized by exaggeration and excessive emotions (humor, happiness, sadness), similar to Indian and Nigerian films. Larkin observes, "The repetitive storylines, grandiloquent dialogue, and outrageous plots represent a world of fantasy and myth that was supposed to atrophy with the rise of a modern, rational world" (171). In *Broken Promises*, the extended family is marked by tension, which is constructed around repetitive, nonsensical plots that result in situations and contexts that are generally audacious. Here the Indian family is marked by both conflict and contestation, yet offers support and love when conflicts have been resolved.

One of the single largest contributing factors to the popularity of these films within specific communities is that the content is heavily informed by the specificities of the regional or local audience's interests: in the case of *Broken Promises,* South African Indians recognize themselves. In terms of thematic concerns, *Broken Promises* and *Rainbow Love* use the genre of family melodrama to explore broader issues in South African society.

The South African film industry has a complex history whose mandate post-apartheid (after 1994) shifted dramatically to focus on national identity formation and nation building. The formal film industry in South Africa is largely aspirational: desiring international visibility and international recognition. This, however, presents similar problems experienced historically with African cinema in the global Market. The criticism being that African films made at a national level rarely appeal to local audiences (if they are seen by local audiences at all), the narratives and visual language serve to appeal to a broader international audience (who have some preconceived notions of what constitutes African cinema). South African cinema relies on official distribution Markets and international film festivals for circulation and exhibition. One of the criticisms of the industry is that it has not been able to develop a South African (local) audience large enough to sustain a local national film industry.

Low-budget films and informal distribution networks have been welcomed and praised as the new way of making African films. Ebewo suggests, "The initiative is a big lesson to other African countries because it demonstrates that a successful film need not have a huge budget" (55). However, Ebewo remains critical of the images and representational politics that these films activate within certain (mainly international) audiences. Ebewo stresses, "Some productions seem to celebrate the evil inherent in the themes, with no serious effort to highlight their moral message" (47). Many African film theorists like Ebewo and Okome have been critical of women's roles in Nollywood films. Ebewo recognizes that "Nollywood films are popular in Nigeria because they have indigenous content and address issues relevant to a mass audience" (47). However, in his article, Ebewo argues that Nollywood filmmakers and producers need to be held accountable for the images they create and the politics their films activate.

In a postcolonial context, Third Cinema's political imperative lent a "transportability" to the ideas of postcolonialism and liberation cinemas that dealt with revisionist histories, cultures, and the use of the medium as a democratizing tool: an instrument for "decolonizing the mind and the image," so to speak. Nollywood in some ways wears the veneer of a democratizing mode of cinematic expression on account of its modes of production. Hence, it is heralded as a vehicle through which Africans can develop a cinema from within (outside of the colonial project; in Diawara's sense, the "technological paternalism" is eliminated).

The emergence of Nollywood is the rejoinder to the democratizing effect of the digital evolution in filmmaking, thus creating a revolution in content creation. Moreover, this shift in technology facilitates circuits of distribution and exhibition that enable new contexts for the consumption of films. Therefore, Nollywood in its mode of distribution has been able to generate a large local and regional audience as it relies on more informal routes for circulation. Nollywood's ability to circumvent official channels of distribution and exhibition has been one of its successes, augmenting its popularity. In West Africa, local markets are essential for the distribution of Nigerian video films. West African markets serve as informal economies that allow for the transnational circulation of films and other goods, creating an alternative circuit of distribution, one that "clearly undermines official forms of globalization" (Diawara, qtd. in Adejunmobi).

In South Africa, the films by Naidoo circulate within informal markets, particularly the Fordsburg cultural market in Johannesburg. The Fordsburg market caters primarily to the cultural needs of the Indian and Pakistani diaspora populations in Johannesburg. It operates mainly as a night market and is characterized by the convergence of cultures and ethnicities. Authentic Indian and Pakistani food, clothing, music, and films are on display and for sale. The market becomes an important location for exchanging different and diverse cultures and represents an informal economy, the success of which is predicated on the Indian and Pakistani diasporas living in South Africa. Located within an African city, the convergence of African and Indian (or South Asian) identities is apparent in the landscape of the marketplace.

Among the cultural products for sale are popular Indian films and sound tracks. The covers of different films and sound tracks are displayed on tables, and when a customer wishes to buy a particular DVD or CD, it is copied from an original, the master copy usually stored elsewhere. Such modes of content circulation reaffirm the relationship between informal economies (markets) and piracy, similar to the African video film markets that have had global reach and challenge global Markets through piracy and copyright violations.

The informal marketplace undermines the official routes of distribution and exhibition that form part of the film industry in South Africa. Unlike Nigeria, South Africa has two well-established distribution and exhibition houses, Ster-Kinekor and Nu-Metro, both primarily focused on commercially viable films exemplified by Hollywood blockbusters. In Johannesburg, the Fordsburg market becomes an important place for diasporic populations to access Indian films. For this minority group, the consumption of these films is a marker of cultural identity and resonates with Appadurai's "ethnoscapes" (6) as a context for group identity.

In interviews, Naidoo claims that his films have been widely distributed and are popular in Pakistan. This claim, if credible, is significant because it demonstrates the manner in which informal markets such as the Fordsburg market ensure the transnational circulation of films. Most of the vendors in this market are Indian or Pakistani nationals who travel between South Africa and the subcontinent extensively. Usually, a few copies of an Indian film are brought from India or Pakistan and are pirate-copied extensively for sale in South Africa. Piracy of Indian popular films and to a lesser extent Hollywood films suggests that there is a parallel, unofficial economy operating in South Africa, aligning the country with "new metropoles such as Dubai, Singapore, and Beirut" (Larkin 221). Like Nollywood's filmmakers, Kumaran Naidoo by and large aspires to succeed in the local market and is keen to compete on the global Market or even pursue any competitive arena such as film festivals or film competitions.

A newspaper article headlined "Banker Breathes Life into Film" claims that illegal sales of Kumaran Naidoo's film *Broken Promises, 2* reached around five hundred thousand in South Africa and approximately two million in Pakistan (Cordeur). As a filmmaker operating on the margins of a well-established film industry that desires international visibility, Naidoo recognizes the role of piracy in the distribution and circulation of his films. Like Nigerian video films and Indian films, piracy in the South African case study functions as an important second- or third-tier distribution network, and piracy boosts the popularity of these video films to a certain extent.

Similar to Nollywood films, the emerging South African video industry has gained local (community-specific) niche audiences on account of the content that addresses the needs, desires, and aspirations of its audiences. The narratives provide a foundation for cultural identification among these particular audiences. Naidoo's films are popular particularly among South African Indians in densely populated Indian areas like Chatsworth, Lenasia, and Laudium.

South African Indians have an ambiguous relationship with the subject matter. First, in a post-apartheid context, for a minority group the narratives articulate fears and anxieties that many can identify with. At the same time, the films are offensive, "audacious" (exploiting Indian stereotypes of masculinity and femininity, Indian accents, and community or local "slangs"), and often humorous to mask the offensiveness of the representations. The offensiveness in turn is excessive, and although it is made palpable (through humor) to a larger Indian audience, it does little to provide space for critical engagement on racial or gender prejudices. Such audacious representations are tolerable and tolerated because they are made by and from within the community. Put simply, South African Indians tolerate the content precisely because it is made by Indians for them to laugh at.

The popularity of these films can also be attributed to the desire among South African Indians for greater representations of themselves in cultural forms like films and theater. It can be argued that the popularity of Naidoo's films among South African Indians bridges the gap between the lack of official media representations of Indians on television (the public broadcaster) and the desire for greater cultural and ethnic representation. Adejunmobi argues that "under certain conditions, such commercial forms offer greater opportunity for autonomous voices from globally minoritized populations to emerge, in dialogue with local publics, and outside the dominant centers of cultural production, than do the non-commercial forms of transnational cultural productivity."

The opportunity for autonomous voices to be activated from minority populations is persuasive, and, in effect, Naidoo's appropriation of the entrepreneurial model of Nollywood filmmaking ensures that he is able to produce content that is immediate to its audience's interests and is able to market and distribute the product directly to the community as well.

IN CONTEXT: HOLLYWOOD, BOLLYWOOD, NOLLYWOOD

In his essay "Nollywood: What's in a Name?" Jonathan Haynes problematizes the term that "implies that Nollywood is an imitation of Hollywood and Bollywood rather than something in itself, something that is original and uniquely African" (106). Although this analogy echoes the aspirations of African video films to be likened and comparable to the North American West Coast studio system of commercial filmmaking or to the predominantly Mumbai, Hindi filmmaking industries, an important aspect is overlooked that is central to the success of both industries. Both Hollywood and Bollywood operate on highly organized economic structures. They are part of a complex ideological apparatus aimed at being fully self-sustainable and that aspires for global reach through organized distribution networks. As Haynes rightly points out, these terms eclipse the diversity of film practices and cinematic representations in India and North America.

To explicate: Bollywood is never conflated with national Indian cinema, nor is Hollywood considered homogeneous American cinema. Both cinematic traditions contain and accommodate diversity – from studio films to independent films, from art house to regional films. Bollywood's aesthetic preoccupation is with the hyper-real, the musical, and often family melodrama. Hollywood too may be described as a popular cinema relying on the star system to cater to mass appeal and is concerned with high production values in the numerous genres it produces. Its economic success is largely predicated on reinforcing audience expectations of genres.

However, both Bollywood and Hollywood are concerned with political registers, either informed by dogmatic Hindu principles and political instrumentalization (as in the case of the former) or (in the case of the latter) serving American values, ideals, and convictions: the significance of the individual's will to triumph over adversity, the importance of the nuclear family, and patriotism. These political persuasions are inscribed in the narratives and are nonetheless produced with an ideological reflexivity that is concerned with some form of political and social self-regulation.

Independent filmmakers in each of these very dominant markets strive to be heard, for an independent voice that subverts, transgresses, or does not conform to the dominant (hegemonic) political position often represented in these cinemas. How often have we heard African Americans decry the representations of black subjects in Hollywood films or that Bollywood films are overtly pro-Hindu and do not reflect India's ethnic and religious diversities? Clearly, the term *Nollywood,* as Haynes points out, reinscribes a homogenizing effect on the diversity and complexity of video films produced in Nigeria (and by implication the rest of the continent, should the term become more synonymous with a broader mode of production in Africa).

It is erroneous and counterproductive to offer simplified comparisons between Hollywood, Bollywood, and Nollywood since their modes of production are markedly different. Issues of aesthetics and content also inform these fundamental differences, as do their distribution networks and Market share. All three (arguably) enjoy success based on their broad mass appeal as part of a system in popular culture. Each of them speaks directly to its immediate local audiences in terms of content and issues reflected in the narratives. Hollywood and Bollywood have developed from complex economic structures that rely on stars for their appeal. Nollywood too has developed highly recognizable stars who facilitate the marketability of content. However, the mode of production, particularly with the former two, is to maintain a distanced relationship between *commandement* structures (producers or studios or both) and audiences (subjects), whereas with Nollywood this distance is a single epistemic mode of production-consumption.

ANALYTICAL CONTEXT: ANTHROPOLOGY AND CINEMA AND FILM STUDIES

The question that remains is one of the (ir)reconcilability of contemporary Nollywood with the historical political sentiments of African cinema and the delimitations of its transgressions and what is compromised

NOLLYWOOD'S TRANSPORTABILITY   63

(or not) in its wake. The uptake of Nollywood in anthropology, social studies, or cultural studies challenges the reluctance in disciplines such as cinema and film studies to recognize the impact of these films. At this point, it would be useful to consider the complexity of the debate from another position. Cinema and film studies, in part, is invested in the connoisseurship of the medium. Its emphasis has historically privileged the *auteur* and demanded that film was read as a mode of artistic expression. After photography, film theorists and practitioners (Sergei Eisenstein, Rudolf Arnheim, Andre Bazin) have battled for its incorporation as the eighth muse among art forms. We hasten to add, though, that cinema scholars have neither neglected popular films and popular culture nor reproduced any high-low art divide between film forms. Instead, what has been more instructive is the analytical uptake of the various cinematic and film phenomena in geographical contexts and at different historical moments. In short, modes of film production are read as part of the zeitgeist and are used as a vehicle to understand complex ideological, cultural, and social conditions in which the films are made and consumed. Moreover, the layers of meanings that become possible are drawn from the transnational circulation of film as a cultural product. Herein lies the more tenuous relationship with Nollywood in this particular discipline.

Nollywood is a popular form for the masses in Nigeria and in the diaspora. Similar to its Bollywood counterpart, its success and visibility have been garnered from its transnational circulation and importance for both the region and the communities in the diaspora. In both these instances, these diasporic communities constitute fairly large populations across different geographic spaces. In this sense, both Bollywood and Nollywood serve as part of the complex "global cultural flow" that is described by Appadurai through the convergence of "mediascapes" and "enthnoscapes": "What is most important about these mediascapes is that they provide (especially in their television, film, and cassette forms) large and complex repertoires of images, narratives, and ethnoscapes to viewers throughout the world, in which the world of commodities and the world of news and politics are profoundly mixed" (35). Thus, the value of Nollywood is precisely that it operates first at the local level and has a transnational life through very niche global networks that speak only to ethnoscapes in the diaspora. Similarly, the sensationalism of Bollywood is about niche audiences in global contexts that enable the transnational circulation of cultural products for communities in the diaspora. This results in greater awareness and visibility but not necessarily greater consumption outside of its niche (once a certain curiosity from outsiders is satiated; see Ajibade, this volume).

To return, then, to the issue at hand: not only the legitimizing of Nollywood in anthropology, but its incorporation in cinema and film studies require further deliberation. The study of national cinemas has often challenged popular cinemas. The study of Indian cinema, for example, has privileged the skill of Satyajit Ray and Ritwik Gatak at the exclusion of popular Hindi cinema. Bollywood as a phenomenon is now studied similarly to mainstream American films, and these movies are considered in relation to genre studies. Alternatively, popular films made in America or India are used as case studies to map out sociocultural and ideological relevance. In this respect, films often are not read as texts, but used as case studies to illustrate a political or sociocultural observation – for example, to show how popular culture either challenges or subverts political or ideological convictions or stylistic considerations.

Moreover, scholars often complain that great African works by, for example, Ousmane Sembène, Djibril Diop Mambéty, and Souleymane Cissé are not available to local African audiences. Similarly, audiences in India might name great filmmakers, but have not had the opportunity to see their works or might find the social realism of Ray and Gatak less accessible than the formulaic melodrama of mainstream Indian cinema. The same applies to cinephiles in Europe who complain that Ingmar Bergman is not as accessible to Swedish audiences or the reevaluation of director Douglas Sirk in American cinema. Succinctly phrased, the role of cinema as popular culture has always been markedly different from its function as artistic expression.

The shift in technologies has enabled more adept producers of content, but the concern for including Nollywood in the canon of African cinema is guided by its politics and artistic merits, and despite its huge popularity, it belies any form of cinematic connoisseurship that promotes reading the films as texts. Nevertheless, the challenge has been met, and cinema and film studies programs consider Nollywood a phenomenon to be investigated, analyzed, and theorized in the larger context of African cinema. Akin to the French New Wave, which posed stylistic challenges to classical Hollywood filmmaking and offered a radical reassessment of production conditions for independent filmmakers or the significance of the short-lived Dogma 95 manifesto, these all contribute to the strategies independent filmmakers have used to subvert and challenge dominant, hegemonic structures of film production, film distribution, and film consumption.

CONTEXTUALIZING NOLLYWOOD'S "TRANSPORTABILITY"

The "transportability" of Nollywood is provocative because it speaks to the historical idea that "a shared sense of a broadly conceived African identity is a prerequisite to true independence for the continent" (McCall 92). For Nollywood to be read as a zeitgeist in (African) cinema, it is intrinsic that it be considered in relation to Adorno's culture industry. As McCall observes: "For Adorno, the most pernicious quality of capitalism was its ability to displace critical reflection and political action with commodity fetishism. Adorno pioneered the theory that a robust culture industry was capable of transforming anything – including authenticity, identity and political resistance – into a marketable product" (95). McCall later concludes: "What positions Nollywood as a catalyst for pan-African discourse is precisely that it has no view, no agenda, no ideology. It is a sprawling marketplace of representations" (96). However, Adorno remains very committed to the idea that "the question of the culture industry is raised from the perspective of its relation to the possibilities for social transformation" (2). At this point, the idea of film as a culture industry finds its most direct connection to Third Cinema. However, the "sprawling marketplace" appears to have its limitations: the pan-Africanism of Nollywood is limited by its political apathy and emphasis on economic ambition.

Naidoo's success echoes the significance of local markets and audiences. It therefore demands the radical reassessment of the importance of ethnoscapes and mediascapes as a significant and vibrant intervention for how digital technology (as a democratizing tool) affords a more direct relationship between content creation and content consumption.

The success of Nollywood (video films in general) in the diaspora reflects the importance of film as a medium for maintaining a relationship with the "homeland" – it is about nostalgia for culture, tradition, and language (no matter how they evolve in the transnational context). It is also about recognizing how fundamental the notion of niche markets has become to the phenomenon of global cultural production.

The African Movie Academy Awards (AMAA) is another context in which the limitation of Nollywood's pan-Africanism is reflected. Its website reads: "AMAA is thus conceptualized as an annual celebration of the brightest and the best in African movie [sic]. It is about class and style, blitz, glitz and razzmatazz. It is the biggest gathering of moviemakers across the African continent and the diaspora. It is to show to the world that the rating of Nollywood (Nigeria) as the third largest producers of movie [sic] is real." Now in its seventh year, the awards offer an interesting conflation of a general African cinema as part of the legitimizing of Nollywood as an industry.

In terms of the traditional canon of African cinema and its desire to produce an African film aesthetic and language, Nollywood films can only be described as "aesthetics of non-aesthetics," or more precisely as an "aesthetics of evolving aesthetics." As to Guneratne, theorists of Third Cinema, such as Paul Willemen, "appreciated 'the historical variability of the necessary aesthetic strategies to be adopted,' even to the extent of suggesting that there are '36 different kinds' of Third Cinema" (14).

The content, its mode of production, and the distribution of Nollywood films reflect an entrepreneurial, grassroots mode. The implication for this model of filmmaking is that it shifts the emphasis away from two important considerations – first, the idea of social transformation and, second, the value of film as creative expression – and instead privileges the economic (capital) over and above all other concomitants.

Nollywood video films reflect an absence of a distance between the *commandement* and the subject. Mbembe describes this absence of a distanced relationship as one of familiarity that results in the "zombification" of both the dominant and the dominated: "This zombification means that each has robbed the other of vitality and left the other impotent" (104).

The impotence of Nollywood might for now simply be the handicap that has been so emphatically outlined by numerous critics, and it is one of content, production value, and its ability to really function competitively on the global Market. Without truly interrogating its political substance, there is no space for Nollywood as a mode of cultural production to evolve. In this sense, its significance would be informed by the role and value of cultural production in the postcolony as an instrument for social, political, and identity politics. This thinking is inspired by the sentiments expressed in Third Cinema and African cinema:

> Wherever there is a filmmaker prepared to stand up against commercialism, exploitation, pornography and the tyranny of technique, there is to be found the living spirit of New Cinema. Wherever there is a filmmaker, of any age or background, ready to place his cinema and his profession at the service of great causes of his time, there will be the living spirit of New Cinema. This is the correct definition which sets New Cinema apart from the commercial industry because the commitment of industrial cinema is to untruth and exploitation. (Rocha 13–14)

This "New Cinema" practice, as proposed by Rocha, continues to inform the interrogation of cinema as cultural production in the post-colony. "New Cinema" offers the political or ideological position to view postcolonial, cultural production as not simply a challenge created from subverting structures of capital that influence production and distribution. It also offers a chance to question the ideological frameworks in which content is produced and consumed. Although Nollywood films have an agenda (and an ideology), their production mode emphasizes the "commodity fetishism" over any social, political transformation in the postcolony. Hence, Adorno's insistence on social transformation remains significant. The pan-African transportability is the challenge for the Nollywood phenomenon. It must find a way to operate within a paradigm that is set on multiple levels: as art, as creative expression, as political tool, and as commodity.

NOTES

1. Achille Mbembe defines *postcolony* in his book *On the Postcolony* as follows: "The notion 'postcolony' identifies specifically a given historical trajectory – that of societies recently emerging from the experience of colonization and the violence which the colonial relationship involves. To be sure, the postcolony is chaotically pluralistic; it has nevertheless an internal coherence.... The postcolony is characterized by a distinctive style of political improvisation, by a tendency to excess and lack of proportion, as well as by distinctive ways identities are multiplied, transformed, and put into circulation" (102, 103).

2. It is important to recognize the difference between Markets and markets. "Markets" refer to commercial, formal economic networks of distribution and exhibition exemplified through Hollywood distribution channels, whereas "markets"

refer to informal traditional markets. See
Adejunmobi.

3. It is important to distinguish between "broad-based audiences" and "niche
audiences." "Broad-based audiences"
refer to a more general "populace" that
is not wholly differentiated by market
categories. "Niche audiences" are defined
by a differentiation or "target" that fore-
grounds ethnic identity, linguistic prefer-
ences, living standards, education, or gender to differentiate its audience appeal. In
the analysis of the success of locally made
South African Indian films, this is a niche
audience, and within this sector the films
have a broad-based appeal.

4. "We need to uncover the use made
of the grotesque and the obscene not just
in ordinary people's lives but (1) in the
timing and the location of those occasions
that state power organizes for dramatiz-
ing its own magnificence; (2) in the actual
materials used in the ceremonial displays
through which it makes manifest its maj-
esty; and (3) the specific manner in which
it offers these, as spectacles, for its subjects
to watch" (Mbembe 104).

5. The V in *Vollywood* takes its cue from
the local suburb of Verulam where Naidoo
lives and makes his films. It is important
to observe that the term is so easily appropriated between the metropolises of Johannesburg, as in "Jollywood," to a more
localized production location like a small
suburb on the north coast of Durban, as
with "Vollywood."

WORKS CITED

Adejunmobi, Moradewun. "Nigerian Video
Film as Minor Transnational Practice."
Postcolonial Text 3.2 (2007): n. pag. Web.

Adorno, Theodor. *The Culture Industry.*
New York: Routledge, 2007.

Appadurai, Arjun. *Modernity at Large:
Cultural Dimensions of Globalization.*
Minneapolis: University of Minnesota
Press, 1996.

Arnheim, Rudolf. *Film as Art.* Berkeley
and Los Angeles: University of California Press, 1957.

Bazin, Andre. *What Is Cinema?* Berkeley
and Los Angeles: University of California Press, 2004.

Cordeur, Mathew le. "Banker Breathes Life
into Film." *Witness,* February 1, 2008.
Web.

Diawara, Manthia. *African Cinema: Politics and Culture.* Bloomington: Indiana
University Press, 1992.

Ebewo, Patrick. "The Emerging Video
Film Industry in Nigeria: Challenges
and Prospects." *Journal of Film and
Video* 59.3 (2007): 46–57.

Eisenstein, Sergei. *Film Form: Essays in
Film Theory.* New York: Harcourt, 1969.

Fanon, Frantz. *The Wretched of the Earth.*
New York: Grove, 1963.

Guneratne, Anthony. Introduction. *Re-
thinking Third Cinema.* Ed. Anthony
Guneratne and Wimal Dissanayake.
New York: Routledge, 2003. 1–28.

Haynes, Jonathan. "Nollywood: What's in
a Name?" *Film International* 5.4 (2007):
106–108.

Larkin, Brian. *Signal and Noise: Media,
Infrastructure, and Urban Culture in Ni-
geria.* Durham, N.C.: Duke University
Press, 2008.

Mbembe, Achille. *On the Postcolony.*
Berkeley and Los Angeles: University of
California Press, 2001.

McCall, John C. "The Pan-Africanism We
Have: Nollywood's Invention of Africa."
Film International 5.4 (2007): 92–97.

Okome, Onookome. 2007. "Nollywood:
Spectatorship, Audience, and the Sites
of Consumption." *Postcolonial Text* 3.2
(2007): n. pag. Web.

Pines, Jim, and Paul Willemen, eds. *Questions of Third Cinema*. London: British Film Institute, 1990.

Rocha, Glauber. "The Aesthetics of Hunger." *Twenty-Five Years of the New Latin American Cinema*. Ed. Michael Chanan. London: BFI Channel Four Joint Publication, 1983. 13–14.

Ukadike, Frank. *Black African Cinema*. Berkeley and Los Angeles: University of California Press, 1994.

Willemen, Paul. "The Third Cinema Question: Notes and Reflections." *Questions of Third Cinema*. Ed. Jim Pines and Paul Willemen. London: British Film Institute, 1990. 1–29.

FILMOGRAPHY

Baara. Dir. Souleymane Cissé. Sisé Filimu (Mali). 1978.

Broken Promises. Dir. Kumaran Naidoo. Vollywood Productions (South Africa). 2004.

Broken Promises, 2. Dir. Kumaran Naidoo. Vollywood Productions (South Africa). 2007.

Camp de Thiaroye. Dir. Ousmane Sembène. Enaproc et al. (Algeria et al.). 1987.

Finyé. Dir. Souleymane Cissé. Sisé Filimu (Mali). 1982.

Heritage Africa. Dir. Kwaw Ansah. Film Africa Production (Ghana). 1989.

Le Mandat. Dir. Ousmane Sembène. Comptoir Français du Film Production and Filmi Domirev (France and Senegal). 1968.

Osuofia in London. Dir. Kingsley Ogoro. Kingsley Ogoro Productions (Nigeria). 2003.

Rainbow Love. Dir. Leonard Ashu. Brain Africa Films (South Africa). 2008.

Run for Your Life. Dir. Kumaran Naidoo. Vollywood Productions (South Africa). 2006.

Sarraounia. Dir. Med Hondo. Direction de la Cinematographie Nationale and Les Films Soleil O (Burkina Faso et al.). 1986.

Wend Kuuni. Dir. Gaston Kaboré. Direction du Cinéma du Haute Volta (Burkina Faso). 1982.

Xala. Dir. Ousmane Sembène. Filmi Domirev and Ste. Me. Production du Sénégal (Senegal). 1974.

Yeelen. Dir. Souleymane Cissé. Atriascop Paris et al. (France and Mali). 1987.

PART TWO

Transnational Nollywood

THREE

The Nollywood Diaspora: A Nigerian Video Genre

JONATHAN HAYNES

THE PRODIGIOUS SPREAD OF NOLLYWOOD FILMS AROUND THE world has been accompanied by the spread of Nollywood filmmaking around the world, as Nigerian actors and directors have traveled abroad to make movies and Nigerian expatriate communities have sought to participate in this most powerful of Nigerian cultural forms. This essay analyzes a number of Nollywood films set partly or entirely overseas. One of my themes is how Nollywood imagines the foreign; mostly, my project is to define the films set abroad as a genre, with a typical story arc, moral and psychological themes, and formal features. It is a distinctly Nollywood genre, directly derived from some of the most fundamental conceptions in Nigerian filmmaking. The distinctiveness is not, however, a matter of melodramatic excess in story or style, or of the prevalence of occult elements – two elements many observers of Nigerian and Ghanaian video films have taken to be defining of this film culture, myself included. I was arguing along those lines in an earlier study of the theme of Africans abroad, contrasting the way the theme has been handled in celluloid African filmmaking with its treatment in the emerging popular video tradition ("Africans Abroad"). The more recent films surveyed here are substantially different on both scores, being generally much more restrained in style and seldom making reference to the supernatural.[1]

The former essay was written just before there was an explosion of videos set abroad, triggered by the phenomenal success of Kingsley Ogoro's *Osuofia in London* in 2003 and Tade Ogidan's *Dangerous Twins* the next year. Other frontline Nollywood directors, including Lancelot Imasuen, Zeb Ejiro, and Chico Ejiro, along with too many of the major stars to mention, went abroad to shoot soon thereafter. This was also a period of large-scale initiatives involving the American and British markets, which involved bringing delegations of Nollywood filmmakers and actors to their fans abroad. These initiatives included the Filmmakers Association of Nigeria, USA, a project intended to organize the American market and encourage crossover projects; the Nigerian National Film and Censors Board–sponsored Road Show in London; and the inauguration of the Nollywood Foundation's series of annual conventions, beginning in 2005, designed to build long-term connections between Nollywood and Hollywood. Two high-profile coproductions came of networking between Nollywood and Hollywood: *30 Days,* written and directed by the United States–based Mildred Okwo, a film set entirely in Nigeria but reflecting an expatriate sensibility in various ways, including a central character who is visiting home from the United States, where he lives; and Lancelot Imasuen's *Close Enemies,* a Nollywood-style film shot in Hollywood with Hollywood equipment and support, financed by a United States–based Nigerian producer.

Preceding and more fundamental than these high-profile professional activities is the enduring basis for films about Nigerians abroad: the existence of many communities of expatriate Nigerians in Europe, North America, and elsewhere, which provide both practical succor and inspiration to their compatriots stuck in the morass of the Nigerian economy. These communities are fully integrated into Nollywood, though the distribution system that irrigates them is dominated by pirates to an unusual extent, even by Nigerian standards. The emotional adhesion of the expatriate communities to Nollywood film culture is strengthened by their circumstances: the films answer a longing for home and serve as a vehicle for showing children and non-Nigerian friends what Nigerian culture is.

The desire to make films about Nigerians abroad has been there since the beginning of Nollywood: the sequel to the very first English-language Nigerian video film, Kenneth Nnebue's *Glamour Girls, 2: The Italian Connection* (1994), is about Nigerian prostitutes in Italy, and half of the film is set in an Italy constructed in Lagos with derisory means.

Soon a system was set up to actually shoot films abroad in collaboration with Nigerian expatriate communities. The basic elements are one or more Nollywood stars brought from home to add glamour and to make the film salable in Nigeria, and an expatriate host community that provides contributions in kind (actors, props, settings, hospitality), as well as funding by local African-owned businesses in return for having the businesses featured on-screen.[2] These contributions allow the film to be made within a Nollywood-style (that is, very low) budget. This limit on the budget is a strict necessity, as the film will have to make its money back in the market for Nigerian films, although the producer may bank on a bonus from the host community, which can be expected to buy a number of copies of the film in hard currency and pay to attend screenings. In many cases, the story originates with an expatriate. Because of the circumstances of production, individuals often perform more functions in the filmmaking process than is normal in Nollywood, where labor is specialized along industrial lines: in *Man on a Mission*, for instance, Romanus Ike Eze is the main actor, director, producer, story and screenplay writer, unit production manager, music editor, and rerecording mixer.

Within this structure of collaboration between the Lagos-based industry and expatriate communities, there is a spectrum of where the impetus and resources for a particular film come from and of where the film's point of view is located. At one end of the spectrum are films like *Dubai Runs*, which is about Igbo women who make business trips to Dubai. In this case, the foreign location is as much a figment of the Nigerian imagination as it is in *Glamour Girls, 2*, with only a few establishing shots of Dubai (and these only in the second part). It looks like the cast stayed home, filming their scenes in hotels in Abuja, the filmmakers acquiring the establishing shots from a film library or some other source. The same is true of another film also directed by MacCollins Chidebe, *Boys from Holland*, which begins with a sequence of establishing shots of Holland, one of them an aerial shot the filmmakers are unlikely to have paid to make themselves; from then on, everyone is sitting on sofas that look distinctly Nigerian. In short, these films have invested very little indeed in representing the reality of their foreign locations. The Yoruba-language film *Omo Eniyan* is indubitably shot partly in London, but has only a sketchy interest in London as a source of wealth; the film's point of view is solidly rooted with the protagonists' families back home in Lagos.

On the other end of the spectrum are films like *Missing in America*, written, produced, and directed by Sola Osofisan, long a resident of New

York, where the point of view is clearly that of settled expatriates. Except for a few brief scenes, the whole film was shot in the United States, and much of it has the character of a somewhat irritable letter home on the subject of all the mistakes and misapprehensions Nigerians suffer from when they try to come to America, burdening their expatriate connections in the process. Nevertheless, in spite of its cool, gray wintry tones and slick New York imagery, *Missing in America* is clearly recognizable as a Nollywood film (see also Hoffmann, this volume).

The integrity of Nollywood, both aesthetically and socially, is spectacularly demonstrated in this genre of films. Whatever the difficulties of defining Nollywood in the Nigerian context (are Yoruba and Hausa films part of it?), its external boundaries are sharp and clear.[3] Nollywood diasporan films tend not to interact with the film cultures of their host countries to produce a hybrid Nollywood-British or Nollywood-German or Nollywood-Brazilian aesthetic, though certainly the Nollywood aesthetic itself has been heavily influenced by transnational media forms since its inception. The purpose of Imasuen's *Close Enemies,* the Hollywood-Nollywood coproduction mentioned earlier, is explicitly to take Nollywood to the next level of professional expertise; it does not aim at producing a culturally hybrid art form, and its theme of an infertile marriage is central within the Nollywood tradition. In the general run of films, the credits sometimes show that some technical personnel have been picked up where the film is made, but this seldom means a difference in the style and quality of filmmaking. (An exception, in this as in other respects, is *This America.* In contrast, French crews and postproduction personnel are mandated in so many French-financed African celluloid films in large part to guarantee technical and aesthetic norms.) Invariably, some local foreigners are cast as actors, but they mostly seem to be nonprofessionals recruited out of the Nigerian expatriate communities' social networks. If they do have training as actors, their professional formation is overwhelmed by the Nollywood style of direction. In general, their performances are worse than those of the locally recruited nonprofessional Nigerians, since the Nigerians are steeped in the Nollywood aesthetic and therefore have an instinctive sense for what to do. (There are honorable exceptions, such as Simone McIntyre in *The London Boy.*) The Nigerian expatriates who scout and manage the locations, provide costumes, and so on are all equally attuned to the Nollywood style.

The one film in my sample that does seem to cross over into another film culture is *Crazy Like a Fox,* written, directed, and produced by Tony Abulu. Abulu has been settled in New York for many years; along with Bethels Agomuoh, the director of *This America,* he was a moving spirit behind the Filmmakers Association of Nigeria, USA. *Crazy Like a Fox* might be thought of as part of a trilogy of Abulu's films with transatlantic themes. *Back to Africa,* the story of a beautiful African American looking for her African roots and the Nigerian father who abandoned her, is patently designed to appeal to an African American audience. *American Dream* is about a Nigerian's desperate attempts to get an American visa to visit a beautiful Americanized Nigerian with whom he has fallen in love; the film's concerns and much of its humor would resonate best with Nigerian viewers. *Crazy Like a Fox* is set entirely in New York, in a multicultural and very upscale Harlem, and is shaped by the genre of black American erotica. Instead of an imported Nigerian movie star to headline the production, we have Angel "Lola Luv" Fershgenet, an African American of Ethiopian descent who is a pinup model and figure in the hip-hop world. The crew is non-Nigerian, and while the credits include extras and secondary producers with Nigerian names and the script is discernibly Nigerian in its perspective on life in America, the film features only one African (played by Karibi Fubara), a Nigerian who speaks Americanized English and has little of Nigeria clinging to him. "Tell me about Africa," commands his employer as she seduces him, but she and the film settle for an extremely perfunctory answer. The film is all about New York, apparently made for an African American audience, with a bit of exotic spice.

As with the American genre of westerns, the genre of Nollywood films set abroad cuts across the grand transcultural genres: it includes comedies (*Osuofia in London*), tragedies (*Dangerous Twins*), and romances (*The London Boy*). It frequently incorporates or is continuous with adjacent genres that are normally set entirely in Nigeria. The flourishing Nigerian genre of crime films often involves drug dealing with an international connection (*Columbia* [sic] *Connection*) or the kind of fraud known as "419" that is often practiced on foreigners whom we see picked up at the airport (*Dollars from Germany*). The "been-to," the African who is recently returned from living abroad, has been a ubiquitous figure in Nigerian culture since colonial times and is extensively represented in

Table 3.1. Themes

	Black Night in South America, 1 and 2	Boys from Holland	The Broken Pitcher (USA)	Coming to South Africa, 1 and 2	Crazy Like a Fox (USA)	Crossing Paths, 1 and 2 (USA)	Dangerous Twins, 1, 2, and 3 (UK)	Dapo Junior (Netherlands)	Dubai Runs, 1 and 2	Goodbye New York, 1 and 2	Home & Abroad (Germany)
crisis driving Nigerian abroad	x										
visa and ticket problems	x						x		x	x	
airport sequence				x			x			x	x
alienation/hardship sequence	x		x	x						x	x
contact with African community	x		x	x						x	x
advertising African businesses	x			x	x			x	x	x	x
discussion of cultural differences	x			x	x		x	x		x	x
crisis: money, courage, morality	x		x	x			x		x	x	
drug dealing	x	x	x	x			x			x	
prostitution	x								x	x	
other criminal activities					x	x	x	x			
tourism sequence	x			x	x		x	x			x
shopping sequence	x		x	x	x		x	x		x	x
romance with foreigner	x	x	x		x	x	x	x		x	
romance with Nigerian				x	x	x		x			
exploitation/racism	x						x	x		x	x
need to send money home	x			x			x				x
illegitimate demands from home	x		x		x			x		x	
betrayal by Nigerian intimates	x			x		x	x	x	x	x	
betrayal by foreign intimates	x			x			x				x
betrayal of foreign intimates	x						x	x		x	x
arrest/imprisonment/deportation	x	x	x	x	x	x	x		x	x	
establishment of life abroad	x	x	x	x		x	x			x	x
return to Nigeria	x				x		x		x	x	x
death				x						x	
direct cautionary advice			x		x	x					
Christianity			x						x	x	
non-Christian occult forces			x								
marital issues	x						x		x	x	x

	The London Boy, 1 and 2	London Forever	Man on a Mission in China	Missing in America	Mr. Ibu in London	A Night in the Philippines, 1 and 2	Omo Eniyan (UK)	Osuofia in London, 1 and 2	The Other Side of Life (USA)	This America	Western Union, 1 and 2 (Germany)
crisis driving Nigerian abroad	x	x	x	x			x				
visa and ticket problems	x	x	x	x							
airport sequence	x	x	x	x	x	x	x	x		x	x
alienation/hardship sequence	x	x	x	x	x	x		x		x	x
contact with African community	x	x	x	x	x			x		x	x
advertising African businesses	x	x	x	x	x			x	x	x	
discussion of cultural differences	x		x	x	x			x			
crisis: money, courage, morality	x	x							x	x	x
drug dealing	x	x									x
prostitution	x	x									x
other criminal activities	x	x	x		x		x	x	x	x	
tourism sequence	x	x	x	x	x	x	x	x	x	x	x
shopping sequence	x	x	x		x	x		x	x		
romance with foreigner	x	x	x		x	x		x	x	x	x
romance with Nigerian	x			x			x		x	x	x
exploitation/racism	x										
need to send money home	x	x	x	x							x
illegitimate demands from home	x	x		x			x				x
betrayal by Nigerian intimates	x	x	x	x	x	x					x
betrayal by foreign intimates	x	x			x			x			x
betrayal of foreign intimates	x		x	x			x				
arrest/imprisonment/deportation	x			x	x		x		x	x	x
establishment of life abroad	x	x		x					x	x	x
return to Nigeria	x	x			x		x	x	x	x	x
death					x				x	x	
direct cautionary advice	x			x							x
Christianity											x
non-Christian occult forces	x								x		
marital issues									x		x

Nollywood films. In the wake of *Osuofia in London, 2,* a subgenre arose of films about Nigerians coming back with foreign wives (*Love from Asia*). *South Connection,* from the venerable video producer OJ Productions, is a concatenation of several of the themes having to do with the foreign that have been central in the Nollywood imagination, with the novel (in 2004) twist that South Africa is the foreign source of exorbitant wealth for those with the stomach to do anything to get it. The film is always located in Nigeria, but it depicts the ardent desire of three ambitious young men to go abroad and the splashy return of the two survivors.

The attached table of themes will I hope do much of the work of establishing the regularities of this genre. Only films at least partly shot abroad are included.[4] Themes are not counted on the table unless they are strongly present: hardship is talked about but not actually shown in *The Other Side of Life,* for example. Some films show up in only a few rows because they concentrate so heavily on a couple of themes. Other films have narrative premises that set them apart from the standard story of a Nigerian struggling to live and make money abroad, obviating some of the typical themes and motifs, though others come roaring in.

The Nollywood diasporan films follow the normal Nollywood pattern of repeating winning formulas, intensified by circumstantial factors: when a director or actor is abroad, he or she is apt to take advantage of the situation to work on several projects. So Jim Iyke and Rita Dominic star in a slew of films set in the United States, and *The London Boy* and *Fateful Love* grew out of *Osuofia in London.*

But – again, this is typical of Nollywood – actual remakes are unusual, and I do not attribute the remarkable similarities among my examples to imitation of some particular original, in spite of what has been said about the inspiration provided by *Osuofia in London* and *Dangerous Twins.* Those two films are in fact atypical in their narrative framing. The remarkable similarities are due rather to the persistence and extension of essential thematic complexes of Nollywood culture as a whole. This argument will be developed as we go along. The similarities could be taken as lack of imagination or as evidence of centeredness, strength, and assertion of identity, a flexible, extendable cultural form that works in all sorts of environments. The films each give a sense of being independent and integral conceptions, with different things on their minds, from patriarchal anxieties about women's independent trading (*Dubai Runs*) to the spiritual direction of the Christian family (*The Broken Pitcher*), scary devouring females (*Crazy Like a Fox*), the triumph of romance over revenge (*Crossing Paths*), the Nigerian personality (*Home & Abroad*), and the question of whether a Netherlands-based drug dealer has sufficient cultural capital to marry a Nollywood star (*Boys from Holland* – he does).

The range of foreign settings is impressive: the United Kingdom and the United States, inevitably; Germany and the Netherlands, not surprisingly; but also South Africa, Dubai, China, the Philippines, and Brazil.[5] But the films generally show a lack of interest in the foreign as such. The far-flung locations are not responsible for the important differences among the films; any of them could easily have been shifted to another continent (with the exception of *This America*, which is centrally about the relationship of Nigerian immigrants to African Americans). There is little interest in the exotic for its own sake; the camera seldom wanders about foreign landscapes with a curious eye.[6] In general, Nollywood has always exhibited a general poverty of intention as well as of means in its representations of the foreign. The "Germans" in *Dollars from Germany*, for example, are played by Nigerians of Lebanese extraction, with Nigerian accents and nothing German about them. The lightness of their complexions is supposed to be an adequate signifier. (Lebanese Nigerians are frequently cast in this way.) This is in line with the tradition established by *Glamour Girls, 2: The Italian Connection*, which contained nothing and no one that looked Italian.

The films' establishing shots tend, as in Nollywood films generally, to be stereotypical rather than exploratory, moving us quickly to the interior scenes where nearly all the action and the talking take place. *London Forever* obsessively flings the same shots of Big Ben and red double-decker buses in our faces. *Goodbye New York* is careless about the image of New York it builds up, including footage of beaches and marinas that look suspiciously Californian. Much of this footage seems found, not shot by the filmmakers: certainly, for one moment we glimpse the Miramax-logo image of the Manhattan skyline. This lack of integration between the establishing shots and the lived experience of the characters takes on ironic meaning: the solid, noble, sunlit spectacle of Lower Manhattan, shot from and including the image of helicopters, stands against the lives of the Nigerians whom we watch loafing and fretting through unemployment, tending bar, shoplifting, pimping, and prostituting themselves, mumbling to one another in dimly, muddily lit interior spaces. Shots of an American flag being carried in a parade are spliced into scenes of rape and murder.

For obvious reasons, the United States, Britain, and a generalized continental Europe loom large in the Nigerian imagination, but that imagination tends to be impatient with other kinds of foreignness. Naira, dollars, pounds, and euros are the only currencies ever mentioned, even when the films are set in Brazil or China. (Rand are mentioned in *Coming to South Africa*.) The police in Brazil (*Black Night in South America*) and in South Africa (*Coming to South Africa*) read suspects their Miranda rights as they arrest them, as in American police dramas. American culture overshadows everything: in *Mr. Ibu in London*, Ibu never shakes the idea that somehow getting to London involves going through the United States, and when he is deported back to Lagos, the culture he flaunts to advertise that he is a "been-to" is American hip-hop ghetto style.

The films' narrative premises also impose tunnel vision. Leaving aside for the moment the comedies, in which the trip abroad tends to tumble into the laps of the central characters, in most other cases the protagonists leave Nigeria because of a more or less desperate need to make money. Sometimes we see a melodramatic crisis that spurs them on; sometimes the films editorialize about the lack of opportunities in Nigeria through opening titles (*Black Night in South America*), voice-over narration (*Europe by Road*), or a montage sequence (*Man on a Mission*); in other cases, casual mention of the desire for a better life, greener pastures, or the golden fleece allude to what the audience understands perfectly well. Wider and softer motives – curiosity about foreign cultures, love of adventure, a rebellious desire to wander, in short, the desire to travel for its own sake – almost never come up, except in the comedies, and the harsh realities of life abroad for those without work permits, which is the situation of most of the protagonists, quickly enforce their undivided attention to the struggle to survive, get established, and if possible send some money home.

Air travel itself reduces the physical traveling to a few unremarkable hours, and the high cost of getting a permit to shoot in Murtala Muhammed Airport in Lagos (which is a tenth the average budget of a Nigerian film) and the daunting process of applying for permissions abroad make the transition almost invisible apart from some standardized shots of planes taking off and landing and people coming out of terminals.[7] Thus, the mythic narrative structure of the journey and its attendant theme of adventure are rarely exploited in this genre, though both are staples in the Nigerian genre of the cultural epic. Characters are simply dumped suddenly into the foreign environment, a new city, where they have to make or keep social relationships in order to obtain the necessary food, shelter, and employment. The only film I have seen that emphasizes the journey itself, *Europe by Road,* a harrowing tale of crossing the Sahara to Morocco and embarking on a disastrous sea voyage to Spain, is (paradoxically) not included in the table since it fakes the foreign locations – the film crew obviously never got farther north than Sokoto – and since the protagonists never manage to set up residence in Europe. Of necessity this film has no establishing shots of foreign cities, but its blinkered vision corresponds to the experience of the travelers, often traveling at night, confined to the smugglers' route and safe houses, too miserable and terrified to think of anything but survival. They do not have the luxury of being tourists.

Most of the films have what I call an alienation/hardship sequence, in which the protagonists trudge disconsolately, carrying their shoulder bags, through the streets of the foreign city, unable to find a foothold and growing increasingly desperate. It is striking that the protagonists virtually never have any contact with poor people in the host country. They mostly come from the Nigerian middle class – the really poor generally cannot even think of airfare and visas, unless they are provided by the organizers of a prostitution or drug-smuggling ring – and they will collapse of hunger or cold on a fancy shopping avenue or on an upscale New Jersey suburban street, their clothes still immaculate, rather than find their way to Harlem, where accommodation is cheaper and the informal economy might offer work. *Man on a Mission* is unusual in offering us a brief glimpse of working-class life, but even in this film the emphasis is all on the endless, gleaming tall buildings of the new China. *Dark Night in South America*'s São Paulo looks entirely and impeccably First World, with no favelas. For that matter, we see no Brazilians who are not of overwhelmingly European extraction. Such systematic erasures are quite a feat. Doubtless, part of the point is to keep the protagonists in visual relation to the object of desire while emphasizing how difficult it is to attain. Insofar as possible, "abroad" should correspond to certain stereotypical signifiers, so Brazil should look as much as possible like the United States.

In one way or another, through fair means or foul, eventually the protagonists get established in the foreign land and are free to look around and enjoy themselves. What I am calling the tourist sequence places the protagonists in iconic foreign landscapes at a moment when they have "arrived." (Carmela Garritano, "New Critical," calls such sequences moments of "cosmopolitan spectacle"; see also Haynes, "Africans Abroad.") Formally, these sequences are distinctive: plot movement is suspended, dialogue largely ceases, and the music is turned up as the protagonists enter in their own flesh the world of travelogues and travel advertising. The images are even more heavily stereotyped than the establishing shots, to which they are related. The tourist sequences are formally similar to the hardship/alienation sequences, but reverse the emotional polarity of the relationship between the figure in the foreground and the background from alienation and suffering to ecstatic identification and a sense of triumph.[8]

The tourist sequence often blends into a shopping sequence, in which the traveler is seen in the landscape of consumerism rather than tourism, giddily celebrating disposable income. Such scenes of "enjoying" are also common in films set in Nigeria; here there is an extra relish from being at a center rather than on the periphery of global consumer culture.

In most cases, there is a new lover on the protagonist's arm in both these kinds of sequences, so both kinds blend into another familiar type, the romance sequence. *A Night in the Philippines,* about a couple on a prenuptial honeymoon and worldwide shopping spree, spends an enormous amount of time on all three types. The lover often represents relief from terrible loneliness and the promise of a new home. In many cases, the lover is foreign, and so the relationship takes on additional meanings: a successful relationship with the host country, a cultural and emotional adventure, the (perhaps ambivalent) prestige of consorting with someone with lighter skin. In the films that are most completely domesticated abroad and are most oriented toward expatriate audiences (*Crazy Like a Fox, Crossing Paths, The Other Side of Life*), romantic sequences take the place of tourist sequences.

Let us return to the narrative arc of these films where we left it, shortly after the protagonists' arrival. What they do, in their initial

isolated desperation, is try to make contact with the African expatriate community. If they do not already have an address, they look for a
neighborhood where there are Africans and then stop black people on
the street and ask if they are Nigerian, and if so, whether they will help.
Someone eventually will, and from this point on, the film will be prin-
cipally set in the African immigrant community. It will include scenes
shot in that community's shops and restaurants, which will have provided sponsorship for the film. The material circumstances of filmmaking
reinforce the social horizon of the diasporic community that supports
the film and the interests of the Nigerian audience at home to produce
a remarkably Afrocentric world. If a couple gets married, the official in
the town hall is apt to have a Nigerian accent; the doctor in a hospital
emergency room is apt to be African (*This America*). African American
and black British characters are often played by actors with Nigerian accents, or, if they have American or British accents, the actors may have
Nigerian names, presumably because they were born to Nigerian immigrants or immigrated long ago. *Crossing Paths* carries this Afrocentrism
to the limit: a collaboration of Nigerian and (mostly) Ghanaian U.S.
residents, it is set in an unnamed and utterly deterritorialized but clearly
American space of McMansions and suburban offices (the credits reveal
it to be Dumfries, Virginia, a suburb of Washington, D.C.), which is
populated almost exclusively by Africans. This fact is never commented
upon: Africa and African identity are never mentioned at all, and there is
no talk of anyone immigrating or traveling or telephoning the continent.
The African immigrants are just there, leading their melodramatic lives.
In *A Night in the Philippines,* the central Nigerian couple, who are in the
Philippines on holiday, run into one of the woman's best friends, and
then into the man's old flame, who is there as a contestant in the Miss
Earth 2004 beauty pageant, chaperoned by the aforesaid best friend,
and also run into the man's former colleague, now a waitress in Manila,
who five years earlier disrupted the relationship with the old flame out
of jealousy. They comment on how small the world is and how Nigerians
are everywhere.

The help the protagonists are offered, once they have made contact with the African community, often comes with strings attached. In
any case, it is soon made clear that for an African immigrant without a
work permit, the options are selling drugs (for men) or prostitution (for

women). (These options lead directly to immersion in the iconography
of those professions, already thoroughly developed on Nigerian soil in
versions heavily influenced by foreign models, especially gangster films
and hip-hop culture. *Man on a Mission* is particularly self-conscious in
playing with this culture; a major character is called "Dogfather.") Sometimes a third option is visible, doing more or less menial jobs under more
or less exploitative conditions, but the protagonist is too ambitious (*Man
on a Mission, The Other Side of Life*), or the need to send money home is
too great (*Goodbye New York, London Forever*), or both (*Western Union*),
so he or she chooses the faster track. This is normally a moment of crisis,
discussed and dramatized at some length. The protagonist is shocked and
dismayed at these options, having come from a respectable background
and having never entertained the idea that life would turn out like this.

So far, in spite of the foreign locations, we are on terrain that is familiar from, and central to, the general video film tradition. If one is not especially interested in foreign cultures or landscapes for their own sakes,
beyond a set of stereotypical images, the social, moral, and psychological
experience of landing in New York, London, or Hamburg is not terribly
different from moving to Lagos from elsewhere in Nigeria. There is the
same overwhelming first impression and the immediate need to find
shelter and employment, which is bound up with the necessity to find
a social network. Then one discovers that social networks follow different and treacherous rules in the intensely individualized and brutally
competitive urban environment. Existing relationships are stressed to
the breaking point. The protagonist moves between extremes of hardship and glamour and suffers tests of endurance and tests of what one is
willing to do for wealth. All this is shown in the first English-language
Nigerian video, Kenneth Nnebue's *Glamour Girls, 1.* Most of these issues are also in play if one is shaken out of one's familiar place in Lagos
through loss of employment (as in *Shame,* which has memorable scenes
of walking the streets looking for work) or through simple dissatisfaction
with one's position, as in the urtext of the Nigerian video tradition, *Living
in Bondage,* also by Kenneth Nnebue. The scenes in which protagonists
try to make contact with the African community abroad are genetically
related to the scene in *Living in Bondage* (initiating a common motif)
where Andy runs into his old friend Paul by accident, which leads to
questions about what he is willing to do for money and his introduction

to a cabal engaged in dark and lucrative business. This business is occult money rituals in *Living in Bondage* and many other films, but it may be drug dealing, prostitution, or 419 fraud schemes.

It is striking, given the general context and reputation of Nigerian videos, that with only one major exception (*The Broken Pitcher*) and two minor ones (*The London Boy* and a very brief, jokey moment in *Osuofia in London* featuring a disappearing pigeon), none of the films in the sample contain any occult element. This is quite different from the films set abroad surveyed in my earlier study ("Africans Abroad"). In a reading of *Glamour Girls, 2,* I have argued that the exorbitance identified with the foreign was closely linked with and analogous to occult powers ("Nnebue"). *The Broken Pitcher,* a collaboration between Mike Bamiloye's Mount Zion Productions, the best known of Nigerian Christian video producers (Ogunleye; Oha), and a church in Texas, is also the only film strongly framed by Christianity. In two other films, *Western Union* and *Crossing Paths,* a Christian framework gradually grows in importance, but with no element of the supernatural. A pastor, fervent prayer, and a winning lottery ticket shape the very end of *London Forever.* Muslim faith and culture are deeply important in *Omo Eniyan,* but there is nothing like spiritual combat.

The decline of the occult element in this genre reflects a gradual evolution across the breadth of Nollywood video production. It is remotely possible that we are finally seeing the effect of the campaigns of the Censors Board against occultism in video films. Perhaps the video public has finally gotten tired of *juju* movies, as commentators have been predicting since 1993 or so. Perhaps the expatriate audiences these films target have more "enlightened," or simply more Americanized, tastes, though they avidly consume cultural epics that are full of magic. Perhaps the actual conditions of life abroad – the hardship, the visible wealth, the temptations to turn to drug dealing or prostitution, and, not least, the existence of functioning police forces that are apt to bring erring characters to account without divine intervention – form a sufficient dramatic structure that makes the occult unnecessary.[9]

In any event, the central theme of psychological, moral, or spiritual trial as the protagonist's personality comes under extreme pressure in the foreign environment is regularly put in predominantly secular terms. One can sometimes discern in the discourse on personality at these moments elements that reflect ultimately religious beliefs shared by the Igbo, Yoruba, and other southern Nigerian ethnic groups that shape the film industry. These beliefs involve the importance of individual destiny, individual spiritual force, and, therefore, individual dynamism and individual achievement as social values. These cultures are of course famous for sending individuals forth to prove themselves and realize themselves, with the result that these cultures are among the most dynamic and far-flung in the world. So the two Igbo protagonists in *Coming to South Africa* are lectured by an Igbo settled in South Africa who offers them a way into drug dealing when they are stranded and desperate: "every man has his own potential. You guys can make it on your own. . . . Are you willing to do whatever it takes to make money? If that's the case, I'll assist you." These values are not overtly ethnicized or traditionalized, however – there is no talk of *ikengas* or *chis* or *ase*.[10] The idiom is more or less that of the self-help books that now crowd the shelves, racks, and tables at the front of Nigerian bookshops, a gauntlet one has to run to get to anything else, except that many of those books have a religious orientation that is remarkably absent in the films.

Sometimes there is a discourse of freedom, as in *Black Night in South America*: "This is not Africa. You're abroad: you've got the freedom to do whatever you want, however you want. The choice is yours." But this sense of freedom is always framed very tightly as a question of what one is willing to do for money and how much money one wants to have. In this example, a woman is counseling her sister to go into prostitution.

In their loneliness and isolation, the protagonists seldom find solace in making contact with home (see Naficy). Contact with home tends rather to remind them of the harsh necessity to make good in their situation on their own. *The London Boy* has poignant scenes of the protagonist calling Nigeria; he is understandably inarticulate in conveying the reality of London life to his family and is constantly met with urgent pleas for money that he cannot meet. The central character of *Western Union*, complaining to a friend about the pressures on him to send money home, is told: "You are right, this is why you are in Europe; you must live up to expectation. What they need from you is a constant flow of cash. This is Europe; you must make use of the only opportunity you have. . . . Get rich, or die trying."

Sometimes the protagonist honorably decides life abroad simply is not worth it, like the heroine of *Missing in America,* who, in spite of what everyone assumes, came to New York to find her missing husband, not for a new life as an immigrant. In her final voice-over, she says, "It takes a special hunger to live in America as an illegal alien. I'm not hungry enough to live here like that. I'll go home where I have friends and family to help me raise my baby. America is a dream. For some it becomes a beautiful reality. For others, that dream is just a nightmare."

Europe by Road and *Coming to South Africa* develop the theme of struggling to get ahead in a social and (apparently) moral void through a contrastive pairing of Nigerian friends who have come abroad together, one of them stronger, harder, more determined, readier to do anything than the other. In the latter case, they both turn to drug dealing, but one pulls out while the stronger one stays in; it is not always clear where the first's weakness stops and his virtue begins, though the plot rewards him with a (white) girl, a job, and freedom after his brush with drug dealing, while the stronger one gets twenty-five years in prison.

The normal way of narrativizing the meaning of the moral crisis is by showing the consequent strain on kin, marital, or romantic relationships. This is, of course, the normal Nollywood procedure: in *Living in Bondage,* Andy's initiation into the money ritual cult requires him to sacrifice his beloved wife, Merit. Betrayal of or by intimates is the most prevalent of all Nollywood themes. What is special about this genre of films set abroad is that the protagonists are largely shorn of intimate relationships by virtue of their situation. But if they are married, there will be adultery (*Broken Pitcher, Dangerous Twins, Dubai Runs, Black Night in South America, Goodbye New York*). If they come looking for a missing spouse (*Missing in America*) or relative (*Black Night, Dangerous Twins*), they will find treachery. Some are betrayed by their families in Nigeria, to whom they are sending money that is wasted in reprehensible ways (*London Forever, Western Union*). A foreign lover may suddenly prove to be treacherous (*Dapo Junior, The Broken Pitcher, Crazy Like a Fox*, and *Osuofia in London*, though in the last case she later redeems herself). More often, the Nigerian betrays a good foreign woman because of inordinate greed (*Man on a Mission, Western Union, Black Night, Dangerous Twins*). Betrayals of Nigerian lovers are routine.

It is worth stressing the extent to which these betrayals happen within the Nigerian community. The principal reason for this is the fact, suggested above, that the films are not very much interested in anything beyond the (extended) Nigerian community. But it is striking how little racism appears in these films. It is fairly often alluded to in passing, as a structuring element in the experience of trying to make it abroad, and is sometimes demonstrated by harsh police officers (a recurring theme in *This America*) or those with depraved sexual interests in black bodies (*Black Night, Goodbye New York*), but in general it is seldom shown. On the other hand, the films include a number of spontaneously generous white people, who are often betrayed or offended (*Home & Abroad*) for their pains (see Haynes, "Africans Abroad"). Only *Dapo Junior* puts white racism at the narrative and emotional center. *Goodbye New York* is awash in bad feelings about being an African in the United States, concentrated in the relationship between a Nigerian and the African American girlfriend off whom he lives. She makes him do things – fix her coffee, rub her feet – which affront his African masculinity, and he responds with a stream of insults and threats in Igbo, pretending all the while they are endearments. But it is not at all clear he actually has the moral upper hand.

This America, by the collaborative team of Oliver Mbamara, Bethels Agomuoh, and Felix Nnorom, is more deeply and systematically about the relationship of Nigerian immigrants and the African American community. Nigerian cousins, one settled in Brooklyn, the other newly arrived, both marry African American women in order to get green cards, and in both cases the relationship goes very wrong. Of all the films in this study, this one is the least structured by Nollywood conventions, though it is rooted in an immigrant community in the standard way, and Agomuoh is closely involved with Nollywood as the owner of the first Internet site selling Nigerian films. But this film is different from the others in many respects and so serves as an important reminder of the openness of the situation of the Nigerian diaspora and its potential to exert a positive influence on Nollywood filmmaking – to make a difference. One of the film's unusual features is that while the others normally contain a very brief and superficial discussion of cultural differences or make them an occasion for simple comedy, *This America* dwells on the subject from beginning to end. (The film is based on an unpublished book Mbamara wrote about the cultural differences faced by African immigrants.) Sometimes the situation is played for laughs – the newly arrived cousin cannot satisfy his simplest needs when he shops for food because what he calls "groundnuts" and "minerals" Americans call "peanuts" and "sodas." Because attention is evenly divided between the cousin who has adapted and the one who doubts he wants to adapt, there is no clear right and wrong as questions arise such as whether a woman should be able to buy a man a drink. The African American society the cousins are faced with is not exactly malevolent toward them, but it is deeply dysfunctional across a range of issues (gun violence, alcoholism, drug addiction, carelessness about women's sexuality and fertility, child raising) in ways that are shocking and dangerous for the Nigerians. The film simply watches and counts the costs of adapting to this utterly unromanticized environment. The establishing shots are brilliant, but the film is never tempted to indulge in tourism, shopping, or romance sequences.

Observation of the Nigerian national character is at the heart of the comedies set abroad. *Osuofia in London, Mr. Ibu in London,* and *Home & Abroad* spend most of their time watching comic Nigerians, who are entertaining masses of low motives and ignorance, goofing around and making fools of themselves in Europe – failing to understand indoor plumbing, waving at themselves in security cameras, and botching relationships with foreign women – but somehow remaining the heroes of their stories. Nkem Owoh's Osuofia is a bushman, a villager, whose long-lost brother has died in England, leaving him an enormous fortune. John Okafor's Ibu is a poor, unsophisticated, and foolish security man working at the Lagos port, who falls asleep in a container and wakes up by the Thames. *Home & Abroad* is about two professional comics (one played by Okafor, the other by Victor Oswuagwu) who are invited to Germany to collect an award and perform. They bring on themselves the hardship/alienation sequence and the need to find Africans in the street because they miss their flight, get distracted by drink and a German lady on their arrival, fail to telephone the promoters who brought them, and do not show up at the awards ceremony. Similarly, Ibu doubles his hardship/alienation experience because he forgets the address of the first Nigerian who has taken him in off the street and needs to be rescued again by a second-chance meeting with another Nigerian. Osuofia has to leave England in a hurry with his brother's English wife, now his fiancée, who was part of a scheme to defraud him but has fallen out with her confederate; part 2 is about their return to his village and her gradual change of heart (see also Okome, this volume). In the other films, the protagonists are deported as manifestly unfit for life in Europe.

Europe is there as a manifold object world to be faced and fooled with, but the relationships that matter are, as usual, largely with Nigerians. Osuofia's experience in London is shaped by his late brother and a Nigerian lawyer who conspires with his brother's wife against him (and who feels his facade of assimilation slipping away in Osuofia's maddening presence). In *Home & Abroad,* the lovable but impossible protagonists' exemplary Nigerian fecklessness, childish greed, irresponsibility, quarrelsomeness, endless wheedling, geniality, humor, liveliness, and sheer force of personality are contrasted not with German rationality but with the rationality of the Nigerian promoters, who are based in Germany and operate according to European standards. They have invested ten thousand euros and their reputations on the awards ceremony, to which they had invited the Nigerian ambassador, and they are understandably furious when the comics do not bother to show up. The Nigerian community in Berlin (which seems to have been deeply involved in the production of the film) is also represented by Lady Suru, whose African grocery store is heavily advertised, but who is an ambivalent figure at the center of an expatriate community prone to rumor, gullibility, and erratic swings between generosity, hypocrisy, and anger. In *Mr. Ibu in London,* the key figure representing the film's point of view is Michael, a Nigerian who takes Ibu in for an extended stay and shows him the sights. Michael is motivated partly by sentimental reasons (there is a slight prior acquaintance, but more important, Ibu generally embodies home), partly because he enjoys Ibu's comic reactions to everything from London Bridge to the London Eye, and partly, doubtless, because Ibu's reactions make him feel superior, measuring how far he has come himself. But when Ibu makes unwanted sexual advances toward Michael's British wife, he is not amused.

All three films lavish attention on the theme of the "been-to." *Osuofia in London, 2* is all about the hero's triumphant return to his village, in a bowler hat, with a white wife in tow. In *Home & Abroad,* before their departure for Europe the comics use the prestige of being "international" men, with passports and visas, to face down landlords and a police officer and to enforce the admiration of their families, and while they are away their families keep at this game in scenes intercut with the men's German misadventures. The general Nigerian population in the film seems uncertain what a visa is, exactly, but is willing to be impressed. Similarly, in *Mr. Ibu in London,* on his return Ibu finds an admiring audience for his implausible lies. The mood is gently satirical – not the kind of satire that is expected to change anything or carry a real message.

The contrast and interplay between a feckless Nigerian personality and the rationality of Nigerians who are used to operating in a foreign environment are at the center of Tade Ogidan's *Dangerous Twins,* the longest (it is in three parts) and richest of the films made abroad, which begins as comedy but quickly turns very dark indeed. Taiye, who lives in London, comes back to Lagos to see his identical twin, Kehinde. They are so much alike even their wives cannot tell them apart (both parts are played by Ramsey Nouah). Taiye tells his brother he has not been able to impregnate his English wife, Judy, and he asks Kehinde to switch places with him to do the job. After some hesitation, Kehinde agrees. In London, Judy is taken aback but pleased by Kehinde's ardent lovemaking and extravagant presents, both so unlike the husband she is used to, and Kehinde makes his brother's business thrive by playing fast and loose with the rules. In Lagos, Taiye is too uptight to touch his brother's wife, Shola, who finds this coldness outweighs the fact that Taiye likes to be a family man at home with the kids, while the husband she is used to was always out chasing other women. Taiye is shocked at the way his brother's business runs and sets out to reform it, firing workers who do not really work, getting rid of equipment he considers unnecessary, and refusing to pay bribes. (Akin Adesokan compares these austerity measures, imported from London, with the structural adjustment program of the 1980s, 410.) Morale suffers, and since Taiye's innovations are so at odds with the local culture, the business declines disastrously. In London, Kehinde succeeds in impregnating Judy, flies her around the world on expensive vacations, and, once the child is born, evades and lies to his brother in order to prolong his new life. In Lagos, Taiye is vexed nearly to madness: he swelters in the dark when the electricity goes off since he refuses on principle to buy a generator, irritated at the neighbors' noisy celebration and furious that no one will listen to his brilliant business ideas. When his home is invaded by armed robbers, he escapes over the wall to call the police, who do nothing since their vehicle is grounded by lack of fuel and the power outage means they cannot phone their men on patrol. Meanwhile, the robbers kill all of Kehinde's children and make off with all the family's money, leaving Shola hysterical.

This is all in part 1, which ends with a fine balance: Kehinde has stolen Taiye's life, and Taiye has destroyed Kehinde's. Taiye is rationality and morality, which evidently do not reign in Nigeria; it is lamentable that Nigeria is a place where trusting law enforcement gets children killed, but Taiye has forgotten or refuses to know how to live there, and he is dead, a sexual and social failure, and therefore an economic failure and a disaster to the family. In the later parts, he becomes a drug courier to return to England to reclaim the wife he loves, now a man of unshakable purpose, willing to get his hands dirty. Kehinde is full of the life force, sexy and fun, but also deeply irresponsible. In the later parts, he completes his betrayal of his brother and goes on to betray Judy and various other women. Finally, he is beyond unforgivable – he is a shell of a man, a compulsive liar and womanizer, a trickster who begins to be tricked over and over, condemned to systematic punishment.

If Taiye seemed in danger of losing touch with his society, the greater danger turns out to be Kehinde running off the rails into a moral, emotional, and social abyss. There is a danger in overestimating Taiye's alienation, in any case; he, like the Nigerian businessmen in *Home & Abroad*, may stand for rationality, but it would be a serious mistake to simply identify rationality with foreign influence and the opposite with Nigerianness. The point is that Taiye and Kehinde are twins, both Nigerian, representing opposite sides of the national temperament. The film is ambivalent toward both sides and is extraordinarily inventive in turning this ambivalence into narrative.

The fact that Kehinde is seen as the greater problem reflects the basic thematic pattern that emerges from these films as a whole. To a remarkable extent, the assimilation of Nigerians abroad to their foreign host cultures does not appear as a major threat. A fundamental point about the Nigerian (and Ghanaian) video films is that they have not been based on the discourses of authenticity and nationalism associated with celluloid cinema and with so much other officially sponsored cultural production in Africa (Meyer; Larkin; Garritano, "Contesting"). African popular culture is comfortable with creolization and foreign trappings used as a marker of African success, and so is apt to react with pride to the sight of a Nigerian living a foreign lifestyle, at least as long as the Nigerian is sending money home, though certainly other reactions may also be in play. The Nigerian diasporic communities, whose points of view loom large in these films, have a sophisticated, lived experience of these issues. Still, it is remarkable how little the inevitable conflicts of assimilation are dramatized. One would think stories about children deserting the values of their parents would be ubiquitous, but there are only two examples in this batch of films: *The Broken Pitcher* briefly turns its attention to a teenage daughter who has begun meeting men in motels and asserts an American independent right to do so, and *The London Boy* is about the conflicts between the claims of a couple's romantic love, situated in London, and the claims on each of them by their families back home. The film conducts a lively and heavily overdetermined debate on the matter without coming anywhere near taking a position. The assimilation theme comes up most frequently in the form of shifting gender roles, either in a relationship with a foreign woman (*London Boy* again) or in a Nigerian marriage where the woman does better than her husband in the foreign economy and he is reduced to domestic labor in the home (*Black Night in South America, Goodbye New York*). Other films refer to missing persons, reflecting a concern that Nigerians abroad may get lost to their families, but cultural assimilation is not usually a prominent part of these stories.

The films are much more worried about two other threats. One is simply the human carnage involved in the dangerous transition to life abroad. If there is one thing these films agree on, it is that Nigerians need to be advised that acquiring wealth abroad is not as easy as they imagine. *Europe by Road* has the character of films made to discourage drug use or unsafe sex, luridly demonstrating the dangers of risky behavior to young people who might be tempted. The theme is sometimes directly expressed at the end of a film through a voice-over, a title, or a scene such as the one that ends *Goodbye New York* in which the protagonist, now back in Nigeria with nothing except very bad memories, advises a circle of young female relatives not to make the same mistake she made. But they do not seem to listen. The frequently sobering fortunes of the films' protagonists are balanced by the visible existence of a Nigerian community abroad, full of people who have made it.

The other threat is from within: that greed, fear, and apparent necessity will lead to moral transgressions with devastating consequences. As I have been arguing, this is the central terrain of the video film tradition as a whole; what the videos primarily see in the foreign is not an occasion for adventure travel but the dangers of a moral holiday during which the thoroughly investigated dark impulses of the national personality can flourish. Betrayal of intimates is in the national character, the videos tell us, though so too of course are extraordinary demonstrations of loyalty and selfless suffering. The moral logic of the diasporan films is the same as that of the video tradition in general, with the same need to punish transgression and the same ambivalence about wealth. In the plot denouements, the protagonists are suitably chastened if their strength has expressed itself in unprincipled ways, or they are allowed to go home if life abroad has roughed them up too badly, or they settle into a successful life abroad if they have passed their tests.

NOTES

1. The previous study was mostly about Ghanaian films, and all the films were made before 2001; this one is all about Nigerian ones (though one film, *Crossing Paths*, is a Nigerian-Ghanaian coproduction dominated by the Ghanaian components), mostly made between 2003 and 2009. I believe historical evolution rather than nationality is responsible for the change in the character of the films.

2. It is possible to do without one of these elements – *A Night in the Philippines* and *Dubai Runs* do not depend on an expatriate community, and *This America* and *Man on a Mission* have no imported star – but most films have both.

3. There are film professionals from Nigeria or of Nigerian descent making careers in the United States and Europe whose work has nothing to do with Nollywood, such as Ngozi Onwurah, Chiwetel Ejiofor, Vigil Chime, and Newton Aduaka.

4. I have given the benefit of the doubt to *Dubai Runs* and *Boys from Holland*.

Some films set abroad that are mentioned in the text are not included in the table because I have not managed to see them in their entirety.

5. I have excluded from my survey a whole category of films made with imported Nigerian stars in other African countries as those countries attempt to establish their own film industries in imitation of the phenomenally popular Nollywood model. See Haynes, "Nollywood."

6. I rush to point out that while Hollywood does like to exploit exotic foreign landscapes, its interest in foreign people is also contained within very strict limits – for example, to some Hollywoodian colorful natives in the background while Robert Redford and Meryl Streep kiss in the foreground (*Out of Africa*), or to a noble savage standing around behind Jennifer Connelly and Leonardo DiCaprio as they explore their rich moral lives and do not quite kiss (*Blood Diamond*).

7. But the top-of-the-line production *Dangerous Twins* has shots of both Murtala Muhammed and Heathrow Airports. For some remarks on airport scenes in Ghanaian video films, see Dogbe 237–40.

8. Hamid Naficy writes of exile, "It is a slipzone of anxiety and imperfection, where life hovers between the heights of ecstasy and confidence and the depths of despondency and doubt" (12).

9. My thinking here has been influenced by Carmela Garritano's careful

argument to the effect that the occult element in the early Ghanaian video films has been overestimated, to the detriment of noticing the fundamental role of economic disparity in those films (*African Video*).

10. An *ikenga* (Igbo) is a small statue representing a man's individual strength; *chi* (Igbo) is a person's daimon or spiritual double, and also his or her destiny; *ase* (Yoruba) is the universal life force contained in every individual as well as in objects.

WORKS CITED

Adesokan, Akin. "Excess Luggage: Nigerian Films and the World of Immigrants." *The New African Diaspora*. Ed. Isidore Okpewho and Nkiru Nzegwu. Bloomington: Indiana University Press, 2009. 401–22.

Agorde, Wisdom S. "Creating the Balance: Hallelujah Masculinities in a Ghanaian Video Film." *Film International* 5.4 (2007): 51–63.

Dogbe, Esi. "Elusive Modernity: Portraits of the City in Popular Ghanaian Video." *Leisure in Urban Africa*. Ed. Paul Tiyambe Zeleza and Cassandra Rachel Veney. Trenton, N.J.: Africa World Press, 2003. 227–48.

Garritano, Carmela. *African Video Movies and Global Desires: A Ghanaian History*. Athens: Ohio University Press, 2013.

———. "Contesting Authenticities: The Emergence of Local Video Production in Ghana." *Critical Arts* 22.1 (2008): 21–48.

———. "A New Critical Architecture for African Grassroots Cinemas: Nigerian Video in Ghana, Pirate Economies, and Transnational Media Flows." Paper delivered to Society for Cinema and Media Studies conference, Philadelphia, 2008.

Haynes, Jonathan. "Africans Abroad: A Theme in Film and Video." *Africa*

e Mediterraneo 45 (December 2003): 22–29.

———. "Nnebue: The Anatomy of Power." *Film International* 5.4 (2007): 30–40.

———. "Nollywood: What's in a Name?" *Guardian* (Lagos), July 3, 2005, 56, 58. Reprinted in *Film International* 5.4 (2007): 106–108.

Larkin, Brian. *Signal and Noise: Media, Infrastructure, and Urban Culture in Nigeria*. Durham, N.C.: Duke University Press, 2008.

Meyer, Birgit. "Popular Ghanaian Cinema and 'African Heritage.'" *Africa Today* 46.2 (1999): 93–114.

Naficy, Hamid. *An Accented Cinema: Exilic and Diasporic Filmmaking*. Princeton, N.J.: Princeton University Press, 2001.

National Film and Video Censors Board. "Film & Video Directory in Nigeria." Vols. 1 and 2, ed. Ferdinand O. Abua. Vol. 3, ed. D. R. Gana and Clement D. Edekor. Abuja, Nigeria: National Film and Video Censors Board, 2002, 2004, 2006.

Ogunleye, Foluke. "Christian Video Film in Nigeria: Dramatic Sermons through the Silver Screen." *African Video Film Today*. Ed. Foluke Ogunleye. Manzini, Swaziland: Academic Publishers, 2003. 105–28.

————. "'That We May Serve Him without Fear': Nigerian Christian Video Film and Battle against Cultism." *International Journal of Humanistic Studies* 2 (2003): 16–27.

Oha, Obododimma. "The Rhetoric of Nigerian Christian Videos: The War Paradigm of the Great Mistake." *Nigerian Video Films.* Ed. Jonathan Haynes. Athens: Ohio University Press, 2000. 192–99.

FILMOGRAPHY

Back to Africa. Dir. Tunde Alabi. Bonag and Tony Abulu Film (Nigeria). 1997.

Black Night in South America . . . Pray Hard Not to Be a Victim, 1 and 2. Dir. Abel Success Erebe. African Oasis and Christian Dior (Nigeria). 2007.

Blood Diamond. Dir. Edward Zwick. Warner Bros. Entertainment (United States and Germany). 2006.

Boys from Holland. Dir. MacCollins Chidebe. Magic Movies (Nigeria). 2006.

The Broken Pitcher. Dir. Mike Bamiloye. Mount Zion (Nigeria) and Northward Film Productions of RCCG Household of Faith (United States). 2008.

Close Enemies. Dir. Lancelot Oduwa Imasuen. Afro Media (United States and Nigeria). 2009.

Columbia Connection, 1 and 2. Dir. Obi Callys Obinali. Hallmark Films (Nigeria). 2004.

Coming to South Africa, 1 and 2. Dir. Paul Louwrens. P. Collins (South Africa) and Emmaco Holdings Films (Nigeria). 2004, 2005.

Crazy Like a Fox. Dir. Tony Abulu. Black Ivory Communications (United States). 2008.

Crossing Paths, 1 and 2. Dir. John Uche. Ghawood Angel Productions (United States). 2008.

Dangerous Twins. Dir. Tade Ogidan. OGD Pictures (Nigeria). 2003.

Dapo Junior. Dir. Tody Dele Akinyemi. No Budget Entertainment (Netherlands) and Double "A" Entertainment (Nigeria). 2000.

Dollars from Germany, 1 and 2. Dir. Nonso Emekaekwue. Deraco Productions (Nigeria). 2004.

Dubai Runs, 1 and 2. Dir. MacCollins Chidebe. Kammadimss (Nigeria). 2007.

Europe by Road . . . Miles Away from Africa, 1 and 2. Dir. Ikenna Ezeugwu. Columbia Production et al. (Nigeria). 2007.

Fateful Love, 1 and 2. Dir. Simi Opeoluwa. Andy Best Electronics (Nigeria). 2004.

Glamour Girls. Dir. Chika Onukwufor. NEK Video Links (Nigeria). 1994.

Glamour Girls, 2: The Italian Connection. Dir. Christian Onu. NEK Video Links (Nigeria). 1996.

Goodbye New York, 1 and 2. Dir. Tchidi Chikere. A2Z Movies International (Nigeria). 2004.

Home & Abroad. Dir. Lancelot Oduwa Imasuen. Lancewealth Images (Nigeria), Videofield International (Germany et al.). 2004.

Living in Bondage. Dir. Chris Obi Rapu. NEK Video Links (Nigeria). 1992.

The London Boy, 1 and 2. Dir. Simi Opeoluwa. Andy Best Electronics (Nigeria). 2004.

London Forever. Dir. Chico Ejiro. Grandtouch Pictures (Nigeria). 2004.

Love from Asia, 1 and 2. Dir. Ugo Ugbor. Deraco (Nigeria). 2004.

Man on a Mission (Making Money Abroad). Dir. Romanus Ike Eze. Kingsdome Entertainment (Nigeria). N.d.

Missing in America. Dir. Sola Osofisan. Creative Chronicles & Concepts and Buky's Place Enterprises (United States). 2004.

Mr. Ibu in London. Dir. Andy Chukwu. Kas-Vid (Nigeria). 2004.

A Night in the Philippines, 1 and 2. Dir. Zeb Ejiro. Zeb Ejiro Productions (Nigeria). 2006.

Omo Eniyan. Dir. Muka Ray Eyiwunmi. Muka-Ray Films (Nigeria). 2006.

Osuofia in London, 1 and 2. Dir. Kingsley Ogoro. Kingsley Ogoro Productions (Nigeria). 2003, 2004.

The Other Side of Life. Dir. Femi J. Babatunde. TFT Entertainment (United States). 2003.

Out of Africa. Dir. Sydney Pollack. Mirage (United States). 1985.

Shame. Dir. Chico Ejiro. OJ Productions (Nigeria). 1996.

South Connection, 1 and 2. Dir. Andy Chukwu. OJ Productions (Nigeria). 2004.

30 Days: Hell Hath No Fury. Dir. Mildred Okwo. Native Lingua Films and Temple Productions (United States and Nigeria). 2006.

This America. Dir. Bethels Agomuoh. African Film Company and United African Artists (United States). 2005.

Toronto Connection, 1 and 2. Dir. Amayo Uzo Philips. Darlington Okonkwo Production and Goodlife Production (Nigeria). 2007.

Western Union, 1 and 2. Dir. Stanley Solomon Phillips and Prince Sam Onyejuwa. Uche 10 (Nigeria) and Damek Comm. Network (Germany). 2007.

FOUR

Nollywood Made
in Europe

SOPHIE SAMYN

THE HISTORY OF NOLLYWOOD CAN BE TRACED BACK TO THE
home video industry that emerged in Nigeria in the early 1990s. The
video films rapidly reached an audience far beyond Nigerian borders,
circulating throughout Africa and beyond and creating a buzz that soon
became a media blitz. Over the past ten years, the Nigerian diaspora has
been gradually integrated into Nollywood, a word that quickly became
shorthand for the video phenomenon in Nigeria. It is now very popular
fare in the diaspora due partly to the fact that some of the films are shot
abroad, often in collaboration with expatriate communities. Nigerians
living in Europe, who do not want to miss out on the success of this
flourishing industry, have seized the initiative and begun producing
their own films. As they live abroad, they feel the urge to tell their stories
and often in the manner of Nollywood. With its distinctive use of cheap
digital technology and video, Nollywood has made this possible. The
main purpose of this chapter is to describe examples of the filmmaking
by Nigerian immigrants in the Netherlands, Germany, and Belgium by
examining the work of Tony A. B. Akinyemi, Leonard Ajayi-Odekhiran, Isaac Izoya, John Osas Omoregie, and Azubuike Erinugha who,
like many Nollywood filmmakers, produce, write, act in, or direct their
films. In this chapter, I aim to discuss their personal lives as migrants
and what drives them to be filmmakers. I will discuss their thematic
preoccupations, bringing into the debate the multiple publics that are
involved in their works with an aim of bringing into sharper focus how
these immigrant filmmakers negotiate the various cultural and national
boundaries they cross. I will also examine the production, distribution,
content, and aesthetics as they are mobilized in these films in order to

uncover the similarities and differences between Nollywood made in Europe and Nollywood made in Nigeria, which I will sometimes refer to as "domestic Nollywood." One key question that will be part of this inquiry is whether they can actually be called Nollywood filmmakers. In this process, the importance of the practices of the Nigerian immigrant filmmakers for African communities throughout Europe and their relationship with Nigeria will be unraveled. I have chosen to examine the work of these filmmakers because of the geographical proximity of their host countries and the connections they share, for they all know and inspire each other. This chapter is based primarily on the interviews I conducted with the five filmmakers in their homes in 2010 and is complemented by my textual analysis of their films with the aim of highlighting their motivations and expectations.

IMMIGRANT FILMMAKERS

The filmmakers I interviewed are Nigerian expatriates who left their country between 1990 and 2000, a period during which many Nigerians aspired to emigrate in the hope of a better life in Europe.

Tony A. B. Akinyemi and Leonard Ajayi-Odekhiran met in the early 1990s, as newly arrived immigrants to the Netherlands. In this respect, Akinyemi says, "It's always going to be two homes for us, whether you like it or not. When somebody asks me what my country is, I always say: I only know of two Ns, Nigeria and the Netherlands." Both men were active in the entertainment sector back in Nigeria. In Europe, they founded Double "A" Entertainment, and in 1998, they made the first-ever Nigerian film to be shot in Europe, *Under Pressure*. The film was a success, and the two men thus paved the way for other Nigerians in Europe to follow in their footsteps. Subsequently, they released *Dapo Junior, Holland Heat,* and *From Amsterdam with Love*. Their most recent Edo-language film is *Eti vbe Holland* (in postproduction and translated as "Trouble in Holland"). Akinyemi and Ajayi-Odekhiran write, direct, and act in all their films. They, moreover, distinguish themselves by highlighting the theme of mixed marriages.

Isaac Izoya left Nigeria around 1993, during the military rule of Ibrahim Babangida. When I asked him why he left, he said: "When you tell someone in Nigeria you left at that time, everybody understands, no explanation required." Currently living in Berlin, he claims: "I can never forget my identity as an African. . . . I'm a Nigerian and I want to be seen like that. I can never forget home, and no matter how long you spend in Germany, you are still *Ausländer* [foreigner]." In Germany, Izoya first made his living as a journalist for the magazine *African Courier*. When he saw *Dapo Junior* by Double "A" Entertainment, he got inspired, believing that Nollywood could help him get his message across to a sizable audience in Europe. To make this idea a reality, Izoya founded his own production company in Berlin, Ehizoya Golden Entertainment. He also set up a partnership with Nigerian-based Nollywood director Lancelot Oduwa Imasuen, and they made their first film, *Sinners in the House.* Izoya produced (and acted in) several films in Germany, always in collaboration with Nollywood writers, actors, and directors. The productions I will consider here are *Zero Your Mind; Love in Berlin . . . the Meeting Point, 1 and 2;* and *Run but You Can't Hide, 1 and 2.* In addition to making films, Izoya is a show promoter and has toured with Nigerian Nollywood stars, musicians, and comedians throughout Europe.

In 2001, John Osas Omoregie settled in Antwerp, Belgium, a city he has made his own. Inspired by Double "A" Entertainment's *Under Pressure,* he made his first film in 2003. Titled *Igho Evbue Ebo,* which is roughly translated as "Money Abroad," the work is filmed in Omoregie's native Edo language and is about the situation of African migrants in Europe. He subsequently founded the Association of Nigerian Actors and Actresses in Belgium (ANAABEL), a recognized nonprofit organization. With ANAABEL, Omoregie has made religiously inspired films, such as *Desperate Heart; Mama, Why Me? 1 and 2;* and *Amazing World. The Immigrant Eyes,* his first documentary, tells the story of a group of immigrants living in Antwerp. Omoregie is a preacher in his local church, and he hopes to fight poverty and inequality with his charitable organization, the JOMOSA International Foundation (JIF), which he also founded.

Azubuike Erinugha is a highly educated Nollywood director who recently settled in Brussels. He left Nigeria in 1997 and lived in the United States, Canada, and Germany before moving to Belgium. He goes back to Nigeria regularly and is very involved in the home video industry in his homeland. He made his first Nollywood film in 1996, when he was still living in Nigeria. In Europe he continues to write, direct, and produce Nollywood films (all shot entirely in Nigeria) as a member of Towncrier International, a Canadian-based production company. Erinugha is convinced that serious subjects can be conveyed to the Nollywood audience through humor and satire. *The Champion Sportsman*, his only film that I will consider in this chapter, premiered in Berlin in 2010. It was Erinugha's first overseas production in collaboration with the German artist collective InterArte. With this film, the issue of migration became Erinugha's primary concern.

MOTIVATIONS AND EXPECTATIONS

Why do these filmmakers do what they do? Making a fortune can't possibly be the goal, as they all struggle financially to continue their work. When I put this point to Akinyemi, he replied, "If we would put ten thousand euro into a film, and we would get back ten thousand without a cent as gain, we'd be happy doing it." Akinyemi and Ajayi-Odekhiran, Izoya, Omoregie, and Erinugha became filmmakers because they wanted to celebrate Nigeria's popular culture, which has a successful popular entertainment industry expressed in music, theater, and film production. They also believe that Europe misses out in the enjoyment of this kind of joie de vivre that is so typical of Africa, and, as a result, they wish to enrich the cultural life in Europe by showcasing art forms. Furthermore, they all want to change Nigeria's bad reputation in Europe. Izoya explained, "It was to show the good face of Nigeria that made me to venture into Nollywood, which is a pride to Africa" (Idowu-Shadrach). The other reason they went into filmmaking is to inform and educate people. According to Erinugha, "I don't believe in just making a movie for making a movie. I think the filmmaker should also play a very important social role in society." This is in line with the narrative intent of Nollywood where stories are a source of information and moral insight. With their films, these immigrant filmmakers mainly want to inform the Nigerian audience about the situation of African immigrants in Europe, and the struggles of migration are a central theme in many of their films. They hope that this will stop desperate immigrants risking their lives to make the journey to Europe and evoke discussions on both continents. Last, these filmmakers seek to promote integration with their films by symbolically blurring the boundaries between Africans and Europeans, black and white, and by dealing with issues such as discrimination and mixed marriages. When they organize screenings, social gatherings, or performances, they bring, very literally, a mixed audience together.

The Nigerian immigrants describe themselves, without hesitation, as true Nollywood filmmakers. Nollywood is, for them, an experience – a genuine Nigerian creation made with little capital and even less time. As Akinyemi put it to me, Nollywood "takes the impossible, and makes it possible. That is what Nollywood is all about." However convinced they are about their being part of Nollywood, can we substantiate the claim in a real sense? How does the work of these filmmakers tie in with the tradition of Nollywood filmmaking? Asking these questions gives significance to the differences that exist between the two forms of film-making, even though they have close affinities. The most remarkable difference between the two groups of filmmakers is that one group is based in Europe and not Nigeria. In what follows, I will be looking at the content of their films as a way of answering these questions.

THEMES AND STORY LINES

Thematically, the movies of the filmmakers living in Europe share many similarities with domestic Nollywood films. Romance, drama, and crime are equally the dominant genres. Love and relationships play an impor-tant role in the stories far more than the reality of life abroad. Foreign settings lend themselves particularly well to crime films in which "the protagonist moves between extremes of hardship and glamour and suf-fers tests of endurance and tests of what one is willing to do for wealth" (Haynes, this volume). In *Holland Heat,* the main character, Fred, played by Ajayi-Odekhiran, and his friend Chris are struggling to survive finan-cially in the Netherlands. Having just spent their last twenty euros on food, Fred finds Don Pedro's wallet. The latter is a member of the Nige-rian mafia. Tempted by the prospect of sudden wealth, he gets himself into trouble. In *Run but You Can't Hide,* set in Berlin, the protagonist, Okuemu, flees Nigeria to escape from the police and arrives in Germany. He decides to improve his life and gets a job. Desperate because money is running out, Okuemu decides to commit one last crime, which in-evitably leads to his arrest. In *From Amsterdam with Love,* the sequel to *Dapo Junior,* the rebellious Risky is released from prison. Dapo contacts Risky from Nigeria and asks him to kidnap his son Dapo Junior. The law always catches up with the criminals, and the message is the same: a life of crime never pays. As Haynes notes, "The moral logic of the diasporan films is the same as that of the video tradition in general, with the same need to punish transgression and the same ambivalence about wealth" (Haynes, this volume). The five immigrant filmmakers, who are all Christians, want to reflect the reality they are living in. As religion is not such a dominant force in Europe, it is less prominent in their films. They also feel the need to downplay the supernatural in order to reach the European audience. The stories, therefore, tend to be more secular and focus less on the occult, although this is a development that is noted in Nollywood productions in general (Haynes, this volume).[1] However, religion is very present in the films of Omoregie, who is also a preacher, and the "supernatural elements" play decisive roles in his story lines. The film *Desperate Heart* is about a prostitute, Naomi, who betrays the people who helped her come to Belgium in order to obtain a residence permit. At the end of the film, she encounters a phantom (made visible by special effects) that comes with a message from God. In *Mama, Why Me?* 1 *and* 2, the Christian agenda is even more present. The film is about Juliet, who lives in Belgium and is constantly being pressured to send home money by her avaricious mother in Nigeria. The film ends with a sequence of constantly alternating shots of the pleading Juliet; the pastor, played by Omoregie himself, and other church members passionately praying for her in Belgium; and the mean mother performing a wicked ritual in Nigeria. The prayers get louder and more intense until, suddenly, a lightning bolt strikes the mother dead.

Nollywood films made in Europe can be distinguished thematically, as they often portray the immigrant experiences and issues that are typical of life in the diaspora. According to Omoregie, "The story depends on what is happening in our environment.... What we see, what we hear, and what we experience is what we portray. That is how our movies differ from those made in Nigeria." Jonathan Haynes argues that Nollywood films set partially (or entirely) overseas constitute a specific genre within Nollywood characterized by similar stories, themes, and aesthetics. Haynes includes all Nollywood films that have some kind of "foreign" imagery (beyond the African continent) in this category of Nollywood diasporic films. Most of the characteristics of this genre that he has identified are remarkably present in the films of the five filmmakers that I consider in this study. Akinyemi's *Under Pressure,* Izoya's *Zero Your Mind,* and Erinugha's *The Champion Sportsman* all tell stories of Nigerian men coming to Europe in the hope of a better future. The films explore everything that a newly arrived immigrant faces in Europe: alienation, loneliness, ignorance, cold weather, and racism. Life is tough, and it is hard to communicate this new reality to the family back in Nigeria. In both *Under Pressure* and *Zero Your Mind,* a Nigerian robs the main characters upon their arrival. Nevertheless, they are quickly introduced to the local African community. In *Under Pressure,* the main character (Victor) marries a Dutch woman (Mandy). Cultural differences, however, are the cause of constant dispute. Although Mandy works, Victor insists that he, as the husband, should manage their money. Moreover, because Victor sends most of their funds to Nigeria, they are unable to pay their bills. In *The Champion Sportsman,* Okoro desperately tries to find a job. Due to a case of mistaken identity, he ends up taking part in a German reality show on television, featuring world-famous sportsmen, and becomes the public's favorite. The confrontation with life in Europe is usually portrayed humorously. The films depict "comic Nigerians, who are entertaining masses of low motives and ignorance, goofing around and making fools of themselves in Europe . . . but somehow remaining the heroes of their stories" (Haynes, this volume). All kinds of misunderstandings, based on cultural differences and clichés, are combined with a theatrical acting style. In *Home & Abroad,* one of the characters locks himself in the refrigerator in Nigeria in preparation for his trip to Germany. In *Run but You Can't Hide,* the main character, played by the comedian Francis Agoda, is startled when, after ringing the doorbell, a voice comes out of the intercom. In *Zero Your Mind,* Teddy doesn't know any better than to put his socks over his hands as gloves, when he feels the cold upon his arrival in Germany. He then continues looking for a pay phone, despite passing many. He finally asks a passerby where he can find a *working* pay phone. In Nigeria, after all, the absence of a line means the telephone doesn't work.

Whereas these films feature Nigerians who have just arrived confronting life in Europe, others simply portray life in the diasporic community. In such films, the relationship with the host country is seen as problematic. Cultural differences, discrimination, and economic difficulties are central themes. Typical of films made in the diaspora is the transposition of the themes of treachery and betrayal, especially between friends and lovers, to the immigrant community (Haynes, this volume). The film *Dapo Junior* appears, at first glance, to be a romantic film about a Nigerian man and a Dutch woman. Although confronted with racism on both sides, their love survives, and they have a baby. The film then takes a drastic turn when his wife reports Dapo to the police. Apparently, all she wanted from Dapo was a colored baby. The films often portray the decadence and immorality of life in Europe, in contrast to the traditional way of life in Nigeria. A secondary plot in *Dapo Junior* tells the story of Risky, a Nigerian student in the Netherlands, who is wasting his life and money, smoking, drinking, and partying at the expense of his studies. His mother is desperate and sends a girl over from Nigeria to be his wife and keep him out of trouble. *Mama, Why Me? 1 and 2* deals with the difficulty of selfish mothers in Nigeria who pressure their daughters to send money home and try to stop them from getting married. *Desperate Heart* is an autobiographical film by Omoregie about the issues of human trafficking and prostitution, made to tell the world his side of the story. All these stories about migration and life in Europe are, in a way, the stories of every African in Europe, and therefore, the films speak not only to Nigerians but also to a broader audience of migrants of all African descent.

PUBLICS AND SPACES

Globalization has not only brought about the physical mobility of people, it has also created new spheres of communication, where people and spaces across the world come together virtually. What public spaces do the practices of these Nigerian immigrants mobilize, represent, and address? In the following, I will examine the extent to which Nigeria, Europe, the Nigerian diaspora, and the city are articulated in the work of Nigerian immigrant filmmakers. By doing so, I will try to determine if there are good reasons – apart from similarities of content (which have been discussed in the previous section) – to include films made by Nigerian immigrants to Europe in the tradition of "Nollywood filmmaking." Are there similarities in terms of financing, production, distribution, and exhibition?

The immigrant filmmakers are connected to the domestic Nollywood industry in different ways. Ajayi-Odekhiran and Akinyemi acted in films by Chico and Zeb Ejiro back in Nigeria. Izoya starred in several

domestic Nollywood productions and collaborated with one of Nollywood's most prolific directors, Lancelot Imasuen. Erinugha made three
films in Nigeria before making *The Champion Sportsman*. Omoregie col-
laborates with his brother's film production company in Nigeria. Moreover, some of these filmmakers have brought Nollywood stars to Europe
to act in their films. Izoya is the most integrated in the industry and has
been interviewed on Nigerian television and received awards for his European tours featuring Nollywood stars.

The immigrant filmmakers mainly aim at a Nigerian, and by extension African, audience. After distributing their films in the diaspora
through African shops, they take their films to Nigeria, where they distribute them "through the same channels as the other Nollywood practitioners in Nigeria – through the marketers."[2] They sell the rights to
their films to a marketer who then distributes them. This is not always
easy. According to Omoregie, "This is difficult, mostly when you don't
have a Nollywood famous actor or actress from Nigeria in your movie.
No marketer wants to market your film because they are afraid that the
movie might not make market."[3] Piracy equally proves to be a challenge.
According to Akinyemi and Ajayi-Odekhiran, even when they release a
film in Europe, by the time they get to Nigeria, they will almost certainly
find illegal copies of the work there.

Often, a number of scenes shot in Nigeria are integrated into the
movies, which are set in Europe. Omoregie uses his brother's production company to shoot his Nigerian scenes. In contrast, Erinugha and
Izoya travel to Nigeria themselves for filming purposes. The alternation
between the Nigerian and European setting can be a problem when the
main actors are unable to travel for filming. In *Desperate Heart*, the main
character, Naomi, is played by two different actresses. This is also evident in *Run but You Can't Hide*, but the actor switch becomes part of the
story, as the main character conveniently has to undergo plastic surgery
before traveling abroad. In terms of geography, the scenes set in Nigeria
are mostly undefined. They are either set in villages or in suburbs or entirely indoors. It is only in *Run but You Can't Hide* that the city of Lagos
makes a recognizable appearance, reflecting a violent environment that
is controlled by the mafia.

The five immigrant filmmakers relate differently to the countries in
which they currently live, and this influences their productions. Akin-

yemi and Ajayi-Odekhiran appear the most integrated in their host country, the Netherlands. The reason for this is that they have been living abroad the longest, and Akinyemi is married to a Dutch woman with whom he has a family. Moreover, there is no real African community in Eindhoven, the city where they live. They have to go to Amsterdam, Rotterdam, or Antwerp to fraternize with other Nigerians and often feel that "they [the other African immigrants] look at us like white people." Double "A" Entertainment works with a number of white actors and crew members, even though their films are always set in African communities. In *Under Pressure* and *Dapo Junior,* the lead female characters are Dutch because mixed marriages are at the center of both stories. *Dapo Junior* was also the first film to be subtitled (in Dutch) for a European audience and was subsidized by the city of Eindhoven. Double "A" Entertainment takes the most interest in the local setting, and the titles of their films are generally linked to the Netherlands: *Holland Heat, From Amsterdam with Love.* The cover of *Under Pressure* reads, "As a bonus, you will get to enjoy the beauty of the Dutch and Belgian scenery, where this epic was filmed," leaving little doubt that this movie mainly addresses an audience back in Nigeria. The opening sequence of the film contains a montage with images of rural and urban Holland. There are shots of typical Dutch city life: busy streets, typical buildings, outdoor cafés, and shots of the classic "flat" Dutch countryside with its canals and woods. Some Dutch symbols are included: bicycles (in the city) and mills (in the countryside). The Netherlands is portrayed as a place that is welcoming, and the main characters easily make contact with Dutch women. In *Under Pressure,* a Dutch woman gives Victor her jacket when he arrives at the airport and says, "Take it as a gift from Holland." Nevertheless, racism is also part of everyday reality, and the characters are often beaten up and deceived by the local population.

Izoya is convinced it was fate that brought him to Germany. Although he is often frustrated with the German way of life, Izoya admires its precision and thinks this has influenced him and caused him to stand out in the industry. When asked what advice he would give upcoming filmmakers, he replied, "Like I always say, they should learn from the Germans.... [A]n average German believes 'anything worth doing at all, is worth doing well and good.' That is the way forward" ("If It's Easy"). Just as Izoya is determined to change Nigeria's bad reputation, he also believes that he can do the same for Germany. Izoya is convinced that Germany has a smeared image in Africa due to vague reminiscences of World War II.

Azubuike Erinugha lived in Germany for three years before he made *The Champion Sportsman* in 2010. He is the only one of the filmmakers discussed who has made an actual coproduction with Europeans. The press folder of *The Champion Sportsman* contains a carefully written synopsis and outline of the film's objectives, which is very un-Nollywood. The collaboration was born out of a shared concern about the issue of migration, as a global reality affecting Europe and Africa in very different ways. According to the press folder, the aim was to show Africans the reality of the immigrant experience and critically review European responsibilities. At the same time, it was an attempt to provoke discussion on both continents. Erinugha is the writer and director of the film, but the rest of the crew consists mostly of Germans. The film has a big German (white) cast, and the German way of acting contrasts sharply with the theatrical and improvisational acting style of the Nigerian actors. Erinugha personally experienced a more hostile environment in Germany than he did anywhere else, and he found the collaboration challenging. According to him, the German sense of precision and preoccupation with planning clashed with Nollywood production conventions. He noted:

> A German wants to sit down for it doesn't matter how long, and then plan what is going to happen next year. Now in Nollywood's tradition . . . there's a small preproduction plan, but the plan always changes. The Germans did not understand why I should stop somebody on the street and say, "Please can you come play this role for me?" . . . At one point, . . . I took the script and canceled some lines, to make it faster to shoot, and it was a big problem.

The financing in Nollywood is mainly an independent venture. Budgets are small and largely derived from one's own savings. But this is certainly not the only way of financing filmmaking in Nollywood. Often the marketer pays for a film, and he or she gets the final cut and then distributes. In this sense, it is best to say that Nollywood films are financed on an ad hoc basis, which makes it lack the institutional structure that many film cultures have in Europe, America, and Asia. I should note in passing that Diamond Bank and UTB ventured into the business of financing Nollywood films but had to withdraw, as it proved unprofitable. The same applies to productions made in Europe. According to Izoya: "That is one of the wonders of Nollywood. We lack government support . . . and even in Germany, sponsorship of Nollywood movie by film board is more or less a mission impossible. Hence, we resolve in collective contribution or donation and borrowings, and of course one's savings to meet up with the production cost."[4] These productions rarely make a profit, which shows the drive these filmmakers have to continue with these projects. Asked about returns, Akinyemi answered: "So far so good. We have produced about seven films and almost all of them were personally financed by us. Ajayi-Odekhiran took a personal loan to finance our first movie *Under Pressure* and for our second film (our most expensive movie ever) I re-mortgaged my house to finance the project."[5] *Dapo Junior* and *The Champion Sportsman* got financial backing from official European institutions, which is unique within Nollywood production.

Nigerian filmmakers in Europe are eager to reach the European audience. Izoya claims his films are made "for all people":

> My movie has two worlds; it comes to both sides. . . . I try to show . . . people back home because everybody wants to come to Europe, because in Africa we believe that once you enter Europe, you see a bunch of money on the street. . . . [W]e don't believe you have to work for your money . . . and then you also choose a movie of Africa to tell people back here we are not only living in trees. . . . We use it to educate the West. . . . [T]hey don't know Africa is a continent; they think Africa is a country. Stupid [laughing].

The idea of wanting to reach "all people" is appealing, but in practice little is done to accomplish this. The films are often unintelligible (due to the use of pidgin English) for a European audience, and they are, moreover, not marketed outside the African community. When I asked him if he intended to reach a Belgian audience, Omoregie responded rather ironically: "Of course, if possible," and laughed. Erinugha admitted he targets predominantly the Nigerian and African audience. This does not mean that no efforts are made to reach Europeans. The producers of *Dapo Junior* and *The Champion Sportsman*, not surprisingly the films financed by European institutions, made genuine efforts to subtitle their films and to attract a European audience through marketing and well-organized screenings. In Izoya's latest film, *Love in Berlin . . . the Meeting Point*, the actors noticeably try to speak a more understandable English.

Omoregie started subtitling his films in Dutch in 2010. It is hard to measure how successful these attempts are in reaching a European audience. In general, however, the films still find their audience within the African diasporic communities. With regard to the screening of *The Champion Sportsman* in Berlin, Erinugha has this to say: "It's a true life story to almost every African. The day of the screening, all the Africans there really identified with this guy [the main character], because everybody has passed through this, maybe not 100 percent, but whatever has happened to this guy in the film has already happened to every African in Germany."

In Europe, films by Nigerian immigrants are distributed via African shops, churches, and personal relations. Small-scale screenings are often held in local community halls when a film premiers. Most of the immigrant filmmakers work with a more or less stable cast and crew of other Nigerian expatriates. Local Nigerian or African businesses often support productions and, in exchange, are featured and promoted in the films. African shops, clubs, and hair salons are also popular settings for these films, which supports Haynes's observation that a certain "Afrocentric world" dominates the foreign setting in diasporic Nollywood films (this volume). In the European location, Nigerians coincidentally bump into each other all the time, or encounter old friends from Nigeria. For the newly arrived Nigerian, the diasporic community offers guidance and comfort. At one end, there is the diasporic community consisting of Nigerians who have "made it" and live in luxury. This is especially true of the films by Omoregie, which are predominantly shot indoors and pay little attention to the specificity of the foreign environment. The characters in the films reside in fancy apartments, wear expensive clothes and jewelry, and frequent parties. They feel superior toward the Nigerians living in Nigeria and frustrated with their ignorance. In *Mama, Why Me?* Juliet complains that her mother keeps calling, to which her friend Susan comments, "African people with their problems, they are too much." When Susan's mother disapproves of the independent life that she is leading, as opposed to starting a family, she tells her mother, "That is in Nigeria. We are in Europe now." In most of the other films, the characters deal with discrimination and economic difficulties in a complex and contradictory manner while at the same time looking back with yearning to their old life in Nigeria.

The cities, where the Nigerian immigrant filmmakers live, are often more meaningful in their work and lives than the country itself. Analogous to the role of Lagos (or other urban centers like Enugu, Abuja, and Benin City) in the Nollywood industry, the European city is more than just the setting in Izoya's and Omoregie's productions. Omoregie feels more like an "Antwerpener" than a Belgian. According to Omoregie, "I think I can't live anywhere else in Belgium apart from Antwerp. I love Antwerp." The two associations that he founded, ANAABEL and JIF, are supported by the city, and a photo of Omoregie and the mayor features on his website. Omoregie has also made a short promotional video for Antwerp, which forms a trailer for his films. His documentary, *The Immigrant Eyes*, tells the story of immigrants and their perception of Antwerp.

Izoya loves the vibrant and multicultural atmosphere of Berlin, and although he does not want to be seen as a German, he loves being a "Berliner." For him, "when you are in Berlin, it's like you're in Lagos. There is no dull moment in Lagos, as there is no dull moment in Berlin." The city offers him "the African way of life," and the glamour reminds him of Lagos. The representation of Berlin in Izoya's films is very similar to that of Lagos in Nollywood films, as described by Haynes ("Nollywood in Lagos") and also Okome ("Writing the Anxious City"). The opening credits of Izoya's films are always accompanied by an elaborate Berlin sequence: a succession of shots of imposing buildings and significant historical and modern places across the German capital. In the film, the same images are reused between scenes. Nevertheless, Berlin is also perceived as a hostile environment for immigrants. In *Zero Your Mind*, the main character is forced to sleep in subway stations, which stand for his "underground" position as an immigrant. Izoya's Berlin is simultaneously a place of luxury, loneliness, and violence (see also Hoffmann's chapter on the representation of New York in American Nollywood films, this volume). Moreover, Izoya's film *Love in Berlin . . . the Meeting Point* was shown (in 2010) as part of Black History Month, an annual festival in Berlin that celebrates the African diaspora.

TRANSNATIONAL AESTHETICS

In *An Accented Cinema: Exile and Diasporic Filmmaking*, Hamid Naficy argues that the distinctive conditions of production, distribution, and

consumption of films made by deterritorialized filmmakers have defining consequences on the style of the films. Elements of this "accented
style" (22) can be found in the films discussed in this chapter, some
of which I will now deal with in more detail. However, as opposed to
Naficy's "accented filmmakers," who "operate independently, outside
the studio system or the mainstream film industries" (10), Akinyemi,
Ajayi-Odekhiran, Izoya, Omoregie, and Erinugha stay very close to the
popular Nollywood aesthetics in their films. This may be partly the result of similar production circumstances and partly because of their
desire to be part of the Nigerian video industry. Moreover, the artisanal
mode of production is characteristic of Nollywood production, and not,
as Naficy argues of "accented cinema," a result of the marginal and displaced situation of the filmmaker. The films are low-budget, shot quickly,
and intended for video distribution, and thus for a small screen. The
stories are dialogue-oriented, and the camera often forms "the fourth
wall" facing the conversing characters. Interior scenes tend to dominate Izoya's and Omoregie's films, interrupted by establishing shots of
the city in the case of Izoya, or symbols of luxury such as close-ups of
expensive alcohol, jewelry, and skyscrapers in the case of Omoregie.
Akinyemi's and Erinugha's films are more complex technically, with a
slightly greater degree of dynamic editing and expressive camera work,
The Champion Sportsman being the most expensive and technically complex of all the productions.

Nigeria is always present in these immigrant filmmakers' films, even
if some of them do not contain sequences shot in the country itself. According to Naficy, the constant reference to "home" is a typical feature
of "diasporic films." He observes that the portrayal of home is generally associated with nostalgic longing and idealization. The meanings
these filmmakers attribute to Nigeria, however, are more complex and
reflect their own ambiguous relationship toward their homeland. It is
important to emphasize that these underlying dynamics can make the
film aesthetically and narratively difficult to read for the untrained eye.
If not present through sequences photographed abroad, Nigeria is virtually integrated through modern technology, letters, memories, and
dreams. For immigrants, the telephone forms the most direct way of
communicating with home. In the films of the Nigerian immigrants,

telephone sequences are frequent and allow Nigeria into the narrative. In Omoregie's films, the scenes shot in Nigeria are almost always part of telephone sequences. In *Mama, Why Me? 1,* approximately half the scenes are telephone conversations between Juliet, the main character, and her mother in Nigeria. These sequences consist of alternating shots between Juliet in Belgium and her mother in Nigeria. In *The Champion Sportsman,* Okoro ends up living in a yellow telephone booth in Berlin but tells his mother (in Nigeria) that he is living in a fancy apartment. The situation is familiar to a much-debated antimigration spot of the International Organization for Migration that seems to have served as a model here.[6] Okoro gives his mother the telephone number of the booth because he does not even have a cell phone. When Okoro is arrested, his mother dials the number repeatedly in an attempt to reach him. Passersby on the street pick up, leaving the mother perplexed.

Scenes involving letters to and from home are as important as scenes of telephone conversations between the homeland and the diasporic home. The protagonists sometimes receive letters from their parents and friends in Nigeria and are often haunted by them. The letters are either read aloud by the characters or voiced by the (Nigerian) sender, and thus form an indirect, nonvisual way of making the connection with Nigeria on-screen. Most often, the letters represent the unrealistic expectations of people back home. Television is another device mobilized to achieve the presence of the absent home country. In Omoregie's films, which are predominantly set indoors, a television is always switched on in the background, showing an African or Nigerian show. Africa thus symbolically enters the apartments through the television screen, a choice consciously made by the director to give the setting a more African atmosphere. Telephones, letters, and television are some of what Naficy refers to as "epistolary media" that "link people across time, space, and cultural difference" (105) and "play a constitutive part in the life-world of displaced people; it is with them that they think and construct their affiliative identities" (120). Finally, the soundtracks of the films include a great deal of African and Nigerian music. This creates an interesting dynamic. The opening credits of *Love in Berlin . . . the Meeting Point,* for example, are a montage of shots of Berlin, accompanied by African music. The viewer is immediately confronted with the transnational character of the film. A

4.1. Postcard advertising *The Champion Sportsman* with John Okafor and Patience Ozokwor (courtesy of Norma Mack).

recurring theme that forms "a major thematic thread" in this immigrant cinema is that of the journey – personal and communal (Naficy 33). It is, of course, present in the recurring narrative of the immigrant who travels to Europe. These journeys can also be "metaphoric and philosophical journeys of identity and transformation" (33). Mama G, in *Love in Berlin . . . the Meeting Point,* overcame her racist way of thinking through her journey to Europe, which made her accept her son's marriage. In addition, symbols of travel such as airports, train stations, trains in motion, taxis, and highways are constantly shown between scenes. These places and objects are symbols of journeying and "act as portals to other places and times" (Naficy 238).

    The Champion Sportsman is aesthetically unique. It emerged from a collaboration with the Braunschweig University of Arts and the German artist collective InterArte. Azubuike Erinugha's story and John Okafor's acting style are unmistakably Nollywood. In contrast, the reality of Berlin is shown through semidocumentary fragments throughout the film. The film integrates the story of three real immigrants living in Berlin. They advise the main character, Okoro, and reflect, among themselves, on their situation in Germany. Other purely informative scenes on migration are inserted, with the use of a voice-over. The artists and film crew are shown while working. One fragment shows David Reuter, the coproducer, being taught by Nigerians how to make a traditional Nigerian dish. This film illustrates a degree of "self-reflexivity" that Naficy attributes to the "accented style" that "involves making visible what the invisible style of the classical realist cinema has traditionally concealed" (276). The nonfictional scenes break up the fictional world of the narrative and create a critical distance with the audience. The result is a film that is meant to be both entertaining and informative and to appeal to both an African and a European audience. Erinugha told me *The Champion Sportsman* was enthusiastically received on its premiere in Berlin. The documentary aspect, however, contrasts sharply with what a Nollywood audience expects and wants. Due to a negative reaction after a press screening in Nigeria, Erinugha is now thinking of cutting out the documentary scenes for the Nigerian market.

In this chapter, I have attempted to examine Nollywood films made in Europe and assess the place of the filmmakers within Nollywood. Departing from the perspective of five Nigerian immigrants, I have developed the story of Nollywood film production in Belgium, the Netherlands, and Germany. Tony A. B. Akinyemi and Leonard Ajayi-Odekhiran, Isaac Izoya, John Osas Omoregie, and Azubuike Erinugha, five immigrants currently living in these countries, all believe in the power of Nollywood, which they harness as a way to get their messages across to a large, primarily African, audience. By exploring the themes, aesthetics, production process, and distribution, I discovered their films are unmistakably part of Nollywood. The filmmakers all collaborate with players in the Nigeria-based video industry and apply the same financing and distribution methods. They use the dominant Nollywood genres and also feature similar themes, motives, and morality in the foreign settings. Aesthetically, the films look very Nollywood-like, which results partly from similar production circumstances: low budgets, cheap technology, and limited time. In addition, the films are marked by the typical "Nollywood" theatrical and improvisational acting style, for the cast is largely made up of Nigerian expatriates, occasionally complemented by Nollywood star actors. Although set in Europe, the settings also have a definite African atmosphere (Haynes, this volume). Consequently, the films mainly address an African audience, in the diaspora and back in Nigeria.

Nevertheless, I argue that the productions are unique within a transnational understanding of the Nigerian video industry. The filmmakers are based in Europe and work with a small, very committed group of other Nigerian immigrants, often complemented by a number of white actors and crew members. The filmmakers are supported in different ways by their host cities and nations, and two of the films made in Europe received financing from official European institutions, which sets them apart from typical Nollywood film production. The filmmakers attempt to reach a European audience, most noticeably by adding subtitles in the languages of their host countries. Because of the alternating shooting locations in some films, the filmmaker, if unable to travel to Nigeria, must depend on others to follow his instructions, and sometimes the same character is played by different actors. On a diegetic level, the films share a preoccupation with the immigration narrative and themes linked to life in the diaspora. The foreign setting, with the exception of Omoregie's films, is generally explored as a touristic sightseeing of Europe. These elements link the films to other Nollywood productions made in the diaspora, as described by Haynes (this volume). In addition, I discovered that the Nigerian filmmakers use similar motives and aesthetics in their indirect portrayal of Nigeria as do other diasporic and exilic filmmakers, marking an "accented style" (Naficy). Finally, Erinugha's *The Champion Sportsman* includes a genuinely European perspective in terms of theme and aesthetics and integrates the idea of self-reflexivity.

In conclusion, I argue that the transnational nature of the productions made by Nigerian immigrants in Europe is a result of the combination of their being a part of the Nollywood industry in Nigeria and of their own displaced reality in Europe. Akinyemi and Ajayi-Odekhiran, Izoya, Omoregie, and Erinugha have put their own mark on the traditional Nollywood style and methods and can consequently be called "accented" Nollywood filmmakers. Through this research, I discovered that through the practices of filmmaking, as well as their products – the films – the immigrant filmmakers have established a means of staying in touch with their home country, and also effectively strengthened the bonds between different communities of Nigerian immigrants in Europe. These "accented" Nollywood filmmakers have created networks that cut across boundaries and give the, otherwise unheard, Nigerian immigrant a voice.

NOTES

1. Nollywood films frequently involve the occult. Macabre rituals take place, and spiritual forces are made visible, representing forces from Christian or "traditional" beliefs. They play important roles in the story lines and take on different forms often characterized by computerized effects.

2. E-mail communication with Tony A. B. Akinyemi, June 30, 2011.

3. E-mail communication with John Osas Omoregie, June 30, 2011.

4. E-mail communication with Isaac Izoya, June 30, 2011.

5. E-mail communication with Leonard Ajayi-Odekhiran, June 30, 2011.

6. The spot has since been removed from the IOM server but can be viewed on this site: http://www.blick.ch/news/ausland/so-schrecken-wir-die-afrikaner-ab-76915.

WORKS CITED

Akinyemi, Tony A. B., and Leonard Ajayi-Odekhiran. Personal interview. Eindhoven, April 24, 2010.

Erinugha, Azubuike. Personal interview. Brussels, May 1, 2010.

Haynes, Jonathan. "Nollywood in Lagos, Lagos in Nollywood Films." *Africa Today* 54.2 (2007): 131–50.

Idowu-Shadrach, Wale. "Nollywood . . . Is a Pride to Africa." *Ehizoya Golden Entertainment.* N.d. Web.

Izoya, Isaac. "If It's Easy, Stress Free, and Lucrative, Let My Critics Venture It." Interview by Shaibu Husseini. *Ehizoya Golden Entertainment*, November 23, 2008. Web.

———. Personal interview. Berlin, May 9, 2010.

Naficy, Hamid. *An Accented Cinema: Exilic and Diasporic Filmmaking.* Princeton, N.J.: Princeton University Press, 2001.

Okome, Onookome. "Writing the Anxious City: Images of Lagos in Nigerian Home Video Films." *Black Renaissance* 5.2 (2003): 65–75.

Omoregie, John Osas. Personal interview. Antwerp, July 10, 2010.

FILMOGRAPHY

Amazing World. Dir. John Osas Omoregie. Jomosa Video World and ANAABEL (Belgium). 2010.

The Champion Sportsman. Dir. Azubuike Erinugha. InterArte, Kulturkontakte, and Towncrier International (Germany and Nigeria). 2010.

Dapo Junior. Dir. Tony A. B. Akinyemi. Double "A" Entertainment (Netherlands). 2000.

Desperate Heart. Dir. John Osas Omoregie. Jomosa Video World and ANAABEL (Belgium and Nigeria). 2007.

Eti vbe Holland. Dir. Tony A. B. Akinyemi. Double "A" Entertainment (Netherlands). In progress.

From Amsterdam with Love. Dir. Tony A. B. Akinyemi. Double "A" Entertainment (Netherlands). 2003.

Holland Heat. Dir. Tony A. B. Akinyemi. Double "A" Entertainment (Netherlands). 2002.

Home & Abroad. Dir. Lancelot Oduwa Imasuen. Lancewealth Images (Nigeria), Videofield International (Germany et al.). 2004.

Igho Evbue Ebo. Dir. John Osas Omoregie. Rainbow Entertainment and Jomosa Video World (Belgium and Nigeria). 2003.

The Immigrant Eyes. Dir. John Osas Omoregie. Jomosa Video World and ANAABEL (Belgium). 2010.

Love in Berlin . . . the Meeting Point, 1 and 2. Dir. Lancelot Oduwa Imasuen. Ehizoya Golden Productions (Nigeria and Germany). 2007.

Mama, Why Me? 1 and 2. Dir. John Osas Omoregie. Jomosa Video World and ANAABEL (Belgium and Nigeria). 2008.

Run but You Can't Hide, 1 and 2. Dir. Peter Gabriel and Taiwo Oduala. Ehizoya Golden Productions (Germany and Nigeria). 2008.

Sinners in the House. Dir. Lancelot Oduwa Imasuen. Ehizoya Golden Productions (Nigeria and Germany). 2003.

Under Pressure. Dir. Tony A. B. Akinyemi. Double "A" Entertainment (Netherlands). 1998.

Zero Your Mind. Dir. Lancelot Oduwa Imasuen. Ehizoya Golden Productions (Nigeria and Germany). 2003.

FIVE

Made in America:
Urban Immigrant Spaces in
Transnational Nollywood Films

CLAUDIA HOFFMANN

FILMMAKERS IN NIGERIA'S MEGACITY LAGOS HAVE PRODUCED astounding numbers of video films in recent decades, but the significance of the city for Nollywood film production does not stop there. Lagos itself is being reproduced, reimagined, and re-created in many of these films. The importance of the Nigerian urban center for the country's English-speaking film production is indisputable, and the production of English-speaking video films in southern Nigeria is inextricably linked to contemporary Lagos.[1] This phenomenon shows that Nollywood is following the cinematic tradition of using the cityscape as a setting and as a symbol of national cinemas, such as Rome for Italian, Berlin for German, and Paris for French national cinema. In the development of Nollywood as a thriving and distinctly Nigerian film industry, Lagos has become the icon and symbol for modern Nigerian filmmaking: "[Nollywood] is a medium of the city. It is only a city like Lagos that could have engineered and nurtured its birth" (Okome, "Nollywood"). In recent years, not only the distribution of Nollywood films, but also their production have become transnational, and Nigerian filmmakers based in cities around North America have produced Nollywood-style videos that are set in urban centers such as New York, Los Angeles, and Atlanta. Through diasporic filmmaking, these globalized cities and their immigrant communities become cinematic manifestations of transnational movements of money, labor, goods, media, and people, and the actual city space, with its buildings, streets, sidewalks, cars, and other symbols of urbanity, is a place where social actors "negotiate the relationship between the local and the global" (Mennel 201).

Jonathan Haynes's essay in this volume has provided an extensive and highly useful overview of the relationship between Nollywood film-making and the Nigerian diaspora in highlighting the specifics of Nol-lywood films that are set abroad. Haynes suggests that diasporic Nige-rian films "answer a longing for home and serve as a vehicle for showing children and non-Nigerian friends what Nigerian culture is." Therefore, Nollywood's uniqueness is not limited to its commercial success, but includes its potential to reach an audience way beyond native Nigeria while at the same time remaining local in terms of themes and aesthetics: "Whatever Nigerian video films may lack in technical quality, acting, and narrative style they make up for in a high degree of localized immediacy" (Adejunmobi). This localized immediacy includes sites that are familiar to the audience such as the aforementioned Lagos cityscape. While dia-sporic films closely follow Nollywood filmmaking conventions, they also share features that are deeply embedded in their transnational mode of production. To illustrate these features, I examine urban spaces in three Nollywood films shot in the United States that have immigration as their central theme and are all predominantly set in contemporary New York City: *Missing in America*, by Sola Osofisan; *This America*, by Bethels Ago-muoh; and *God's Own Country*, by Femi Agbayewa. All three directors are immigrants from Nigeria, and their films reflect their transnational filmmaking identities. Osofisan, Agomuoh, and Agbayewa have not only produced truly transnational Nollywood films in terms of production locations, but also taken on the theme of Nigerian immigrants who enter the United States and attempt to gain legal status or otherwise create a life for themselves as immigrants in a city that has become the iconic place of migrant realities and multiplicities of diasporic identities.

NOLLYWOOD AND THE DIASPORA

Diasporic spaces consist of the local and the transnational within glo-balscapes or pockets, and the essence of their interplay depends on the nature, purpose, and form of the respective community. These "diasporic pockets" are created through what Arjun Appadurai describes as "a form of negotiation between sites of agency (individuals) and globally defined fields of possibility" (31). The global pockets at the heart of this discus-sion are the urban Nigerian immigrant communities in several U.S. Nigerian Nollywood films. They share a space because individuals sought a new life in the United States and with that vision became part of the diasporic community. Many transnational Nollywood films depict the Nigerian immigrant who travels abroad, but finds him- or herself not only in a community of Nigerians, but in almost the same cityscapes (albeit different cities) and interior spaces, which make the film, once again, relatable. I argue in favor of a trend in diasporic Nollywood that uses the city as a cinematic site within which the transnational identity of the filmmaker and the diasporic mode of production manifest. I place the city in the foreground because the diversity of Nigerian video film production is linked to the cities in which their bulk is produced, such as Lagos for the English-speaking Igbo films of southwestern Nigeria and Kano for Bollywood-inspired Hausa films in Nigeria's North. The "transnational" in the films discussed here is as much linked to the global urban centers of filmmaking, from Lagos to New York in this case, as it is to the respective nation-states, Nigeria and the United States.

Despite the primary intention to entertain, Nollywood films re-create issues, conflicts, and tensions that are specific to a contemporary Nigerian reality, such as gender inequalities, religious and ethnic tension, cults and the occult, and so on. Through Nollywood films, Nigerian expressions, fashion, food, and other cultural expressions are exported throughout Africa, adopted, re-created, redefined, applied, and appropriated, but are still largely identified as Nigerian. The expansion of Nollywood filmmaking into the diaspora blurs the borders of Nollywood's exact location and what it consists of, and I am sure this discussion will continue for a while. However, the diasporic films I am discussing clearly follow Nollywood traditions of aesthetics while reflecting the transnational identity of the diasporic filmmaker who introduces the anxieties and challenges associated with life and film production in the diaspora.

Despite the overwhelming entertainment factor in Nollywood films in general, critics have warned against assuming that Nollywood films are largely nonpolitical and made only for entertainment (McCall; Haynes, "Political Critique"). John McCall urges critics to "be careful not to condemn [Nollywood] because it departs from intellectual formulations of what progressive political thought is supposed to look like" (94). McCall asks critics to take into consideration the impact of Nollywood on the formation of African identities and pan-Africanism.

In addition, domestic and transnational Nollywood films address issues and concerns that reflect societal anxieties and postcolonial conditions, even if they are not obviously situated within an overall political condition, but rather are individual reactions on a localized or immediate level. The familiarity of the setting as well as the relevance of the issues improve the ability of domestic Nollywood films to relate to their audiences. In contrast to domestic Nollywood films, many films made in the diaspora, even the ones that are more obviously made for entertainment, are quite noticeably political in that they address the tension between the diasporic community and Nigerians back home.

The transnational Nollywood films I will discuss below formulate even more overt criticism against national and transnational processes and are not primarily made to entertain, but made to inform and educate a Nigerian and African community from within (see also Samyn, this volume). Furthermore, diasporic films in general have more leeway in being critical toward the home nation-state because the filmmaking process and distribution of the final product are physically removed from Nigerian censorship. Diasporic Nollywood filmmakers create political messages by establishing the immediacy I have mentioned before. While European filmmakers have highlighted the hardship endured by many African immigrants who navigate the diaspora from an outsider's perspective, Nigerian expatriate filmmakers have taken on the issue from a different, an inside-out, point of view. European films tend to emphasize the challenges of the migrant in a stylized way, and much is conveyed through elaborate and carefully manipulated cinematography, which also places the film into a visual culture that is largely defined by its aesthetics (European Art House Cinema).[2] But although the immigrant seems to be at the center of the plot, they are often just the vehicle of a macrolevel political statement about the oppressive global structures and inhumane immigration practices of individual nation-states. In contrast, through their conventional reliance on dialogue, diasporic Nollywood films that are concerned with immigration quite literally give the immigrant a voice.

THE CINEMATIC CITY AND IMMIGRATION

The three transnational Nollywood films discussed herein are all set in New York, and the urban setting gains significance within the narrative that follows the immigrant who navigates the cityscape. As I have mentioned before, the Lagos cityscape is a recurrent image in Nollywood films because, as Haynes points out, "[location] shooting . . . creates a common realism, a mass of interchangeable, conventionally framed shots of Lagos streets and compounds, lavish parlors and ordinary bedrooms, hospitals and offices" ("Nollywood in Lagos" 138). This interchangeability of how locations and spaces are represented is a feature that transcends into transnational Nollywood films as well, in which case they represent how immigrant characters negotiate the local and the transnational space while (physically and mentally) navigating the diaspora.

Okome maintains that "Nollywood is the medium of the Nigerian city" and goes on to describe the Nigerian megacity Lagos as a "quintessential postcolonial city" that is "heavy with a burden of the past but light-headed in its . . . drive to look ahead" ("Introducing"). Okome labels the urban video films "city video films" and maintains that the "city is foregrounded in the narrative as an ordering system, which is inescapable and all the characters must sign into its system of apprehending reality that is at once dubious and indescribable" ("Introducing"). In the immigrant experience, the foreign city is not only dubious in terms of being an unknown space and difficult to navigate, but also indescribable because of the ever-changing tension of expectation and reality. According to Haynes, "This cityscape is a resource that the films share and an environment that shapes them materially" ("Nollywood in Lagos" 133). The reputation of Lagos as a place where everything is possible attracts young people with a lot of visions from all over Nigeria, but it also has a more universal appeal of the vibrant, diverse, and worldly urban center. Surely, Lagos is more chaotic, less structured, and more flexible than most of its global counterparts, but nevertheless the notion of the city as a place where one can achieve something is translated into transnational Nollywood films by re-creating New York as a multicultural and cosmopolitan place.

The three films herein feature a similar type of urbanity as Nollywood films set in Lagos, but foreground a typical New York landscape to mark the diasporic setting. The appeal to expatriate audiences lies in their emphasis on the immigrant's struggle to which diasporic audiences can relate, either because they have experienced this struggle or because they know people who have. The films establish urbanity as an important feature of the story in that it represents the urban immigrant space and its opportunities as well as its dangers. The cinematic city has historically been a setting that goes beyond the actual city. In his discussion of New York as a cinematic site of urban alienation, James A. Clapp suggests that writing about "cities and film inevitably involves a conflation of images, of the city actual and the city virtual." Images of New York at once reflect the real place and mark the narrative that occurs there. That is to say that the very selection of urban visuals is informed by the significance of places for the story and the filmmaker's particular aesthetic. Lori Maguire summarizes the appeal of New York for film settings and otherwise by drawing on its significance as an entry point to the United States:

> New York succeeded because it was a great port: the nation's products poured out of Manhattan to Europe while Europe's immigrants poured into New York. For this reason, New York became the American city. Furthermore, around that port, all the things necessary for trade grew up: insurance companies, stock exchanges, businesses and banks. New York became the seat of American economic power and may have been the first city in the world in which the temples to Mammon were larger and more striking than the temples to God. (514)

New York has been and continues to be the one American city most associated with immigration, signified by its famous landmarks such as the Statue of Liberty and Ellis Island. In addition, the city has become a place of blatant consumerism, signified by places like Fifth Avenue, where shopping temples reign, and symbols of capitalism, such as Wall Street. As we will see in the three films, cinematic New York represents consumerism and freedom that immigrants want a share of, the point of entry from which they must find their way – an alienating urban jungle that can make or break them.

MISSING IN AMERICA

The maker of *Missing in America,* Sola Osofisan, is an award-winning, New York–based Nigerian author and filmmaker who immigrated to the United States in 1997. Osofisan has published collections of poetry and short stories and regularly writes for newspapers, including contributions about the Nigerian immigrant experience. He re-creates this experience in his 2004 film *Missing in America.* In the film, protagonist Agatha travels from Lagos to New York with forged documents under the pseudonym Tonia to find her husband, Fela (played by Sola Osofisan himself), who has been in the United States for five years, but recently visited Nigeria. During this visit, Agatha became pregnant, and unable to reach her husband by phone or letter, she now tries to find and inform him of the pregnancy. She goes to the address he gave her, only to learn that he has not been there in years. Unable to find shelter after being turned down by a Nigerian expatriate who used to be Fela's roommate but wants nothing to do with newly arrived compatriots, she wanders aimlessly through a hostile New York and New Jersey landscape. Eventually, she collapses at the doorstep of Bimbo, an established and successful Nigerian immigrant who reluctantly takes her in. Bimbo suspects that Agatha is an illegal immigrant who wants to stay in the United States, but eventually believes her story and helps her to track down Fela. Agatha is soon successful and discovers that he is now married to an American woman in a bid to obtain a green card. After revealing the truth to Fela's "green-card wife," who in turn threatens to report him to the authorities, Agatha decides to return to Nigeria to raise her child with the help of her family. In a parallel plot, Bimbo falls in love with another legal and established Nigerian immigrant.

Missing in America qualifies as what Okome labels the "city video film." The opening credits are accompanied by establishing shots of the urban center in which the plot is set, but the sequence also reflects the transnational journey of the protagonist. A fade-out shot of New York's Statue of Liberty is replaced by a train arriving at the station and then again by shots of fairly generic New York street scenes, presumably of Times Square. These images then again fade into overhead shots of Ellis Island and what might be Manhattan Bridge, as well as several New York street scenes. The sequence ends with an overhead shot of Manhattan, which fades out slowly and into the beginning of the narrative. In this opening sequence, the emphasis is on New York as a travel destination for immigrants. Osofisan sets up the migration narrative by panning over landmarks, such as the Statue of Liberty, and images associated with immigration and journeying, such as Ellis Island and the train station, as well as travel images of, for example, tourists snapping pictures. This overall portrayal of the urban space creates an impression of openness, vibrancy, consumerism, and hospitality. Furthermore, it evokes the significance that Maguire ascribes to New York as "the most popular setting for American films and, as such, many of its landmarks are instantly recognisable to people all over the world" (516).

After the opening sequence, the film immediately cuts to a medium shot of Agatha at the doorstep of a New Jersey apartment. Although the transition might be abrupt, it also highlights that the personal immigrant story is embedded in the larger picture of the "American Dream." After learning that her husband is not at the address, Agatha makes her way back to the city. She walks through a dreary New Jersey suburb along a street that is completely empty except for the occasional car. It is raining, and Agatha is obviously not dressed warmly enough. Haynes has identified similar scenes in other Nollywood films set abroad as "an alienation/ hardship sequence, in which the protagonists trudge disconsolately, carrying their shoulder bags, through the streets of the foreign city, unable to find a foothold and growing increasingly desperate" (Haynes, this volume). The nondiegetic music emphasizes a sense of alienation and loneliness to highlight how disconnected the new immigrant feels in this diasporic space. Symbols of movement and journey reappear, such as train stations and the passenger cars of the train, when Agatha travels back from New Jersey to New York. When she leaves the station, Agatha finds herself in a changed cityscape. The weather is dark and dull, and it is raining. Despite all the hustle and bustle, Agatha is still lonely and isolated. Not only her suitcase but also her slow walk, as if searching for something, mark her as a nonlocal. We now look at the city from her perspective, and instead of looking down through overhead shots, we are forced to look up at the skyscrapers that rise up almost threateningly under a dark, gray sky. The images of New York as a dream destination for hopeful immigrants at the start of the film have now turned into a confusing, alienating, oppressive, and claustrophobic representation of urbanity.

Unable to find Fela in New York and kicked out by Fela's former roommate, Agatha returns to New Jersey, and once more we see her walking along the street, only this time the scenery seems even more hostile, and on top of it all, it is now snowing. It seems as if with every disappointment the protagonist experiences and the prospect of finding a place for the night fading, the outside shots become more dreary and depressing. Interestingly, the portrayal of the city changes once again in a later scene. Agatha is in a taxi on her way to where Fela supposedly lives.

During her conversation with the taxi driver, who speaks to her as if she were an immigrant who will "understand in a few months" what it means to be more established, a sequence of urban images appears, including shots of New York skyscrapers and a rather beautiful overhead shot of the city and the river. But as soon as the taxi driver leaves her behind, taking with him her suitcase and purse, we see her once again walking through rainy and dreary New Jersey suburbia.

Although the film does not actually show Agatha's journey from Nigeria, the theme of navigating the foreign space is quite obviously represented through prolonged scenes of Agatha walking through different landscapes. Haynes observes that in both domestic and diasporic Nollywood films set abroad, the "characters are simply dumped suddenly into the foreign environment, a new city, where they have to make or keep social relationships in order to obtain the necessary food, shelter, and employment" (this volume). While *Missing in America* features the typical establishing shots of urbanity that are so often seen in Nollywood films, it also includes more outside scenes in which the character literally navigates the cityscape, which is not typical for Nollywood films, but fairly typical for migration cinema. The explicit positioning of Agatha in New York street scenes and empty suburban New Jersey sceneries emphasizes Agatha's foreignness and her detachment from the transnational location for which she is not prepared. On the other hand, Bimbo's suburban home along with her expensive car suggest that the all-American life is accessible for immigrants, but only for those who arrive with a plan.

At the end of the film and after learning about her husband's green-card marriage, Agatha's voice-over informs us that she is going back to Nigeria while shots of New York street scenes fade into each other. Her offscreen voice suggests that she does not participate in the street life of American consumerism and potential success. She remains aloof from the urban space because she does not want to become part of the diaspora. She does not believe she could cope as an illegal immigrant because she lacks what she calls the "special hunger." The images of New York that accompany the voice-over are heavily marked by consumerism and show the typical New York shopping scenery with flashy and classy storefronts and pedestrians carrying large shopping bags. This is a variation of Haynes's observation of the shopping sequence, "in which the traveler is seen in the landscape of consumerism . . . , giddily celebrating disposable income" (this volume). Instead of embracing the consumerism, however, Agatha physically removes herself because she is not willing to pay the price. The emphasis on urban consumer culture is an emulation of a similar portrayal of Lagos in domestic Nollywood films: "Wealth in the most tangible, desired forms is fundamental to the lure of Lagos and is at the heart of Nollywood imagery and thematics" (Haynes, "Nollywood in Lagos" 140). Although the film acknowledges through Bimbo that it is possible to settle down and live the American Dream even as an immigrant, it emphasizes that this does not apply to everyone.

THIS AMERICA

Bethels Agomuoh, director of *This America* and author of the screenplay, is a pioneer of diasporic Nollywood. Originally from Nigeria and now based in New York, Agomuoh is president and cofounder of the United African Artists Incorporated and is also a director with the African Film Company. *This America* is set in New York and also spotlights the immigrant experience. Nigerian banker Ozobio has just arrived from Nigeria to visit his cousin Eddie (Bethels Agomuoh himself), who is married to an American citizen and waiting for his green-card application to go through, which does in the end. Upon learning that he lost his job in Nigeria due to a political coup, Ozobio decides to try his luck in New York. However, he soon learns that without proper immigration papers, a suitable job is hard to come by. In addition, Eddie's African American roommate resents Ozobio's staying in their apartment. Eddie convinces Ozobio to marry for the green card, and he reluctantly weds an African American single mother and moves into her apartment, although he has a girlfriend back in Nigeria. The cultural tension between the couple escalates into violence, and the film ends with Ozobio's lifeless body after his green-card wife has shot him.

This America opens with a view of a New York neighborhood in which street vendors sell CDs. A police car arrives and stops right beside them, and as the vendors take off, two policemen chase them. Urbanity is shown as a place of undocumented foreign workers. The film suggests that the movie itself is sold somewhere in urban America by an immigrant trying to survive. This metanarrative of illegal labor introduces an important part of the relationship between immigration, labor, and the informal urban economy created by immigrants in American cities and the sub-version of American consumerism into an urban underbelly of piracy, illegal trade, and illegal employment. Immigrants can survive, but they are constantly under scrutiny. From here the film cuts to another scene in which protagonist Ozobio flees from his American gun-wielding wife. After a gunshot, the screen fades to black. These seemingly unrelated scenes (the end of the film reveals the connection) take a fairly complex look at immigrant realities and introduce one of the central themes of the film, namely, the vulnerability of migrants in the diasporic situation of difficult survival, illegal employment, and subsequent dependence on shady characters such as crazy green-card wives for help.

From here, similar to the opening sequence in *Missing in America*, the urban setting is established through a series of shots of New York, but in this film they are more realistic and feature fewer stereotypical New York landmarks. Apart from busy street scenes and people hurry-ing through Grand Central Station, the camera moves up to skyscrapers and shows an American flag. The images are less romanticized than in *Missing in America*, but they, too, include the train station as a symbol of transportation. Eventually, the scene cuts from the top of a skyscraper to the protagonist, Eddie, in his taxi. The transition from the establishing shots of the city to the beginning of the narrative is once again abrupt, going from long to medium shots and close-ups without transition and creating a sense of moving from the larger transnational context, signi-fied by the cosmopolitan urban center, to the more personal and intimate story (which is typical for Nollywood films). Unlike most other Nolly-wood films, and like *Missing in America*, much of the plot-related action takes place outside, once again emphasizing the significance of the urban setting. There are plenty of brief establishing shots of different parts of the city, and not all of them are related to the migration theme of the film. In the end, however, the film comes full circle. As Ozobio flees from his wife, Jeanie, and her gun, he runs into one of the CD hawkers who are be-ing pursued by the police. We hear an offscreen gunshot as the two men run into each other and remain motionless on the streets. The outlook on migration is just as pessimistic as it is in *Missing in America*. Agatha never truly gets "inside" America and instead remains on the border of both American consumer culture as well as the Nigerian expatriate com-munity in New York. Ozobio, on the other hand, manages to integrate himself into this space through his green-card marriage, but he remains vulnerable and ultimately becomes a victim of this vulnerability.

This America also suggests that a part of the American Dream remains completely foreclosed to the immigrant without proper papers. While the transnational urban setting offers the migrant opportunities to integrate into a community that shares both the transnational vision and the localized purpose and design with others – for example, Bimbo, her girlfriend, and her lover as part of a well-off Nigerian expatriate community – this cannot happen detached from the immigration regulations imposed by the nation-state. For the transnational subject who does not have legal status or has gained legal status through illegal action, agency is severely limited and visions crushed as the imagination meets reality. *This America* re-creates this through Ozobio, who is highly qualified for a position on Wall Street, but is unable to find one because he does not have the proper documents. When he is looking for work, Ozobio walks past a Barclays Bank building, and we see a sequence of signs and buildings, including a Wall Street sign, JP Morgan Chase, Guardian, and One New York Plaza. Not only is the diasporic setting therefore implied to be a transnational place in its physical form, but in its representation it is also tied to the immigrant's attitude toward this particular location and his or her view of it – for example, the imagination of Wall Street as a place that promises wealth and success. Ozobio does have a successful job interview, but soon learns that he can work only with a green card. After the interview, the city scenery changes from Wall Street images to more general street scenes, as if to signify the uncertainty that lies in this space for the immigrant and the accessibility of some spaces versus others. On the other hand, however, the city is yet again presented differently when Eddie receives his green card: we see the colors of the American flag reflected on a building next to which there is a pantomime of the Statue of Liberty. Again, and similar to *Missing in America,* the portrayal of the city reflects the opportunities available to the migrant, their attitude toward it, and their position within the urban space.

GOD'S OWN COUNTRY

Femi Agbayewa wrote, directed, and produced *God's Own Country,* a film that reflects on his own experience as an immigrant in America

("Filmmaker"). As he points out on his MySpace site, Agbayewa terms his films and others like it "Nollywood USA" to set them apart from mainstream Nollywood. In an interview with Nigeria International, Agbayewa addresses the appeal of Nollywood films to Nigerian expatriates: "When you come over to America, you want a piece of home. . . . It has a lot to do with nostalgia because you want to be part of where you are from" ("Filmmaker"). In *God's Own Country,* protagonist Ike leaves Nigeria, hoping for a better life. Upon arrival in New York, he looks for his uncle, who allegedly owns a hotel in the city. However, as soon as Ike arrives at the hotel, he finds out that his uncle is not the owner of the hotel, but instead works as a dishwasher in the hotel kitchen. After taking residence with his uncle, Ike unsuccessfully looks for work as a lawyer, his trained profession, and eventually begins to work in the same hotel kitchen as his uncle, along with several other immigrants who are also overqualified for the job, but are unable to find work that matches their credentials. After a quarrel with his boss who insists that the workers not use the front door, Ike quits his job. Later Ike learns that his sister in Nigeria is very ill and needs a significant amount of money for treatment. Unable to find legal work that could pay enough to help her, Ike participates in 419 credit card fraud, but soon becomes the victim of a scheme himself.[3] He confronts the 419ers and, after shooting one of them, is able to retrieve the money, which he sends to his ill sister in a blood-smeared envelope.

Unlike the previous two films, *God's Own Country* starts out with images of a Nigerian cityscape. Filmed from a car with a handheld camera, the focus of this introductory shot is the street that presumably leads the way to the next destination – the United States. The diegetic street sound creates the immediacy and familiarity that we associate with Nollywood. As the scene accelerates, the street images become blurred, and eventually the screen fades to black before we see a landing aircraft. While Ike moves into the picture on the escalator and walks through the airport, his offscreen voice tells us the reasons for his journey (a promise to his dying mother). The cityscape of New York, in which the migration plot is situated, comes into view as Ike steps out of the airport. The film cuts back and forth as Ike looks around and up at the skyscrapers and shaky, blurry images of the nighttime cityscape, accompanied by nondiegetic street sounds that are oddly similar to the ones we have heard before in the Nigerian city scene. The urban images are out of focus and blurry, and details are not recognizable. As Ike starts walking, the film moves into a rapid succession of New York scenes, which creates a dizzying and anonymous urbanity, signifying the underbelly of the urban center within which the protagonist eventually gets involved in 419 scams. Urbanity in *God's Own Country* is in many parts characterized by speed, and the urban setting is not as clearly recognizable (as New York) as it is in the other films. The city soon symbolizes dread and fear. Ike moves mainly within largely invisible or unrecognizable spaces in the underground of the city – for example, the hotel kitchen in which only immigrants work and the bar and strip club in which 419 scams are plotted.

The connection between the cityscape and immigrant labor that I have already addressed in *This America* appears in this film, and Ike's search for work closely resembles Ozobio's unsuccessful attempts to do the same. When Ike sets out to find work, he, like Ozobio, looks very professional in a business suit and confidently walks through the doors of what appears to be an office building in an area that could be Wall Street. The scene cuts to another, but this time Ike is walking along a street that is lined with strip malls, car dealers, restaurants, and nail salons in a part of the city that does not at all resemble Wall Street. Ike looks desolate. His suit jacket is gone, and whereas his gait was purposeful in the previous scene, he now walks slowly, looking down and appearing defeated. The move from one cityscape to another resembles Ike's initial hopefulness and his eventual disillusionment when he realizes the city does not live up to his expectations. Fittingly, it is in this scene and cityscape that Ike is picked up by his friend's younger brother Kwame, who offers to work with him on 419 scams involving credit cards and drugs. While Kwame offers Ike the opportunity to join him in the schemes, they are standing on a highway bridge overlooking traffic and the skyline in the background. The fast-moving cars give an impression of urgency and speed. As the cars quickly drive by on the highway below him, Ike considers a career in crime.

God's Own Country is the only film, except for a very brief scene in *Missing in America,* that is partially set in Nigeria. However, apart from the opening shot of the Nigerian city street, all Nigerian scenes are in rural settings and form a stark contrast to American urbanity. The rural images are accompanied by narratives about slavery, which add to the film's concern with exploitation and race. Ike's mind wanders back to rural Nigeria, and the accompanying voice-over marks it as a place of solace: "Where I once found chaos, I now find focus." After experiencing America as a place of betrayal and lies, he longs for the peace and familiarity of Nigeria represented through the calmness of villages and nature that contrasts with the busy American urban center, which for him represents 419 scams and deceit. The "truth" about "God's own country" is significantly spoken in a graffiti-covered alley near the back entrance to a strip club. The crime boss who schemed against Ike tells him, "I would have told you the truth about God's own country. How we are treated like dogs." Throughout the film, America is a hopeless place for immigrants, and there are no established well-to-do Nigerian expatriates to be found anywhere.

Transnational Nollywood films evoke the homeland Nigeria even if it is not always represented on-screen. This is apparent in *Missing in America* when Bimbo suspects Agatha of being a potential illegal immigrant and her annoyance with Nigerians in her homeland who do not understand that things are different in America. At the same time, Nigeria is a place of consolation for Agatha, and she can return there to raise her baby among her family and friends. Ozobio is more or less forced into exile by the chaos and upheaval in Nigeria. It is a place to which he would return if things were different. Equally, in *God's Own Country*, Ike longs for home, which vis-à-vis America turns into a place of peace and solace. All films juxtapose America and Nigeria, as both countries can be havens or out of the migrant's reach. No film explicitly states that life is easier or harder in either country, and all three films are intriguingly balanced in their portrayal of opportunity and setback. All three films explicitly show how the protagonists navigate the urban space, which is presented in unison with the respective migrant's position in the respective host society. *Missing in America* portrays the alienation between Nigerians at home and in the diaspora. *This America* shows the desire of migrants not to return to the chaos and unpredictability of Nigeria. Finally, *God's Own Country* highlights the problem of 419 scams that thrive within the film's Nigerian immigrant community and corrupt the desperate newcomer. In addition, the cinematic sentiments toward the home country are ambiguous, which creates dissent and tension within the immigrant community. A sense of loss pervades the films. Agatha and Ozobio lose their husband and fiancée, respectively, and Ike sacrifices his integrity.

The films come across as unrelentingly realistic, and the dramatic effect of typical Nollywood acting style and dialogue is considerably subdued. Furthermore, the films feature symbols of global transportation, such as airplanes, airports, taxis, trains, and so on. Like other recent Nollywood films set outside of Nigeria and that are largely about Nigerians abroad, these three transnational films are "more restrained in style" (Haynes, this volume). Moreover, the films make remarkably similar use of urban establishing shots of New York. In all cases, the city is unmistakable through the portrayal of well-known landmarks. This almost seamless transition from the Lagos cityscape to American urbanity not only suggests an adherence to Nollywood conventions, but also localizes the transnational space by situating it within the transnational experience of the protagonists. Other diasporic Nollywood filmmakers have done the same, but in different American urban settings. Pascal Atuma's comedies – for example, *Only in America* and *My American Nurse, 1 and 2* – are largely set in Los Angeles, while Eve Ikuenobe-Otaigbe's *The God Daughter* takes place in Atlanta. Urbanity therefore remains recognizable and very much connected with the filmmakers' identities in the diaspora, but the interplay between the local and the transnational adapts to the immigration theme of the respective diasporic Nollywood films. Last, the immigrants' experiences are often tied to cities because of the existence of immigrant communities, better work opportunities, and, especially in the case of undocumented immigrants, greater ease of blending in with the masses and remaining unrecognizable as an illegal.

There is a development from the Nollywood national cinema toward films that are still very much recognizable as Nollywood, yet distinctly marked by their close affiliation with the diaspora. Nigerian expatriates raise the money, manpower, and resources to make films that follow Nollywood modes of conventions, but create the typical immediacy for their intended, mostly diasporic, audiences. Therefore, these films occupy a position between Nollywood and global cinema, as they "are interstitial because they are created astride and in the interstices of social formation and cinematic practices" (Naficy 4). The films are created within global pockets with specific social formations (immigrant communities) and at the same time follow conventions to appeal to an audience that has made their predecessors produced in Nigeria successful. The diasporic films occupy a cinematic space, which identifies with Nollywood conventions in terms of being dialogue heavy and having a seeming lack of cinematographic sophistication by common standards. However, to be stripped of layers of expressions can be part of the immigrant experience. In other words, Nollywood films that are transnational in production exemplify the migration experience not only through the stories they tell, but also in terms of their production environment. Nollywood films have established themselves firmly throughout Africa and in the African diaspora, and they have become easily accessible in many parts of the world. While the term *Nollywood* evokes the film industry's connection to the nation-state of Nigeria and the city of Lagos, Nollywood has become a transnational phenomenon in both distribution and production. The film industries of Hollywood, Bollywood, and Nollywood have so far always been clearly connected to the nation-states of production and specific locales within the nation-states, such as Los Angeles, Mumbai, and Lagos, respectively. With the production of films by expatriates, however, the boundaries are blurred and shifted, and national cinemas become transnational and newly creative in their own right. In filmmaker Agbayewa's words, "I felt Nollywood is more independent and more backing and things of that nature, but I wanted to put my spin on it and take it beyond just being Nigerian and open it up to being as open as possible" ("Nollywood or Bust").

NOTES

1. The same is true for the northern Nigerian city of Kano with its thriving production of Hausa films. For more information, see Brian Larkin's groundbreaking book *Signal and Noise*.

2. For example, Stephen Frear's *Dirty Pretty Things*, Luc and Jean Pierre Dardennes's *La Promesse*, Montxo Armendáriz's *Las Cartas de Alou*, and Frieder Schlaich's *Otomo*, among many others.

3. So-called 419 (four-one-nine) scams are confidence tricks named after the relevant section of the Nigerian criminal code.

WORKS CITED

Adejunmobi, Moradewun. "Nigerian Video Film as Minor Transnational Practice." *Postcolonial Text* 3.2 (2007): n. pag. Web.

Agbayewa, Femi. "Filmmaker Femi Agbayewa Interview." YouTube, June 2008. Web.

———. "Oluwa Femi Agbayewa: Nolly-wood or Bust." *Hip Hop Cosign* (June 2007). Web.

Appadurai, Arjun. *Modernity at Large: Cultural Dimensions of Globalization.* Minneapolis: University of Minnesota Press, 1996.

Clapp, James A. "'Are You Talking to Me?': New York and the Cinema of Urban Alienation." *Visual Anthropology* 18 (2005): n. pag. Web.

Haynes, Jonathan. "Nollywood in Lagos, Lagos in Nollywood Films." *Africa Today* 54.2 (2007): 131–50.

———. "Political Critique in Nigerian Video Films." *African Affairs* 105.421 (2006): 511–33.

Haynes, Jonathan, and Onookome Okome. "Evolving Popular Media: Nigerian Video Films." *Research in African Literatures* 29.3 (1998): 106–28.

Larkin, Brian. *Signal and Noise: Media, Infrastructure, and Urban Culture in Nigeria.* Durham, N.C.: Duke University Press, 2008.

Maguire, Lori. "The Destruction of New York: A Recurrent Nightmare of American Cold War Cinema." *Cold War History* 9.4 (2009): 513–24.

McCall, John C. "The Pan-Africanism We Have: Nollywood's Invention of Africa." *Film International* 5.4 (2007): 92–97.

Mennel, Barbara. *Cities and Cinema: Critical Introductions to Urbanism and the City.* London and New York: Routledge, 2008.

Naficy, Hamid. *An Accented Cinema: Exilic and Diasporic Filmmaking.* Princeton, N.J.: Princeton University Press, 2001.

Okome, Onookome. "Introducing the Special Issue on West African Cinema: Africa at the Movies." *Postcolonial Text* 3.2 (2007): n. pag. Web.

———. "Nollywood: Spectatorship, Audience, and the Sites of Consumption." *Postcolonial Text* 3.2 (2007): n. pag. Web.

FILMOGRAPHY

Las Cartas de Alou. Dir. Montxo Armendáriz. Elías Querejeta Producciones Cinematográficas (Spain). 1990.

Dirty Pretty Things. Dir. Stephen Frears. BBC Films et al. (UK). 2002.

The God Daughter. Dir. Eve Ikuenobe-Otaigbe. Afrimedia Entertainment (United States). 2006.

God's Own Country. Dir. Femi Agbayewa. Real Livin' Films (United States). 2006.

Missing in America. Dir. Sola Osofisan. Creative Chronicles & Concepts and Buky's Place Enterprises (United States). 2004.

My American Nurse, 1 and 2. Dir. Pascal Atuma. Pascal Atuma Productions (United States). 2006, 2010.

Only in America. Dir. David DeCrane. 360 World Pictures (United States). 2005.

Otomo. Dir. Frieder Schlaich. Filmgalerie 451 and Zweites Deutsches Fernsehen (Germany). 2000.

La Promesse. Dir. Jean-Pierre and Luc Dardenne. Eurimage et al. (Belgium et al.). 1996.

This America. Dir. Bethels Agomuoh. African Film Company and United African Artists (United States). 2005.

SIX

Reversing the Filmic Gaze: Comedy and the Critique of the Postcolony in *Osuofia in London*

ONOOKOME OKOME

COMEDY IN NOLLYWOOD

SOMETIME IN 1999, I RAN INTO ONE OF THE ICONS OF NOLLYWOOD, Sam Loco, at a bar located close to the University of Calabar, and I engaged him in a lively discussion about everything from his drinking history to his place in Nollywood. I asked him to explain why Nollywood dubs one category of film as "epic" and another "religious video film" when it is obvious these categories are hardly different in any significant way.[1] His response was: "You university people are always asking questions that do not make any sense." In his explanation, he made reference to *Battle of Musanga, 1 and 2* as the major "epic video film" in Nollywood, explaining that the phrase is an illustration of a certain category of film in the industry. He insisted that the "naming" came from those who work in the industry. The "epic video film," he told me, is "like the history film. It deals with history, things of the past." He emphasized the *pastness* of this kind of film, stressing that it is merely a dramatization of history as *truth*. To make the point stick, he said, "dis na how we dey describe dis kin film in the industry, no be how una see am."[2] Sam Loco's definition reiterates the possibility of thinking (and writing) about the emergence of *genre* in the art of Nollywood, and the acknowledgment of the "epic film" as a separate narrative entity is interesting for the reason that it explains the presence of a set of formal rules, which is consciously articulated by those who make Nollywood films. I would argue in this chapter that the recognition of the "genre" of the "epic video film" demonstrates "an area of agreement between audience and the text" (Kitses 24) that releases a distinct "pleasure" of *seeing*. Indeed, as E. Bascombe argues, "popular arts, in fact, have always depended on this" (qtd. in Neale 8), the manipulation and enhancement of its own language of articulation. It follows, then, that *Battle of Musanga*, which is the exemplar of this genre of Nollywood film, entails the reiteration of certain qualities of the pro-filmic world in Nollywood. In other words, like other forms emerging, my main argument is that *Osuofia in London*, the subject of this analysis, codifies and establishes the format of comedy in Nollywood. This argument pays special attention to the exploration of its peculiar narrative signs, outlining how the singular and distinct narrative item, the reversal of the filmic gaze, is ordered as a discourse that uses Osuofia as the agent of that narrative reversal. The intention is to discuss how the spoken and narrative languages of this film articulate a specific sense of the postcolonial discourse. Can we, for example, read *Osuofia in London* as the comedy of the rustic fellow who is conscious of the history of colonialism? How is he framed as the vehicle of this discourse?

To be clear, *Osuofia in London* is not the first comic film in Nollywood, but it is certainly the most engaging since the rather less known film *Holygan* (1999) was released. As a comic film, the significance of *Holygan* lies in the self-reflexive ways that it is framed as a narrative and in its ability to reiterate a sense of social critique belonging to the lower class by calling attention to the duplicity of the church, the corruption of the police, and the gullibility of women in the city. Uncannily close to the social reality of the pro-filmic world of the film text, a fact that the film consciously calls into attention, *Holygan* lays bare and reiterates this pro-filmic text as a discourse by giving accent to instances of the socially incongruous and the culturally ludicrous. It does this by deploying the full range of parody in order to restate what is already known to the local audience, and thus gives the impression that the social critique it deals with comes from and is sanctioned by this class of people. To achieve this, pidgin English, which is the language spoken in the film, is retooled to meet the demands of the seriousness of the social issues at the heart of the film's narrative. What *Osuofia in London* brings to this emerging genre is that it solidified its character as genre.

OSUOFIA IN LONDON: THE STORY
OF THE "BUSHMAN FROM AFRICA"

Parody is central to the narrative of *Osuofia in London,* and it is deployed as the incongruous in both the narrative and the linguistic coding that the film adopts. Although noting in passing that the structure of this film is exceptional in Nollywood, and that it dispels the notion that after the "first 5 minutes the story of Nollywood becomes predictable," it does provide ample evidence to show that Nollywood has left the ways of "mad" improvisation behind.[3] Structured as a travel tale, *Osuofia in London* is told in three distinctive but narratively integrated parts. The first part deals with Osuofia's life in the village of Neke Ama Nasa and the second with Osuofia in London. In the third part, the story returns Osuofia to Neke Ama Nasa with pomp and ceremony. The title of the film privileges the second part of this narrative of travel, signifying its importance as the site of contestation where *difference* is played out in the travel of discovery. The third part, which deals with his triumphant return to his village, having seen "Eliza," the queen of England, is laced with the symbolism of an imagined conquest and points to the reversal of the colonial gaze. Osuofia's marriage to an English woman, Samantha Wood, the fiancée of his late brother, is significant in this regard. Each part of this narrative triangle has precise implications for the plot as a journey of discovery.

Osuofia in London is by every account deeply embedded in the social history of its pro-filmic locality, which is rural Nigeria, and the narrative investment in the idea of the subgenre of "crazy comedy" cannot be fully understood outside of this culture. For this reason, the full range of linguistic expression boldly written into its structural pattern becomes a crucial site of knowledge and functions as a guide to a proper reading of the layered texture of the film text. Rather than merely paying attention to the debate between rural and urban Africa, the narrative also privileges the connection between rustic Africa and the colonial metropolis, thereby giving a larger accent to the discourse of colonialism. The story line is simple. Upon receiving an unexpected letter from the fiancée of his dead brother, Osuofia sets out to London to inherit what the brother left behind. He imagines that this inheritance includes

the dead brother's fiancée, and this makes him happy, for, after all, the
fiancée is a white woman, different. In a series of comic skits before this
triumphant departure to London, Osuofia dazzles the people of Neke
Ama Nasa with his knowledge of London even before he has visited the
place. As a clever comic backdrop, which is constructed to prop up the
eventual visit to London, the story registers his *difference* from the other
villagers. As he performs for the bewildered villagers the peculiar way
people in London walk and talk, he reinvents himself in hyperbolized
movement and gestural codes only a comic of the status of Nkem Owoh
can muster. Complementing these symbolic gestures is the stylized outfit that he designed for himself and consciously displays just before he
leaves for London. Bizarre as it may seem, the villagers are taken in by
the sheer outlandishness and audacity of the costume, which adds color
to the paralinguistic codes of his body gestures.

In London, Osuofia takes the viewers through a number of important public spaces, exploring these urban spaces as he is explored as an
outsider by the viewer. But as he explores these spaces, he is seen exercis-
ing his sense of propriety in the actions he deems inappropriate in his
culture, an act that lands himself in trouble with Londoners who know
little or nothing of his culture. For instance, he approaches a young girl in
one such public place and then tries to cover her up with his coat for the
reason that she sits indecently in the public, exposing herself. He is dis-
graced as the girl slaps him in the face. The most consequential part of his
trip around London happens in a park when he attempts to "catch" one
of the pigeons in the park for "pepper soup," a local Nigerian soup that
goes with beer drinking. The police are called in, and after the bizarre
interrogation, he is led to the home of his late brother. He meets the late
brother's fiancée, Samantha Wood, who initially treats him condescend-
ingly. After a series of hilarious encounters with the local shopkeeper and
with Samantha, Osuofia is revealed as someone whose sense of *self* and
of his culture is stable, sometimes uncannily stable.

Meanwhile, Osuofia is taken to meet the lawyer who managed the
business of his brother. The meeting does not go as Samantha and the
dubious lawyer planned. The "bushman from Africa" does not fall for the
tricks they had set him up for. Trying hard to convince Osuofia to sign
the document needed for the lawyer and Samantha to lay their hands
on the money left behind by the dead brother, the lawyer fails at first.

Upon the renewal of the flirtatious antics of Samantha, Osuofia signs the document, but the lawyer then tries to double-cross Samantha. She fights back, offering to marry Osuofia and to go to "Africa" with him.

Osuofia's return to Neke Ama Nasa is a veritable carnival and his formal marriage to Samantha Wood a communal festival. But while Osuofia celebrates his marriage to Samantha, it is clear that all is not well in his household. There are familial squabbles to contend with, and his "local wife" is more than becoming intransigent. Osuofia's daughters, who take sides with their mother, are making life unbearable for him. Samantha, who is becoming ever more restive because she has not been able to get what she wants from Osuofia, designs yet another plot as she gets deeper and deeper into the ways of life of the local people. Desperate beyond reason, she tries to poison Osuofia. This plot is revealed by Nkechi, Osuofia's favorite daughter, who is also Samantha's only friend in this troubled household. Osuofia confronts Samantha, who confesses to the crime, providing reason for her attempt to kill Osuofia. She had loved his brother, Donatus, very much, she confesses, and gave all she had so he could begin and have a thriving business. The promise of marriage, which did not materialize because of the death of the brother, is the reason for her generous offer. Osuofia, "the bushman from Africa," does not buy the story, but in a show of magnanimity, he returns the sum of five hundred thousand pounds sterling to Samantha Wood but not before telling her, "but I loved you so much." Samantha is overwhelmed by this act of generosity and says to him, "We make judgment about people without actually knowing them. . . . I heard so many things about your people and thought they were true." Amid this passion of self-discovery, she kisses Osuofia genuinely and generously for the first time, saying, concluding this act of self-discovery, "I just wish more people would experience this. . . . Thank you for everything. Thank you for making me see the truth." A lavish party is given by Osuofia and the community of Neke Ama Nasa, and Samantha leaves for London afterward. Osuofia returns to his "local wife," and the life of the community is made whole again, as is the case with all comedies.

The main point of the story is made in the final remarks by Samantha. She is taught her lesson, which is that she must not take this "bushman from Africa," and by extension the whole of Africa, for granted. As the representative of the *other*, the self-discovery can be linked to the reversal of the colonial episteme about African people. The story ends in the same way that the famous African novel *Things Fall Apart* does, giving a continental twist to the story of Okonkwo of the little, unknown fictional village tucked away in the Igbo country of Nigeria. It is Obierika, the friend of Okonkwo, the novel's protagonist, who instructs the white district commissioner on the cultural practices of the Igbo people of Umuofia, an act that reverses the symbolic power balance of the story of colonizer and the colonized in the text.

The plot of *Osuofia in London* is revealing as a postcolonial text. It calls into the debate the *modus* of the write-back that Okonkwo's travails mean to postcolonial studies in Africa. In the same way, *Osuofia in London* reverts the narrative gaze typical of colonial discourse by taking over and insisting on the retelling of the archetypal story we find in empire films.[4] The narrative gaze is framed as local and the ordering reversed in favor of local episteme. This reading of the story is supported by Nkem Owoh, who plays Osuofia. He is quoted as saying, "Being part of the production was very fulfilling for me. It was an interesting experience because it was a cross-cultural production in which we explored the culture of the white man to see where we have agreements and where we disagree. It was such a production that is far from demeaning to the African sensibility."[5] Reacting to those who have contrary views, he replies, "Those who say they have become so European in their own ways that it becomes extremely difficult for them to even appreciate the fact that in Osuofia's home land to capture a pigeon and prepare it in a pot of soup as the rule deserves our sympathy and not condemnation." Perhaps this is the most interesting point that he makes: "So despite all his clowning, Osuofia in the midst of murky and dangerous waters ferried back his late brother's money into Nigeria. The movie showed once again, like in Wole Soyinka's *Lion and the Jewel,* that most often, native intelligence has a way of surpassing book knowledge." Owoh enjoins "people to see the movie again and they will be very proud that Osuofia went to London."

These comments are a reaction to critics who interpret Osuofia's bizarre behavior as a reaffirmation of the savage and uncouth behavior of the "black man from Africa." Owoh's defense throws light on the way this film was received in Nigeria. Although it is still popular with Nollywood fans, the points that Owoh makes are crucial. The emphasis on the "native intelligence" is a way of saying that "intelligence" comes not

from studying the "Oyinbo man's book" but from the resources of human intellect, which every human being is endowed with. Owoh reacts
directly to some of the opinions that the film generated. Here is the
summary of what one observer has to say:

> There is a danger to argue that the message of a movie does not really matter if
> the movie is a fiction. True fiction is based on some reality. The opposite of this
> would be false fiction. A movie based on false fiction should not be seen at all.
> The fictional comedy "Osuofia in London" is unpatriotic to Africa. The movie
> portrays Osuofia as being more interested in the brother's wealth rather than the
> brother himself. Africans are presented in this movie as timid and uncivilized
> people who have no idea of what it means to use a rest room, a confirmation of
> what the West believe already about Africans. Mr. Okafor the London based
> solicitor of Donatus is seen as a corrupt man, another Euro American image of
> Africans. Osuofia is portrayed as a dumb idiot who would sign off every of his
> brother's property for a kiss from a white lady. To show the producer's willing-
> ness to sell this false identity of the African to West, the movie is produced with
> a Western audience in mind. This is seen clearly in the narrations before and at
> the end of the movie.

It seems to me that this reading is mediated by the larger discourse,
which the relationship between Neke Ama Nasa (rural Africa) and London (Europe) provokes. Nkem Owoh does not read the film in the same
way. He reads it from the very opposite end, that is, from the perspective
of the popular, which is the way that a lot of viewers who saw the film
in Nigeria conceived of it – as a narrative of conquest, and the symbolic
trophy is Samantha, the white wife, whom Osuofia acquires. Can we read
this obvious idea of "trophism" as the conquest of whiteness motivated
by greed on the part of Samantha, and if we do, what would be the implication of such a reading?

   I do think that Owoh's comment drags the viewer into the larger
postcolonial context of the text as well as the transnationality of its narrative purpose, reversing the power of the gaze from the perspective of
the colonizer to that of the (post)colonized subject. In this regard, *Osuofia in London* can be read at the ideological and cultural levels, both of
which privilege the politics of culture and *difference*. In this regard also,
what the film does is to deregister one episteme, the colonial discourse,
and to reframe another in its place. In other words, *Osuofia in London*
momentarily confirms what Bekeh Utietang argues, which is the "confirmation of what the West believes already about Africans," but it quickly

reverses this discursive construction that creates and institutionalizes this episteme as discourse. Indeed, Samantha's final remarks about getting to know a people before making value judgments about them are part of this reversal of the discourse that sees Africa as a place of human negation. Unlike empire films, *Osuofia in London* provides a multilayered discursive platform to do this act of deconstruction. It gives the viewer the critical view of Osuofia's gaze as it is positioned as a critique of what is alluded to. Playful as this gaze may seem, the viewer comes into its system of knowledge from the language of laughter, which the character of Osuofia deliberately inaugurates and fosters.

THE LANGUAGE OF COMEDY: THE
COMEDY OF *OSUOFIA IN LONDON*

As a crazy comedy, *Osuofia in London* is the hyperbolic narrative of the rustic character, Osuofia, who challenges the very idea of rusticity, compelling the viewer to rethink this taxonomy but within a larger discourse of the postcolonial situation. As a type, Osuofia represents the rural archetype of the postcolonial, and as a character, he functions as one who is designed to reverse the stereotype of the rustic who is seen as the epitome of the unintelligent being. In this way, the diegetic and nondiegetic aspects of the narrative compel the viewer to rethink him as a character and as type, even as the diegetic template of the main narrative competes with the nondiegetic in the carefully plotted journey undertaken by Osuofia. This offers multiple ways of reading the significance of the journey he undertakes. Part of the design of the visual and verbal languages of the narrative is also organized around the social grotesque and the drama of incongruity. This is consciously done to plot the incongruous acts and then to reverse that which is socially incongruous, acts that are mainly constituted in the personhood of Osuofia, and this allows for a reading that hyperbolizes the construction of the actions of Osuofia. In other words, if genres are part of the "signifying processes of cinema," as Stephen Neale argues convincingly, as an object of "crazy comedy," Osuofia's subjectivity becomes the vehicle through which the social texts in the narrative and the narrative conventions are viciously fractured and then reassigned new meaning. While he must mobilize the act of the grotesque as an essential aspect of this exaggerated comic show – generally defined here as a system of social performance that is at odds with social norms – this narrative of social disjuncture is recognizable as socially aberrant, one that seeks to reduce the ordinary, the known and the quotidian, to new ways of apprehending the world. In doing so, the filmic version of the pro-filmic compels the spoken and filmic language to yield to the true meaning of what it is to be socially grotesque so that one of the defining characters of *Osuofia in London* as a "crazy comedy" is the transgressive act of the agent of the narrative itself, which is, in this case, Osuofia. He is at once the act of parody as well as the agency of the parodic act itself. As the agent of parody, he affects the process of transformation in significant ways. In this narrative order, Osuofia "articulates order and disorder across the very mechanism of discourse, producing incongruities, contradictions and illogicalities at the level of language and codes" (Neale 24). As part of this experiment, the true meaning of *Osuofia in London* must then be construed in this sense – the transformation of a local gnosis. As a way of "making some kind of sense out of its own hieroglyphics" (Gottesman 1), this film is therefore deliberately self-reflexive. He is the main text of the story, and through him, and in his language, the viewer is able to unpack the other texts embedded in the story. Focused as the film is on his character, Osuofia allows the viewer to see him as a narrative point that transforms the debate on the use of language in African cinema to a new level. In other words, this film is transformative in the ways that it is able to localize the spoken and filmic languages at the same time. This is because Osuofia is both the diegetic instance and the narrative center through which all else happens. Through him, and by the way he inserts and activates his presence in the social events of this story, he is able to parody and critique his society as well as the *other* discourse connected to the "oyinbo people" of the story.[6] The uniqueness of the language with which this is done can be scrutinized on two levels: its compelling deliberateness and the formation of the social meanings that are compelled to reveal different discursive formations in the text as well as the subtexts of the main text. Yet it is important to point out here that it is not just the spoken language alone that gives Osuofia, and indeed the story, this sense of uniqueness. As a comic character who is appropriately constructed in the genre of comedy, especially the subgeneric category of the "crazy comedy," his personhood elicits – even in the less than comic situations – the sense of the comic incongruous. Part of what elicits this sense of "craziness" are his physical gestures as well as his manner of dress – his costume. Both combine to form the *crazy persona* of Osuofia. Deploying the "bush English" as the spoken medium, Osuofia is never without ideological and cultural baggage, and this linguistic choice cannot be construed as a narrative oversight, either. Rather, it is deliberately done to align Osuofia to a social class while at the same time positioning this class status (the peasant class of the rustic category) in contrast to one of its "other" (the intellectual class). What Osuofia takes us through in his journeys is then brought together as oppositional in the discursive template of the story to this "other." As the narrative formulates this aspect of the story, it is Osuofia's linguistic coding that is given valence, signaling the narrative upper hand of Osuofia's personhood within this framing. The mobilization of this category of the spoken language functions then to signal and establish the iconoclastic presence of Osuofia as "the man from Africa." Stripped of the "cultural sophistication" of the English language, the colonial language, resorting to the "bush English" offers a reading of the iconoclastic presence of Osuofia as the main text of the narrative – a text from which other texts emerge. While the vibrancy of the language holds the attention of the viewer, the discursive narrative it elicits makes reference to other kinds of ideological texts without explicitly naming them. One such ideological text is the discourse of colonialism. Reading the story of Osuofia's journey is incomplete without making the linkage to this other text – the colonial presence.

Osuofia is the primary image and the language of the main text. In him, the other texts of the story are configured and made readable. In the first major event of the film, just before the extradiegetic sequence of the main text is completed, Osuofia is shown on a hunting trip with his children, all of them girls. As a hunting band, they look ludicrous, if not outlandish, but this is meant to be. It is part of the distinction that the story makes in order to set Osuofia and his family apart from others in the village, in this idyllic and pristine African setting. This is the first part of the journey in the story, the journey around pristine Africa. From the hunting proceedings, it is clear that Osuofia is not good at the job. Rather than focus on the job at hand, he engages in meaningless banter with his daughters, on whose heads he sits as he takes aim at game. Ruffled because he is unable to take steady aim, he exclaims, "I am going to shoot

one of you, o!" He fails to kill the game, saying, "We will cook one of you
... because it is one of you that has been bringing this bad luck." It is not
just Osuofia's *difference* that is registered in these actions. His family is
also singled out, so that when out of frustration he tells his daughters, "If
you do not know how to flash your torchlight to young men, you better
learn, o!" the viewer recognizes at once a man who is at odds with his
community and with his family. The localized reference of this language
of frustration expresses an aspect of the local episteme that the uniniti-
ated may not immediately decipher. To "flash your torchlight" simply
means to display that body part in a way that is tantalizing to those for
whom the performance itself is directed.

Perhaps even more compelling is Osuofia's lack of communal one-
ness when he prevents his friend Ibekwe, an official of the Igwe's palace,
from partaking in his lunch. Ibekwe is visiting to summon him to the
Igwe's palace for some urgent matter. It is about Osuofia's refusal to pay
the communal levy as prescribed by the orders of the Igwe. In what is
clearly a tepid show of uncharacteristic incivility, the kind that is not part
of the usual discourse of African hospitality, the viewer is left with the
picture of Osuofia as a selfish man. The film registers this by narratively
insisting that Osuofia reverses the episteme of common civility by asking
the visitor to join in a meal when he declares to Ibekwe, "You nearly meet
me well," meaning the visitor cannot eat with him because he has just
finished eating. The making of this local iconoclast is finally sealed when
Ukpaka, another official of the Igwe's palace, describes him as "a difficult
man" after Osuofia makes an uncommon remark at the Igwe's council.

But the most dramatic event in the formation of Osuofia as a character type is cemented in his reaction to the news of the death of his
brother, Donatus. Informed by teacher Charles, the village school head-
master, that his impending trip to London is urgent and required, Osuofia's response is characteristically predictable: "Do you want me to
take his dedi bodi?" he asks teacher Charles.[7] However, convinced of
what he stands to gain, his language and physical comportment change.
He is happy to "journey to London," where, according to him, "you will
become ice block," a reference to the cold in London. In one of the final
moments before Osuofia leaves his village, he parodies the imagined life
in this European metropolis, which sets up the obvious line of narrative
contestation between both worlds. As he embarks on the journey into

"the unknown," the nondiegetic aspect of the narrative, the sound track, reiterates this sense of a new spatial location and notes the transition from the village in Africa to the city of London, connecting Osuofia's bizarre attire to a world that is unknown to him but one that is likely to clash with his sense of cultural wholeness. Once in London, the sound track changes to reggae music from the deep traditional rhythm of Igbo music as Osuofia screams, "Wonderful, wonderful!" The fast cut in this sequence accentuates what he sees and the magic of seeing. The viewer is not left in doubt as to who is in control of what is privileged in the story. It is certainly Osuofia's cultural gaze.

In London, Osuofia reveals the wondrous delight of the postcolonial coming into contact with a colonial metropolis, a narrative trope that has become ubiquitous in postcolonial literary and critical formations in Africa and the Caribbean. He does this on his own terms and with the "exotic" facility of the "bush English." He never gives up his cultural integrity even in the city of London. He is as firm in his conviction as he is of his person. His cultural references are solidly local. His reckless encounter with the liberal city is indeed magical, but it does not offer the preferred way of life. He makes this clear to the viewer in more ways than one. He rebukes a teenager who would not "sit like a woman" in what looks like a train station, he is taken by the presence of the cannonball gun in another public space, and he is awed by the order and serenity of the parks he visits. If these encounters are cultural testimonies of his sense of difference, the narrative reiterates how his "native culture" governs the way he sees and interprets London. Consciously ignoring the "other culture," he insists on this sense of cultural integrity, making it clear that unlike the colonial subject who exists in the spatial category of the first and second registers of Frantz Fanon's description, he is never caught up in either category.[8] This trip around London may indeed read as incredulous, if not incongruous, but it is the conscious display of the ridiculous and the preference of a distinct cultural being that define Osuofia as "the man from Africa."

The high point of the performance of this sense of cultural specificity is staged when Osuofia arrives at a public square full of pigeons. He catches one for the purpose of "making pepper soup," an intention that causes concern for those present. The police are called, and Osuofia is taken to Scotland Yard. His interrogation displays yet another level of the comic incongruity of his person. His exuberant declaration of this personhood manifests itself quite clearly. He demands the proper pronunciation of his name during this interrogation and sternly rebukes the interrogating officers for not doing so. Exasperated but not ready to give in, the interrogating officers manage to get the information about his mission in London. But this is after one of the most bizarre and anachronistic moments of the interrogation unfolds. Osuofia summons the aid of "black magic" in the form of a wand to ward off the aggression of the interrogators. It is unclear if he succeeds in this act, but on its own, this act is significant. One way to read this act is that it is simply a demonstration of the response from Osuofia confronted with another worldview that relies heavily on the rational. Is it possible, then, to read this act as a way of peppering the content of the narrative in order to appeal to the discourse of the "noble savage" doing savage things? The narrative provides very little cues for us to make any valid conclusions in this regard.

There is a lot to say about the paralinguistic coding of Osuofia's traditional Igbo attire, which he adorns proudly when he visits the lawyer, Ben Okafor, for the first time. Complete with the red cap that is the privilege of chiefs, his costume serves as the counterpoint to that of the lawyer, who is in a European suit. If, as part of the *difference* that Osuofia performs in his homeland, he seeks a personality that is unique, in London the performance of this *difference* has other aims. At home, the performance is all about repositioning himself, seeking a social uniqueness at the level of individuation. He gets it even if teacher Charles points out the "ridiculousness" of his desire to parody the way that the English language is spoken and used in everyday conversation in London. In London, the cultural politics, which his attire elicits, is radically different. He is no longer the bearer of the ways of the English. This conscious display of his "Igboness" in London is, I would argue, a reiteration of his cultural well-being. In this cultural frame, he is no longer himself. He does not represent himself. He represents something more and other than himself. He is an assertion, a cultural assertion. In this sense, Osuofia's performance of culture, especially during this meeting with Ben Okafor, demonstrates the politics of cultural reproduction of the homeland. A postcolonial subject, Osuofia recognizes his national culture as his social and cultural anchor. He is self-conscious about it. He adequately performs it. If Osuofia is the "stubborn goat" from Africa because he refuses to sign the papers that would give legal backing for Samantha and give the lawyer access to the money of the late brother, he remains steadfast. He does this by expressing his line of resistance in one of the most eloquent expressions of bush English, saying, "How can I pay the bride price when I have not seen the bride?" His triumph is complete when out of desperation, Samantha agrees to be his wife and to accompany him to "Africa." Conquering Samantha means conquering London and by extension the colonial past. The narrative symbolism is not lost on the student of postcolonialism.

Osuofia's return to his village with Samantha is an epiphany. It concretizes the triumphant metaphor of this story of travel and conquest. But as Osuofia retells his trip to the bemused people of his village, this sense of conquest becomes a communal success, even if the viewer knows that Osuofia's narrative is imagined to the last detail. The "imagined" becomes part of the sense of communal worth. Extraordinary as it may seem, part of this narrative, which includes the introduction of Samantha as "the daughter of the President of the United Kingdom," is not taken at face value by the villagers. As part of his narrative package, Osuofia lets it be known to the villagers that he actually met with "Eliza," the queen of England. Away from the glare of the community, he relives his life in London in a series of flashbacks, all of which do not correspond to the experience that he relates to the villagers, and this allows the viewer to come to some knowledge about the purpose of this invention. Transformed in the eyes of the villagers by this credulous narrative, Osuofia makes capital of his imagined visit to Buckingham Palace. He convinces himself that his imagined trip to London has made it possible for him to make the distinction between what is "overall" and "all over."

But the most telling event in this narrative of conquest comes at the end, when Osuofia sabotages Samantha's plot to poison him. Visibly displeased by this act of sabotage, Osuofia feigns illness in order to prove the veracity of the claim on his "deathbed." Samantha is shaken when she realizes that Osuofia knows the truth about the plot. In a dramatic show of magnanimity that smacks of patronage, Osuofia offers to return the sum of five hundred thousand pounds sterling, which Samantha claims she gave to his brother to begin his business. Osuofia tells her, "And to think that I loved you. I really loved you." Samantha's declaration that she will no longer look down on the people of Africa, even "though she has heard so many bad things about them," shows that she is part of the discourse of that metropolis, which privileges the infantalization of the formerly colonized people of Africa. This encounter, which reiterates the connection of the discourse of the local and the colonial global, signals the tension between the two epistemes in the narrative construction of this story. Osuofia wins only because he is able to display an uncanny wit and sense of humor.

OSUOFIA IN LONDON AND THE
REINVENTION OF FILM LANGUAGE

The filmic language deployed in *Osuofia in London* is one of a kind in Nollywood. It is self-conscious. The special and unique qualities of the film language are carried through by two nondiegetic constituents of the narrative – the voice-over and the musical score, both of which are uncommon narrative features in Nollywood. As commentaries on the journey of Osuofia, these nondiegetic aspects of the narrative are configured to heighten this sense of exploration as well as to demarcate the narrative focus of each segment of the story, giving each a different and distinct ideological valence. The special use of the voice-over is established in the opening sequence. As the credits come to an end, the voice-over privileges Osuofia's "Africa" that is "vast, still, and largely unknown." In this "pristine" stillness, the turbulent household of Osuofia is introduced. Osuofia is different in every conceivable way. This visual narrative of peace and quiet is quickly juxtaposed with a visual antithesis, the "concrete jungle" of London, so that the viewer is given a contrastive sense of the two worlds, while at the same time his or her attention is drawn to the narrative possibility of collision between the two. The visual *pleasure* that this contrast generates privileges Osuofia's world in an unambiguous way, making it possible for the viewer to read it as part of another code of discourse. As a parodic strategy of the main text, the insertion of the voice-over proclaims clearly that "we can never escape from the voices that shape our experience even as we parody them, because they are part of our heteroglossia" (Rush 11). It is impossible, then, to read Osuofia's world outside this "other," which it privileges in this visual formation of contrast. By inserting the voice-over in such a way, the strategy is set for it to compete with the main narration for attention, thereby calling the attention of the viewer to it in ways that are difficult to ignore. Yet the reference to Osuofia's village, and indeed the whole of Africa, calls into the discussion the stereotype of anthropological Africa. Osuofia's activities subvert this narrative intention intentionally and show the deconstructive potentials of the narrative strategy itself. Neke Ama Nasa may be "pristine" and Africa "a vast, unknowable jungle" safely tucked away in some inconsequential corner of the world, but Osuofia's humanity is not in question at all. The deliberateness of the strategic and nuanced intention of the narrative is similar to Chinua Achebe's reversal of intention that governed the ideology of his novel *Things Fall Apart*. He argues, for instance, that it is important to recognize that "Africans are people in the same way that Americans, Europeans, Asians, and others are people. . . . Although the action of *Things Fall Apart* takes place in a setting with which most Americans are unfamiliar, the characters are normal people and their events are real human events" ("Teaching" 21). *Osuofia in London* obliquely makes the same argument.

If the voice-over registers the contrast between the two worlds in the film text, the musical score directs the viewer to the intentionality of the story of Osuofia's journey as a postcolonial narration of conquest – the conquest of the rationality of the metropolitan European logic. This is especially apparent in the second part when Osuofia goes to London. The refrain of the musical score, "Osuofia don enter London," is important, and the lyrics, which inform the viewer that "Oyinbo carry wayo come," because "they think say we be moomoo," register Osuofia's intention as the maker of the journey on behalf of the postcolony.[9] Even though "dem think say we be moomoo," the sound tract insists, Osuofia defies this definition, and the affirmation of this rejection is registered as the journey of conquest, which contains references such as "there is no place like home" and "Osuofia don return home," bringing "money and Oyinbo wife."

Osuofia in London is much more than the parodying of society, even if this is done in meaningful and sustained ways. The transnational debate, which it institutes as part of this narrative order, marks it out as one of the most telling narratives in Nollywood so far. Equally significant is the retooling of the hybridized language, pidgin or "bush English," which is stylistically compelled to yield much more than what it has been assigned as a literary means of cultural production. In *Osuofia in London*, this language option is given cultural currency and duly invested with critical purpose. Thus far, some of the criticism of Nollywood, which is reminiscent of the criticism of the Onitsha market pamphlets, has focused on the inability of this language to provide such a critical gravitas for understanding social order and cultural life in the postcolony. This, I argue, is the critical atmosphere in which we must contextualize the reading of *Osuofia in London*. Indeed, this film makes full use of the hybrid popular language and proves that it is possible to press it to deal with serious social, political, and cultural issues. The point, then, is that *Osuofia in London* successfully puts to use this language of the street to invoke one of the most significant subjects of the postcolonial debate by pressing it to yield its intrinsic parodic qualities that trouble "the dominant metaphors – those social, political, economic, and expressive conventions that always threaten to choke" it (Gottesman 1). This film presents us one example of a local cultural machine that "is simultaneously maintaining continuity and making something new and valuable out of the eternal tension between imagination and reality" (ibid.). *Osuofia in London* offers us evidence that the Nollywood film culture has not despaired of making something "out of its own hieroglyphics" (ibid.). As parody, *Osuofia in London* gestures toward a self-reflexivity that reveals internal tension as well as the connection to an external world, which it contests. In the act of self-criticism, we follow Osuofia's hard-hitting critique of his own society while he simultaneously draws the attention of the viewer to the relationship between the local and the global. What his social fight offers the viewer – at least in my reading – is a new way of looking at, a fresh way of seeing, what is presented in that tension between what the text of *Osuofia in London* privileges and the reality of the pro-filmic world as we know it. In this regard, I wish to argue that this film fights the notion that is fashionable in some quarters that popular arts cannot be pressed to yield any sustained critique of the postcolonial condition because of the rowdiness of their uncritical push toward hybridity. *Osuofia in London* offers a critical reading of the pro-filmic world from a postcolonial standpoint. Its semantic intention as parody is directed not only at itself and its social and cultural milieu but also at a larger historical community. That larger concern is framed by the discourse of colonialism, which the narrative of *Osuofia in London* rephrases as a gaze that is returned by Osuofia. By marking the discourses of the meeting between the West and Africa as "intentional quotation marks" (Simon 23), this film reminds the discerning viewer – and this point is important – that popular arts can and indeed often do deal with matters that are serious beyond what is commonly ascribed to them in the scholarship. Although the primary purpose of the story is the attempt to "decrown" the "intentional quotation marks" that are the unchanging sameness of the postcolonial subject in popular arts, it cannot do so profoundly without referencing the "other discourse," that is, colonialism. Even if Osuofia's gaze sufficiently provokes a self-reflection that supervises the attention of the viewer, the paradox is that it also calls attention to a narrative double, that which Osuofia's social actions do not privilege.

Osuofia in London is a remarkable popular text. It is able to take on a serious debate about the connection between the postcolonial object and the complicated presence of the European metropolitan culture in his history. Certainly, this is not the only way to read one of the *classics* of Nollywood. Why, for instance, is Samantha objectified as the representative of the "alien discourse" when any casual reading of the colonial enterprise shows its masculine industry? Isn't there something to be said about the gendering of the privileged discourse in *Osuofia in London*? It is worthwhile to pay attention to what Nkem Owoh says about this film: "So despite all his clowning, Osuofia in the midst of murky dangerous waters ferried back his late brother's money into Nigeria."

NOTES

1. In my essay "Women, Religion, and the Video Film in Nigeria," I gave a brief but tentative categorization of genres in Nollywood, pointing out that the so-called religious films can be reliably referred to as "hallelujah films."

2. This is the pidgin English phrase that roughly translates as "This is how we describe it in the industry, not how you do outside the industry."

3. See "The Nollywood Debate," in *NEH African Cinema Institute Reader* (private circulation, 2005). Reference is also made to this in my essay "Nollywood and Its Critics" (33).

4. My definition of *empire film* is very akin to the definition of *empire* and *colonial literature* in Elleke Boehmer's *Colonial and Postcolonial Literature*. Like colonial literature, the signifying practice of any empire film is designed to promote the political and cultural ideology that supported empire building. At the heart of this ideological apparatus, for that is what it was, is the idea of racial difference, cultural superiority, and narrative eloquence.

5. See the discussion on the website http://www.kwenu.com/nollywood /osuofia_london.htm. All references to this debate are found on this website.

6. This is the pidgin English word for all white people and, in some context, the very idea of whiteness.

7. *Dedi bodi* is the pidgin English reference to a corpse.

8. See Fanon. His analysis of the different phases of the conversion of the colonial subjects from being totally colonized to the search for national culture is significant in this regard.

9. Pidgin English: *Carry wayo* translates as "cunning," and *moomoo* is an expression for "being foolish."

WORKS CITED

Achebe, Chinua. "Teaching *Things Fall Apart*." *Approaches to Teaching Achebe's "Things Fall Apart*." Ed. Bernth Lindfors. New York: Modern Language Association of America, 1991. 20–24.

———. *Things Fall Apart*. New York: Doubleday, 1994.

Bascombe, E. "The Genre in American Cinema." *Screen* 11.2 (1975): 42–45.

Boehmer, Elleke. *Colonial and Postcolonial Literature: Migrant Metaphors*. Oxford: Oxford University Press, 1995.

Fanon, Frantz. *The Wretched of the Earth*. New York: Grove, 1963.

Gottesman, Ronald. "Film Parody: An Immodest Proposal." *Quarterly Review of Film and Video* 12 (1990): 1–3.

Kitses, Jim. *Horizons West: Directing the Western from John Ford to Clint Eastwood*. London: British Film Institute, 1969.

Neale, Stephen. *Genre*. London: British Film Institute, 1980.

Okome, Onookome. "Nollywood and Its Critics." *Viewing African Cinema in the Twenty-First Century: Art Films and the Nollywood Video Revolution*. Ed. Mahir Şaul and Ralph A. Austen. Athens: Ohio University Press, 2010. 26–41.

———. "Women, Religion, and the Video Film in Nigeria." *Film International* 7 (2004): 4–13.

Rush, Jeffrey S. "Who's in on the Joke: Parody as Hybridized Narrative Discourse." *Quarterly Review of Film and Video* 12 (1990): 6–12.

Simon, William G. "Welles, Bakhtin, Parody." *Quarterly Review of Film and Video* 12 (1990): 23–29.

Utietiang, Bekeh. "Osuofia in London: A Philosophical Perspective." *Nigerians in America* (2005). Web.

FILMOGRAPHY

Battle of Musanga, 1 and 2. Dir. Bolaji Dawodu. Gabosky and Chezkay Film (Nigeria). 1996.

Holygan. Dir. Tony Muonago. Infinity Merchants (Nigeria). 1999.

Osuofia in London, 1 and 2. Dir. Kingsley Ogoro. Kingsley Ogoro Productions (Nigeria). 2003, 2004.

SEVEN

Nollywood and Postcolonial Predicaments: Transnationalism, Gender, and the Commoditization of Desire in *Glamour Girls*

PAUL UGOR

AS I REVISED THIS CHAPTER FOR FINAL PUBLICATION, CNN, America's international cable TV network and perhaps the world's most powerful media empire, aired a heart-wrenching documentary titled *Nepal's Stolen Children,* featuring the American film star Demi Moore and Anuradha Koirala, India's anti–sex trafficking activist and CNN's 2010 Hero of the Year.[1] The documentary itself was part of a larger global campaign mounted by CNN, CNN Freedom Project, aimed at eliminating the transnational trafficking and sexual exploitation of women and girls all over the world.[2] According to the documentary, at least 3 million women and girls from Southeast Asia are being exploited by powerful and vicious cartels that lure innocent and trusting females into forced prostitution all over the world. Obviously framed as a politically motivated media war against modern-day slavery, *Nepal's Stolen Children* came fifteen years after Nollywood took up the same social concern in one of its earliest power movies, *Glamour Girls, 2* (1996). Appropriately subtitled *The Italian Connection,* this first Nollywood English feature dealt with what has come to be known internationally (although coined in Italy) as "the Nigerian woman problem" – the transnational sex trafficking of girls and women from southern Nigeria to Europe and North America.

Since the 1990s, Nigeria has suffered the terrible reputation of being at the forefront of the global trafficking and commercialization of women for sex work and emotional care in Europe and North America (Monzini; Elabor-Idemudia). Studies indicate that approximately 105,000 people are trafficked from Nigeria for sex work in western Europe every year, and Italy and the Netherlands are the main destinations.

In fact, roughly 60–80 percent of girls involved in the sex trade in Italy are Nigerian youths with an age average of between fifteen and twenty (Ejalu). Most of the girls come from southern states like Edo, Delta, and Akwa-Ibom as well as the Lagos area. Often these youths not only send back remittances that sustain siblings, parents, and other extended family members, but at times also return to their homesteads for annual Christmas holidays with flashy cars and designer apparel from Western cities. In some cases, it has been reported that the returnee sex workers even build huge mansions for their parents. Indeed, so popular was this business of the flesh that parents in Benin City, Warri, and Uyo were selling or mortgaging family plots to support their young daughters' flying abroad for prostitution. *Glamour Girls, 2: The Italian Connection* is thus a cultural representation of the sickening but huge global business of the flesh that now constitutes the "third largest moneymaking venture in the world, after illegal weapons and drugs" (Malarek 4).

The point needs to be made, however, that the crisis of transnational sex trafficking of young women and girls as explicitly represented in *Glamour Girls, 2* is not one entirely disconnected from the failed socioeconomic policies in Nigeria since the 1980s. The global economic decline of the 1980s forced most developing countries like Nigeria to resort to short-term loans from international financial institutions such as the World Bank and the International Monetary Fund. These loans required borrowing nations to restructure their local economies to fit in with the global liberalization order of free trade and competitive markets. Thus, cost cutting in key sectors such as education, health care, and other social services, combined with the rationalization of the nation's federal workforce, spawned huge unemployment rates and consequent large-scale poverty affecting mostly women, children, and youth. The joblessness that is at the center of the recurrent frustration in *Glamour Girls, 2* and its reason for the recruitment and abuse of innocent girls in the film had in fact reached its climax by the mid-1990s when the film was released. The film thus puts a precise hand on the subterranean and dangerous cultural economies that had begun to take shape as a response to the postcolonial life of chronic want and endemic scarcity that had become the daily reality of young people in the country from the late 1980s onward. *Glamour Girls, 2* therefore offers a poignant visual signature of the social struggle of young women in most of sub-Saharan Africa where poverty became "the major incentive in forcing people to move to other countries in search of employment and to better lives" (Ejalu 170).

Released in 1996, at a time when the emerging underground transnational business in the trafficking of young women and the commercialization of sex had gained international attention but eluded the surveillance and mitigating efforts of sovereign states and even international organizations such as the United Nations, the movie unraveled the hidden transcripts of a global sex market that had begun to tap into the global "feminization of poverty" by preying on innocent girls all over the Third World. Even for early academic researchers interested in having a handle on transnational sex trafficking at the time, the phenomenon posed a huge challenge, because most of the pertinent population sample relevant to the study, such as sex workers, traffickers themselves, and their victims and survivors, constituted a hidden population very difficult to identify (Tyldum and Brunovskis 18).

But *Glamour Girls, 2* essentially blew the lid off this underground industry by providing concrete details of how the industry operates. Having been tricked abroad and forced into prostitution, the girls in *Glamour Girls, 2* are expected to work for two to three years each to pay back the forty-five thousand U.S. dollars expended by their "madams" in taking them abroad. This means grueling sex encounters with different men for countless hours every day. Security agents monitor the girls day and night, and any attempt to escape is met with stiff penalties, even death. The syndicate has connections with the Italian police, so lodging a formal report isn't helpful, as the information is channeled back to the "madams." The film thus reveals not just the sordid details of a particular instance of the commercialization of intimacy within a specific postcolonial context (Nigeria), but also the gritty details of the true mechanisms of a transnational vice ring, graphically illustrating the causes as well as the complex processes of recruitment, transportation, exploitation, and enslavement of young girls doing forced sex work in the dark bellies of the world's global cities. As we see in the movie, while Doris (Gloria Anozie) is in Lagos recruiting young, beautiful, but jobless girls who are desperately searching for alternative avenues of making headway in life for commercial sex work in Western cities, at the other end of the transnational spectrum is Maureen (Dolly Unachukwu), who runs a sophisticated escort service–cum–sex brothel in Italy. Both Doris and Maureen fund these new transnational travels by procuring passports, processing visas and flight tickets, and securing final accommodation in Italy for the girls to work. As soon as the girls arrive in Europe, their passports and other immigration documents are confiscated and stored away or recycled.[3] Whereas the "madams" get paid directly for the girls' services, the girls themselves are responsible for their own general welfare. This sordid reality is conveyed to us in an encounter between Sandra and two white patrons. We see Sandra awkwardly sandwiched between two white men, suggesting of course that she's been involved in a demeaning sexual encounter with them overnight. As Sandra leaves the hotel room the next morning, she demands her money, only to be told that her "manager" (Maureen) had already been paid for the services she rendered to the young clients. Here then is a great example of how "the bonded laborer is made responsible for his or her own upkeep, thus lowering the [modern-day] slaveholder's cost" (Bales 17). *Glamour Girls, 2* therefore exposed the real mechanisms – mobilization, implementation, and insertion and integration – of a deadly dimension of a new transnational dynamic that had begun to prey on the vulnerabilities surrounding the lives of young women in Nigeria and other marginal economies of the world.

In this chapter, therefore, I explore how *Glamour Girls, 2: The Italian Connection* (and by extension Nollywood) privileged insights into the gruesome world of this thriving but underground industrial complex currently estimated to be worth well over thirty-two billion U.S. dollars. In pursuit of this agenda, the chapter takes up the familiar theme of sex and violence, two key thematic threads in the Nollywood repertoire, but in particular relation to the transnational context.[4] As Nollywood's first English-language feature, *Glamour Girls* (especially the sequel, *The Italian Connection*) is important not only because it widened the local audience base for Nollywood video movies by opening up a new "sociocultural territory and a new market," as Jonathan Haynes ("Nnebue" 33) argues, but also because it marked the decisive beginning of the complex relationship that this West African screen media practice has had with the wider world on many different fronts, culturally, technologically, economically, and politically. Using *Glamour Girls, 2,* I thus propose to draw a link between Nollywood as a specific regional media practice in Anglophone West Africa and the uniquely powerful ways in which this marginal media tradition both inaugurated an important humanistic debate and facilitated deep insights into an entrenched subversive global economy that has remained pervasive and almost indomitable for more than three decades, and for which CNN, supposedly a politically sensitive First World media conglomerate, is now waging a belated media war.

GLAMOUR GIRLS: TRANSNATIONAL TRAFFICKING IN WOMEN AND THE COMMODITIZATION OF DESIRE

Glamour Girls is one of the very early video films to come out of Nollywood, and its narrative is familiar but also different in many ways. First, both segments of the movie embody the prototype of women in the Nollywood oeuvre in which, whether as helpless or hapless objects or as autonomous agents, "women don't fare well" (Garritano 167). As I will show later in my analysis, most of the female characters are almost always doomed to failure. Second, its sequel, *The Italian Connection,* embodies a recurrent theme in African cinema and video – "Africans abroad" – a subject that Jonathan Haynes has so well theorized ("Africans Abroad"; this volume). As with all Nigerian and Ghanaian video films concerned with transnational migration, *Glamour Girls, 2* suggests that the entire project of "establishing oneself abroad is extremely arduous" (Haynes, "Africans Abroad" 4). Third, both *Glamour Girls, 1* and *Glamour Girls, 2* generally fit the bill of Nollywood films that visually articulate what Jonathan Haynes ("Nnebue") describes as "the anatomy of power" in Nigerian society and culture. However, I want to argue that *Glamour Girls, 2* is different in some ways, because it dramatizes the dynamics of social power by gliding away from both the domestic and the local realms we see in other Nollywood classics to the international arena (however obliquely), linking power to sex and violence in the context of a global neoliberal economic arena. Thus, if *Glamour Girls, 1* anatomizes the immense contradictions and challenges of urban life for young women in Nigerian cities, *Glamour Girls, 2* brings to light the morass and oftentimes ironic side of the centrifugal forces of globalization for young women from developing economies of the so-called Third World who encounter the world (or enter the global domain) on unequal terms and in an unfamiliar terrain and hence whose lives are almost always completely fated to end tragically. Although originally conceived as a cultural representation of the fallen city woman, a trope very typical of early African popular art, the narrative of *Glamour Girls* generally conveys the dreadful side effects of the intractable crisis of widespread economic decline for young Nigerian women and the new subjectivities that they have begun to develop as inevitable responses to the dire socioeconomic circumstances around them.

Infused with other subplots that mirror the nebulous contours of Africa's urban experience, the central plot of *Glamour Girls, 1* revolves around Sandra (the late Jennifer Emeka-Ossai), a jobless university graduate who moves from Enugu, a regional city in the Southeast, to Lagos, Nigeria's megacity in the Southwest. Having completed her undergraduate education and one year of compulsory national service, Sandra can boast of nothing but three years of joblessness and mean treatment by different men. Her life mirrors the familiar tale of terror and tears often led by most hardworking but exploited women in Nigeria and other parts of sub-Saharan Africa. Desperate to make headway in life, Sandra decides to move to Lagos to try her luck in the big city. On arriving in Lagos, her friend and former schoolmate Doris (Gloria Anozie) introduces her to a small clique of urban socialites made up of businessmen and -women, politicians, and other powerful forces in the city. Essentially, Doris and her cohort of senior girls in Lagos are courtesans who cater to the sexual desires of prosperous politicians and business moguls with huge amounts of disposable income stolen from the state treasury. Sandra soon hooks up with a rich politician (a senator) who buys her a house and a car and basically pays her everyday bills. The reversal in Sandra's fleeting fortune happens, however, when she makes the mistake of falling in love with a younger man. Doris, now engaged in a power game with her friend Sandra, betrays her by reporting the illicit affair to the rich politician, and Sandra is ultimately kicked out of her exquisitely furnished home by the politician's thugs and her car impounded. As if her woes are not enough, her young lover disappears, leaving only a letter that says he has gone to meet his childhood love in the United States. What happens to Sandra in *Glamour Girls, 1* is perhaps typical of a global gendered space in which we often see a double standard whereby men are permitted sexual variety, while women are not. The politician's adultery as a married man, keeping a mistress outside his marital home, is perceived as one of those regrettable but "understandable foibles" of men, while Sandra's only relationship as a single girl to another single boy is interpreted as an "unpardonable breach of the law of property" and propriety, where discovery brings "highly punitive measures" (Giddens 7).

It is in *Glamour Girls, 2: The Italian Connection,* however, that we meet head-on the dark underside of a new order of both the commercialization of femininity and the wholesale feminization of transnational migration that has become one of the most pronounced socioeconomic trends since the 1990s. The film opens on what is supposedly a university campus, and a multifaceted plot structure unravels immediately. A female student, Stella Okafor (Susan Patrick), returns from an overnight date with a rich oil magnate (the Alhaji) and flaunts twenty thousand naira in front of her bewildered friends. Intent on making her own money from the Alhaji, Stella's friend Cecil (Uduak Johnson) sabotages Stella's date with the Alhaji the next day, but dies after the Alhaji hypnotizes her into making love to a snake, a powerful scene that emblematizes Nollywood's obsession with the theme of "occult economies" (Comaroff and Comaroff) in urban Africa. In this opening segment of *Glamour Girls, 2,* we also meet Fred (Zack Orji), who has just returned from abroad to take his childhood love, Jessica (Tina Amuziam), to Italy, where they both hope to lead the good life. But as we will learn later in the film, Fred is a failed "been-to" who has returned home to lure an innocent woman into prostitution as a way of generating capital for him to begin business in Nigeria. In the very opening segment of *Glamour Girls, 2,* therefore, what we see and feel is a general atmosphere not just of modernity, youth, and hedonism, but also of fast life, love for sale, betrayal, and urban danger. Indeed, the horrifying love scene between Cecil and the snake in the Alhaji's house prefigures the central theme of the whole movie: how the interiority of femininity is ransacked by a ruthless modern patriarchy bent on squeezing both pleasure and wealth from young women.

In spite of the multidimensional plot structure of *Glamour Girls, 2,* the main plot of the film still rotates around Sandra, the protagonist in part 1 of the movie. Jobless, homeless, and now completely frustrated, Sandra returns to her old friend Doris, who now heads a powerful underground sex trafficking network in Lagos known as the "Women of Substance International." Founded and constituted mainly by women, this club lures innocent girls to Europe with the promise of a good job and a better life, one supposedly removed from the travails and anxiety of a precarious urban life in Lagos, as we see in *Glamour Girls, 1*. It is Sandra's entanglement with this cruel sex-trafficking racket and her final transnational movement to Italy that ultimately bring us to the fate of a new generation of young girls trapped in Europe's hellhole of sex work marked by exploitation, violence, and modern-day slavery. As the second segment of the movie opens, we see Doris distributing green passports and tickets to a group of girls who are preparing to travel to Italy. She tells Sandra that the girls are "unemployed graduates of this country" (meaning Nigeria) and that she has sent more than twenty thousand to different places in Europe. Doris's reference to joblessness and poverty is very significant to the travel motif in the text, because all movements by women and girls in the film, both within and outside Nigeria, whether voluntary or forced, are essentially animated by the desire to clinch better economic opportunities that do not exist at the point of departure for the characters. Thus, the city space and its very magnetism as a site of economic opportunity for youth, both in the postcolony (Lagos) and the West (Italy), become central to the narrative of the film. *Glamour Girls, 2* thus participates in a broader global discussion about how the feminization of poverty in the global South now pulls young women into seeking new niches of survival in precarious zones where they have neither rights as citizens nor protection as humans.[5]

Supposedly set in both Nigeria and Italy (although with no conscious effort to realistically represent Italy), *Glamour Girls, 2* offers disturbing images that resonate with recent scholarly arguments linking globalization, postindustrial megacities, and the phenomenal rise in new survival economies by women (Ehrenreich and Hochschild). Saskia Sassen has in particular drawn on the concept of globalization and global cities in formulating arguments about global gender inequities and the dramatic rise in "survival circuits" (30). The concept hints at the novel informal and alternative modes of survival stratagems developed by young women from the global South in the face of a global economy in which the asymmetrical allocation of economic resources and opportunities has ensured that the rich get richer and the poor get poorer. And we see this dynamic eloquently dramatized in *Glamour Girls, 1 and 2*. Whereas all the significant male characters are invested with both economic and political capital to allow them a decent living, all the female characters often have to turn to their bodies as the last resort in their quest to secure a living both for themselves and for their families. The case of Jessica is quite interesting in this regard. On her arrival in Italy, she discovers that Europe is not as rosy as Fred had presented it. Confronted with the crude realities of life abroad, she capitulates to her husband's plea that she gets into sex work to generate the liquid capital that they need to begin business back home in Nigeria. Even when the couple makes US$350 from Jessica's demeaning sex with a dog in a porn movie, she offers to stay back and make more money to enable Fred to finish their house project in Lagos. Jessica's complicity in her own exploitation and abuse is beside the point here. What is important in her story, I think, are the ways in which it elaborates the extended length and depth of humiliation and abuse that women from peripheral economic zones like Nigeria, and by extension other developing economies, must go through in the fluid transnational arena in their quest to find economic independence and support for their families. Jessica's tribulations in Europe negate the dominant conception of globalization in our social imagination as a moment of the democratization of wealth and indicate a different reality in which modern-day transnational movements predominantly involve workers from impoverished nations "searching the globe for resources for themselves and their families" (Zimmerman, Litt, and Bose 10), and, if I may add, under very mortifying and hideous conditions.

What *Glamour Girls*, 2 articulates, then, is a new global order in transnational emigration, with women as the new working-class migrants who crisscross the globe from poor to rich countries, desperately seeking to make better lives out of their precarious economic situations.[6] Once in global cities in the North, however, this new generation of transnational migrants, devoid of the legal status or professional skills to function in a competitive electronic economy, now takes up odd jobs in the informal sectors of the global economy as care workers, domestic servants, and sex workers (Ehrenreich and Hochschild). *Glamour Girls*, 2 thus dramatizes powerfully the idea of "survival circuits" but does so in the context of global cities and the concomitant large-scale commercialization of women's bodies.

At the heart of the search for an improved life by young women in the movie is the urban space, but an urban space whose specific significance is hinged on its place as a "facilitator of sexual transactions" (Laumann et al. 6). Whether in Lagos or in Italy, the sole means of survival for the young women whom we encounter in the film is through the commoditization of their bodies and sexuality. There is never a need or opportunity for the girls in the film to do anything else but sex work. The sense one gets from the narrative is that all social fronts, whether domestic or public, have been covered; the personal emotional needs of the mass of male population in the city are lacking, though. The global city is, then, constructed as a social domain with an acute emotional deficit for which the girls must now provide needed bailouts. And the shift in the narrative universe of the film – for example, from Lagos to Italy – is significant in many ways, because it suggests that what the film narrativizes is not a uniquely Nigerian phenomenon. Indeed, as a number of insightful scholarly efforts have already shown, sex work is perhaps now the most thriving job available in big European cities for young women from poor countries in eastern and central Europe, South America, Asia, and the Middle East (Beeks and Amir; Monzini). But *Glamour Girls, 2* is particularly unique in its elaboration of the new economy of desire in global cities, because it is a potent postcolonial narrative of how international movements for young women from Africa struggling for a better life can become ugly and nasty, trailed not only by gender objectification but also by gratuitous violence and inhuman treatment.

The film goes beyond untying the mechanisms of the emerging objectification and commoditization of young women's bodies, indicating precisely how violence, according to Bales, has become the "one critical dimension" in modern-day types of slavery (19). The case of Laura (Thelma Nwosu) in the movie is indeed pertinent in this regard. Years earlier, Laura's parents had taken in Maureen (Dolly Unachukwu) at the age of thirteen, when her parents died. From Maureen's own personal discussion with her friend Doris, we know that Laura's parents pleasantly raised her. Now thriving in Europe (Italy), she returns to Nigeria with enormous gifts of clothes and exotic perfumes for Mama (Buki Ajayi), her benefactor. As a sign of her gratitude, especially at a difficult time when Mama has lost her husband, who was the main breadwinner in the family, Maureen offers to take young Laura (approximately eighteen years of age) abroad for further education and a better life. In Italy, however, Laura comes face-to-face with the rude reality of her new life and the truly demonic side of her trusted aunt. A stern-faced Maureen tells her that prostitution is her new life and that everyone is doing it, including Italians. Thoroughly grounded in her neo-Pentecostal faith and passionately reminded by her mother on leaving Nigeria to remain true to her Christian faith, Laura resists her aunt's orders. For refusing to obey her boss, the brothel's thug smashes Laura's head against the wall on the orders of Maureen. When the film ends, we do not know Laura's final fate; all we know is that Maureen orders the thug to take "this thing" (Laura's lifeless body) away. Laura's tragic end is a classic example of the new global dynamic in the international sex trade in which young women and teenage girls in vulnerable positions from developing countries are tricked into a new model of indentured labor in global cities. It is a concrete narrative of the real-life stories of numerous innocent girls whose lives, according to Gilbert King, get "snuffed out by violence and betrayal at the hands of someone they trusted, and sometimes by members of their own families" (8). *Glamour Girls,* 2 thus reveals the brutal force often associated with the social reality of countless young women who are now the victims of an atrocious and wicked intercontinental business in human lives in which well more than ten million innocent teenage girls are manipulated and tricked into forced sex work. Indeed, the thoughtless manner with which Laura's body is dispensed after her brutal murder tells a lot about how young women now constitute the huge crop of disposable people who make up the new global economy.

Kevin Bales has observed, for instance, that the mass of new disposable people who mark the modern-day global economy are unified by their suffering, "among them the abuse and death of their children, the damage to their bodies through trauma and untreated disease, the theft of their lives and work, the destruction of their dignity, and the fat profits others make from their sweats" (viii). One particular instance in *Glamour Girls,* 2 allegorizes this cruel dynamic of the new global economy in the commoditization of sex. Maureen and Vera (Clarion Chukwura-Abiola) are both members of the notorious Women of Substance International, the all-female club in which, as Doris tells us, "you'd meet the women of the new era, the women who rule men, women with power in this country." While in Italy, Maureen contacted Vera in Nigeria to help her get a "black girl who could make love to a chimpanzee in a blue movie" being shot by an American film agency.[7] Maureen has been offered US$150,000 for the deal. Although Vera is initially apprehensive about the health consequences for the young girl who might take on this apparently deadly job, she is tempted by her own cut of the contract (70 percent of the total sum). Combined with additional pressure from Maureen, she sends one of her girls (Judith) to Italy. According to Vera's own account, the poor girl "became a working corpse" after the deal was successfully completed. Instead of trying any medical options to redeem the girl's failing health, Maureen gives Judith a fatal injection as a form of mercy killing done to save the dying girl from prolonged suffering and pain. The fate of Judith and others in *Glamour Girls, 2* is indeed the real destiny of many young girls who have become the tools and objects for others to make money in the new global sex economy in which profits are prioritized over human lives.

Therefore, unlike the glamorized version of global city life often attributed to *Glamour Girls, 2*, the film actually uncovers the invisible and dark undersides of a seemingly pleasant worldwide subculture in which young women have become crucial pawns in an emerging economy of desire. By doing this, *Glamour Girls, 2* particularly marked the earliest beginnings of Nollywood's engagement with social issues that cut across both local and international lines. It not only unveiled the complex systems and forces associated with the new specter of sexual exploitation of innocent women that had begun to take shape in the late twentieth century, but also unraveled the rude realities of violence, trauma, exploitation, dehumanization, remorselessness, and even racism associated with this new phenomenon and demonstrated how all of these dynamics intersect with a new but asymmetrical global economic and social order that intensifies privileges and hope in one place (the North) and chronic scarcity and hopelessness in another (the South). Poverty, according to Parrot and Cummings, "was and continues to be the key in the development of [the new] sexual slavery" (6), and at the very center of all this (as we see in *Glamour Girls*) is the stereotypical victim – the innocent, young, and sometimes naive and helpless girl from the developing world like Nigeria, India, or even Nepal, as we see in CNN's *Nepal's Stolen Children*.

But one must add in the final analysis, however, that as depressing and scandalous as *Glamour Girls, 2* seems, there are also crucial moments in the film when we encounter interesting identity politics by the young women, often resulting in new agency and powerful subjectivi-

ties. I understand precisely how this might seem contradictory to the
analysis I have drawn so far to buttress my point about the mistreatment
and exploitation of young women in the movie. But the point really is
that young women may not be as entirely helpless as it appears under
very vulnerable and inauspicious conditions. As Hubbard has argued,
people who find themselves in the global sex industry whether voluntarily coerced or tricked "may resist, rework and use their confinement
to recast their identities" (180). These are the emancipatory moments,
often constructed and negotiated by exploited young women, in which
they gain command of both themselves and their environment in very
symbolic ways.[8] Thus, although I do not mean to trivialize the excru-
ciating conditions under which the young women in *Glamour Girls, 2*
live, we must recognize that there are indeed those who consciously
choose this path as a way out of not just dire economic straits but also a
stereotypical patriarchal world in which women's freedom and economic
independence have remained a problem. So sex work, like every other
job, as we see in the movie, has its own risks and challenges. For some it is
empowering, for others exploitative, and hence it can both be a "life-line
for some" and "a life sentence for others" (Hubbard 8). The young girls in
Glamour Girls, 2 who dance lasciviously in the sitting room, drinking and
flaunting dollar bills on their bodies, are perhaps representative of those
who consciously choose the path of selling their bodies for purposes of
making money to support both themselves and their families. As one of
the girls tells Maureen, she hopes the new arrivals from Nigeria know
they are here to "make money." Various studies show that the majority
of the girls who engage in transnational sex work do so as a means of
supporting extended families back in the postcolony (Ejalu; Monzini). A
recent World Bank report estimated that in 2008 alone, Nigerians abroad
remitted approximately US$3.3 billion (about 400 billion naira) to the
country, the highest in sub-Saharan Africa.[9] While this sum includes
the remittances of professionals doing legitimate work all over North
America and Europe, one may never know how much of this came from
the young women who stride the streets and brothels of Europe and
North America doing sex work. For some, this is their moment of empowerment in which they can secure for themselves and their families
the exclusive pleasures of the First World that their home country may
never allow them to even aspire to.

Although Laura's life ends tragically, apparently murdered under the watchful eyes of her own aunt, her protest against Maureen and her thug also privileges insightful moments of subjectivity and agency in this movie. Even though she has been tricked into the dark belly of Europe's underworld of sex work and slavery, she is still adamant in spite of the apparent violence and uncertain circumstances in which she finds herself. In spite of her aunt's vehemence and eventual violence, her refusal to capitulate and be exploited under what seems an apparently inescapable circumstance is a symbolic gesture of control over her body, senses, and dignity. Although Laura is eventually brutalized and silenced, that moment of violence does not go unchallenged. As the brothel's thug attempts to touch her, she smashes an empty bottle of beer on the thug's head, a sign of resistance to being stampeded into a subservient cultural positioning that she did not consciously choose. The thug, Maureen, and, symbolically, the entire global sex market may have succeeded in silencing Laura, but while alive, she took control of her body, soul, and dignity.

GLOBALIZATION, NOLLYWOOD, AND MINORITY DISCOURSES

In her essay "Nigerian Video Film as Minor Transnational Practice," Moradewun Adejunmobi argues that Nollywood is a perfect example of how commercial forms of marginal culture production "offer greater opportunity for autonomous voices from globally minoritized populations to emerge, in dialogue with local publics and outside the dominant centers of cultural production." Although Adejunmobi is more concerned with production processes rather than the discourses embedded in what she calls the new "global ethnic" productivities, it is undeniable that the thread of her analysis gravitates toward a shift from one of production and circulation of texts by peripheral media cultures to the "minority discourses" engendered by such alternative production practices. Therefore, in response to Marjorie Stone's challenge about paying attention to what cultural texts in the form of films, prose fiction, plays, and other art forms might tell us about the global malaise of transnational sex trafficking and its policy implications (36), I have demonstrated how Nollywood, as a particular instance of a minor transnational practice, has extended its cultural reach beyond its immediate context of production, inaugurating and actively participating in the international debate about the inequities that predominate the new transnational mobility patterns that now trail globalization's history. And by shifting the debate from one of the production and circulation of Nollywood films transnationally to one that emphasizes the "minority discourses" embedded in the texts, I have reinvented the debate about the "beyondness" of Nollywood from transnationalism to focus on transnationality, what Okwui Enwezor has described as the experience of "diasporicity." Enwezor uses the term in referring to the associated forms of violence such as "fragmentation, dislocations, reterritorialization [that accompany postcolonial exilic experiences and how] all these motifs of transnational human culture and fraught modernity, collude to make new meanings of [postcolonial] identity" (33). In this chapter, therefore, I have been concerned with demonstrating how Nollywood – as a particular form of local-global cultural practice – made inroads into the global cultural arena, initiated a sophisticated humanistic debate about the social and economic injustices associated with the new feminization of transnational travels, and thus privileged insights into the squalid social transcripts of what it means to be an ethnic "Other" in a bizarre global modernity where the strong prey upon the weak.

John McCall hinted at this revelatory power of Nollywood during the conference in Mainz when he talked about the industry's great potentials for visually articulating what it means to be African, or, as he puts it elsewhere, "what it means to be Nigerian" (109), in an uncertain, fluctuating, and risky global modernity. I have therefore used *Glamour Girls, 2* in specifically signifying Nollywood's discursive potential, especially the transcending of its humble beginnings as an unrefined and rejected peripheral popular art form, in taking on a global discourse of the marginalization, exploitation, and abuse of postcolonial subjects from sub-Saharan Africa who make their entry into global cities as disadvantaged global citizens. My particular intent has been to recalibrate the debate about Nollywood's beyondness by illustrating not only how it unraveled the dubious and invisible transnational economy of modern sex slavery, but also how these representations offer one of the most fruitful cultural sites for understanding how countless postcolonial subjects from all over the developing world come to experience what Iain Chambers has described as "the violence of alterity" (4). I argue that to experience that moment of violence, especially for young women from the African postcolony, is essentially to encounter what Chambers himself describes as the "language of powerlessness" (6–7). In general, therefore, the main objective of my critique has been to illustrate a particular example of how the Nigerian video industry, long before even its deriders and admirers acknowledged its discursive power, had extended its tentacles to the international domain, contributing acutely to the understanding of how postcolonial African subjects have become "collateral casualties" in a new global economic and cultural order. What *Glamour Girls*, 2 shows is a graphic social portrait of not only how young Nigerian (African) girls are now the victims of economic decline from within the continent itself, but also how they have become the major victims of emerging global postmodern sexual cultures where there has been a shift from procreative intimacies to modern-day models of sexuality in which, Bernstein argues, "recreational sexuality bears no antagonism to the sphere of public commerce" (7).

NOTES

1. The documentary premiered on June 26, 2011.

2. The 2010 *Trafficking in Persons Report* compiled by the U.S. State Department indicates that 56 percent of the 12.3 million people forced and tricked into bonded labor and prostitution around the world are women and young girls.

3. Here I am referring to the process by which passports once used for entry into the West are sent back to the home countries for other entrants under false names (see Monzini).

4. See Frances Harding's "Appearing Fabulous" for a detailed analysis of sex and violence in African cinema and video.

5. For a fuller discussion of the concept of the feminization of poverty and its consequences for new immigration

patterns, see United Nations; Melrose and Barrett; Parrot and Cummings.

6. The new movements by women from poor to rich countries are what scholars now refer to as the feminization of transnational migration (Massey, Arango, and Hugo; Sweetman).

7. These are the exact words of Vera in her account of the deal to the Women of Substance International.

8. There are those who argue that sex work and other modern-day erotic-care duties are indeed imbued with powerful moments of agency and empowerment (see, for example, Egan; Hubbard).

9. "Nigerians abroad remitted Naira 400 billion home in one year – World Bank" (*Nigerian Tribune*, April 7, 2008).

WORKS CITED

Adejunmobi, Moradewun. "Nigerian Video
  Film as Minor Transnational Practice."
  Postcolonial Text 3.2 (2007): n. pag. Web.
Bales, Kevin. *Disposable People: New Slav-
  ery in the Global Economy.* Berkeley and
  Los Angeles: University of California
  Press, 1999.
Beeks, Karen, and Delila Amir, eds. *Traf-
  ficking and the Global Sex Industry.* Lan-
  ham, Md.: Lexington Books, 2006.
Bernstein, Elizabeth. *Temporarily Yours:
  Intimacy, Authenticity, and the Com-
  merce of Sex.* Chicago: University of
  Chicago Press, 2007.
Chambers, Iain. *Migrancy, Culture, Iden-
  tity.* London and New York: Routledge,
  1994.
Comaroff, Jean, and John Comaroff. "Oc-
  cult Economies and the Violence of Ab-
  straction: Notes from the South African
  Postcolony." *American Ethnologist* 26.2
  (1999): 297–303.
Egan, Danielle. *Dancing for Dollars and
  Paying for Love: The Relationship be-
  tween Exotic Dancers and Their Regulars.*
  New York: Palgrave Macmillan, 2006.
Ehrenreich, Barbara, and Arlie Russel
  Hochschild, eds. *Global Woman: Nan-
  nies, Maids, and Sex Workers in the New
  Economy.* New York: Owl Books, 2004.
Ejalu, A. E. William. "From Home to Hell:
  The Telling Story of an African Wom-
  an's Journey and Stay in Europe." *Traf-
  ficking and the Global Sex Industry.* Ed.
  Karen Beeks and Delila Amir. Lanham,
  Md.: Lexington Books, 2006.
Elabor-Idemudia, Patience. "Race and
  Gender Analysis of Trafficking: A Case
  Study of Nigeria." *Canadian Women
  Studies* 22.3–4 (2003): 116–23.
Enwezor, Okwui. "Between Localism and
  Worldliness." *Global Encounters in the
  World of Art: Collisions of Tradition and
  Modernity.* Ed. Ria Lavrijsen. Amster-

dam: Royal Tropical Institute, 1998.
  31–42.
Garritano, Carmela. "Women, Melodra-
  ma, and Political Critique." *Nigerian
  Video Films.* Ed. Jonathan Haynes.
  Athens: Ohio University Press, 2000.
Giddens, Anthony. *The Transformation of
  Intimacy: Sexuality, Love, and Eroticism
  in Modern Society.* Cambridge: Polity
  Press, 1992.
Harding, Frances. "Appearing Fabulous:
  From Tender Romance to Horrifying
  Sex." *Film International* 5.4 (2007): 10–19.
Haynes, Jonathan. "Africans Abroad: A
  Theme in Film and Video." *Africa e Med-
  itarraneo* 45 (December 2003): 22–29.
———. "Nnebue: The Anatomy of Power."
  Film International 5.4 (2007): 30–40.
Hubbard, Philip. *Sex and the City: Geogra-
  phies of Prostitution in the Urban West.*
  Aldershot: Ashgate, 1999.
King, Gilbert. *Woman, Child for Sale: The
  New Slave Trade in the 21st Century.* New
  York: Chamberlain Brothers, 2004.
Laumann, Edward, et al., eds. *The Sexual
  Organization of the City.* Chicago: Uni-
  versity of Chicago Press, 2004.
Malarek, Victor. *The Natashas: Inside the
  New Global Sex Trade.* New York: Ar-
  cade, 2003.
Massey, Douglas, Joaquin Arango, and
  Graeme Hugo, eds. *Worlds in Motion:
  Understanding International Migration
  at the End of the Millennium.* Oxford:
  Clarendon Press, 1999.
McCall, John C. "Nollywood Confiden-
  tial: The Unlikely Rise of Nigerian
  Video Film." *Transition Magazine* 13.1
  (2004): 98–109.
Melrose, Margaret, and David Barrett,
  eds. *Anchors in Floating Lives: Interven-
  tions with Young People Sexually Abused
  through Prostitution.* Dorset: Russell
  House, 2004.

Monzini, Paola. *Sex Traffic: Prostitution, Crime, and Exploitation.* Trans. Patrick Camiller. London and New York: Zed Books, 2005.

Parrot, Andrea, and Nina Cummings. *Sexual Enslavement of Girls and Women Worldwide.* Westport, Conn.: Praeger, 2008.

Sassen, Saskia. "Global Cities and Survival Circuits." *Global Dimensions of Gender and Carework.* Ed. Mary K. Zimmerman, Jacquelyn S. Litt, and Christine E. Bose. Stanford, Calif.: Stanford University Press, 2006.

Stone, Marjorie. "Twenty-First Century Global Sex Trafficking: Migration, Capitalism, Class, and Challenges for Feminism." *English Studies in Canada* 31.2–3 (2005): 31–38.

Sweetman, Caroline, ed. *Gender and Migration.* Oxford: Oxfam International, 1998.

Tyldum, Guri, and Anette Brunovskis. "Describing the Unobserved: Methodological Challenges in Empirical Studies and Human Trafficking." *International Migration* 43.1–2 (2005): 17–34.

United Nations. *Resolution Adopted by the General Assembly on the Report of the Second Committee (A/50/617/Add.6) – Women in Development.* New York: United Nations, 1996.

U.S. State Department. "Trafficking in Persons: Ten Years of Partnering to Combat Modern Slavery." June 2010. http://www.state.gov/j/tip/rls/tiprpt /2010/.

Zimmerman, K. Mary, Jacquelyn S. Litt, and Christine E. Bose, eds. *Global Dimensions of Gender and Carework.* Stanford, Calif.: Stanford University Press, 2006.

FILMOGRAPHY

Glamour Girls. Dir. Chika Onukwufor. NEK Video Links (Nigeria). 1994.

Glamour Girls, 2: The Italian Connection. Dir. Christian Onu. NEK Video Links (Nigeria). 1996.

Nepal's Stolen Children. Written by Neil Curry. CNN International (United States). 2011.

PART THREE

Nollywood and Its Audiences

Nollywood in Urban Southern Africa: Nigerian Video Films and Their Audiences in Cape Town and Windhoek

HEIKE BECKER

ON A BALMY SPRING EVENING IN SEPTEMBER 2008, I WENT TO visit Kondjeni Nghitevelekwa, a young engineer working with NAM-POWER, the state-controlled Namibian electricity provider, in his apartment in Windhoek's Dorado Park. This is one of several residential areas for lower-middle-class people and young upwardly mobile professionals that have been built on the outskirts of the Namibian capital since independence in 1990. These relatively new residential developments are designated "multiracial," which means that – unlike in the racially segregated townships of the apartheid era – both black and colored people live there; only rarely, however, will white singles or young couples consider them a place to start out.[1]

On entering Dorado Park from the older, formerly "white" suburb of Hochland Park, this area at the foot of the hilly Khomas Hochland appears almost barren. Dorado Park, like other similar residential developments, comprises modestly sized bungalows and blocks of apartments, locally known as "courts." These apartment complexes are closed off from the street by a remote-controlled gate. About half of the apartments in Evamaria Court had a satellite dish on the roof, I noticed when I arrived, and in front of many apartments were parked medium-size, relatively new sedans, such as Kondjeni's Opel.

We sat in my host's spacious living room on couches near the front door; facing a wall unit built around a large-screen television set. Decorations were few except for a couple of photographs of Kondjeni and his girlfriend on the wall unit. One picture showed him at his graduation from Stellenbosch University near Cape Town, where he had qualified two years earlier in electrical and electronics engineering. Another picture showed his partner graduating from the University of Namibia (UNAM). Evidently, Kondjeni was proud of both their academic achievements.[2]

When I arrived just after five o'clock, the television was tuned into the DStv Africa Magic channel, which was showing a Nigerian video film. None of us was familiar with this movie. Kondjeni did not show much interest in the story line. Most of the movies' plots were actually rather boring, he exclaimed; instead, he loved the African movies because he could "relate" to them and the kind of life they depict. (He described himself as a "huge fan" who had taken out the subscription to the pay-TV DStv purely for its "African channels.") He added that they gave him an opportunity to see what was going on in village life, which "we who are living in the city" are missing out on. He stressed: "They teach us about the past and about the retention of African culture in city life."

Kondjeni's friend Hangula Haipinge, who had recently been appointed as a lecturer at UNAM, joined us later.[3] While we settled down with our beers and soft drinks, Kondjeni did a running commentary on the scenes flickering across the screen: "Look, they've got big houses – like in Cape Town!" "Nice cell phones, hey!" He also pointed out differences between the images on-screen and "Westernized" urban environments: "Look, here a guard is opening the gate [to the mansion's premises]; in Klein Windhoek, people have remote-controlled gates."[4] Kondjeni and Hangula considered this to be far from trivial, but rather an expression of rural difference to Westernized city life in urban Namibia, or in South Africa, where they both had attended college.

AFRICAN MOVIES AND AFROMODERNITY
IN SOUTHERN AFRICA

This vignette opens up my discussion of Nigerian video films and their audiences in urban southern Africa.[5] The years since the mid-2000s have seen a marked increase in the popularity of Nigerian video films across the southern African region. In Cape Town, where I live and teach at the University of the Western Cape (UWC), a plethora of outlets all over the metropolitan area have sprung up, where the films are for sale and rent. In 2007, during a random half-hour drive around the Bellville part of the UWC campus alone, I came across three "Nigerian video shops." Several others could be found in central Cape Town and in other suburbs. Conversations with shop owners and employees revealed that although immigrants from across the African continent constitute one ready market for the West African film productions, they are also extremely popular among South Africans. Similarly high levels of popularity of Nigerian video films I began to observe in 2006 in the Namibian capital, Windhoek, during one of my regular professional and personal visits to that country.

Observations and conversations revealed that in both South Africa and Namibia, the films were particularly popular among young well-educated elites.[6] I wanted to determine the reasons for this popularity, especially as well-educated people in Nigeria had initially shunned the video films, which were regarded as cheap mass entertainment.[7] In southern Africa, Nollywood productions apparently appealed particularly to college students and young professionals. The films had also begun to shape speech patterns and habits, in a Bourdieuian sense, of young highly educated people. I wondered, what was at stake in the encounter between the southern African audiences and the West African video films? How did consumers negotiate their meaning? This chapter explores the films' audiences in Cape Town and Windhoek as sites of meaning production through the appropriation of representations in the "African movies" as a form of popular art.[8] It draws on several stints of fieldwork in Cape Town and Windhoek between 2005 and 2008,[9] as well as the analysis of selected Nigerian video films that were popular among college students and young professionals.[10]

The transnational dimensions of the West African video industry raise a set of intriguing questions about how films travel in terms of the transnational expansion of their audiences and local consumption. How can we account for the striking appeal that these movies from another geographically distant part of the continent have for young people in contemporary southern Africa? Why do they seem particularly attractive to emerging young elites? What do these video films mean to those who consume them? How does their meaning translate as they move in circulation and live in different media environments? What is the meaning that is being produced through the encounters between the movies' content and those involved in their consumption in particular in historically situated social, cultural, and political contexts?

In the early 1990s, Brian Larkin studied the attraction of Indian films in northern Nigeria. He suggested that, for Hausa viewers, Indian films offered images of a parallel modernity to the West, because they could re-work Indian films in relation to their existing cultural experience "with-out engaging with the heavy ideological load of 'becoming Western'" ("Indian Films" 410). Hence, the films opened up an imaginary "third space," concurrently similar to and sufficiently different from the view-ers' own cultural environment to allow them to reimagine themselves. Does Larkin's argument allow us to begin understanding the attraction of Nigerian video films for young emerging elites in southern Africa?

There is suggestive evidence that young people in contemporary South Africa seek and espouse new forms of conscious African identities through various forms of popular culture, including African-language hip-hop, or Rastafarianism, which link them, concurrently, to global nodes of cosmopolitanism and pan-Africanism (Becker and Dastile). Similar processes seem to be revolving around the consumption of the Nigerian video films, which, I argue, constitute a brand of cultural pan-Africanism on-screen that, through its transnational circuits, has be-come an opening for young highly educated, cosmopolitan people in southern Africa to forge their own brand of "Afromodernity," to use a term coined by the Comaroffs.

Afromodernity, the Comaroffs argue, is taking shape in the inter-stices between the democratic institutions of the (South African) postcol-ony and the "kingdom of culture" (200). The emerging living, vernacular modernity they identify is fashioned out of a wide range of (re)sources and is changing the terms in which postcolonial realities are experienced, understood, and negotiated. African modernities, thus, comprise signs, practices, and dispositions that have come about in the encounters be-tween the local and its elsewheres, in the process forging conceptions of "culture" as the "language of difference spoken in the active voice" (188). Afromodernity emphasizes the insistence on different ways of being in the modern world, particularly the notion of marrying global technolo-gies and learning from the African past. The localized form that the trans-national consumption of Nigerian video films is taking among emerg-ing young elites in southern Africa should be considered as one sphere where the processes of Afromodernity are currently taking place through the audiences' form of imag(in)ing Africa – its primordial difference as a timeless and whole "cultural" identity, that is – in their appropriation of this popular art form's representations.

"THE VILLAGE LIFE": AFRICAN MOVIES
AND THE YEARNING FOR HOME

Listening to Kondjeni and Hangula commenting that evening, I was rather surprised about their emphasis on the Nigerian movies' capacity to "teach" young Namibians like them about "village ways" and "African culture," for at least two reasons. First, both men – who were in their late twenties but still considered themselves youths – had grown up in rural Owambo and regularly visited their home villages in northern Namibia. Second, while many of the movies indeed have "traditional village" settings, and some are set in a historical past, most are set in contemporary Nigerian cities, especially Lagos. Signs of urban wealth such as luxurious mansions, fancy cell phones, and big shiny cars stand out in the films and appear "ubiquitously as the symbol of the desired good life, the reward of both good and evil, the sign of social status and individual mobility" (Haynes, "Introduction" 2).

Yet if we went by the verbal appreciations of the movies to which Kondjeni, Hangula, and other young men and women I spoke to in both Windhoek and Cape Town kept returning, one got the impression that the "African movies" were characterized mainly by "traditional" village settings and that their characters' actions and behavior were generally determined by a reified African culture in manners, values, and materiality. It was precisely these two aspects that students and young professionals mentioned on many occasions when they lauded the movies as "realistic," unlike American films, which they considered "exaggerated," "fake," and bent on "creating an image of what they want the world to think their [Americans'] lives are like." Nigerian movies, in contrast, were said to depict "real life in Africa," as UWC student Natalie put it, "especially the hardships and trouble that we [Africans] face on a daily basis: issues of witchcraft, relationship issues, family issues, all issues pertaining to African lifestyle."[11] Fellow UWC student Laurein added: "They show people as they really are. Most of the [Nigerian] movies I have watched show life in the rural areas, which is never shown in other films. When I watch these movies, I am able to relate with what I see." Laurein explained that while she personally had no experience of the more mundane aspects of village life, "like going to the toilet in the bush," she knew of people "who do this, right here in South Africa."

Petunia, an undergraduate in UWC's Commerce Department, appreciated the rural settings, because she grew up in a village, "even though,"
she explained, her home community was "more advanced than the ones
they show in the movies."

The students' comments made it very clear that the movies fulfill a
nostalgic yearning for an idolized African village "home" among young
upwardly mobile southern Africans. This seemed to be equally true for
those who actually had identified rural homes and for some of the South
Africans, though none of the Namibians, who came from entirely urban
backgrounds. Even for those students and young professionals who laid
claim to rural "homes," urban and rural spaces had become less distinctive in their everyday lives; as Romie Nghiulikwa has shown for Namibia,
popular youth cultures have begun blurring rural-urban divides in the
lives of young people. The movies, on the other hand, clearly distinguish
between the rural and the urban by emphasizing the representation of
practices, which southern African audiences identified as "rural," "traditional," and "cultural."[12] These practices were not so much a part of
their lived experience, even when on a visit "home" to the postcolonial
hinterland, as a repertoire of images and imaginings of the village as the
pivotal "African reality." The participants evidently yearn for a return to
"the African village" as a past they never knew. The village thus signifies
the post-apartheid era's claims to and reinventions of "African identity,"
which build on these modern restorations of the idea of Africa as a whole,
intact, and timeless cultural entity.

AFRICAN MOVIES AND THE EVERYDAY MEDIA CULTURE

Many of the UWC students emphasized that the movies portrayed
"African realities" and bolstered "African culture" in the face of foreign (Western) cultural domination. In other words, they perceived
the Nigerian and African movies as spaces of cultural alterity. Some
explicitly said they were a welcome "change" from their everyday media
consumption.

Which images do young people in post-apartheid South Africa and
Namibia encounter on-screen when they do not watch Nigerian movies?
Going to the movies is not a part of the everyday practices of the young
people I worked with in Cape Town and Windhoek; the generation of

today's twenty- to thirty-year-olds grew up saturated by, chiefly American, soap operas on the South African and Namibian public broadcasters' television programs, which are the most popular form of everyday visual entertainment.

Ten years ago, UWC academic Teresa Barnes found to her dismay that "young black South African university students are learning to think like 'the [slender, rich] Yankees of Africa' partly by religiously imbibing daily doses of *Days of Our Lives* and *The Bold and the Beautiful*" (355). She noted that while South African–produced soap operas like *Generations* and *Isidingo*, which were introduced in the 1990s to promote nation building and multiracialism, were growing in popularity, students still found the American soaps "more real" than the South African productions, despite the fact that their characters were almost always white (352).

It appears that the fascination with American soap operas is now largely a thing of the past. Television rooms in the UWC student residence halls fill up when South African–produced soaps come on, especially *Isidingo* and *Generations*.[13] *Generations* dropped its original multiracial ambitions some years ago and is pure melodrama, with all the glitz and glamour of American soaps; its setting is superaffluent, and the cast is entirely "black" (in the narrow sense). Often those students, who call themselves fans of *Generations*, say they appreciate the soap because it shows that "black people, too, can be filthy rich."

By contrast, *Isidingo* is conceived as the exemplary nation builder, and although it also has its moments of glitz and glamour, its settings and characters are more varied. They feature, among others, a township *shebeen* (informal tavern) and some ordinary lower-middle-class homes. The series frequently takes up local and global current issues, including those related to the reproduction of gender and sexuality in the new world order, such as HIV/AIDS or same-sex relationships.[14] Conflicting relationships revolving around contestations of normative, traditional "culture" also feature regularly in what the *Isidingo* producers and writers perceive as urban life in contemporary South Africa, with all its manifold connections to both rural "homes" and South Africa's global elsewheres. Arguably, the ways in which the characters of the soap's multiracial cast are portrayed reinforce commonly held beliefs that "black people have more culture than whites," yet the series, despite its fair share of soap-style melodrama, incorporates an unusually open repertoire of styles, values, and modes of conduct, which make the South African postcolonial reality appear to be under constant (re)construction.

For many students, the fascination with *Isidingo* stems from its intriguing mélange of contemporary real-life "issues" – not in the least intergenerational "culture clashes" – and the utopia it presents in its portrayal of the "new South Africa" as a hypermodern, multiracial, multicultural kaleidoscope. Interracial and interethnic couples are the order of the day on *Isidingo,* whose relationship issues arise from a wide range of sources except racial and ethnic differences. Barnes describes it aptly: "Africans, whites, coloureds, and Indians cavort on these programs as if they inhabited a society where reconciliation is an unquestionable success" (351). To some extent, soaps like *Isidingo* appear to draw their popular appeal from the fact that they address a longing for another set of "home," a nostalgia for an as yet unrealized future: contrasting, but complementing, rather than denying the nostalgic, idolized African village, yearned for by many of the African movie lovers in Cape Town and Windhoek. "The 'new South Africa' does not yet exist," argued one of the students in my Culture, Media, and Globalization class, "except on *Isidingo.*"

Elaine Salo suggests that the post-apartheid years have seen the emergence of "an imagined cosmopolitan South African youth culture" (358). Programs such as *Isidingo* appear to satisfy some of the desires and fantasies that have emerged from this new cultural formation. Viewers draw on images of global cultural forms, which are being circulated through mainstream media, the Internet, global forms of consumption, and youth culture, in relation to local histories, available practices, and ideals, as shown by Salo's study of post-apartheid youth in a Cape Town township. In different ways, young people in post-apartheid southern Africa appear to relate to both South African soaps and Nollywood productions as part of the processes of re-creating modernities, which include yearnings for past and future returns "home."

SITES AND ROUTES OF NOLLYWOOD
IN SOUTHERN AFRICA

Nigerian video films made a serious impact on the southern African markets in 2004. Several of the UWC students and young Namibian professionals remembered their first encounter with the films that year.

Some had heard of the Nigerian video films and then noticed that they had suddenly become "big." Petunia, a UWC student who was then in her final year of boarding school, recalled that in mid-2004, "when I got home [to the eastern Cape] for the holidays, I realized that Nigerian movies were 'in.' Everybody was talking about them." From early on, a lively culture of exchanging DVDs sprang up among fans of Nigerian and African movies. After facilities for copying DVDs became fairly accessible, it became common. One Namibian woman said that she first watched African movies in 2005 during her last year at UNAM. A friend had copied DVDs of Nollywood films, which they watched together on a computer.

Although the public, state-owned broadcasters in South Africa and in Namibia no longer screen African video movies, the Namibian Broadcasting Corporation broadcast them for some time in the late 1990s on Saturday evenings, which the Namibian interviewees all recalled vividly (they were teenagers then); this visual form aroused plenty of curiosity.[15] Those movies were not Nigerian productions, though; they were mostly slow-paced Zambian and Ghanaian films, which were often set – fully or partially – in rural settings (I particularly recall long, drawn-out "traditional court" hearings). Common lore has it that these programs were eventually discontinued at the personal intervention of then Namibian president Sam Nujoma, because he objected to their depiction of "too much witchcraft and violence."

In the mid-2000s, English-language productions of the Nigerian video film industry appeared in Cape Town, and almost concurrently in Windhoek, when DVDs became available for sale through a range of channels, which were initially of an entirely informal nature. It appears that Nigerian expatriates figured prominently in the early promotion and distribution of the productions. Namibian cultural performer Shali Kapepo was introduced to them during a cultural festival in Swaziland in 2003 by a Nigerian musician, who proudly told him that in Nigeria "we have our own movies" and took him to watch some films. Afterward, Shali, who was then an undergraduate at the University of Namibia, purchased DVDs from Nigerian students at UNAM, who brought them from their home country for sale in Windhoek. Everyone remembered that before the advent and access to the satellite pay-TV Africa Magic channels and the multiple Internet sites that allow legal or illegal downloads, street vendors in the townships, especially in Cape Town, and stalls near taxi ranks were the primary suppliers of the movies.

In Cape Town, the vendors were generally described as Nigerians, which in the local lingo has come to be used as a generic term for any "Africans from up north." Thus, not all vendors were Nigerian nationals. In both Cape Town and Windhoek, the roving street and stall vendors and those operating more formal businesses selling or renting African movies are generally immigrants from West, Central, and East Africa. However, once during a chance encounter near a busy taxi rank on the outskirts of Windhoek, I met a Zimbabwean woman who traded in seven-in-one Nollywood DVDs. She said she shuttled back and forth on business between Harare and Windhoek. Except for one shop owner in Katutura who got his stock from suppliers in South Africa, the vendors and shop owners in both cities claimed that they received the films straight from Nigeria, including both the single movie discs sold in hardcover cases and colorful printed sleeves and the five-in-one or seven-in-one discs, which are sold in plastic mesh sleeves. In 2008, video films were sold according to two different pricing categories; either the price was per DVD (50 rand/ Namibian dollars; US$7.50), irrespective of whether the disc contained a single film or multiple films, or the price was per movie (100 rand/Namibian dollars; US$15); for the price of a movie, the buyer received parts 1–3 of the respective miniseries, usually shot as parts 1–3.[16]

DVDs were also widely available for rent in both Cape Town and Windhoek, at prices between 7 and 10 rand/Namibian dollars (US$1 to US$1.50) in various mixed businesses in townships and areas near central traffic nodes or with a substantial immigrant population.[17] Such outlets sold and rented African movies and, in some cases, also mainstream American and South African films, in addition to selling (West) African fashion and hair extensions; they often also offered shoe-repair, braiding or barbershop, and Internet facilities as well as scan, fax, photocopy, and lamination services.

The South African video rental chain stores, such as Mr. Video, or Vee's Video, that dominate the formal market in South Africa and Namibia did not stock Nigerian video films. In an affluent, commercial part of Windhoek, near the main branches of mostly big South African banks and businesses, I noticed an independent outlet called Video Zone offering mostly American films for rent. I also spotted two stands labeled

"African Movies." When I entered the shop to take a closer look, only half the movies on one of the stands were Nigerian productions; the rest of the films were South African or South African–themed block-busters such as *Sarafina* or *Tsotsi*, as well as African American movies. For example, I found *Boyz n the Hood* and several Spike Lee films. The shop assistant told me that the African movies were popular mostly with "black people," who worked in the city and picked them up after work.

The sale and rent of DVDs are still popular among people in Cape Town and Windhoek who want to access Nigerian films. For those who can afford them, the satellite pay-TV DStv Multichoice African channels have become vast sources of the movies. Africa Magic (DStv Channel 114) was originally launched in December 2003, broadcasting seven hours daily. Since April 2007, it has been broadcasting a continuous flow of Nigerian films to subscribers in South Africa and across the continent twenty-four hours a day. Africa Magic Plus (DStv Channel 115), which has been broadcasting since June 2008, is focused on movie productions of African countries other than Nigeria, such as those of Ghana and Uganda. The channel has become particularly well known for its popular Tanzanian Swahili-language soaps. Both channels come with the DStv Multichoice Compact option. In March 2009, a monthly subscription in South Africa cost 219 rand (US$32). Subscribers have to pay an additional onetime cost of 399 rand (US$59) for a standard decoder.[18]

In December 2008, Multichoice DStv had 2.3 million subscribers, of whom 1.7 million were in South Africa.[19] A substantial section of the South African middle class hence has continuous access to Nigerian video films, as a popular art form read by many as embodying the idea of "Africa" and "African culture," through a media technology that epito-mizes the post-apartheid society's insertion into global mediascapes.[20]

CONNECTING "MY CULTURE TO THE REST OF AFRICA"

I have shown that the considerable attraction of Nigerian or African movies for young upwardly mobile people in urban southern Africa is their potential for nostalgic imaginations of a return to an idolized "Afri-can village." Although it is commonplace that nostalgia is part of moder-nity, nostalgic yearnings for a "traditional" past they never knew is only part of the movies' appeal for young women and men in post-apartheid southern Africa.

One chilly September morning in Windhoek, I met another self-professed lover of Nigerian video films in a shiny downtown South African coffee-shop chain. Twenty-seven-year-old Shali Kapepo came across as sophisticated and widely traveled; he had spent time as an exchange student in the United States and had visited Britain and other European countries, as well as having been "all over southern Africa," including Malawi, Lesotho, Swaziland, and Angola. This very worldly young man – in his day job an auditor in the Namibian government services – has been a member of a well-known Namibian cultural performance group for a number of years, which has been a chief reason for his frequent travels on the African continent and beyond. When I asked Shali why he was so fond of the films, he did not hesitate to dictate into my notebook: "The African movies serve as a connection of my culture to the rest of Africa." He then paused for a moment and rephrased: "No, wait: I see them as a way of how I, or my culture, are connected to the rest of Africa."

The notion that by watching Nigerian movies they could literally see that "our culture" in southern Africa was connected to and "not so different" from "African culture" elsewhere on the continent appeared as a recurrent theme in Cape Town and Windhoek alike. They seemed to have also inspired the adaptations of the accent when speaking English, which several participants reported as the main influence the movies have had on their everyday manners. Shali told me that he frequently copied the "Nigerian jokes," which he had enjoyed while watching the films, in his conversations with friends; some young South African students even proudly proclaimed that they spoke with a "Nigerian English accent" in their everyday lives, irrespective of the common connotations with anti-Nigerian – epitomizing anti-African "foreigner" – sentiments in their country.[21]

Shali's insistence on his "culture's" connections with "the rest of Africa" is partly due to a contemporary process in post-apartheid southern Africa to claim an African identity. Owen Sichone argues that "for many South Africans the end of apartheid has involved becoming African [again]" (6). He maintains that this "re-Africanization" was a trend shared by South Africans of different hues, who generally had assimilated the belief that "Africa begins at the Limpopo myth" (ibid.). I have observed similar types of intentional re-Africanization in Namibia since independence in 1990; already in the 1980s, a Namibian oppositional newspaper's telling byline was "Bringing Africa South."[22] The emphasis on Africanity in contemporary South Africa and Namibia is to some extent thus owed to historically derived political reclamations of identities and citizenship, which the people in these countries previously did not have when they were cut off from the continent during the apartheid years in South Africa and Namibia.

WITCHCRAFT, THE MALL, AND THE INTERNET

A view of African culture as a narrative of difference – different from the young urbanites' daily experience of "Westernization" through brightly lit shopping malls, branded clothing, and their professional and personal engagement with cellular and digital technologies – is produced through encounters between the contents of Nigerian video films and the southern African spectators and their viewing contexts. The narrative of alterity provides for a powerful identification with the Nigerian movies. This was brought home to me during a conversation with Kondjeni in Windhoek who, like others, said that the films, "even those with an urban setting," always had "so much culture" and portrayed life from "a cultural angle." By "culture," Kondjeni was referring to reified cultural practices, which were derived from "African tradition" and distinct from "Westernization" – his everyday life in the city.[23]

Brian Larkin recently argued that Nigerian video films provide a metacommentary on the place of "culture" in contemporary Nigerian society. In "a society at once rapidly modernizing and still deeply traditional, . . . [t]hey represent the fantasy of playing with other forms as a way of interrogating local norms. In this way, Nigerian films depict and embody the daily 'experiments' that constitute the practice of everyday urban life" (*Signal and Noise* 216). While urban life, synonymously understood as modernity, is present in the films in the slick surface of shining German sedans, lavishly furnished mansions with all the technological trappings (stereo systems, computers), sumptuous clothing, and fancy cell phones, "aesthetically, these films dramatize structural transformations brought about by the architecture of insecurity in melodramatic terms, by objectifying and reifying an idea of culture . . . as a sign" (173).

The movies were made "for Africans, featuring Africans, showcasing African customs," as anthropology major Lerato put it. Laurein, another bachelor of arts student, elaborated:

> The messages in the movies are produced for Africans by Africans to educate them about issues that are rife in Africa and how to solve their problems in an African way. They teach *ubuntu*, peace and unity.[24] People are concerned about each other's well-being; they care for their neighbors and help them where they can. Respect is another aspect, especially respect of elders by children. The movies also convey commitment to marriage. They show acceptance of one's self, one's situations and circumstances, acceptance of one's body. They mirror Africa's way of living.

Jean-Claude, a Rwandan master's student in UWC's Tourism Studies program, was especially concerned about women's physical comportment: "The Nigerian movies show how very different Africa is from Europe. It's a different lifestyle, and people have different behaviors. Africans have more culture than Westerners. . . . Western girls expose their bodies on the beach not wearing much beach clothing. In Africa it is not normal exposing the body, only nowadays they are starting to imitate Westerners. . . . It is bad copying other people's culture."

Although the representation of the African difference in attire, values, and everyday cultural address was thus much cherished, "witchcraft" was the main aspect of discussions on "culture" as portrayed in the movies. Some made clear that they regarded the images of witches and magic as a dark underside, rather than as a valued part of African culture. Everyone agreed, however, that they presented realistic portrayals and challenges of contemporary Namibian and South African society and the conceptual uniqueness and unity of the continent. Shali in Windhoek said that one of the reasons he liked African movies was "because one sees that some concepts are the same all over Africa," "especially witchcraft," although he regarded witchcraft as an "idea or concept. I don't even know whether it is a practice."

It was brought home to me time and time again that for my young upwardly mobile interlocutors, the movies provided an opportunity to insist on forms of different "being in the world," without ceasing the historical and mundane connections with "Westernized" consumption and the associated cultural styles from elsewhere. In other words, they felt drawn to the Nollywood productions precisely because of their por-

trayal of supposedly "African" cultural practices within a familiar material "Western" world in what many regarded as a major challenge: to
engage in global forms of modernity in terms of consumption and knowledge – the mall and the Internet – in ways that will not compel them to
"abandon our culture."

NIGERIAN VIDEO FILMS AND AFROMODERNITY

Nollywood has become a major source of African identification in postcolonies such as South Africa and Namibia. The consumption of Nigerian video films provides young highly educated, cosmopolitan men and
women in Cape Town and Windhoek with the opportunity to claim,
reinvent, and debate their Africanity, thus imagining a contemporary
brand of Afromodernity on-screen.

I have demonstrated different ways in which the movies provide
a space for their southern African audiences to engage with the complex postcolonial realities that they experience and negotiate and to
forge their own prospects of vernacular Afromodernity, which appears
prevalent in both urban Namibia and metropolitan South Africa. First,
their reinventions of Africanity are connected to historically specific
efforts to "bring Africa south" in the former apartheid postcolonies, as
expressed in the wistful aspirations of "connecting my culture with the
rest of Africa." Second, nostalgia, which I define as a sentimental yearning for a period of the past and the memory of an earlier time, plays a
prominent part in the imagined on-screen realism of African village
life, which participants in both South Africa and Namibia said was a
major attraction of the movies; they offered a sociocultural reality, that
is, of which the participants have no actual experience or only in the
twisted shape of late-apartheid and post-apartheid rural poverty and
"underdevelopment." Thus, their yearnings appear to be less for relics
of a "traditional past" they never knew than for a home of their own,
as Africans, in the contemporary world, hence taking nostalgia rather
literally from its etymological relation to the notion of home.[25] Third,
and most significantly, the Nollywood productions' representations of
Nigeria as a society at once rapidly modernizing and still deeply traditional appeal to southern African audiences. As I have argued along the
line of the Comaroffs, African postcolonial modernities comprise signs,

practices, and dispositions that have come about in the encounters between the local and elsewhere in ways that may only be insufficiently
described in the conventional understandings of hybridity as a cultural
form, which has been created out of the interaction of two or more preexisting cultures. Instead, Afromodernity allocates a central place to
the "kingdom of culture" as an active language of difference. In this
respect, I have shown the complex ways in which the consumption of
Nigerian video films among emerging young elites in southern Africa
revolves significantly around the audiences' appropriation of the representations of Africa as primordially, culturally different from Western
modernity. The young men and women in Cape Town and Windhoek,
without exception, appreciated the movies as an effective medium for
the promotion, propagation, and even preservation of "African culture,"
in order to demonstrate the necessary cultural morales of the crises of
African modern life.

Their imagination of the movies as a metanarrative of African difference indicates that the consumption of Nigerian video films constitutes one sphere where the processes of Afromodernity are taking place.
Repeatedly, the young women and men referred to a sense of similarity
and difference, however, when they related the films to their everyday
experiences. Similar to Larkin's Hausa informants, they referred to a reified culture that "acts as a foil against which Westernization in its myriad
form can be defined" ("Itineraries" 344), yet they also demonstrated an
awareness of an "other" modernity that has begun to do away with the
internalized traditional-modern dichotomy. The reconceptualization
of "witchcraft" as "cultural capitalism" – as Kondjeni in Windhoek put
it – that is, the practice of "modern traditional doctors from all over Africa," who have set up shop in cities like Cape Town and Windhoek and
cater for significant monetary remuneration to the needs of the urban
elites and middle class, presents an interesting detail of how Nigerian
video films offer young southern African audiences a way of being modern that does not necessarily mean being Western. In this sense, they
provide spaces of alternative African modernities, similar to Larkin's notion of a "third space," which he argued that Indian films offered Hausa
viewers between Western modernity and the reified poles of tradition
("Indian Films").

NOTES

A note on the use of the racial categories "African," "black," and "colored" (in the following without quotation marks) is necessary: The persistence of the apartheid racial categorization is ubiquitous in contemporary usage in both South Africa and the apartheid state's former colony, Namibia. Although I do not wish to support the apartheid-induced usage, I use the categories as they are commonly understood in Cape Town and in Windhoek: "African" and "black" are used interchangeably by most residents of both cities to denominate people who speak an African language as their first language, whereas "colored" is the persistent designation of people of mixed descent, who mostly speak Afrikaans as their first language.

1. I am indebted to Waseema Barendse and Romie Nghiulikwa for their formidable assistance with the research in Cape Town and Windhoek. The U WC Research Fund provided much-appreciated financial support.

2. Kondjeni's partner, Romie Nghiulikwa, was at the time completing her master's degree in anthropology at UWC.

3. Name changed.

4. Klein Windhoek is an upper-middle-class, formerly white suburb of Windhoek.

5. From the 1990s, in Nigeria "Nollywood" has been widely used for the country's video film industry (Haynes, "Nollywood"); academic usage originally preferred "Nigerian video film" (Haynes, "Introduction"), in order to emphasize the technology ("video") and the feature-length dramatic narratives ("film"). In southern Africa, the term *Nollywood* has no currency outside academic, media, and artistic circles (see, for example, Stevenson). The South African students mostly used the tag "Nigerian movies"; some

also referred to "African movies," which was the sole appellation I ever heard in Namibia. I remain as close as possible to the research participants' respective usage when I directly speak of their perspectives; otherwise, I use the terms *(Nigerian) video films* and *Nollywood productions* interchangeably.

6. I use *emerging elites* and *upwardly mobile* interchangeably to refer to young black university students and young university-educated professionals.

7. In the 1990s, the movies were regularly taken to task by Nigeria's cultural establishment for being escapist and politically irresponsible and for being too open to baleful foreign influences, both in the lifestyle they represent and in their aesthetic form (Haynes, "Introduction" 9).

8. Following Karin Barber, I understand *popular art* to mean "new unofficial art forms which are syncretic concerned with social change, and associated with the masses. The centers of activity in this field are the cities, in their pivotal position between the rural hinterland on the one hand and the metropolitan countries on the other" ("Popular Arts" 23).

9. During fieldwork, I found only minimal differences between the receptions of the movies in the two cities, which are more likely to be owed to the slight differences in the audiences' demographic profiles than to those of the research sites; the Cape Town research participants were university students, whereas in Windhoek I conducted research with young professionals. All Namibian participants were oshiWambo speakers (the closely related languages spoken by about half of Namibia's population); among the U WC students were a graduate student from Rwanda and one colored Capetonian (who described herself as being "anti-colored" and "pro-

African"); the other participants spoke African languages, mostly isiXhosa, as their first language.

10. At the time of research in 2007 and 2008, the most popular video films in southern Africa included the multipart *Mr. Ibu* comedies, as well as the two parts of the iconic comedy-drama *Osuofia in London*. *Mr. Ibu* (part 1 released in 2004) features the hilarious escapades of divorcé Mr. Ibu (John Okafor) and his mischievous son, Muo (played by Osita Iheme), in Lagos and occasionally up-country. *Osuofia in London* (part 1, 2003; part 2, 2004) portrays the adventures of a "traditional" villager, Osuofia (played by megastar Nkem Owoh), in London, where he travels to claim the bountiful inheritance left to him by his deceased brother. Part 2 features Osuofia back home in the village with his brother's white fiancée as a second wife. The *Osuofia* narrative thrives on fish-out-of-water humor but also has its deeper moments of cultural critique (see also Okome, this volume).

11. The research participants in Windhoek generally were eager to have their full names included in the paper, whereas some of the UWC students asked for anonymity. I thus use first names only for the UWC students (some of which are pseudonyms), while referring to the Namibians by their actual first names and surnames, except for Hangula Haipinge, whose name has been changed per his request.

12. "Traditional courts" were mentioned specifically. Hearings at chiefs' courts are indeed a common feature of Nollywood productions in rural settings.

13. *Generations,* but not *Isidingo,* is broadcast also on the Namibian Broadcasting Corporation's only television channel, but seemed to be of little interest to most of the Windhoek research participants. Unlike Cape Town, the programs on the national public broadcast were hardly ever mentioned during discussions in Windhoek.

14. For example, just a few days after December 1, 2006, when South Africa became only the fifth country worldwide to make legal provision for same-sex marriages, *Isidingo* broadcast a gay wedding into millions of South African homes.

15. When I lived in Windhoek during the 1990s, most of the city's intellectuals and media people were rather disparaging of those movies and said that they were not up to the professional standards to which they were accustomed.

16. The Namibian dollar is pegged to the South African rand. Popular films go for less on the South African Internet book- and media store Kalahari Net. In March 2009, Nollywood blockbusters were available from Kalahari Net "on special" for 36.05 rand (US$5.36).

17. In Cape Town, outlets were found at the city's central train station and in several residential areas; in Windhoek I visited several places where African movies were for sale or rent in the city's large Katutura township area, as well as one business, which traded from a slightly run-down shopping center, located near a central taxi rank.

18. In Namibia the costs were slightly higher, at 238 Namibian dollars (US$35.40) per month in September 2008.

19. Most of the remaining 600,000 were in "the oil-rich states" of Nigeria and Angola. Nigeria, with a population of 120 million, has been identified as the major potential growth point, according to the managing director for Multichoice Africa (Zvomuya).

20. Multichoice DStv's managing director for Nigeria has claimed that the screening of Nigerian video films on its Africa Magic channel – "such a huge draw around the continent" – has contributed much to the movies' promotion across the African continent (including Nigeria itself). He also referred to the proliferation of "Nigerian shop[s] selling Nigerian mov-

ies with so much patronage" in formerly white middle-class suburbs of major South African cities (Enyadike).

21. A twenty-one-year-old bachelor of commerce student at UWC told us: "Most people that I'm surrounded with like the American English accent, so I love being different with my Nigerian English accent. I have watched a lot of movies, so I've mastered the way they speak. Usually when I'm with my friend who also likes to speak the Nigerian English accent, we speak like we are straight from Nigeria. A lot of people mistake us that we are from that side of the world. We get people who are from Nigeria calling us their home sisters because of the way we speak."

22. The *Namibian,* which was published in Windhoek from 1985, used this slogan.

23. This reference to "culture" appears to be similar to what Brian Larkin describes for northern Nigeria in respect to the fascination with Indian movies, which Hausa people related to the fact that Indian films, unlike American movies, had "so much 'tradition'" (*Signal and Noise* 196), which they understood in a very similar way to contemporary southern African discourses about "culture" as reified, essentializing, and often objectified practices and values.

24. Laurein translated *ubuntu* as "humanity"; the Comaroffs describe the notion of a specifically African form of interpersonal humanity as "a fundamental sociomoral tenet of Afromodernity" (200).

25. Nostalgia is derived from the Greek *nostos,* meaning "return home."

WORKS CITED

Barber, Karin. "Popular Arts in Africa." *African Studies Review* 30.3 (1987): 1–78.

Barnes, Teresa. "'Days' and 'Bold': The Fascination of Soap Operas for Black Students at the University of the Western Cape, South Africa." *Leisure in Urban Africa.* Ed. Paul Tiyambe Zeleza and Cassandra Rachel Veney. Trenton, N.J.: Africa World Press, 2003. 343–56.

Becker, Heike, and Nceba Dastile. "Global and African: Exploring Hip-Hop Artists in Philippi Township, Cape Town." *Anthropology Southern Africa* 31.1–2 (2008): 20–30.

Comaroff, John L., and Jean Comaroff. "Criminal Justice, Cultural Justice: The Limits of Liberalism and the Pragmatics of Difference in the New South Africa." *American Ethnologist* 31.2 (2004): 188–204.

Enyadike, Emeka. "DStv Mobile Launches in Nigeria." *Biz Community,* August 20, 2007. Web.

Haynes, Jonathan. "Introduction." *Nigerian Video Films.* Ed. Jonathan Haynes. Rev. ed. Athens: Ohio University Press, 2000. 1–36.

———. "Nollywood: What's in a Name?" *Film International* 5.4 (2007): 106–8.

Larkin, Brian. "Indian Films and Nigerian Lovers: Media and the Creation of Parallel Modernities." *Africa* 67.3 (1997): 406–40.

———. "Itineraries of Indian Cinema: African Videos, Bollywood, and Global Media." *The Anthropology of Globalization: A Reader.* Ed. Jonathan X. Inda and Renato Rosaldo. Malden, Mass.: Blackwell, 2008. 334–51.

———. *Signal and Noise: Media, Infrastructure, and Urban Culture in Nigeria.* Durham, N.C.: Duke University Press, 2008.

Nghiulikwa, Romie V. "Re-situating and Shifting Cultural Identity in Contemporary Namibia: The Experience of Rural-Urban Migrants in Katutura

(Windhoek)." Master's thesis, University of Western Cape, 2008.

Salo, Elaine. "Negotiating Gender and Personhood in the New South Africa: Adolescent Women and Gangsters on the Cape Flats." *European Journal of Cultural Studies* 6.3 (2003): 345–65.

Sichone, Owen. "Africanization: An Alternative Perspective on Africanness

in Global Identity Politics." Paper presented at the "New Social Formations" seminar series, University of Stellenbosch, May 4, 2004.

Stevenson, Michael. "Pieter Hugo: Nollywood." *Stevenson* (2009). Web.

Zvomuya, Percy. "Africa's Movie Factory Foreman." *Mail & Guardian Online*, December 6, 2008. Web.

FILMOGRAPHY

The Bold and the Beautiful. TV serial. Creators: Lee Phillip Bell and William J. Bell. Bell-Phillip Television et al. (United States). 1987–.

Boyz n the Hood. Dir. John Singleton. Columbia Pictures (United States). 1991.

Days of Our Lives. TV serial. Creators: Ted Corday, Irna Phillips, and Allan Chase. Corday Productions et al. (United States), 1965–.

Generations. TV serial. Creator: Mfundi Vundla. Morula Pictures (South Africa). 1994–.

Isidingo. TV serial. Creator: Gray Hofmeyr. Endemol (South Africa). 1998–.

Mr. Ibu in London. Dir. Andy Chukwu. Kas-Vid (Nigeria). 2004.

Osuofia in London, 1 and 2. Dir. Kingsley Ogoro. Kingsley Ogoro Productions (Nigeria). 2003, 2004.

Sarafina. Dir. Darrell Roodt. Hollywood Pictures et al. (United States et al.). 1992.

Tsotsi. Dir. Gavin Hood. The UK Film and TV Production Company et al. (South Africa). 2005.

NINE

Religion, Migration, and Media Aesthetics: Notes on the Circulation and Reception of Nigerian Films in Kinshasa

KATRIEN PYPE

MEDIA AESTHETICS IN KINSHASA HAVE SEEN TREMENDOUS changes since President Mobutu opened up the Zairian mediascape in 1996. This newly declared freedom of the press made possible alternative patterns of media patronage. At the same time, and coinciding with the charismatic renewal in urban centers throughout sub-Saharan Africa, Kinshasa's public culture, and in particular its broadcast media, have become more and more charismatic.

The gradual charismatization of Kinshasa's public culture is inherently related to the movement of people. Many charismatic Christian leaders travel back and forth between Kinshasa and Nigeria. When they return to Kinshasa, these pastors show Nigerian films in their churches and on their television channels. The influence of West African video films is so significant that it has even altered the aesthetics of local television drama in Kinshasa. Following the tremendous influence of Nigerian films on Kinshasa's daily life worlds and also media production, this chapter scrutinizes the meanings of "Nigeria" in Kinshasa and its media world and considers in particular the various media brokers who control the arrival and interpretation of Nigerian films in Kinshasa.

The data I present offer empirical evidence on current central African media products, allowing us simultaneously to refine interpretations of the interaction between media and migration. First, this material enables us to correct persistent ideas about African migration, which is not always South-North oriented nor always economically inspired. Apart from commerce, religion motivates Africans to move, and it inspires them in particular to travel within the continent. Second, South-South migration co-occurs with the circulation of electronic media, which in turn modifies local aesthetic regimes and challenges assumed Western cultural dominance in postcolonial Africa.[1]

This chapter explores how media aesthetics travel around the African continent. With this essay, I attempt to contribute to the burgeoning literature on the dynamics of African media worlds (see, among others, Abu-Lughod; Ginsburg, Abu-Lughod, and Larkin; Hackett; Harding; Larkin; Meyer; Nyamnjoh). I do so by focusing on Kinshasa, the capital of the Democratic Republic of the Congo, where I spent seventeen months between 2003 and 2006 conducting research on the production of local TV serials (called *maboke* in Lingala).

The TV serials, as they are produced in post-Mobutu Kinshasa, cannot be compared to the earliest television serials of Kinshasa's media history. As I have written elsewhere, while the serials filmed between 1981 and the mid-1990s were incorporated into Mobutu's propaganda politics, those produced and screened since the mid-1990s no longer glorify the national citizen. Rather, the *maboke* are now fully immersed in a religious discourse pitting the Christian God against the devil, thus offering an apocalyptic explanation for the hardships of life in a society governed by a weak state and surviving on a precarious economy.

Several political and social changes have contributed to transform the aesthetics of Kinshasa's television dramas.[2] One factor is circular migration to and from Nigeria, where Kinois (inhabitants of Kinshasa) move mainly for economic reasons. Christian leaders also travel back and forth between Congo and Nigeria, but, apart from commercial initiatives, religious motives inspire them as well.[3] These migrants bring Nigerian films to Kinshasa, where the latter easily find audiences. Second, around the mid-1990s, Mobutu's power waned to some degree, resulting in greater political leniency by the state toward broadcasters. In 1996 the president granted freedom of the press, thus enabling private patterns of media patronage. Immediately, all sorts of entrepreneurs took advantage of the new climate. Among them, in particular, were commercial and political TV patrons, who established private TV stations. Finally, Pentecostal-charismatic pastors, who, like elsewhere in urban sub-Saharan Africa, have gained increasing influence in Kinshasa, founded a significant number of Kinshasa's local TV channels.

As I will show, the triangular of migration, religion, and media liberalization relates dialectically to the establishment of a new social and moral imagination, which in turn favors the reception of Nigerian films in Kinshasa and even goes as far as impacting the aesthetic conventions of local TV serials. Local teleserials are enriched and transformed through the visualization and integration of Nigerian films. Plots, protagonists, and morality, thoroughly sensationalized in the Nigerian films, have contributed in Kinshasa to a spread of the apocalyptic imagination; the pervasive understanding of the city as inhabited by occult beings – an interpretation shared by many Kinois – also enhances these films' appeal.

In their introduction to *Media Worlds*, Ginsburg, Abu-Lughod, and Larkin contend that "the dominant frameworks for thinking about the transnational reach of media have been either globalization or cultural imperialism; both tend to privilege media originating from or dominant in the West, with less attention paid to other circuits" (14). The influence of Nigerian video films on Kinshasa's public culture and media production presents concrete evidence that imaginary landscapes are not always rooted in Western hegemonic image systems but sometimes, also, are based in alternative transnational circuits. An analysis of the role played by Nigerian films and the history of their arrival in Kinshasa offers interesting insights into the ways public cultures are reconfigured by moving images and by the circulation of alternative global master narratives.

The following investigation into the meanings and impact of Nigerian films on Kinshasa's public culture is situated within the context of a globalized world where people and media images move together. Media aesthetics also travel alongside flows of consumer goods, money, and bodies. The social trajectories of videotapes and DVDs, as so many sources of identity formation, the dynamics of signification these films provoke, and the processes of legitimization and social control brought about by the circulation of Nigerian films in Kinshasa are all located within the framework of African media-reception practices, themselves aspects of wider economic and political flows. I am not arguing that the South-South circulation of aesthetics is a new phenomenon. Rather, the revolution in communication and information technologies, and its effects in reducing distances and accelerating flows, is unprecedented. Narratives and symbols have circulated by emulation for many centuries, and Nigerian film is but a contemporary instance of this dynamic.[4]

It is important to emphasize, therefore, that the reception of Nigerian films in Kinshasa takes its place within a long history of cultural
politics that runs counter to Western cultural hegemony and links the
Democratic Republic of the Congo to other African countries. During
Mobutu's regime, African films were often shown in movie houses and
on state television channels, as part of the president's authenticity campaign and political efforts to distance Zaire further from its former colonial power (and Western imperialism more generally). Often, when
Nigerian films are compared to American blockbusters, which are also
broadcast in Kinshasa, Kinois hail the "Africanity" that Nigerian films
emblematize. In this discourse, the Nollywood industry is praised as a
welcome strategy of resistance against Western cultural imperialism. Yet
the promise of an African film industry countering Western hegemonic
semiotic systems is only one aspect of how these films are valued in Kinshasa. First, it is not so much the yearning for a "genuine African" cultural expressive form that accounts for the wild popularity of Nollywood
films in Kinshasa; rather, it is the fact that Nigerian films are so easily inserted into the apocalyptic narratives zealously proclaimed by born-again
Christians. In addition, the "Africanity" that these films suggest needs to
be subjected to serious questioning, as born-again Christianity energeti-
cally demonizes ancestral cultural heritage. As I will show, in Kinshasa,
Nigerian films occupy ambiguous positions on the boundaries of the
familiar and the strange, or between the socially and morally acceptable
and that which is rejected; popularity of the Nigerian films showcases
shifts in the nature of symbolic capital in present-day Kinshasa.

WATCHING NIGERIAN FILMS IN KINSHASA

Kinshasa's inhabitants can view Nigerian films on several of the more
than thirty local TV stations, from early in the morning until midnight.
And because these films are frequently repeated, they are able to engrave
themselves in Kinshasa's cultural memory. Besides being screened on
private television stations, Nigerian films also circulate through the
city on DVDs and VCDs, which swiftly pass among friends, relatives,
and neighbors.[5] These electronic media carriers are sold in the streets
by peddlers or vendors (bashayeurs), but can also be obtained in small
shops.[6]

Nigerian films are watched in domestic spaces (living rooms and courtyards inside compounds) and in semipublic spaces such as churches and prayer groups. This contrasts strikingly with Nigerian and Tanzanian reception modes, where audiences flock to video parlors (see Krings, this volume). In Kinshasa movie houses usually screen action and pornographic films, thus constructing these sites as masculine spaces. As I will show below, Nigerian films are to a large extent embedded in a Christian universe, so movie houses are not the appropriate venues for these films. The audiences of Nigerian films, as intended by those who control their circulation to a large extent, are not assumed to ever set foot in movie houses, as these are, from a Christian perspective, deemed immoral.

Although Nigerian films constitute only one genre of the various "foreign" mass-mediated narratives (serials and films) that make up Kinshasa's television programs in the post-Mobutu mediascape, they now form an essential aspect of the viewing experiences of Kinshasa's population.[7] These films have become so ingrained both in the public sphere and in the life worlds of Kinois that no study of the urban social imagination and the city's public sphere can ignore them.[8]

Despite the great thematic variety of Nollywood productions, most Nigerian films (*films de Nigeria*) watched in Kinshasa show demons and witches. This is not particularly surprising, because Nigerian witchcraft films are notorious for staging human sacrifice rituals, as Okwori mentions. These Nigerian visualizations of evil are very similar to the video films Birgit Meyer studied in Ghana, although the obsession with the demonic and the wicked contrasts strikingly with series from Côte d'Ivoire (in particular *Ma Famille*) and other foreign films screened in Kinshasa. The Nigerian films are designed according to a particular Pentecostal style (Meyer 101) that seems to attract Kinois.

Despite the fact that these films are usually in English, or at times in local Nigerian languages, Kinois are drawn to them. Understanding dialogue does not seem necessary, as the actors' body language and the films' special effects speak for themselves. And when these films are broadcast on Kinshasa's TV channels, they are simultaneously translated into kiKinois, the language of Kinshasa.[9]

Regardless of socioeconomic standing, urban women and youth in particular respond enthusiastically to Nigerian films. Private conversations often deal with the films' contents and characters, nicknames given among friends often derive from fictional characters in Nigerian films, and women postpone domestic chores when these films are broadcast. The aesthetics of Nigerian films also influence fashion and home decoration. Seamstresses say that they receive requests to sew dresses and skirts in Nigerian styles, similar to what they saw in the films. A newspaper article, moreover, reported that architectural styles in Nigerian films increasingly inspire new styles of buildings in Kinshasa (Kongo). Ordinary viewers, political and religious leaders, as well as local media celebrities are all familiar with the *films de Nigéria,* and all have opinions on their merits and meanings.

CORRUPTING KINSHASA

Despite the strong appeal of Nigerian films for Kinois spectators, the strange mixture of pleasure and rejection that accompanies so many different kinds of desire also underpins the public discourse about these films. The excessive dramatization of occult practices has especially led to much public controversy. The depiction of occult dances, ritual incantations, as well as the (temporary) successes of traditional healers in these films is perceived by some as a means of introducing spectators to the world of the occult. Viewers, as well as local leaders like politicians and Christian priests and pastors, publicly question the morality of these films.

Kinshasa's leading dramatic artists, in turn, voice other concerns in criticizing these films' dominance of local broadcasting schedules. Troubled by the loss of viewers for their own television dramas, Kinshasa's television actors often demand that the minister of culture order the broadcasting of Nigerian films curtailed. To support their arguments, Kinshasa's artists encourage the search for an indigenous Congolese culture.

But state officials also fuel protest. While I was conducting fieldwork in Kinshasa, the Nigerian ambassador requested that Nigerian films no longer circulate in the city, as they gave an incorrect image of Nigeria. Furthermore, as De Boeck and Plissart (186) argue, these films may have contributed to the spread of witch hunts, targeting in particular child witches. Between 2002 and 2006, the national media censorship board (Haute Autorité des Médias) twice outlawed these films. The films' adversaries (local TV actors, the Nigerian government, and "the public") articulated concerns about the role of visual media in the construction of national identities; they discussed the threat foreign media products pose to the preservation of local culture, and they expressed the need to supervise the instructional value of television programs.

However, state bans did not put an end to the broadcasting of Nigerian films. Despite political decisions, several new channels have started up, and Nigerian films, broadcast without any state interference, almost exclusively dominate their programming. Frequently, political and religious talk shows, American films and series, and even locally produced series lose their viewers when other TV stations show Nigerian films.

These different perspectives on the merits of imported Nigerian films illustrate the ongoing struggle for an authentic Congolese culture. This quest for authenticity also pervades the religious realm, where conflicts between Kimbanguist and Pentecostal-charismatic Christianity center around the skin color of the material embodiment of the Holy Spirit. Given these considerations, Nigerian films are clearly in line with the born-again Christian communities, which do not show pride in local African heritage. The cosmopolitanism that both Nigerian films and the discourses of born-again leaders promote thus challenges the possibility of an "authentic African cultural revival," and at the same time demotes the cultural relevance of American narratives for Kinois spectators.

MEDIA, MIGRATION, AND RELIGION

Migration is inscribed into Kinshasa's media landscape. When I visited the offices of some television station directors in Kinshasa, I often noticed illegal VHS copies of American and Western films, sent by Congolese in the diaspora, which were then broadcast on Kinshasa's television channels. Most of the money required to set up a TV station also comes from abroad. The pirated copies of Western and Nigerian films arrive in Kinshasa through channels that escape state control. Perhaps surprisingly, the owners of TV channels do not perceive this as problematic, but, as some of them have told me in interviews, they are forced to take these "illegal routes" in order to obtain broadcast material. The following discussion about the importation and circulation of Nigerian films in Kinshasa is therefore situated in the context of a society where the state and its officials exert little control over people's movements and economic activities. Although several censorship committees have been installed, and media entrepreneurs can set up a television station only after agreeing to comply with the authorities' rules, there is nearly no state interference in nonpolitical broadcasting. Nigerian films are obviously not perceived as threats to the ruling parties, and therefore film traders and broadcasters rarely meet with political resistance.

There has been much research on the interaction between media and migration. Yet most of this literature has remained focused on media reception, the production of minority media, and its impact on the construction of identities and subjectivities among diasporic publics. There are additional aspects of these media and migration interfaces that require careful analysis and theoretical elaboration. In particular, I want to point to two matters of contention, which are inspired by recent work on cultural globalization from scholars like Arjun Appadurai, Jonathan Friedman, and Ulf Hannerz. First, in addition to the social contexts in which media products are watched and consumed, we need to pay attention to the communities and individuals who direct the circulation of print magazines, audiotapes, and DVDs. These groups, entrepreneurs, and other individuals often commission the production, acquisition, and distribution of print and broadcast media for socially significant reasons. It is important to analyze how images and sounds travel along flows of money and other forms of capital. Such a reconstruction of the "social biographies" (Kopytoff) of visual media will yield a better understanding of how media shape identities. The Nigerian traders (about four thousand, mostly Igbo) who reside in Kinshasa do not control the circulation of Nigerian films in the city. Rather, it is Kinois themselves, who travel to Nigeria, come back with these films, and offer them either to local TV stations, to music and video shops in town, or to the *bashayeurs* who sell them on the streets. It is clear that the local circulation and reception of Nigerian films are embedded in the migration practices of Kinois themselves, and thus cannot be reduced to the presence of Nigerians in the city or to the qualities of skilled Nigerian traders.

Second, framing these media products within larger contexts of narratives and audiences merits careful analysis as well. Local considerations determine the interpretations of televised narratives and images, as Katz and Liebes have already shown. Yet if we aim at a fuller understanding of what exogenous media images and stories offer to particular publics, our attention needs to shift toward the hermeneutic work of intermediaries. The meanings of commodities and cultural products, previously attributed to these media images and stories in their social contexts of production, can be reframed in surprising ways. Adding new layers of meanings to cultural expressions or artifacts, however, takes place through the hermeneutic work of social agents. Focusing on the individuals who direct this appropriation can be a starting point for exploring the social relevance of migrated commodities and cultural expressions and the aesthetic perceptions of viewers.

In the following, I attempt to address both issues by identifying the different kinds of brokers who act as intermediaries between Kinois spectators and Nigerian films and the ways in which these intermediaries engage in the localization of culturally foreign media texts. The brokers bring the films to Kinshasa and make them accessible to Kinshasa's spectators; they also make the narratives meaningful for these audiences. The success of the Nigerian films – and thus their local translation – relies in part on product marketing, organized within different networks, especially the Christian and media networks, both of which overlap to a great extent in Kinshasa. So, instead of privileging Nigerian film narratives in my analysis, I treat practices of movement as well as the localization strategies enacted by media brokers as the primary sites for the intersection of global flows and the local receptions of these narratives.

Pentecostalism, a new type of Christianity pervading the public spheres of many African cities, plays a significant role. It is only recently that the role of religion in African diasporic contexts has received scholarly attention (among others, see Adogame and Weissköppel; Ter Haar; Kalu). There is now a significant body of literature on the active role of Pentecostal communities in the organization of migration. Rijk A. Van Dijk, for example, has argued that both in Ghana and in the Netherlands, Pentecostal leaders tend to act as brokers, not only linking information and flows of interaction between different cultural contexts, but also organizing transnational marriages between Ghanaian Christians at home and those in the diaspora, as well as intervening actively in migrants' pursuit of residence papers and work opportunities abroad. The involvement of Pentecostalism in the mobility and experiences of migrants is, as

I will show, not confined to the movement of people and commodities, but also concerns popular culture. Pentecostalism is the axis of circulation for Nigerian films in Kinshasa.

THE LAND OF THE PLENTY

Currently, Kinshasa is the largest city in central Africa. Although it is difficult to give accurate population figures, the total population is usually estimated at around nine million. Most of them are connected with the Kongo ethnic group, who occupy the area just southwest of Kinshasa, and the Luba ethnic group, whose territory is located in central Congo. Due to the enormous economic and political influence of this ethnic group, Luba people play a significant role in the city's public culture. Yet despite the cultural and economic dominance of the Kongo and Luba ethnic cultures, Kinois claim that their city is a mosaic of Congolese ethnic groups. This attitude seems justified and is evident in particular at funerals and wedding ceremonies, where ethnic languages, songs, and performances are used, thus linking the protagonists of the ceremonies to an ancestral homeland.

Two main social forces pull Kinois away from ethnic registers and draw them into supraethnic communities. The first one is known as La Kinoiserie, an urban atmosphere that defines someone as a Kinois. A "Kinois" is not so much someone born and raised in Kinshasa, but more someone who behaves "like a Kinois," that is, someone who knows the latest Congolese songs and dances, who enjoys the culture of the bars and nightlife, and who knows how to find money to survive (débrouillardise). The second social force that transcends ethnic boundaries is what is known as the charismatization of Kinshasa society, or an understanding of Kinois as participants in a spiritual battle between God and the devil. This symbolic frame pushes people to interpret others, their behaviors and words, as either Christian or demonic. A hegemonic notion of Christian citizenship has become established according to which Kinois are subjects with origins in other parts of the world and continuing commitments to diasporic ancestral cultures. Accordingly, full membership in Kinois society is achieved by cultivating Christian performances, whose perceived authenticity provides crucial support for claims to a legitimate place within the nation. For Kinshasa's Christians, therefore, Christianity represents the official culture through which membership in the Congolese nation is defined.[10] The key significance of contemporary Kinois Christianity is that churches can offer city dwellers a new moral horizon, which in turn recasts individual and collective aspirations. The "Other," without which no imagination of the Self can exist, is, for Christian Kinois, embodied by the pagan: the heathen, as Devisch has it, who lives a hedonistic life, enjoys the pleasures of Afromodernity and its sensual *Sitz-im-Leben*, follows the rhythm of urban dance music, and dwells in bars and other spaces where lavish spending and female eroticism go hand in hand. The new Christian churches preach zealously against this "urban life," which, in any case, is not within most people's reach. Those who feel left out of the pleasures of city life are comforted, therefore, when pastors demonize a lifestyle beyond their reach. This, together with the "democratic" character of the churches (everybody can receive a call from God, and everybody can receive a special spiritual gift), accounts for the popularity of this type of church among Kinshasa's women and youth, in a society where gerontocracy remains the main social structuring principle of authority and social mobility.

Still, these churches cannot counteract the deplorable economic circumstances of many of their followers. Poverty, along with political instability, produces a desire among many Kinois to leave their country.[11] Following the economic crisis of the early 1990s, Laurent Kabila's attempt to boost the local economy failed. The result has been massive unemployment, devaluation of academic degrees, a flourishing informal economy, and a burning desire for many to try their luck abroad. Western Europe and the United States especially are perceived as El Dorados where wealth and prosperity are far easier to attain than at home. This feeling could not be better described than by the terms Kinois use: "Europe" is called *lola*, Lingala for "heaven," or *mikili*, "better world" or "paradise." Unsurprisingly, then, migration is a regular topic of conversation, as well as a reality affecting most people in Kinshasa. Everybody has at least one relative living abroad who sends money or goods home. Being mobile or knowing how to traverse territorial and cultural boundaries invests individuals with symbolic capital. The social prestige of the city's Big Men and Women derives to a large degree from their mobility. One of my key informants, who was desperately seeking to make contact with *mikilistes* (people who dwell in *mikili*), had very little information about a Congolese man who traveled back and forth between Kinshasa and Brussels and whom the young man considered his patron. He had no idea how his patron obtained his money, though the frequent journeys, the expensive car with which the patron would come for the young man, and the designer clothes the young client received on those occasions proved the patron's skill at benefiting from the Western economy. Such patrons are perceived as "good hunters," who travel to Europe, South Africa, or any other country where the economy is reasonably strong and return with their game, which they must share among kin and other networks.

International movement is so deeply rooted that the prospect of transnational movement becomes normative. One could even say that Kinshasa has a "culture of migration" (Kandel and Massey). The hunting metaphor, mentioned earlier, is apt, as it underscores the expectation of migrants and their kin that those who leave eventually come back. This is very common. Migrants do not wish to settle in foreign lands, but they expect to return home once they have gathered a significant amount of cash.[12] Kinois also speak about leaving home as just "having a look" (*kotala*) and then coming back. Even those who migrate using false documents (*kobwaka nzoto*, "to throw away the body") also hope to eventually return home.

Although most people aspire to move to the West, the strict immigration rules enforced by embassies makes this virtually impossible for most Kinois. In fact, more people tend to move to neighboring countries such as Congo-Brazzaville, Cameroon, Nigeria, Zambia, and Angola, either in search of diamonds or to work in petty trade. Many, however, perceive these countries as stops en route to Europe or the United States.

Nigeria, as one of several African countries where Kinois migrate, occupies an important place in the urban imagination. Although only a small number of Kinois have actually visited this West African country, many have particular preconceived ideas and opinions about it and its inhabitants, often based on Nigerian films and the narratives of returned migrants. Nigeria is considered to be a nation of plenty, where access to all kinds of commodities is easier than in Kinshasa. Take, for instance, the case of Bienvenu, the leader of Kinshasa's most popular drama group, who was abroad between 2003 and 2007. Bienvenu was born and raised in Kinshasa. At the age of twenty-five, and as his family's eldest son,

Bienvenu's mother sent him to purchase goods, which she then resold at a local market in Lemba, one of Kinshasa's communities. Bienvenu spent two years in Angola and then traveled to South Africa, before arriving in Nigeria. There, he bought mattresses, soap, and wax. During his stay in Lagos, he approached local filmmakers and learned their skills. Each time he traveled back to Kinshasa, he brought piles of Nigerian video films, which he tried to sell with the help of his maternal cousin in Kinshasa's streets and churches, as well as in the city of Matadi in the Lower Congo, his mother's hometown. After he had been in Lagos for three years, Bienvenu's mother became ill. The family decided to send her to France for medical treatment. This ended Bienvenu's residence in Nigeria. After he returned to Kinshasa, Bienvenu felt inspired by the Nigerian filmmakers with whom he had spent much of his time and set up a drama group of his own called Cinarc. This theater company, now one of Kinshasa's most popular troupes, is much appreciated for the striking resemblance their TV serials bear to the Nigerian video films.

Bienvenu's story is only one example of how the lure of Nigeria's affluence affects local media in Kinshasa. The biography of Thony Best, one of Kinshasa's best-known translators of Nigerian films, is another example of how Nigeria influences local media. When he initially left for Lagos in 1999, Best's top priority was to earn money. As he told me in the course of several interviews, he might easily have chosen another African country, but he was very much attracted by Nigeria's booming film industry. So, along with other commodities, Thony Best made Nigerian films one of his main trading items. His most important clients are not individual buyers so much as local television stations and smaller media shops. When he decided to relocate to Kinshasa, Thony Best started working as a dubber at one of Kinshasa's private TV stations. Nowadays, he earns a living as a simultaneous translator of Nigerian films on local TV screens.

THE LAND OF THE SPIRITUAL BATTLE

Yet there are also many rumors of illicit wealth creation in Nigeria. For Kinois, Nigeria is at once an African El Dorado and a dangerous country, similar to the place Nigeria occupies in the imagination of other Africans. In a study of the image of Nigeria among villagers from neighboring Niger, Adeline Masquelier describes how, according to rural dwellers in Nigeria, Nigeria is, on the one hand, a land of plenty, with a huge potential for daring traders, and, on the other hand, a country of death and destruction because of the thieves, killers, and other immoral people presumed to exist in large numbers among the population. The pervasiveness of this reputation is reinforced when Kinois speak about the Nigerian merchants on Avenue de Victoire and Avenue de Gambela, two important streets in Kinshasa bustling with economic activity. This area is known by many for cheap car parts and as a place where one can obtain these goods at half price, or sometimes even less, than one might pay in Kinshasa's other markets. Yet these goods are also known to be of lesser quality, to be cheap imitations. It is a commonly held belief that Nigerians do not shy away from fraud, reselling stolen goods and trafficking drugs in their bids to earn money and profits.

Nigeria is both fascinating and repulsive (see Masquelier 87). Significantly, the negative aspect of Nigeria's status is embedded in Christian apocalyptic ideology. Consider, for example, the discourse of Nene, a young woman in her late twenties, who leads the children's group in her Pentecostal church. According to her, it is common knowledge that the spiritual battle between God and the devil is more severe in Nigeria than in the Democratic Republic of the Congo. Although she herself has never visited Nigeria, her aunt has done so as a businesswoman and has told these stories to her relatives. Nene's aunt, who spent some time in Lagos, was surprised to observe people reciting incantations on beaches or in parks. She found it equally strange that one could easily purchase magical objects in the markets. Thony Best, the film trader, voiced similar observations, though he did not view them negatively. According to him, by allowing traditional religious practices to be performed in the open, Nigerian society shows itself to be far less hypocritical than Kinshasa's. Thony Best thus rejected the commonly held opinion that in Kinshasa, everybody calls himself a Christian. According to him, many Kinois continue to perform so-called traditional rituals, use herbal medicines, and consult *féticheurs*. Because of public pressure to identify as Christians, though, most Kinois do not speak about their contacts with traditional practitioners.

In the discourse of Kinshasa's Pentecostal Christians, Nigeria is at the forefront of a spiritual battle between God and the devil. It is said that God is more present in Nigeria than in Kinshasa and that he realizes many miracles and fights against the overwhelming presence of magic and evil in Nigerian society. Narratives that cast Nigeria as a nation with "much evil" are confirmed once more when Kinois watch Nigerian witchcraft films. In this stereotyping, Nigeria is reduced to an image that fits Kinshasa's hegemonic apocalyptic atmosphere. Just as they obliterate the various ethnic and religious groups present in Kinshasa, these hegemonic Christian narratives do not take the Yoruba, Hausa, Igbo, or other ethnic origins of Nigerian people into account. Every "Nigerian" is reduced to being either a Christian or a pagan. This kind of stereotype, of course, provides little information about the country described, but says much about the speaker. Beliefs about the difference between Christians and non-Christians, which flourish in Kinshasa, are transposed to Nigeria: a country that has become the "Other" in Kinshasa's modern Christian imagination. Tales of death and overt occultism are part of a wider discourse of otherness through which Kinois articulate local experiences of power, violence, and uncertainty.

The spiritual battle, as it is perceived in Pentecostal circles, is not a localized conflict, but one transgressing both international borders and the boundaries between the material and the immaterial. Christians in Kinshasa believe themselves to be in the same battle as Christians elsewhere on the continent and beyond. The strong cosmopolitan tendency within Pentecostal-charismatic circles (see Corten and Marshall-Fratani) likewise urges Kinois pastors to travel, preach, and perform miracles elsewhere. Both the expansion of African churches and the high mobility of born-again Christian leaders are encouraged by a spiritual cosmopolitanism that understands the entire planet as being involved in spiritual warfare. In Kinshasa, for example, many foreign born-again Christian pastors lead services in the city's largest football stadium. In June 2006, for example, Nigerian prophets were invited to lead a gathering of Kinshasa's Christian women praying for the upcoming elections. Their presence contributed to the event's spiritual significance or efficacy, and thus also bolstered the Christian reputation of its organizers. A few months earlier, in February 2006, South Korean doctor Jaerock Lee starred in that same football stadium as the principal guest of the "Festival of Miraculous Healings" (*Festival des Guérisons Miracles*). He had been invited by Pastor Sikatenda, head of the Pentecostal church "Church of the Living God" (*Eglise du Dieu Vivant*), who had himself traveled to South Korea the previous year. Pastor Sikatenda promotes himself on his TV station and website as "the Prophet and Servant of God in all Nations" (*l'Apôtre et Serviteur de Dieu dans toutes les Nations*). The Church of the Living God seeks to establish branches all across the world. In early 2009, the church's website claimed to possess "102 churches in Kinshasa, 232 churches in the Congolese provinces, 12 churches in Angola, 2 churches in Congo-Brazzaville, and one church in France, Belgium and Italy."[13]

Kinshasa's Pentecostal pastors are also very mobile and in their Sunday sermons boast about visits to France, South Africa, Nigeria, and the United States. As Nigeria is perceived as the place of the most difficult spiritual battle, Kinshasa's spiritual leaders are eager to learn from Nigerian prophets.[14] For Kinshasa's Christians, a visit to Nigeria has become a mark of prestige and a measure of success more desirable than building social capital by leaving for Europe or South Africa. On their return, Kinois pastors during sermons are very eager to speak about miracles witnessed and strong spiritual men encountered abroad. Often, these pastors present themselves as "Nigerian prophets" (*prophètes nigérians*), and they regularly incorporate English words and sounds in their preaching, especially when speaking in tongues, but also in their sermons and daily rhetoric. They perform this Anglophone cosmopolitanism because the attribute "Nigerian" has become a quality label that guarantees the strong spiritual powers and capacities of spiritual men. Equipped with this "Nigerian" stamp, Kinois pastors produce a "Nigerianity" that works, above all, by fixing identity and thus expectation. Going to Nigeria and working with Nigerian pastors give Kinois clergy authority and charisma and draw larger audiences to their meetings. People expect even greater acts of healing and to see more miracles.

Significantly, this orientation of expectation is also present among local interpreters of Nigerian films. As I will show, when Nigerian films are broadcast on Kinshasa's TV channels, they are simultaneously dubbed into kiKinois. It has been noted that interpreters are even granted the status of spiritual leaders, who not only instruct but also heal viewers. Franck Baku Fuita and Godefroid Bwiti Lumisa, two Congolese journalists, have described how viewers contacted José de Jésus with requests to be delivered from sterility and from other illnesses with "mysterious" origins. They write: "The audience, mostly women, told [José de Jésus] about their own experiences and asked to be delivered from an evil with 'mysterious' origins. One woman we met when visiting José de Jésus confirms having been cured of her sterility thanks to an undoing of bewitchment operation (*désenvoûtement*) performed by the famous television host she came to know through the Nigerian films" (112; my translation).

TRANSLATING NIGERIAN FILMS

Both the arrival of the Nigerian films in Kinshasa and the ways in which these films are rendered meaningful to Kinois spectators are embedded in the evangelizing mission of Pentecostal pastors. Pasteur Kutinho, leader of the revival church "the Army of Victory" (*l'Armée de la Victoire*), first screened the Nigerian video *Karishika* on his own TV channel (De Boeck and Plissart 186).[15] This film tells the story of a young girl named Karishika who is sent by Lucifer into the world to destroy humanity. She uses her beauty as a weapon to sow death and despair and brings disorder to many households. At the end of the film, the "real" Christians are saved thanks to their strong faith, while the sinners die, and Karishika returns to the world of the devil. Today, for Kinois, the word *karichika* indicates a genre of West African film depicting the spiritual combat between God and the devil. Once Nigerian films have arrived in Kinshasa, different social categories undertake various cultural strategies to render their narratives comprehensible and meaningful for Kinshasa's spectators.

The role of Pentecostal pastors seems fundamental to the process of appropriation. Pastors use the Nigerian films, at times, as a means of instructing their followers. Similarly, viewers believe Nigerian films teach them lessons. When Nene, the young woman I described earlier, was going through a difficult time because her fiancé had canceled their wedding plans, her aunt gave her a Nigerian film. The film dealt with jealousy about the marriage prospects of siblings and seemed to carry a significant lesson for Nene. In the film, a young woman envied the frequent marriage proposals received by her older sister. Determined to counter her sister's luck, she killed each one of the suitors. Witchcraft played a significant part in her ruses. In the end, however, one of the youngest sister's accomplices was troubled by what she had done and confessed to all of their attacks. This led to a prosperous marriage for the older sister. Nene, who believed that God had sent her the film so she would not lose her faith in marriage, decided to show it in the church group for young women that she leads. She framed the film as a warning: one should not envy the success of other girls on the marriage market, because envy may lead to jealousy, shame, and possibly death. As Nene's use of the film illustrates, through a connection with the born-again Christian leaders' ability to promote Nigerian films, these movies make their way into local reception structures.

Here, it is interesting to reflect upon the staging of the occult within Nigerian films and their relationship to education. Several Christian leaders told me they were worried that the messages of Nigerian films were not always clear to viewers. Bemoaning the fact that film broadcasts are often interrupted by sudden power cuts, or simply knowing the viewing habits of Kinshasa's spectators, who might suddenly switch channels and start watching another show, several evangelizers voiced concerns about the primordial role of witchcraft and magic, which dominate the plotlines of these films. Several pastors have told me that they feared these films were instructing viewers in the ways of the occult, instead of leading them toward the Christian way of life. Nevertheless, there seems to be a tension between the ubiquitous staging of the occult in Nigerian films and the Pentecostal agenda, which firmly rejects these practices. This contradiction lies at the very heart of the evangelizing discourse, which is utterly polarizing. However, in order to glorify the Christian way of life, a meticulous description of its counterparts seems necessary before the merits of the "Christian God" can be shown. Persuasion in favor of any particular program thus requires its "Other."

The other social category bringing Nigerian films to Kinshasa's spectators is that of the dubbers (*animateurs*), or video narrators, as Krings (this volume) calls their Tanzanian colleagues. There are a handful of dubbers, working for Kinshasa's television channels, who perform simultaneous translations of all speaking parts. The television stations have their own translators (José de Jésus, for example, or Thony Best), and these are always male. They interpret all parts (men, women, children, and adults), explain the dramatic events, and comment on them, thus bringing these "foreign" narratives closer to Kinshasa's reality. Dubbers achieve this in the first place by translating English dialogue into kiKinois. Another important localizing strategy is the insertion of *mabanga*

(Lingala, sing. *libanga*). Literally, *libanga* means "stone" or "rock" but also refers to diamonds. In the context of Congo's precarious economy, *libanga* now also points to the economic struggle for survival.[16] In Kinshasa's popular culture, economic survival has a particular form: mentioning the names of local Big Men and Women. This "name-dropping" occurs in popular music (see White) and in local TV drama and is also sprinkled throughout the simultaneous translation of Nigerian films. It is not at all uncommon to hear the dubber suddenly mention "XXXX très très très fort," which then becomes a marketing strategy. "Throwing persons" confirms and creates personal networks that are socially, and at times financially, rewarding, since performance of *mabanga* in the sphere of popular arts entails an obligation from the person whose name was cited. The individual thus mentioned is expected to offer monetary or other material gifts to support the actor's performance.

In addition to making Nigerian films more familiar by interspersing the names of well-known local leaders, dubbers use an additional strategy to make Nigerian films more accessible to Kinois viewers. Aware of the hegemonic value of Christianity in Kinshasa, translators also endorse the apocalyptic battle, which they publicly express by interpreting the film scenes along that same framework. Often, dubbers go further than merely translating protagonists' dialogues. In the film *Magic Love* (this was the title given by the local channel), the opening scene shows a young couple walking around the university campus. For about five minutes there is no speech, only instrumental music underscoring images that evoke their love. While the couple picnics on the lawn, or strolls around the campus, the dubber shouts: "Oh, look at this. *Lisumu* [sin], *Lisumu!* You will see, this is the beginning of their fall. I warn all the young people who are watching this film. Such behavior invites the devil. You will see, you might think now that they are really in love and that there is no harm in touching and kissing, but you will see at the end of this film that the devil is already among them." Such discourse foretells that this love story will end badly and is entirely in line with the apocalyptic ideology of the Pentecostal churches. This example suggests that the requalification process of Nigerian films in Kinshasa consists in the ascription of a series of local significances to these films' narratives and images, thus permitting their integration into various local strategies of reception. It is exactly such practices that transcend the Nigerian films' status as simple objects of entertainment, making them into meaningful clusters of icons and symbols that lend themselves to various hermeneutic practices.

"AFRICANITY" AND NIGERIAN FILMS

As I have argued, the success of the Nigerian films does not merely reside in the specialization of a so-called genuine African film industry that can "speak back" to the metropole and counteract the cultural imperialism imposed by Western cinema. Rather, it is the establishment of an African Christianity that accounts for the popularity of Nigerian films among Kinshasa's spectators. I have identified three categories of media brokers: the petty trader, the Christian pastor, and the dubber. It should be emphasized, moreover, that these three categories are not strictly separate. Pastors also engage in petty trade, while traders can become dubbers. The latter may at times acquire the charisma of pastors.

I have also shown that religious networks, which act, above all, to structure the product's meaning, largely shape the means by which Nigerian films reach their audiences in Kinshasa. Nigerian films are integrated and taken up in a set of transformational units that orchestrate their reframing within contexts of local meanings. Nigerian films participate in Pentecostal evangelizing practices and are culturally assimilated by their brokers and spectators in several ways. It appears that, in the current Kinois context, imported Nigerian films have become embedded objects of charismatic Christianity. The insertion of Nigerian films into local viewing cultures is informed by local cultures of authority and power, and in particular by charismatic pastors' new positions of authority. Most new Christian leaders have gained their positions of power from the appeal of charismatic Christianity, as well as from their proximity to Nigerian Christian culture.

Finally, Nollywood films appeal to Kinois for their "Africanity": the cultural similarity displayed by Nigerian films with Kinshasa's lifestyle. Their "Africanity" lies in the fact that people do not trust their own judgments and prefer to visit pastors and relatives when faced with important matters. Yet, as I argued at the beginning of this chapter, it is exactly the kind of cosmopolitan Christianity Nollywood films seem to promote that attracts Kinois. The "Africanity" framed in the discourses surrounding Nollywood films (even those that do not necessarily focus on witchcraft and magic, as discussed above) is a particular construction, fitting within the Pentecostal rejection of certain parts of the "African tradition" (magic and witchcraft). Given their influence on fashion and architecture (noted earlier), Nollywood films thus are embedded in an agenda that promotes certain aspects of "African culture" while rejecting other features of "the African way of life." Rejection and pleasure coincide once more, rendering the Nollywood films consumed in Kinshasa into very complex cultural objects, the meanings and values of which undergo continuous reframing.

Migration and the Christian renewal in Kinshasa have transformed the local media world in unprecedented ways. All in all, Nigerian films function along ambiguous lines: they sometimes unfold as "good" Christian narratives, belonging to the Christian community, while at other times, they are rejected and constitute objects of the antisocial.

NOTES

1. I thank Filip De Boeck, Birgit Meyer, and Olykoya Ogen, who have read earlier drafts of this text, and the participants of the "Nollywood and Beyond" conference for their stimulating comments. I am also indebted to the anonymous reviewers of Indiana University Press for their comments. In Kinshasa, various TV actors, Pentecostal pastors, dubbers, and spectators were willing to share their opinions about and experiences with Nigerian films. I wish to mention explicitly the Cinarc troupe, the church group of "the Holy Mountain," Mr. Six and his relatives, and the dubber Thony Best. In addition, I gratefully acknowledge the support of the faculties of Psychology and Educational Sciences and also of Social Sciences at the Katholieke Universiteit Leuven, which have provided the financial support for the fieldwork. I finalized this text while a Newton International Fellow (British Academy) at the Centre of West African Studies at the University of Birmingham.

I thank Isabelle de Rezende for her editorial work.

2. Elsewhere, I offer a detailed ethnography of the production of Kinshasa's evangelizing television serials (*Making of the Pentecostal Melodrama*).

3. Often, the person who travels for religious reasons will also engage in petty trade.

4. The dissemination of Congolese music and the Mami Wata figure (the female mermaid) is probably the best example of the spread of aesthetic regimes in Africa. Drewal as well as Szombati-Fabian and Fabian have studied the latter.

5. "VCD" stands for "video compact disc" and is a CD with audiovisual images and sounds. The technology is Chinese.

6. Mostly, these street vendors sell cassettes and DVDs of music shows of local stars such as Koffi Olomide, Werrason, and Papa Wemba or international stars such as Julio Iglesias and Céline Dion. They often also sell pornographic films.

7. Others include in particular Ivorian, Nigerian, American, and Chinese films. In contrast to the early 1990s, Brazilian *telenovelas* are not being broadcast in the early twenty-first century.

8. Significantly, Kinois do not so much remember the titles of the Nigerian films, yet the protagonists' names seem to be far more influential.

9. KiKinois is a mixture of Lingala, French, and Hindubill (youth slang that originated during the early postcolonial period).

10. Although other religions, like Islam and Hinduism, are practiced in Kinshasa nowadays, these attract only a minority of Congolese.

11. I refer here to work by De Boeck; Kadima; Morris and Bouillon; Ngoie; Ngoie and Vwakyanakazi; and Sumata.

12. Of course, this situation is different for political refugees, who mainly come from the eastern Congo.

13. http://www.egliseieuvivant.org.

14. Nigerian pastors have a strong reputation for other Africans as well. African politicians often undertake pilgrimages to Nigeria in order to acquire conditions for success during elections.

15. One other film, *Nneka,* is also imprinted in the visual memories of Kinois. The film recounts the story of a young girl who owes all her success (beauty, money, and lovers) to a mystical relation with a snake. The snake, symbol of the devil, in return asks for her help in his fight against humanity.

16. The creativity of Kinois in the daily struggle for survival has generated "new jobs" in the informal sector. Well-known examples of this are the *Khadafi,* who sell fuel; the *chargeurs,* who look for passengers for public transportation; or the *bana ya vernis,* the pedicure boys from the townships who walk about the city all day long rattling their small bottles of nail polish and remover and calling out for clients.

WORKS CITED

Abu-Lughod, Lila. *Dramas of Nationhood. The Politics of Television in Egypt.* Chicago: University of Chicago Press, 2005.

Adogame, Afe, and Cordula Weissköppel, eds. "Religion in the Context of African Migration." *Bayreuth African Studies Series (BASS)* 75 (2005).

Appadurai, Arjun. *Modernity at Large: Cultural Dimensions of Globalization.* Minneapolis: University of Minnesota Press, 1996.

Corten, André, and Ruth Marshall-Fratani, eds. *Between Babel and Pentecost: Transnational Pentecostalism in Africa and Latin America.* Bloomington: Indiana University Press, 2001.

De Boeck, Filip. "Domesticating Diamonds and Dollars: Identity, Expenditure, and Sharing in s w Zaire." *Global-ization and Identity: Dialectics of Flow and Closure.* Ed. Peter Geschiere and Birgit Meyer. Oxford: Blackwell, 1999. 177–209.

De Boeck, Filip, and Marie-Françoise Plissart. *Kinshasa: Tales of the Invisible City.* Ghent and Amsterdam: Ludion, 2004.

Devisch, René. "Frenzy, Violence, and Ethical Renewal in Kinshasa." *Public Culture* 7.3 (1995): 593–629.

Drewal, Henry. "Mami Wata Shrines: Exotica and the Construction of Self." *African Material Culture.* Ed. Marie-Jo Arnoldi, Chris M. Geary, and Kirstin L. Hardin. Bloomington: Indiana University Press, 1996. 308–33.

Friedman, Jonathan. *Cultural Identity and Global Process.* London: Sage, 1994.

Fuita, Franck Baku, and Godefroid Bwiti Lumisa. "Kinshasa: Quand les vidéos nigérianes chassaient les démons." *Nollywood: Le phénomène video au Nigéria*. Ed. Pierre Barrot. Paris: L'Harmattan, 2005. 111–16.

Ginsburg, Faye D., Lila Abu-Lughod, and Brian Larkin, eds. *Media Worlds: Anthropology on New Terrain*. Berkeley and Los Angeles: University of California Press, 2002.

Hackett, Rosalind I. J. "Charismatic/Pentecostal Appropriation of Media Technologies in Nigeria and Ghana." *Journal of Religion in Africa* 28.3 (1998): 1–19.

Hannerz, Ulf. *Cultural Complexity: Studies in the Social Organization of Meaning*. New York: Columbia University Press, 1992.

Harding, Frances. "Africa and the Moving Image: Television, Film, and Video." *Journal of African Cultural Studies* 16.1 (2003): 69–84.

Kadima, Kalonji D. "Motivations for Emigration and Character of the Economic Contribution of Congolese Emigrants in South Africa." *African Immigration to South Africa: Francophone Migration of the 1990s*. Ed. Alan Morris and Antoine Bouillon. Pretoria: Protea and IFAS, 2001. 90–111.

Kalu, Ogbu. "African Pentecostalism in Diaspora." Paper delivered to the GloPent Conference, Birmingham, February 2009.

Kandel, William, and Douglas S. Massey. "The Culture of Mexican Migration: A Theoretical and Empirical Analysis." *Social Forces* 80.3 (2002): 981–1004.

Katz, Elihu, and Tamar Liebes. *The Export of Meaning*. Oxford: Oxford University Press, 1991.

Kongo, Ne. "Architecture et couleurs nigérianes à la mode à Kinshasa." *Forum des As*, April 13, 2007. Web.

Kopytoff, Igor. "The Cultural Biography of Things: Commoditization as Process."

The Social Life of Things: Commodities in Cultural Perspective. Ed. Arjun Appadurai. Cambridge: Cambridge University Press, 1986. 64–91.

Larkin, Brian. *Signal and Noise: Media, Infrastructure, and Urban Culture in Nigeria*. Durham, N.C.: Duke University Press, 2008.

Masquelier, Adeline. "Of Headhunters and Cannibals: Migrancy, Labor, and Consumption in the Mawri Imagination." *Cultural Anthropology* 15.1 (2000): 84–126.

Meyer, Birgit. "'Praise the Lord': Popular Cinema and Pentecostalite Style in Ghana's New Public Sphere." *American Ethnologist* 31.1 (2004): 92–110.

Morris, Alan, and Antoine Bouillon, eds. *African Immigration to South Africa: Francophone Migration of the 1990s*. Pretoria: Protea and IFAS, 2001.

Ngoie, Germain Tshibambe. "Devenir caméléon ... les jeunes Congolais et les réseaux des migrations clandestines vers l'Europe." Paper delivered to the conference "Migration internationale clandestine en provenance d'Afrique vers l'Europe et développement durable." Centre d'Etudes et de Recherche sur les Migrations Internationales et le Développement Durable (CERMID). Casablanca, 2008.

———. "Les femmes en mouvement: Morphologie d'une catégorie émergente dans la mobilité africaine. Cas de la République démocratique du Congo." Paper delivered to the conference "L'atelier sur les migrations africaines: Comprendre les dynamiques des migrations sur le continent." Accra, 2007.

Ngoie, Germain Tshibambe, and Mukohya Vwakyanakazi. "Profil migratoire par pays: Cas de la RDC." Paper delivered to the conference "Perspectives Africaines sur la Mobilité Humaine." Lubumbashi, 2008.

Nyamnjoh, Francis. *Africa's Media: Democracy and the Politics of Belonging*. London: Zed Books; Pretoria: UNISA Press, 2005.

Okwori, Jenkeri Z. "A Dramatized Society: Representing Rituals of Human Sacrifice as Efficacious Action in Nigerian Home-Video Movies." *Journal of African Cultural Studies* 16.1 (2003): 7–23.

Pype, Katrien. *The Making of the Pentecostal Melodrama: Religion, Media, and Gender in Kinshasa*. New York and Oxford: Berghahn Books, 2012.

———. "'We Need to Open Up the Country': Development and the Christian Key Scenario in the Social Space of Kinshasa's Teleserials." *Journal of African Media Studies* 1.1 (2009): 101–16.

Sumata, Claude. "Migradollars & Poverty Alleviation Strategy Issues in Congo (DRC)." *Review of African Political Economy* 29.93–94 (2002): 619–28.

Szombati-Fabian, Ilona, and Johannes Fabian. "Art, History, and Society: Popular Painting in Shaba, Zaire." *Studies in the Anthropology of Visual Communication* 3.1 (1976): 1–21.

Ter Haar, Gerrie. *Strangers and Sojourners: Religious Communities in the Diaspora*. Leuven: Peeters, 1998.

Van Dijk, Rijk A. "Negotiating Marriage: Questions of Morality and Legitimacy in the Ghanaian Pentecostal Diaspora." *Journal of Religion in Africa* 34.4 (2004): 438–67.

White, Bob. "Modernity's Trickster: 'Dipping' and 'Throwing' in Congolese Popular Dance Music." *Research in African Literatures* 30.4 (1999): 156–75.

FILMOGRAPHY

Karishika. Dir. Chika Onu. Tony Jickson (Nigeria). 1998.

Ma famille. TV serial. Creator: Akissi Delta. LAD Production (Ivory Coast). 2002–7.

Nneka: The Pretty Serpent. Dir. Zeb Ejiro (Nigeria). 1992.

TEN

"African Movies" in Barbados: Proximate Experiences of Fear and Desire

JANE BRYCE

"NIGERIA? I HEAR IT'S BEAUTIFUL," ENTHUSES JULIET GASKIN, an ardent Nollywood fan who lives in Bridgetown, Barbados. Her passionate response may at first mystify the listener, since, in many ways, Barbados could not be more different from Nigeria. An island in the eastern Caribbean, its landmass, at fourteen by twenty-one miles, is three-quarters the size of Lagos, and in that space live only 250,000 people, as opposed to roughly 12 million – a ratio of 1:50.[1] Like Lagos, Barbados was named by early Portuguese explorers, but unlike Lagos it had no prior status as a functioning and integrated social entity. Until the British declared it a colony and began settlement in 1627, it had been intermittently settled by small itinerant Amerindian groups from South America. It therefore came into being as a modern entity under the overlordship of the British Crown, a condition that lasted for more than three centuries, as opposed to Nigeria's less than six decades. And though the population of Barbados is overwhelmingly of African origin, the long history of enslavement and unbroken colonization by one power – the longest in the Caribbean – has meant the virtual effacement of recognizable African cultural elements such as are to be found elsewhere in the region. Traces do, of course, exist, as I shall discuss, but the contiguities between Nigeria and Barbados in the twenty-first century derive more from a common experience of postcolonial marginality in the face of global capital than from any superficially identifiable kinship relation. While it has been the task of pan-Africanism to reimagine and revalorize the latter, "Africa" remains a contested figure in the popular imagination, as often negative as it is nostalgic and heroic.

One connection can perhaps be found at the institutional level – in higher education systems bequeathed by the British. The University of the West Indies (UWI), like the University of Ibadan, began as a college of the University of London. Its first campus, at Mona, in Jamaica – founded, like Ibadan, in 1948, to create an educated cadre to serve the colonial administration – became the basis of an autonomous regional university, with other campuses in Trinidad (St. Augustine) and Barbados (Cave Hill). My perspective in writing this account is that of someone whose life has been indelibly shaped by this colonial bequest: after gaining a doctorate at Obafemi Awolowo University–Ile-Ife (an offshoot of Ibadan) at the end of the 1980s, I became a lecturer at the Cave Hill campus of UWI in 1992. As I arrived there the same year that saw *Living in Bondage* launched in Lagos, I had effectively left Nigeria just as the Nollywood boom took off. In a belated attempt to update myself, I went to Lagos in 2006 to talk to Nollywood practitioners and learn about the industry. When I left Barbados in June, Nollywood was nowhere to be seen; by the time I returned a month later, a revolution had taken place. I walked into my local video store – source of pirated copies of recently released Hollywood films – and there was a new section labeled "African Movies." In amazement, I looked at the titles and realized that not only were these "African," but they were the same films I had been seeing on sale in the Surulere video market, by some of the same people I had been talking to. Suddenly, Nollywood movies were everywhere. My dressmaker, who was watching one when I came by, said she loved them: they were "different from what you usually see," the stories were exciting, they were well acted, and above all they were cheap. She was concerned about the cheapness, because she couldn't see how the filmmakers were making any money. This, however, was a huge advantage in terms of their accessibility. It seemed that almost overnight, Nollywood had conquered Barbados.

Why was I amazed? Nollywood is watched in most places where there are diaspora communities, so why not Barbados? My surprise arose from my own experience of trying to create an audience for African cinema over the previous eight or so years, in a media context overdetermined by our proximity to the United States. I had started by introducing a course in African cinema at the university, which I had been teaching for a couple of years when I attended the Noir Tout Couleurs Film Festival in the French island of Guadeloupe in 1999. As a result of contacts made at that festival, I conceived the idea of what became the Barbados Festival of African and Caribbean Film, which ran in one form or another from July 2002.[2] Today there are a number of festivals in Barbados, but this was the first, run as a collaborative effort between the university and the community. It gave us the opportunity to bring a number of prominent African and Caribbean filmmakers and scholars to show their films and talk about them in person, creating an interregional dialogue that was an important aspect of the event.

The festival was one part of the local context of cinema reception in Barbados; it has subsequently been replaced by a number of other festivals, most recently the annual Caribbean Tales Festival, run by the Toronto-based Trinidadian filmmaker Frances-Anne Solomon. The university also hosts a number of film seasons and a fortnightly Film Society. However, such events, though popular and well received, are patronized by a typically middle-class audience, many of whom are expatriates or locals who have lived overseas. The majority of the population prefers to patronize the two local cinemas, both of which are firmly sutured into the Hollywood distribution system and show almost exclusively current box-office, blockbuster, and mainstream films. The Globe offers a more old-fashioned approach to cinema-going. Its two venues, one a centrally located urban theater, the other a suburban open-air drive-in, are both single screen, and each program is a double-bill. In the indoor movie theater, the audience is divided by a self-selected choice of seating: either upstairs in the balcony (more expensive and more sedate) or downstairs in the pit (cheaper, rowdier, and more interactive). The Olympus Theatre is a modern multiplex located in an out-of-town shopping center, boasting several screens as well as a separate "VIP" viewing space with in-seat refreshment service. The Olympus is open to varied programming, was the venue for our festival screenings, and has since hosted European film seasons as well as occasional Caribbean films during festival seasons, which otherwise fight for visibility.[3] With increasing education and training opportunities through UWI, as well as support from official cultural organizations and government ministries, there have been determined attempts in Barbados to create a local film industry, and a small number of films have been made locally.[4]

There is, however, little crossover in terms of class, with locally made as well as "foreign" films remaining the specialized interest of an edu-

cated minority and American popular cinema being the main alternative
to television for the rest of the population. Despite a government ruling
that there should be 60 percent local content on the single local channel,
and despite the occasional appearance of South African soaps, the tastes
of most ordinary viewers are formed by television soaps and films seen
on cable TV.[5] It is easy to see, therefore, how the situation I have outlined
above supports prevailing stereotypes of Africa as primitive, inferior,
and able to express itself, if at all, only in song and dance and traditional
culture. This stereotype appears in Cropover (the local Carnival) bands
in Barbados in the form of Zulu warriors dressed in skins and shaking
spears. In the popular imagination, Africa vacillates between an idealized repository of unchanging traditions, as in *The Lion King*, or permanently at war, as in *Black Hawk Down, Blood Diamond, Hotel Rwanda*,
and innumerable others. The screening on local television of a series of
feature films by resident Senegalese filmmaker Moussa Sene Absa, who
at the time of writing had spent three years teaching film at UWI–Cave
Hill, has not made much of a dent on this impression. Absa attributes
this to the influence of Nollywood, which, he says, "has harmed [the
audience] so much. . . . They know only about polygamy, witch doctors,
the oppression of women, not culture or the resistance to colonialism,
multinational exploitation, et cetera."

Absa's complaint overlooks the fact that African art house cinema
had, as I have shown, been promoted for several years before the Nollywood takeover. Moreover, 2006 was not the first appearance of Nollywood on the island. It was an integral part of the Festival of African
and Caribbean Film, with presentations by cultural scholar Onookome
Okome in 2003 and 2004, and – though he maintains his distance from
Nollywood – the participation of Tunde Kelani in 2004. His film *Thunderbolt*, a drama centered on occult practices, struck a chord with an
audience acquainted with folk beliefs in the local setting. In general,
however, Nollywood films were too far outside audience expectations
of African cinema, and too strange to their experience of movie genre,
to be taken to heart by a middle-class audience. As a result, by June 2006
African cinema was arguably as marginal to the island's culture as it had
been when we started the festival. The emergence of "African movies" as
a cultural phenomenon took place only once a working-class audience
became involved.

Over the following months, the press began to pay attention to the craze for Nollywood that was sweeping the country. Asking "what is it about these intriguing movies that have Barbadians hooked on them?" the *Sunday Sun* reported, "Many now have a better understanding and grasp of African lifestyle and feel a closer affiliation with the Motherland" (Bradshaw, "African Movies"). Invoking the motherland brings into view another perspective on "Africa" that circulates in Barbados among heritage-conscious individuals: Africa as the site of an ancient royal lineage, the Lion of Judah and Emperor Haile Selassie. Pre-Nollywood, therefore, "Africa" as sign oscillated between the prevailing stereotypes of primitivism and the site of origin lost in the mists of a romanticized past. The arrival of Nollywood as a commercial entity – not confined to the rarefied atmosphere of a film festival – did more to challenge and destabilize these myths than years of painstaking work on the part of academics and festival curators. As one interviewee put it: "We are accustomed to seeing Africans living in huts and dirt poor; but now we know that some also live in some really big houses with exquisite furniture. The dress, the music and dancing are just as modern as we have here in the Caribbean" (ibid.). Not only that, but Nollywood was soon embedded as an aspect of local enterprise in the form of a new business sector dealing with its reproduction and marketing. The videos had become so popular that several people have rented small spaces in malls, selling them exclusively for 5 Barbadian dollars (US$2.50). According to the *Sunday Sun,* the proprietors of these outlets "were selling hundreds of African movies weekly." One of the proprietors who was interviewed put it this way: "I have to keep on top with the new releases because people love them and I have customers who buy about three a day" (ibid.).

Piracy, from the outset, was recognized as a problem that could be addressed only at its source. Though Barbados has stringent piracy laws, they can be applied only when the copyright owners assert their ownership, and they then have to appear in person to make a case. This is the reason pirated copies of Hollywood films are reproduced and sold with impunity in Barbados and across the Caribbean – the market is too small to warrant the expense of asserting ownership on the part of the producers. How much more difficult, then, to police piracy in the case of a product already pirated at its source, and where production costs are too low to make pursuing pirates viable. The head of the then recently formed

Government of Barbados Trans-African Centre for Trade, Nigerian Ntui
Okey, lost no time, however, in capitalizing on the unprecedented level
of interest in his country occasioned by Nollywood. A plan was hatched
to bring Nigerian actors to Barbados to participate in "the local film festival" (then the Bridgetown Festival). These included Patience Ozokwor,
Ramsey Nouah, and the very popular "two rats," Osita Iheme and Chin-
edu Ikedieze (ibid.). Okey also claimed that "plans were in the works
to shoot a combined film with Nigerian and Barbadian actors" and to
sell broadcast rights to the Caribbean Broadcasting Corporation. These
plans never came to fruition, as a result, it appears, of demands by the
actors concerned that would have pushed the costs too high.

THE APPEAL OF NOLLYWOOD: "BLACK LIKE US"?

Though the buzz surrounding Nollywood has waned somewhat since
its initial impact, there is still, many years later, a loyal and committed
audience serviced by numerous outlets importing and selling films. Two
of these are to be found in the busy commercial area of Roebuck Street in
central Bridgetown, in the vicinity of the towering Central Bank building. Roebuck Plaza, a small indoor shopping mall with hairdressers and
cheap clothing stores, contains one. It has been in operation since 2008,
when the owner diversified his clothing import business by bringing in
movies from New York, where he has a Nigerian supplier whom he visits
once a month. A space about twelve feet square is filled floor to ceiling
with sleeve inserts and poster images, which customers browse to make
their choices. Brightly lit with a glass-topped counter and Christian messages interspersed among the video inserts, it is run by the owner's sister,
herself a fan. Like all the fans I spoke to, she called her favorite actors
familiarly by their first names ("Patience, Genevieve, Mercy, Richard,
Ramsey"), and when asked what she liked about the movies, she said,
"They show the life we live." Pressed to explain what she meant, she
shrugged, before adding, "Backbiting, maliciousness, greed, and all the
rest" (Patricia). At the same time, her preferred genres were "comedies,
action, and drama; I don't like the voodoo ones." A second outlet in an
adjoining street is quite different: a large dusty room containing mostly
empty shelves, it evidently used to function as some sort of small su-
permarket. The fact that it is now given over to peddling movies is pro-

claimed by a notice on the door advertising newly arrived Nollywood hits. On the walls hang several posters, while at the front near the entrance is a desk covered in sleeve inserts. Customers cluster around the desk, leafing through them before making their choices. In both stores, the films sell at three for 10 Barbadian dollars (US$5), a little more than the price of a bottle of beer in a rum shop. A middle-aged male customer laughed when I said I thought it was mostly women who watched them. He said they were just as popular with men and that he had a collection of five hundred films that he watches on a specially bought large flat-screen TV. He confided that he was "tired of cursing and violence in American films" and preferred Nollywood because anyone could watch them, one did not have to turn them off when there were children around, and they emphasized marriage rather than sex and divorce. The one thing he did not like was the depiction of witchcraft, "because I'm a Christian." He had been in New York recently, "and they don't have better or different. And they charge more. You pay five U.S. dollars for a bootleg in a case. Here we don't care about the case; we just want the movie."[6]

What accounts for Nollywood's enduring popularity in this far-flung diasporic community? According to Ntui Okey, "People in the diaspora and the Caribbean can identify with the storylines, themes and the language used. They like the fact that black actors star in the main roles. It is the first time they have seen all the roles performed by Blacks and this is uplifting" (Bradshaw, "African Actors"). This brings to mind the title of an essay by Tunde Giwa, "Black Like Us," in which he recalls the craze for comics like *Boom* and *African Film* in the 1960s and '70s. These comics with their African superheroes, he says, "brought many of us joy and not a little pride in the blackness of [their] characters . . . [and] helped create a hitherto unseen shared, Anglophone pan-African, cultural frame of reference that spread beyond the continent all the way to the Caribbean."

How likely is it that racial identification is the primary force of attraction for the Barbadian Nollywood audience? Pan-Africanism has certainly been influential in creating "some idea of a shared, collective African identity in opposition to European identity" (Zeleza 4), but it is debatable how far this has been internalized in an island subjected for centuries to a racist ideology of white supremacy, resulting all too often in a self-preserving distancing from "Africa." To counteract this effect, the Commission for Pan-African Affairs was founded in 1998 to represent a more positive view of Africa's relationship to the island and "mandated by the Government of Barbados to address and rectify that deficiency in Barbadian institutions and national life which is manifested in the relative dearth of relationships, exchanges and interactions with the nations, population groups and institutions of the continent of Africa and the world-wide African Diaspora."[7] As Paul Zeleza has pointed out, and the mandate of the Barbados Commission makes clear, pan-Africanism is closely identified with nationalism and the construction of the postcolonial state. Of the six versions he identifies, "trans-Atlantic, Black Atlantic, continental, sub-Saharan, pan-Arab and global," the version espoused in Barbados is trans-Atlantic, that is, it "imagine[s] a pan-African world linking continental Africa and its diaspora in the Americas" (ibid.). In "African Modes of Self-Writing," Achille Mbembe deconstructs these categories, demonstrating the ways in which they determine the limits of an "African" identity. He cites the use of "Marxist and nationalist categories to develop an imaginaire of culture and politics in which a manipulation of the rhetoric of autonomy, resistance and emancipation serves as the sole criterion for determining the legitimacy of an authentic African discourse . . . [and] an emphasis on the 'native condition' . . . [that] promoted the idea of a unique African identity founded on membership of the black race" (240–41).

It is quite evident in Barbados that there is a divide between official and unofficial, or governing-class and popular, perspectives on this notion of a "unique African identity." The rhetoric of regionalism calls on Caribbean people to see themselves as one family in different islands, at the same time as borders are increasingly policed and illegal migration highlights economic inequalities between the territories. Just as Barbadians used to travel for work to Panama in the 1950s, Guyanese now flock to Barbados, where they live under the immigration authorities' radar and work at jobs scorned by the better-educated and more aspirational local population. Furthermore, few of the territories are as homogeneous as Barbados; in the Anglophone Caribbean, succeeding occupations by the French, Spanish, and British imperial powers, as well as indentured labor arriving from Scotland, India, and Portugal, and Chinese, Lebanese, and Jewish immigration, have resulted in a rich cultural layering of which "Africa" is only one element. Pan-Africanism, therefore, is more often an ideological position adopted by politicians than an identification freely felt by ordinary people. It serves official purposes well where certain kinds of credentials are called for. For example, the new administration building at the Cave Hill campus, designed to replicate an Ashanti stool, was opened by the *Asantehene* himself in 2007, complete with trumpeters and parasol bearers. The interior decor of the building reflects the emphasis on traditional Africa and precolonial royalty, in the form of carved wooden masks and tribal photographs. The question of Ashanti slave ownership is overlooked in favor of a spectacularized Africa that speaks to ruling-class linkages.

This is not to say that Africa has not left its trace in the region, but that this trace is to be found not in conspicuously engineered nationalist occasions, but in belief systems and practices that sustained people during slavery and still thrive today. Religious practices like Shango (Orisha) worship and the Spiritual Baptist church in Trinidad, Kumina in Jamaica, Vodun in Haiti, and Santeria in Cuba all owe their form and substance to African cultural memory. The New World experience has also produced a specific spiritual and social movement in the shape of Rastafari, which continues to attract people who seek an alternative to establishment notions of citizenship and spirituality. In Barbados there are both adherents of the Spiritual Baptist Church and a minority following for Rastafari.[8] The fact that Rastafari is perceived as a fringe religion and its followers marginalized or at times penalized differentiates it from official pan-Africanism. Its goal is less a liberated state than a spiritual kingdom, and its iconography stresses royalty, genealogy, and dignity. What they have in common, however, is a basis in what Mbembe calls "Africanity," the belief in the power of the Return to Africa to substitute for what has been lost. This "Return," however, is not to Africa as it has been shaped by modernity, but to the African past.

In this light, the question of the nature of Nollywood's appeal is all the more provocative in that what the audience responds to is precisely the revisioning of Africa as fundamentally *not* separate, but a participant in the global project of modernity. The difficulty with this view is that it challenges the pieties of racial distinctiveness and requires a relinquishing of race as the ultimate signifier of "Africanness," the promise of recovery of a lost identity. The solution proposed by Mbembe to this dilemma is as follows: "Because the time we live in is fundamentally fractured, the very project of an essentialist sacrificial recovery of the self is, by definition, doomed. Only the disparate, and often intersecting, practices through which Africans *stylize* their conduct and life can account for the thickness of which the African present is made" (292–93).

Instead of focusing on an unchanging essence, Nollywood's emphasis is precisely on "the thickness of the African present," on what people in Africa *do* with and *make* out of cultural forms that compete in the contemporary global marketplace. The popular audience in Barbados has been acculturated over decades by superannuated American soaps (*The Young and the Restless, Days of Our Lives, The Bold and the Beautiful*) that play on television every day, predisposing them to an acceptance of melodramatic plots, a heightened emotional atmosphere, cliffhanger endings, sequels, and recurring motifs and characters – an exact match with Nollywood melodramas. One interviewee said watching a single film was "like watching a whole season of *Desperate Housewives.*" Moreover, the title by which Nollywood is known in the Caribbean – "African movies" – testifies to the absence of interest in Nigerian specificity. Another interviewee asked, for example, if Ghana was in Nigeria, and though the movies imported to Barbados are exclusively from southern Nigeria, and most are from the East, none of those interviewed had the faintest idea of the different groups in Nigeria or their cultural differences. Interest is entirely focused on two spatial dimensions: the city, with its trappings of modernity, and the rural village settings, which are seen as both exotic and familiar. While a respondent expressed a preference for rural over urban settings, "because it's strictly Nigerian, not American," Nigeria's dramatic rural-urban divide is replicated in two ways in the Caribbean: one is through migration to the metropolitan cities of the United States and Britain, which make Caribbean cities look like villages in comparison, the other through a microcosmic parallel within the territories themselves, where the city is viewed as synonymous with both upward mobility and antisocial tendencies like increased violence and lawlessness. In Barbados (I am told), despite its size there is a clear division between the church-based morality that rules in the country areas and the "slackness" of the urban areas, where "town girls" are recognizable by their hairstyles with weaves or gel, French-polished nails, makeup, and gold jewelry. Dialect words – *sketelle, jamette* – highlight this difference.

The lack of recognition by Barbadian viewers of the significance of Nigerian geographical distinctions like "East," "Southwest," and "North"

means that "Nigeria" (which subsumes Ghana) has become a sign for
"Africa." Under this sign, audiences take pleasure in what they perceive
as learning more about Africa as elsewhere: "It all boils down to education – you learn a lot because you get to see that part of the world and how
people live." Also: "I like how they emphasize education in the movies.
You have to go to school to get a job." This argument was used in a focus
group of young Guyanese immigrants in Barbados, all of whom were
members of Pentecostal churches, to counteract the fear expressed by
some of "negative" elements such as *obeah* and *voodoo*: "We know it's
coming out of Africa, but the movies don't show how really evil it is. It's a
bare joke, because *obeah* can be really bad." A man in his thirties rejoined,
"That's part of the culture, so I don't have a problem with it." Similarly,
when one person complained the films focused too much on fashion, he
countered, "But that's how Nigerians live. It's a cultural thing. You can't
expect them to behave like Americans."[9]

Another point on which there was general agreement was that the
actors are "real people" with human imperfections, "not like Hollywood
actors." One woman in the Guyanese group told me, "I like how the
women fight for their men. You can get really emotional." A focus group
of students at the Cave Hill campus noted the realism lent the movies
by the fact that "the actors aren't all young and glamorous. More mature
people carry the plot, even if it's sexual. The imperfections mean people
can identify with the characters, to the point where they think it's real
life."[10] All the women I spoke to approved of the portrayal of an assertive
femininity. According to the student group, "The women are sexually
voracious, but they have power and autonomy. Feminine empowerment
comes through sexuality." A middle-aged woman especially endorsed
the roles played by Patience Ozukwor: "She's the only one I've seen who
actually beats the husband and refuses to cook for him. She's in control.
I would love to meet her." One UWI graduate, now an officer with the
Government Information Service, who has done her own research on
audience attitudes, told me, "It's not that we dress like them, it's that they
dress like us. They look like real people. The mass media make you feel
bad about yourself. In *Handsome* [the film we watched together], Mrs.
Benson is plump and older. If that was Hollywood, she'd have looked
like Meryl Streep in *The Devil Wears Prada*" (Harper). Despite the overwhelming influence of foreign media and advertising on local audiences,

the predilection for plumpness distinguishes body image in the Caribbean from Western concepts of beauty. Beauty queens and models may be conventionally slim, but popular culture still privileges the kind of "big batty" sexiness on display at Carnival.

These testimonies indicate the extent to which a Caribbean audience responds simultaneously to both the familiar ("black like us") and the exotic (not "like us") in Nollywood movies. In other words, both similarity and difference are equally appealing and necessary ingredients. As we watched a movie together, genre recognition enabled the members of the Guyanese focus group to "read" the narrative as they watched it, constantly commenting on the action and predicting what would happen next. They recognized the characters and correctly identified their roles in the plot. At the same time, they wanted to know why Nigerians always drink water and not, as here, fruit juice with food; why they don't seem to eat vegetables; why they use their hands to eat; whether women are really subservient to men; and whether it's true that the extended family can make demands on married couples.

In her article "Charting Nollywood's Appeal Locally and Globally," Moradewun Adejunmobi addresses the issue of cross-cultural appeal and argues: "What is at stake in the appeal of Nollywood . . . is not cultural proximity in the sense of shared cultural heritage, shared cultural patrimony or devotion to a common store of values. . . . [V]iewers may or may not recognize *akpu* and bitter leaf soup displayed on screen, but they understand when meals are meant to be read as signs of excessive consumption, and when they are meant to be read as signs of indigence and poverty" (109). As opposed to cultural proximity, she proposes "phenomenological proximity" or "substantive relevance" as audience drivers, alongside the appeal of foreignness and "vicarious displacement" (110). Her conclusion that "these films travel so well across state and cultural boundaries in Africa because the conflicts they represent and the resolutions they offer are perceived to be experientially proximate for postcolonial subjects" holds true equally for subjects in the Caribbean. In particular, the Manichaean moral universe, in which wrongdoing is punished and evil is ousted by good, as well as "the seemingly unstoppable manifestation of excess" typical of melodrama, can be shown to be experientially proximate for Caribbean viewers (111, 113).

10.1. Interviewee Juliet Gaskin in one of her "African" outfits.

CARIBBEAN PROXIMITIES: STYLE, MONEY, MAGIC, RELIGION

"I love the dresses. People have changed their style since African movies." The speaker is Juliet Gaskin, a retired lady who, when interviewed by the *Sunday Sun* in January 2007, already had a collection of five hundred movies. When I interviewed her in May 2011, she had nine hundred and another two hundred brought by her lodger that she hadn't seen. She watches all day on weekends, up to five or six movies a day. All the titles are recorded in a ledger, starting with *Blood Sisters* in 2006. This, by common assent, was the first Nollywood film to appear in Barbados, and "I was hooked. I'm still hooked. The essence of African movies is 'Don't mind how rough life gets. In the end you'll get through.'" What was it about the film that appealed to her? "It shows people in general. Jealousy between sisters: I want what you have, and I want it at any cost. It's true to life. What happened to Esther [the woman who murders her sister and takes over her husband] was good because she didn't treat the children well. Children don't let you go. As a mother you still look after them; you don't want people to treat them bad." Though Juliet's level of identification is not unusual, she has both leisure and resources to indulge her obsession, as her wardrobe shows. The local shops, she says, all have the same styles, "so if you wear a nice gold dress, someone will step in with the same dress." As a prominent member of her Pentecostal church, Juliet has many occasions when she needs to dress up, so she has started wearing "African" fashion. A Christmas tradition in Barbados is to gather in Queen's Park, an open space in the center of Bridgetown, to parade in your festive clothes. In 2009 Juliet and a group of friends met there in African outfits and posed for tourists to take pictures. "They thought we were real Africans!" A Nigerian friend brings her material, or she gets it in London and has an outfit made, often copying a style she has seen on a Nollywood actress. Now, she has around twenty outfits. "It makes you look different. If you go to a function and twenty people have on African wear, you won't find two people in the same outfit."

Juliet says that before she started watching, she didn't know anything about Africa, and what attracted her beside the fashion were the rituals and the lavish interiors. This fascination with furnishings was borne out by other viewers, who confirmed, "We all enjoy looking at the houses." At a shoot I attended in Osapa London, Lekki Peninsula, Lagos, in 2006, to watch Chico Ejiro directing an episode of the TV soap *Treasures*, I made an inventory of the living room where the action was taking place. The decor was new-rich and ostentatious: on the floor a fake tiger-skin rug, with head; on the walls, factory-made art reproductions on pink board in highly decorated white picture frames; displayed around the room, a collection of plaster figurines, a white china plinth with bunches of grapes containing spray-painted pampas grass, a huge plasma TV screen. There was glass everywhere, including a glass-block bar with an array of liquor bottles on glass shelves and on the counter plaster figures contorted so as to hold bottles aloft on their feet. Opposite me was a washbasin with the drainpipe exposed, as though the money had run out when it came to finishing. Though both of the Barbados houses in which I watched movies with volunteers were typical modest middle-class dwellings in dense residential neighborhoods, this decor would not have been out of place. Fewer and fewer people today live in the simple post-Emancipation wooden chattel houses, balanced on blocks so they could be removed from the owner's land if necessary. Upward mobility decrees "wall houses," built of cement blocks and lacking some of the more attractive features of the earlier postslavery housing that used to open straight onto the road. Instead of the open porch where occupiers used to lounge and greet passersby, small verandas with concrete balustrades enclose entrances that lead into formally furnished parlors, almost always dominated by an oversize television. Juliet's wall house was painted pink on the outside, and inside the carpeted living room had white gold-embroidered curtains, two chandeliers, and a white teddy bear on an upholstered sofa with plump throw pillows. A large sideboard decorated like a shrine had as a centerpiece a reproduction of a painting of Niagara Falls, flanked by a photograph of the recently deceased prime minister, David Thompson. Several photos of Juliet in different African outfits sat alongside china ornaments and fake flowers on various shelves.

The contiguities in taste are one example of the way Nollywood movies play on the familiar, surprising viewers with the similarity between "us" and "them." In Barbados, as in Nigeria, most people do not live in lavishly furnished pillared houses with a gate attendant and electric gates, but they are aware that others do. In an island that has traditionally been a holiday resort for British aristocrats, their discreet West Coast villas hidden in secluded gardens have over the years become an organic part of the landscape. The traditional "great houses" of the old plantation owners tend also to be hidden away down driveways and are not usually very ostentatious, their style in keeping with the older popular architecture of the island. The tourist hotels, however, the island's major employers, bring local people into contact with a level of luxury to which they cannot aspire, while the various gated and guarded communities that have increasingly colonized acres of Barbados's best real estate are like a parallel world. One of these, built around the world-famous Royal Westmoreland Golf Course, is landscaped so that every villa has a view of an artificial lake with tinkling fountain, the golf course, or a vista of the Caribbean Sea sparkling in the distance. With names like Big Tree House, Idyll Moments, Cuckoo Land, Lazy Days, Bali H'ai, and Bougainvillea, each one costs five million U.S. dollars to build and is serviced by an army of maids, cooks, and gardeners. All the

villas are privately owned, many by celebrities, and rented out for fourteen thousand dollars a week on behalf of their owners by Royal Westmoreland. In the dry season, the only patch of green you can see from
the air on the whole island is the golf course. In the Caribbean, tourism
plays the role of oil in Nigeria – it makes visible conspicuous consumption apparently unattached to any logic by which ordinary people live
their lives. This magical wealth both fascinates and repels, providing a
vicarious exposure to luxury and power while simultaneously highlighting the contrast with a world governed by insecurity and the fluctuations
of global capital.

As Comaroff and Comaroff and others have shown, millennial capitalism is universally characterized by "occult economies and new religious movements" that come about precisely in response to the anomie
of powerlessness, the impossibility for most people of ever participating
in the fabulous riches of the global marketplace, and the inability of
the state to maintain or protect civil society. While so-called developed
societies are equally subject to "the allure of wealth from nothing," another proximity between the Caribbean and Nigeria is the turn to fun-
damentalism, particularly Pentecostalist Christianity, which bolsters
belief in the occult and hidden powers (313). The secret sources of wealth
that underpin the excessive display on which Nollywood thrives have
their counterpart in the Caribbean not only in tourism but also in the
off-shore banking sector, where the super-rich hide their wealth to protect it from taxation. The review of a recently published study, *Treasure
Islands: Tax Havens and the Men Who Stole the World,* shows how the
best tax havens are places with an air of respectability – Switzerland, the
City of London, the Channel Islands, and certain Caribbean territories.
"What such places offer are . . . plenty of the trappings of respectability
and democratic accountability . . . somewhere with British values but
without its unfortunate tendency to raise either taxes or regulatory standards in response to political pressure" (Runciman). Barbados, with its
nearly four-hundred-year-old parliament and statue of Admiral Nelson,
is just such a place, affectionately known as Little Britain or Bimshire.
By contrast, other places very close by are conspicuously corrupt. The
neighboring island of Antigua, for example, sold its entire economy to
Texas billionaire Alan Stansfield and is now bankrupt as a result of his
arrest for fraud and the collapse of his empire. According to Runciman,

"Islands make good tax havens . . . because they are close-knit communities, in which everyone knows what's going on but no-one wants to speak
for fear of ostracism." Meanwhile, another hidden current in the ocean
linking Nigeria to Barbados is what the study's author, Nicholas Shaxon,
calls "tides of looted or tainted oil money [that] sluice into the offshore
system, distorting the global economy in the process" (8).

VOODOO ECONOMICS MEETS VOODOO RELIGION

As many scholars have observed, in the face of this confusion, this dis-
junct between sign and referent, religion and the occult steps in to fill
the gap. The role of religion in shaping viewer expectations, noted by
Nollywood scholars (Agorde; Dipio; Meyer; Mohammed; Ogunleye;
Okome) is no less important in Barbados than in Nigeria. The established church in Barbados – the officiator at all state occasions – is the
Church of England, and the island is administered as a collection of
parishes, each centered on a church named after a saint, such as Saint
Michael, Saint Thomas, or Saint Lucy. Although church attendance is
generally decreasing, the Church of England, along with other historical
congregations such as Catholics, Moravians, and Methodists, is losing
adherents to the newer charismatic churches that are sweeping the Caribbean. As in Africa, this division between "mainline and clap-hand
churches" (Edmonds and Gonzalez 14) speaks to "the tension between
the rational-ethical and confessional religious traditions from Europe
and the vernacular religious traditions oriented more strongly toward
ritual healing and possession" (7). Preceding the American-based Evangelical churches, the Spiritual Baptists, a local syncretic church that
originated in Trinidad, was established in Barbados in 1957; its adherents
are distinguished by the wearing of symbolically colored robes, tying
their heads, and "catching the spirit." Like Pentecostalism, the Spiritual
Baptists provide a space for African-inflected worship practices in a
context where these have traditionally been suppressed and demonized.
During slavery, a range of African-derived beliefs were grouped together
and dismissed as *obeah,* a term used in the Anglophone Caribbean with
similar negative connotations to the misnamed *voodoo* in Haiti. Cultural
anthropologists have shown how *obeah,* an essentially neutral system
"related to the channeling of supernatural/spiritual forces," was reduced

by Europeans in the West Indies to "a kind of virulent witchcraft, aug-
mented by the administration of poisons," "a type of sorcery or witchcraft which may be broadly equated with West African 'bad medicine'"
(Bilby and Handler 154, 156, 157). So entrenched was the belief that *obeah*
was evil that linguists claimed it was derived from terms such as Asante-
Twi *obayi-fo*, "evil witches"; Bilby and Handler make the case for its
being derived from Igbo or a related language, in which "*dibia* refers to
a 'doctor' or 'healer' . . . and a related term, *abia*, denotes various kinds
of esoteric knowledge" (163). Although the practice of *obeah* has been
treated with varying degrees of stringency by the law – from a capital
offense in 1806 to a felony characterized as vagrancy in 1944 – legislation
against it was repealed in Barbados only in 1998 (168–69).

    Obeah, therefore, though its traces are far more rudimentary, as far
as the Pentecostal churches are concerned has today the same status in
Barbados as traditional religion in Nigeria. As Birgit Meyer has shown,
"Pentecostal-charismatic churches owe much of their appeal to the fact
that they easily, and seemingly effortlessly, tie into popular understandings and, in particular, take seriously anxieties about the evil machina-
tions of demons and witches, whom they represent as vassals of Satan" (9).

    There is no doubt that part of the appeal of Nollywood in the Carib-
bean arises from the deep-rooted belief in evil, and in the devil as a living
reality, that local audiences share with their West African counterparts.
Meyer's analysis of how video embodies the struggle between good and
evil applies equally to the Caribbean, as does her characterization of
Pentecostalism as itself a form of entertainment spectacle in which "be-
lievers are addressed as audiences and consumers" and church leaders
emphasize "prophecy and vision and frame church service as a spectacular performance where the presence of the Holy Spirit can be witnessed" (11, 14). Dominica Dipio confirms this when she says the public
performance of miracles leads to an expectation of quick solutions to
problems, seen as the consequences of witchcraft, and notes, "Theatre,
art and spiritual experience are all combined in the rituals" (79).

    Interviewing respondents in Barbados, I found that *obeah* was one
of the first things they wanted to talk about in relation to Nollywood
movies. They all, spontaneously, referred to the occult as *obeah* and saw
it variously as something to fear, something to avoid, or something you
might watch with impunity if you have adequate protection. Respon-

dents in the student focus group, asked how widespread belief in *obeah* was in Barbados, replied: "If you believe in good, you have to believe in evil" and "We believe, and because we believe we don't want to watch, because we're afraid." Though there was some disapproval among respondents at the way the occult element "buys into a stereotype – if you don't know better you'll think that every African practices or knows about witchcraft," others were of the opinion that "even when people don't believe in it, it's real." Respondents divided into those who didn't mind watching movies containing occult practices, because "I don't think watching voodoo on-screen can affect you. We don't have the know-how to make that happen," and those who warned, for example, "There are *obeah* men who could learn from it. You're looking for a solution so you can turn to it. It's the same as pornography – it can influence you." Both responses bear out Meyer's and Dipio's claim that the representation is taken for the reality and that the dramatization of the occult is itself seen as an aspect of occult practice. The Pentecostalists, however, felt that they were protected from its evil effects by belief in God. Juliet Gaskin was one of these: "It's just cinema. If you sit down and watch with intent, you'll see that *obeah* backfires. Nothing beats prayer." When Juliet watched *Blood on the Altar* with her pastor and a group from her church one Sunday afternoon, the lesson the pastor drew from the portrayal of a corrupt priest was not to put all your faith in pastors, but to read the Bible for yourself and live by it. In other words, the foundational principle of Pentecostalism, embodied by the movie, was endorsed and mediated by the pastor.

The question of what constitutes Nollywood's appeal in Barbados (and the Caribbean in general) is complex and many layered, but it goes well beyond a straightforward racial or pan-African identification. Indeed, it is far more interesting than that and speaks to a common experience of global flows of popular culture, capital, and religion that simultaneously erase and exoticize difference. I have said nothing here about other shared cultural features – orality, the interactive reception of cinema, or local varieties of English that operate on a continuum from standard Nigerian or West Indian English to the pidgin, patois, dialect, or Creole that so often mark the speaker as poor, working class, or powerless. But from the evidence here, we can see that the magic of Nollywood, conjured out of nothing (as filmmaker Bond Emerua jokes in

This Is Nollywood), exerts a multifarious fascination that can no more be reduced to a single element than culture itself.

NOTES

1. The exact population of Lagos is not known. Interviewed on the BBC World Service program *One Planet* (June 20, 2011), an expert gave it as "somewhere between ten and sixteen million." I have taken a figure somewhere in the middle for this calculation.

2. Its mission statement declared: "The Barbados Festival of African and Caribbean Film is the latest manifestation of a growing phenomenon – a recognition of the importance of visual media to the region, and an enthusiastic engagement with the processes of production, distribution, spectatorship and criticism. In other words, we in the region, recognizing the overwhelming power of the media networks of our much larger neighbor, are actively working to assert our own identity, as filmmakers and movie audiences. This involves exerting a choice over what we see, creating awareness of the 'other' cinemas of the world and bringing them to local audiences."

3. In the Anglophone Caribbean, until recently, the emphasis has been on promoting the Caribbean as a location over support for local filmmaking. Two recent examples of location shooting by foreign companies are Merchant Ivory's *The Mystic Masseur* (based on a V. S. Naipaul novel) in Trinidad, with negligible local participation, in 2001, and the shooting of Disney's *Pirates of the Caribbean: The Curse of the Black Pearl* in St. Vincent (2003) and its sequel *Dead Man's Chest* in St. Vincent, Dominica, and the Bahamas (2006), where the significant short-term boost in local casual employment overrode the niceties of self-representation and cultural nationalism.

4. *Hit for Six* (2007); *A Handful of Dirt* (2011); *Sweet Bottom* (in process); parts of a documentary, *Yoole: The Sacrifice* (2010); and many digital shorts.

5. Even before the advent of cable, the Guyanese director Michael Gilkes declared: "The perception of the average Caribbean citizen is that it is 'de people' television, i.e. it belongs to someone else; the government, private enterprise, foreign interests. *Them,* not us" ("Inside the People TV" 1).

6. Customer at video outlet, May 28, 2011, Bridgetown.

7. Statement of the Inter-American Cultural Policy Observatory, which also declares the objectives of the commission as the following: "To ensure that the Government and institutions of Barbados establish concrete political, economic and cultural links with the Governments and institutions of Africa and the African Diaspora; to assist in the development of the African derived segment of the Barbadian cultural landscape; to be available as a pan-African resource institution to be drawn upon by other Government departments and private sector agencies."

8. Rastafarian precepts are well known: the belief in the divinity of Emperor Haile Selassie, the desire for a return to "Africa" figured as Ethiopia, the rejection of materialism, and the practice of rituals and a way of life specific to the faith.

9. Farida, Kenrick, Makeba, Maloney, Mark, Rachel, and Shevawn. Focus-group discussion with people belonging to a Pentecostal community in Barbados, ages twenty to thirty-eight, Bridgetown, May 4, 2011.

10. Edghill, Cassandra, Jonathan Cho Fook Lun, Danielle Harford, and Ria Scott. Focus group with students in their twenties, Cave Hill, May 19, 2011.

WORKS CITED

Absa, Moussa Sene. Personal interview. Barbados, September 14, 2010.

Adejunmobi, Moradewun. "Charting Nollywood's Appeal Locally and Globally." *African Literature Today* 28 (2010): 106–21.

Agorde, Wisdom. "Creating the Balance: Hallelujah Masculinities in a Ghanaian Video Film." *Film International* 5.4 (2007): 51–63.

Bilby, Kenneth, and Jerome Handler. "*Obeah:* Healing and Protection in West Indian Slave Life." *Journal of Caribbean History* 38.2 (2004): 153–83.

Bradshaw, Maria. "African Actors Are Coming." *Sunday Sun,* January 28, 2007, A16.

———. "African Movies the Rage." *Sunday Sun,* January 28, 2007, A23.

Comaroff, Jean, and John Comaroff. "Millennial Capitalism: First Thoughts on a Second Coming." *Public Culture* 12.2 (2000): 291–343.

Dipio, Dominica. "Religion in Nigerian Home Video Films." *Westminster Papers in Communication and Culture* 4.1 (2007): 65–82.

Edmonds, Ennis B., and Michelle A. Gonzalez. "Caribbean Crossroads: Historical and Theoretical Considerations." *Caribbean Religious History: An Introduction.* Ed. Ennis B. Edmonds and Michelle A. Gonzalez. New York: New York University Press, 2010. 1–14.

Gaskin, Juliet. Personal interview. Bridgetown, May 18, 2011.

Gilkes, Michael. "Inside the People TV." *Reflections 1991.* Paris: UNESCO, 1991. 1–4.

Giwa, Tunde. "Black Like Us." *Chimurenga Library,* June 2008. Web.

Harper, Paula. Personal interview. Bridgetown, June 22, 2011.

Inter-American Cultural Policy Observatory. "Barbados: Cultural Institutions." N.d. Web.

Mbembe, Achille. "African Modes of Self-Writing." *Public Culture* 14.1 (2002): 239–73.

Meyer, Birgit. "Impossible Representations: Pentecostalism, Vision, and Video Technology in Ghana." Working Paper 25, Department of Anthropology and African Studies, University of Mainz, 2003. Web.

Mohammed, Aminu Fagge. "Women, Religion, and Guilt in Hausa Home Video." *Film International* 5.4 (2007): 98–105.

Ogunleye, Foluke. "Christian Video Film in Nigeria: Dramatic Sermons through the Silver Screen." *African Video Film Today.* Ed. Foluke Ogunleye. Manzini, Swaziland: Academic Publishers, 2003. 105–28.

Okome, Onookome. "'The Message Is Reaching a Lot of People': Proselytizing and Video Films of Helen Ukpabio." *Postcolonial Text* 3.2 (2007): n. pag. Web.

Patricia. Personal interview. Bridgetown, May 28, 2011.

Runciman, David. "Didn't They Notice?" Review of *Treasure Islands: Tax Havens and the Men Who Stole the World,* by Nicholas Shaxon. *London Review of Books* 33.8 (2011): n. pag. Web.

Shaxon, Nicholas. *Treasure Islands: Tax Havens and the Men Who Stole the World.* London: Bodley Head, 2011.

Zeleza, Paul Tiyambe. "Imagining and Inventing the Postcolonial State in Africa." *Contours: A Journal of the African Diaspora* 1.1 (2003). Web.

FILMOGRAPHY

Black Hawk Down. Dir. Ridley Scott. Columbia Pictures (United States). 2001.

Blood Diamond. Dir. Edward Zwick. Warner Bros. Entertainment (United States and Germany). 2006.

Blood on the Altar. Dir. Mike Bamiloye and Elvon Jarrett. Mount Zion (Nigeria). 2006.

Blood Sister. Dir. Tchidi Chikere. Great Movies (Nigeria). 2004.

The Bold and the Beautiful. TV serial. Creators: Lee Phillip Bell and William J. Bell. Bell-Phillip Television et al. (United States). 1987–.

Days of Our Lives. TV serial. Creators: Ted Corday, Irna Phillips, and Allan Chase. Corday Productions et al. (United States). 1965–.

Desperate Housewives. Creator: Marc Cherry. Cherry Productions and Touchstone Television (United States). 2004–.

The Devil Wears Prada. Dir. David Frankel. 20th Century Fox (United States). 2006.

A Handful of Dirt. Dir. Russell Watson. Gate House Media (Barbados and United States). 2011.

Handsome. Dir. Ebere Onwu. Aka God Productions and Andy Iyke Production (Nigeria). 2003.

Hit for Six. Dir. Alison Saunders-Franklyn. Blue Waters Productions (Barbados). 2007.

Hotel Rwanda. Dir. Terry George. United Artists and MGM Home Entertainment (United States). 2004.

The Lion King. Dir. Roger Allers and Rob Minkoff. Walt Disney Pictures (United States). 1994.

Living in Bondage. Dir. Chris Obi Rapu. NEK Video Links (Nigeria). 1992.

The Mystic Masseur. Dir. Ishmael Merchant. Merchant Ivory (UK and Trinidad). 2001.

Pirates of the Caribbean: The Curse of the Black Pearl. Dir. Gore Verbinski. Walt Disney Pictures (United States). 2003.

Pirates of the Caribbean: Dead Man's Chest. Dir. Gore Verbinski. Walt Disney Pictures (United States). 2006.

Sweet Bottom. Dir. Gladstone Yearwood. Imagination Films (Barbados). In progress.

This Is Nollywood. Dir. Franco Sacchi. Eureka Film Productions (United States). 2007.

Thunderbolt (Magun). Dir. Tunde Kelani. Mainframe Productions (Nigeria). 2001.

Yoole. The Sacrifice. Dir. Moussa Sene Absa. Absa Films (Senegal). 2010.

The Young and the Restless. TV serial. Creators: Lee Phillip Bell and William J. Bell. Bell Dramatic Serial et al. (United States). 1973–.

ELEVEN

Consuming Nollywood
in Turin, Italy

GIOVANNA SANTANERA

"THE VIDEOS MAKE YOU UNDERSTAND THAT WHEN YOU LEAVE
a country and, as a foreigner, go to another, you have to respect the laws,
the people, and their way of life, as well as the culture. There are a lot of
things we don't do in Nigeria – they're not important – but here, instead,
we have to respect them. Most of the videos teach you how to behave well
in Italy, so I think they're a very good thing for us who are here." This is
how Peter, a Nigerian man who arrived in Turin in 1996, explained the
importance of Nollywood in the context of migration.[1] Like him, many
of his fellow compatriots in Turin say they watch Nigerian video films
because they resonate with their lives in Italy to a certain extent. In what
way are Nollywood videos related to immigrants' experiences in Turin?
What relationship do they establish with the homeland? How does this
relationship vary with migration?

In this chapter, based on the results of ethnographic research that I
carried out in Turin in 2008 and 2009, I will try to answer these questions
by analyzing the models, criteria, and procedures by which Nigerian
viewers interpret Nollywood video films and attach significance to the
surrounding world starting from the reality seen on the screen. In so
doing, I will draw on the idea of the "map of experience" as conceived
by Karin Barber ("Introduction" 5) in her definition of African popular
culture. In the author's view, African popular culture serves as a map of
experience in the increasingly unpredictable postcolonial society as it focuses on matters of great interest and concern to the people who produce
and consume it, giving collective voice to common fears, suffering, and
aspiration for a better life. Recalling Haynes and Okome, I will apply this
notion to Nollywood in the context of migration, and I will look at the

videos as a map of experience by which Nigerians name the difficulties and hopes for their diasporic condition.

I will argue that the Nigerians in Turin watch Nollywood films daily not so much to avoid the hardships of the present and reconnect themselves with an idealized homeland, but more to measure themselves against a familiar, symbolic, and discursive order to cope with feelings of disorientation in a foreign society. On the one hand, confronting the well-known habits, beliefs, and values of the homeland provides anchors and reference points to manage in the confusing new country. On the other hand, it encourages reflections on the homeland and the social experience of migration, thereby enabling immigrants to reassess their own history and identity and master its multiple transformations. Within this general framework, I will identify specific interpretative procedures, since the common condition of displacement explains the shared passion for Nollywood, while the various migration paths motivate different consumption practices. In the first part of the chapter, I will show how Nigerians, who have recently arrived and are in precarious socioeconomic conditions, tend to cling to Nollywood plots to deal with the feelings of cultural dislocation and personal failure that they often experience in the host society. Watching Nigerian video films offers familiar interpretive schemes and structures through which to decipher the alienating new context and give an acceptable meaning to their tough situation. In the second part of the chapter, I will show how those who have been in Italy for decades critically rethink their own culture through Nollywood, thus distancing themselves from certain parts while reaffirming the validity of others still considered appropriate in the new environment. In so doing, they integrate the video consumption in the dialectic between assimilation and resistance characteristic of their lives in the host country. Obviously, the distinctions I propose based on length of migration, socioeconomic condition, degree of integration into the foreign society, and the like are clearly defined explanations in a situation that is far more nuanced and complex. Therefore, they must be considered only tools of general orientation aimed more at identifying trends rather than the norm.

Turin represents a key place for observing these dynamics for several reasons. First, Italy is one of the main destinations for Nigerian immigrants. The country has almost forty-eight thousand legal and an estimated nine thousand illegal immigrants of Nigerian origin.[2] Even though individuals heading to Italy are not as well educated as those heading to Anglo-Saxon countries, one of the most substantial cash flows to Nigeria originates here (Desiderato 378). Second, Turin hosts one of the largest multifaceted Nigerian communities in the country, with more than four thousand individuals. This is a considerable size given the low territorial concentration of Nigerians in Italy. During the oil boom, young well-to-do Igbos and Yorubas came to study, while the end of the 1980s saw the mass arrival of young Edo men and especially Edo women, of low to medium socioeconomic class, looking for easy money to support their families back home. The various ethnic backgrounds and different social extractions, as well as the high crime rate, particularly drug dealing and pimping, have given rise to a fragmented and heterogeneous community where some are well integrated and have a satisfying job and a family, while others live in precarious conditions, supporting themselves through illegal activities or occasional work.[3] This multifaceted panorama constitutes an ideal place for those wishing to study the relationship between migratory paths and media consumption.

The findings on which this chapter is based draw on fieldwork that I carried out in Turin, using primarily discursive interview and participant observation. A fundamental part of the work consisted in watching and discussing the films together with the Nigerian immigrants. I always left it up to them to choose the titles and the places for the screenings.

WATCHING NOLLYWOOD VIDEO FILMS IN TURIN

Nigerian immigrants, regardless of their ethnic origins, length of migration, education or economic and family situation, are passionate about Nollywood video films. They all eagerly await the latest releases and know the names of the actors and directors by name. Hardly any of them have satellite dishes, so most of them purchase or rent the films in the many video stores across the city run by conationals, who get them directly in Lagos markets either personally or through intermediaries.[4] The video stores are located in neighborhoods with substantial immigrant populations, such as San Salvario, Porta Palazzo, and Barriera di Milano. Often these stores sell wigs, cosmetics, and food and offer services such as Internet usage and international telephone calls mainly to African customers as well. Usually, the video CDs cost 5 euros (US$7.20) each, but since the first and second parts are often sold together, the price may reach 10 euros (US$14.40).[5] In any case, negotiating is easy when buying several films at once or if one is a regular customer or a friend of the shop owner. Finally, loans among friends are other important channels for circulating films in Turin. In particular, Sunday get-togethers in church pose an opportunity to exchange video CDs and discuss them together.

Usually, Nollywood films are watched at home alone, with family or at most with a few friends. Unlike Nigeria, collective screenings are rare, and the audience is scattered across private homes. The immigrants do not organize public screenings for a cheap fee, such as those in African video parlors, nor do they meet at a friend's house to watch movies in groups. There are several reasons for the tendency toward isolation. The small homes, sometimes one-room apartments, make it practically impossible to organize community screenings, while the social disintegration and dispersion throughout the area are reflected in the consumption habits. Finally, the very format of the video CDs seems to favor solitary use because of the small television screen and the inexpensive equipment needed, generally within the reach of most.

Even though various Nollywood videos are shot in Nigerian communities of the diaspora and tell stories of the difficulties in a foreign society (see Haynes, "Africans Abroad," and this volume), Nigerians in Turin prefer films set in Nigeria and dealing with complex family events and occult forces.[6] In particular, they ardently watch "Pentecostalite-style" films (Meyer, "Praise the Lord" 92) that center on the affairs of a character who gets rich quickly and effortlessly because of pacts with diabolic spirits, to then fall into ruin (generally going mad, overwhelmed by guiltiness) and ultimately finds serenity by converting to the Pentecostal religion. On the other hand, they rarely watch the videos in the original local languages, which are also sometimes found on the market in Turin (in particular VCDs in Yoruba), largely preferring those filmed in English.

"HOW CAN YOU NOT BELIEVE IN SPIRITS?"

Even though all Nigerians in Turin are passionate about Nollywood video films, the movies have different roles and meanings in their lives. In this section I will consider video consumption among recently arrived

11.1. One of the many video stores in Turin.

Nigerians who often live in precarious social and economic conditions. I would like to open up my discussion with the following vignette.

One afternoon in February 2009, Steve, an Ishan boy who had been in Turin since 2006, took me to his friends' home in the Barriera di Milano neighborhood. He said that they were unemployed like him, and spent their afternoons watching Nigerian movies, chatting and drinking beers. The apartment was small and cozy. The large flat-screen television dominated the living room and was surrounded by sofas. We discussed religious beliefs in Nigeria and watched one of several videos about a young man who was successful through a pact with diabolical forces. During the final scene, where special effects showed the struggle between the Pentecostal pastor and the evil spirits, Steve pointed out, "See how powerful God is? How can you not believe in spirits now? What you see is true! This is how voodoo works in Nigeria. I'm not afraid of evil forces because I believe in God."[7] Basically, Steve was trying to convince me of the existence of spiritual forces. During our talks, he was always astonished and baffled by the lack of faith among Italians: "What can I do without God? Nothing. But I've seen that many people like you don't go to church. Yet certain things are weird; they can't be scientific." Therefore, he turned to Nollywood Pentecostalite-style videos to seek validation of his convictions, unlike Italy's cultural environment in which he felt they were disregarded. One afternoon, while we were in a video store, he asked the salesman if he could use the shop television to show me *The Holocaust* – a movie about a woman who goes to a native doctor, an imam, and a Pentecostal pastor in her efforts to have a child – to make me trust in God: "This movie is going to change you," he said.[8]

Steve's anxiety in using Nollywood videos to prove the reasonableness of his Pentecostal faith recalls the broader semantic uncertainty experienced by many immigrants. In fact, those who have been in Italy for a few years find Italian beliefs and habits strange, incomprehensible, and arbitrary and feel they threaten their own beliefs. The encounter with alterity undermines the objectivity and naturalness of the homeland's belief system, even before the symbolic universe of the host society is familiar enough to be able to offer alternative anchorages and reference points (Beneduce, *Frontiere dell'identità* 84; *Etnopsichiatria* 249). This results in doubts, dilemmas, and perplexity that run the risk of becoming what De Martino (105) has defined as the "crisis of presence," that is, a critical moment of existence in which "historicity stands out," preventing the unification in the conscience of all the memories and experiences needed for an adequate response to a given situation.

In such a state of uncertainty and confusion, Nigerians often cling to the familiar Nollywood plots not only to find the well-known environments of their homeland, but also its customs, beliefs, and value system. In this regard, Nollywood films slow the erosion of the relevance of the home country's systems of meaning and give the immigrant the chance to feel at ease in the confusing host society, as they show both a geographical territory and a "rhetorical country," to use Descombes's meaning of the term (qtd. in Augé). In fact, as the author writes: "The sign of being at home is the ability to make oneself understood without difficulty and to follow the reasoning of others without any need for long explanations. The rhetorical country of a character ends where his interlocutors no longer understand the reasons he gives for his deeds and actions, the criticism he makes or the enthusiasm he displays" (108). In this regard, the viewers' habit of predicting aloud characters' lines and acts is important. During the screening of a movie about a young widow forced to live in the village with her mother-in-law, for example, Frances predicted the kind of harassment the girl would suffer, "because in Nigeria, things go exactly like this." To some extent, through these acts of anticipation the viewers reconnect with a familiar rhetorical country and corroborate their interpretational skills, in a context that forces them to question themselves instead.

Nollywood video films are a particularly effective response to the challenges of a foreign culture, as many Nigerians in Turin perceive them as "docufiction." A Yoruba woman explained: "Nigerian videos tell true stories. Even though they didn't happen to you, you can't say they don't happen in the real world. Sometimes they do; otherwise they wouldn't be on the screen. That's why Nollywood gives you an idea of things that can happen" (Jane). As this remark points out, the videos are considered faithful accounts of the world: the stories are testimonies of real events that the filmmakers, for a variety of reasons, want to share. More precisely, the audience believes that directors and scriptwriters are warning the audience about dangerous situations through this medium. In that respect, some viewers compare Nollywood to Hollywood, which they claim makes fantasy films, not realistic ones. One Ijaw boy put it as follows: "Nollywood is different to Hollywood because Hollywood movies show much more fiction than fact. Certainly, in Nollywood there's more documentary. . . . Nollywood films the reality; it shoots things that have happened somewhere and that the public couldn't see" (Michael).

The perception of Nollywood stories being like documentaries affirms the validity of the practices and beliefs depicted. This is particularly evident in the case of Pentecostalite videos, within which mimesis and reality tend to blend so much they are considered true testimonies from the invisible world, where a battle is raging between the forces of good and evil. As the opening vignette shows, viewers consider God and the spirits the driving force of the event, which they take part in alongside the actors.[9] These stories not only confirm divine power and often end with a pastor defeating the forces of evil, but also uphold the power of the spirits. As Okwori (14) points out, although the cruel rituals on the screen lead to ruin, they can work as the characters achieve the instant, desired wealth.[10] This was brought home to me with particular clarity during the following conversation with Michael:

> M.: Have you ever experienced something strange while watching Nigerian videos?
>
> G.: What do you mean?
>
> M.: I mean, have you begun to believe that spiritual powers do exist in the world?
>
> G.: I know that certain people believe in spiritual powers, but in my culture we usually don't.
>
> M.: In Africa we do, because in Africa some people love spiritual powers. This is why instead of telling you "Look, this man is a wizard," they warn you through a Nollywood movie.

Such confusion between mimesis and reality is favored by certain ploys wisely used by Nigerian directors. As several authors pointed out (for example, Haynes, "Introduction"; Okome, "Writing the Anxious City"; Ugor), to ensure success, these filmmakers take the inspiration for their films from rumors about the occult circulating in Nigerian cities that are often reported in local newspapers. Moreover, they sometimes tell the audience about the characters' fates, as if they really existed, and present the event like a confession. The appropriation of video technology by some of the Pentecostal churches blurs the line between fiction and reality even further. The churches use the telecamera to visualize the secret forces that govern life and shape the global struggle between God and the devil that characterizes their cosmology. Thus, the content of the video can easily be compared to a dream or trance always considered true.[11]

In short, I wish to stress here that in view of semantic uncertainties that often characterize immigrants' experiences, the consumption of Nollywood video films can provide a symbolic platform from which to reaffirm the validity and legitimacy of beliefs and customs of the native country in the new context.

ABSURD MIGRATIONS AND NOLLYWOOD VIDEO FILMS

Many Nigerians recently arrived in Turin find themselves facing not only an alienating cultural environment, but also financial uncertainty in a host society that is far from being "the country where the money tree grows," to recall a remark by Alice, an Edo girl. Their qualifications are not recognized in the labor market, and usually the only legal occupations within their reach are temporary jobs, paid under the table. According to Alice, "Life is hard. We have to toil for everything. Here is not how people in Nigeria think. Especially in the past, Italians were seen as 'stars' in Nigeria. Also because people who were in Italy used to lie, saying that there was money and work, but there wasn't actually." Many of them feel pinned down between economic and social insecurity and the urgent request for money from the family in Nigeria, which often does not believe the stories of hardship and sacrifices. The family in Nigeria feels fooled by relatives viewed as reluctant to share the wealth accumulated in the West – hence, the numerous immigrants' lies pretending "to have made it" so they can live up to their relatives' expectations and avoid the shame of defeat.

Nigerians often claim that Nollywood videos reflect their struggle for survival in Turin. It is common to meet people who say that they have seen a film that tells their own story exactly. Andrew, an Edo boy who has been in Italy since December 2004, for example, quoted a Nollywood video to illustrate his financial straits: "I saw a film called *Blood Billionaires*, and I realized immediately that the story concerned me. I thought the same thing had probably also happened to me." To give a sense of this overlap between Nollywood plots and immigrants' hardship, I would like to briefly recall the "absurdity" of the immigrant's condition as conceived by Abdelmalek Sayad (139). In accordance with the author, when the immigrant's illusions have been shattered, a wide gap between the initial plan and what one can realistically do in the host country opens up. Immigrant life can become pointless and may seem senseless. So it has to become "intellectually tolerable" by constantly giving it new meaning. Controlling one's experiences without compromising personal integrity requires solid hermeneutic practice. Such interpretive effort is particularly pressing in Turin, where poor Nigerians, unable to escape poverty despite all their sacrifices, are constantly faced with many fellow countrymen who got rich quick, but by illegal means. Steve's experience shows the urgency of making sense of their vain efforts. He has been unemployed for more than a year despite his degree in economics. He left a good position in a bank in Benin City to try his luck in Italy. But even after completing several training courses, he still cannot find work here.

Initially, he wanted an office job, but now, he would take any job, even an unsuitable one: "Many people here in Turin feel trapped. They have their backs to the wall. They can't go back to Nigeria because they can't afford the airfare, but also because they'd be ashamed to return without having made their fortune. Some left behind a good life in Nigeria, others, no, but all of them ask themselves: why, why?"

When faced with such doubts and questions, watching Nollywood videos is helpful. When immigrants feel lost and disoriented, the absurdity of their lives hits them hard; they often cling to these plots to find meaning for their plights. More specifically, viewers of Pentecostalite-style videos watch plots where getting rich quick plunges the main character into ruin because the wealth is obtained with the aid of occult forces. At the same time, they see the happy conclusion of characters who resisted the temptation to get rich quick and put up with privation and suffering in the hopes of divine recompense and lasting economic success. Used by the subjects to tell their own stories, these plotlines offer a key to interpreting the real-life situation that makes poverty and privation tolerable. Their fellow Nigerians' wealth becomes the fruit of pacts with the forces of evil that soon lead to ruin, while their own "empty" condition of being unemployed is no longer the result of errors and personal shortcomings, but is a prudent wait-and-see situation, with a view to a future and lasting success. The absurdity of the immigrants' condition thus becomes intellectually tolerable. It acquires that constant reattribution of meaning essential to making their existence governable. These interpretative strategies are evident in the following interview: "The main character in the film was very sad because he didn't have a job. All his friends had abandoned him or tried to convince him to join a cult. He always refused and prayed to God. Isn't this the same thing that happens in Italy? In the end he finds a job in an oil company and gets married. That's what happens to a lot of us in Turin" (Steve). Taking a closer look at the particular story of Michael helps to clarify the interpretative strategies described thus far. Michael has been in Italy since 2004 and still has not found a stable job. He has great ambitions and dreams of becoming a famous Nollywood director. For some time, he has been trying to get financing for his projects, but he has received nothing but refusals from Turin production companies. He interprets his own situation based on what he saw in *Blood Money* and transforms his personal setback into a brilliant fate. In the video, he finds meaning for his continued failures, which otherwise, short of admitting his own incompetence, are incomprehensible. The story of a bewitched banknote that causes the downfall of anyone who receives it leads Michael to consider the small sum of money received from a compatriot like a spell to take possession of his future success. His defeats, therefore, take on a new meaning that is perhaps easier to accept: "It's the only way to understand why others go higher and higher, while I always go further down."

WATCHING NIGERIA THROUGH NOLLYWOOD

In this final section I would like to consider the consumption of Nollywood video films among those immigrants who have been settled in Turin for several years and who have families and steady jobs. As we will see, this applies to the first group who arrived in the late 1970s and 1980s and to those who came in the early 1990s with far fewer resources. Yet they managed to achieve a certain amount of stability in the host country. Both groups had discovered Nollywood when they were already living abroad and welcomed it as an opportunity to "watch" Nigeria from far-off Italy. Lydia, a Hausa woman who arrived in 1990, explained: "Thanks to Nollywood I'm carried back home. I see the latest things happening in Nigeria. I keep up, so to speak, because it's been seven years since I've been there.... Since I only rarely hang out with Nigerians now, I refresh my memory of what they say, how they behave, their way of doing things." Her comments are not unlike Victoria's, an Igbo woman who came to Italy in the early 1990s: "We watch Nigerian films.... [W]e discuss them, we criticize them, we exclaim 'Wow, what a house!' and then 'But that's Nigeria, it's Enugu, our city!' Just think if there weren't Nollywood videos! I listen to music, but it doesn't carry you back home like films do; it doesn't let you get close like films. Seeing is another thing than hearing!"

What I wish to argue in this section is that Nigerians like Lydia and Victoria perceive the consumption of Nollywood videos as a virtual journey from Italy to Nigeria. Like every other journey, it evokes nostalgia, but also critical awareness, assessments, and comparisons of habits and beliefs, thus turning media consumption into one of the signifying forces that articulate the subjectivity of the immigrants. To see why, we have to look at some of the viewers' comments during the screenings. On the one hand, the viewers notice those features of the homeland that they miss in Italy. John, an Igbo man who has been living in Turin since 1982, for example, says: "[In Nollywood] you see a typically African way of being together and communicating: we always talk and we have a sense of community. Spending time with others and talking with others is part of everyday life. . . . You can't do that here with the work commitment and all the problems you have to face." David, an Igbo man who arrived in Italy in 1983, agrees. He is watching the Igwe, the village chief, on the screen who reaffirms the importance of cooperation in the village: "It's right, because competition doesn't always reward you."[12]

On the other hand, the viewers criticize those features that they consider surpassed by the new context. Lydia laughs at an elderly man's comment on the importance of respecting tradition, for example, while David reflects on the difficulty of village life and uses the cold reception that a newcomer from the city receives to illustrate his point: "The village doesn't forgive. If someone judges you as a bad person, you're marginalized by everyone. You have to be very careful, and you suffer a lot."[13] His wife, Victoria, adds: "They judge you on your appearance. Just because you're wearing a miniskirt doesn't mean you're a prostitute! You can't judge people like this. You [Italians] don't do it, for example. Everyone can dress the way they like!"[14]

As the comments show, watching Nigeria through Nollywood in Turin encourages reflections and comparison of the home culture with the host culture rather than a nostalgic idealization of the native country. In light of the comparison with Italian customs, the immigrants ponder the values and habits of their own tradition that they would like to keep in the new juncture. As such, the consumption practice becomes part of complex processes through which the immigrants negotiate their presence in the recipient country. In these dynamics, a central role is played by the integration policies adopted by the nation-states and referable to two major models, assimilationism and multiculturalism. Briefly, the former calls for individuals to give up their traditions to adopt those of the host country, while the latter encourages the birth of ethnic communities and the conservation of the "intact" cultural heritage. Both models are based on an essentialist view of culture, considered a compact and organic whole that is rejected or maintained in its entirety according to a sort of zero-sum logic. Many authors have emphasized the inapplicability of these models and have described immigrants as "indociles" (Mbembe) who do not allow themselves to be limited to the universe of origin or to that of arrival. In particular, Sayad recounts the "broken" lives of people experiencing an inner conflict in which they are torn between the desire to wipe out the past and integrate, and a simultaneous desire to seek refuge in the past to escape from the difficulties of the present: "It is the desperate attempt to reconnect the threads that existed before the rupture, to put the broken pieces back together that supports life, sustains life and fills all of one's life, in such a way that this effort finally comes to be totally identified with life and to constitute life to such an extent that the author of this attempt eventually forgets that there is another way to live, and forgets that life means living other than by striving to live" (143).

Watching Nollywood videos seems to help people with this arduous task of "restitching," promoting a negotiation with the native and the host culture that helps heal the wounds of migration. Indeed, seeing parts of their tradition in the videos that they would like to revive in the new context can be considered part of that acculturation without assimilation that, according to Falola and Afolabi, helps immigrants achieve a precarious balance between "the old self" and "the newly formed self," avoiding an unmanageable splitting in two (4). Only through a continual mediation of language, norms, and social and symbolic ties can immigrants forge a sense of identity that does not start from a loss or even from a replica of the past, but rather as a bricolage taken from both the country of origin and the host country. In this sense, the "selective acculturation" (Portes and Rumbaut 194) that Nollywood stimulates falls within the more general attempt, always provisional, to arrive at a satisfying synthesis between valid elements of the new environment and those parts of their legacy that immigrants want to preserve with a view to their present needs.

Notably, some viewers see a comparison of cultures in the Nollywood stories that characterizes their own lives as well. In the stories, they reinterpret the efforts of mediation between symbolic universes and attribute the integration strategies they have experienced to the characters. This overlap is favored by plots that present conflicting values, habits, and beliefs rather than coherent systems of meaning. As Okome points out, for their social and economic survival, the characters select those traits that are useful to them, at times turning to "tradition," at times to "modernity," thus dissolving the dichotomy between the two ("Onome" 161). Through the everyday practice of improvisation, they creatively combine the elements and elaborate subjective views of the world starting from their own individual experiences.[15]

From this perspective, David's interpretation of *The Native Son* is enlightening because it clearly shows the identification with the character that selects cultural traits from the heterogeneous environment. The film is about attempts by Nerissa, a cultured student from Enugu, to win over the boyfriend of Toanchukwu, a village girl. Initially, the two girls appear very different. Several scenes show the city girl strolling around the countryside in miniskirts, sunglasses, and high heels, while the other girl is working in the fields, wearing the traditional *obi akwa*. Nevertheless, their interaction sparks a reciprocal transformation. The sophisticated, educated girl decides to move to the countryside, while her rival in love starts smoking and wearing the latest fashions. The film suggests not a simple inversion of roles but rather a process of hybridization, a mixing. Nerissa, for example, invokes the right to leave Enugu "to return to tradition" according to a strictly urban, individualistic logic that does not give her father an opportunity to question her choice.

The characters, who have to deal with cultural diversity and elaborate personal synthesis, prompt my interlocutor, David, to reflect on the tactics for survival in a foreign society: "The film is based on a comparison between two cultures, the city and the village. Like when you, Italian, go to America, what do you do? You start to compare the two cultures, yours and the one you find among the people you meet." In the film, he identifies two strategies of adaptation to cultural diversity: the passive opening up to the alterity and the practice of selecting cultural traits. In his eyes, the village girl is "succumbing to herself" because she "wants to be completely different," but "you can't leave your origins completely. If you completely change what you are ... in the end you find yourself ruined." The city girl, on the other hand, embodies the second strategy, since she "is modified, but does not change radically.... [S]he only takes what she needs from village life."[16] Significantly, in his words, Nerissa's urban lifestyle becomes that of Turin, while the rural universe, personified by Toanchukwu, overlaps with his Igbo one. He compares himself with the city girl and confirms that he selects from the Italian and Nigerian repertoire only those traits that help him in his present life. Referring to this mechanism as a "game," he emphasizes, albeit implicitly, the creative qualities used in negotiating a hybrid identity:

> What you can do is to change yourself, like the city girl does, but you can't change completely. This is what I did: I adapted. I see what I need to add to what I already am. For example, I don't need to adopt your way of viewing elderly people. I don't need to because I think our way is better. But there are some traits in Italian culture that are useful and that it's good to adopt. A little modern culture, a little traditional – by playing these two games, I eventually manage to be complete.

In this chapter, I have tried to explain why Nigerian immigrants in Turin consider watching Nollywood a way to reflect upon their experiences in Turin and what relationship with the homeland such a consumption practice implies. I have suggested that the viewers cling to Nollywood stories set in Nigeria, not so much to remember the good old days as to relate to a familiar discursive and symbolic order in the confusing foreign country. Video films represent a map of experience by which they shape and signify their own history, identity, and social universe. The immigrants entertain a dynamic and vital relationship with the home culture that is reinterpreted in the light of present needs and is not fossilized in a fixed and idealized image. Such a dynamic relationship varies with the changing condition of migration. First, Nigerians who have arrived recently watch Nollywood videos to reconnect with a familiar rhetorical country, although they are in an alienating, host society. In the videos they find systems of meaning for interpreting Turin and confirmation of the validity of the homeland's habits and beliefs. Particularly the Pentecostalite-style videos, which juxtapose rapid but ruinous success with patiently waiting recompensed in the end by God, enable those immigrants who have not reached their desired goals in the host country to reinterpret their existence positively. Second, through the consumption of Nollywood videos, those who have been in Turin for many years with their families and have steady jobs connect nostalgically with their homeland, but are also critical of it. They distance themselves from some elements and reaffirm the importance of others that are still valid in the new environment. In so doing, they integrate video consumption in the dialectic between assimilation and resistance that characterizes their lives.

The dynamics described above highlight an active audience that interacts creatively with transnational media flows. Still capable of providing a map of experience for Nigerian viewers in Italy, the videos demonstrate their elasticity and their openness to alternative interpretations. Fundamental in this regard are the shallow characters and plots typical of African popular culture. As Karin Barber writes, stereotypes are a "way of making models" that can be applied to the viewer's own specific circumstances because "stereotypes, like proverbs, are abstracted from the mesh of specificity and given peg-like properties" ("Preliminary Notes" 357). The loopholes, the evasiveness, and the ambiguity that Nollywood videos have been criticized for on occasion (see Okome, "Nollywood and Its Critics") are actually factors of flexibility and stimulate the creative role of the public in constructing meaning. Called upon to fill the gaps, the audience appropriates the content of the films, interpreting it in light of its personal, social, and cultural context. It is thanks to this active consumption that the transnational videos of Nollywood become relocated and take part in the dynamics of cultural change in the predicament of migration.

NOTES

1. Most of the Nigerian immigrants I interviewed asked that their identities be concealed. Therefore, I will use pseudonyms when referring to them. Furthermore, I will use the ethnic categories because they are the ones that the people interviewed always use to talk about themselves.

2. Data taken from *Indagine Nazionale Ismu* (2009) (qtd. in Desiderato 373). However, there is no real consensus on the numbers. In 2009 the Italian Ministry of the Interior counted just three thousand illegal Nigerians in Italy, although the considerable flow of remittances to Nigeria would suggest that the number is vastly underestimated.

3. For a detailed history of Nigerian migration in Turin, see the work of Pietro Cingolani.

4. Nevertheless, among those who have a computer and a sufficiently fast Internet connection, it is now becoming increasingly common to watch the films online, and for free, often as clips on YouTube.

5. From what I could see, in 2008 and 2009 Nollywood video films sold in Turin video shops were always in the VCD format.

6. A Nigerian immigrant and an Italian filmed a Nollywood-style film in Turin titled *Akpegi Boyz*. The screenplay is about drug dealing, pimping, and spiritual battles and was meant to faithfully follow an event that really happened among Nigerians in Turin. The production of the video was financed by a young Nigerian immigrant, while friends, both Italian and Nigerian, created an improvised cast

of actors. Filmed in pidgin English and subtitled in Italian, the film was shown during film festivals in Italy but was not distributed on the Nigerian market, as the directors had hoped. It is unlike the videos analyzed by Haynes in several ways: the presence of an Italian director, a plot focusing on occult forces, and the failed distribution in Africa. Currently, the two filmmakers are working on a Web series titled *Blinded Devil,* in which Nollywood actor John Okafor was given a small role thanks to money from an acquaintance of the Nigerian director.

7. Participant observation in a private home, Barriera di Milano neighborhood of Turin, February 25, 2009.

8. Participant observation in a video store, San Salvario neighborhood of Turin, March 4, 2009.

9. Throughout her work, Birgit Meyer has noted something similar in Ghana, where the actors fear the altars in the scene, believed capable of attracting spirits, and are reluctant to play the role of the "bad guys." They imagine satanic

influences on the action. In particular, see "Impossible Representations."

10. There are countless films on the subject. Among the best known, see *Living in Bondage* (1992), *Rituals* (1997), and *Blood Money* (1997).

11. As mentioned by Hackett; Oha; and Okome, "The Message."

12. Participant observation in a private home, Strambino (Turin), June 14, 2009.

13. Ibid.

14. Ibid.

15. Emblematic in this regard is the film *The Master* (2005), in which the main character passes from one disguise to another to carry out his scams. Playing creatively with "modernity" and "tradition," he pretends to be a priest, politician, and finally – in his words – "the cultural king of Nigeria, traditionally speaking," a title invented to fool a Western businessman.

16. I would like to clarify that, unlike David, I did not notice any difference in behavior between Toanchukwu and Nerissa regarding cultural alterity.

WORKS CITED

Alice. Personal interview. Villar Perosa (Turin), November 29, 2008.

Andrew. Personal interview. Turin, February 29, 2009.

Augé, Marc. *Non-places: Introduction to an Anthropology of Supermodernity.* London: Verso, 1995.

Barber, Karin. "Introduction." *Readings in African Popular Culture.* Ed. Karin Barber. Bloomington: Indiana University Press; Oxford: James Currey, 1997. 1–12.

———. "Preliminary Notes on Audiences in Africa." *Africa* 67.3 (1997): 347–62.

Beneduce, Roberto. *Etnopsichiatria: Sofferenza mentale e alterità fra storia, dominio e cultura.* Rome: Carocci, 2007.

———. *Frontiere dell'identità e della memoria: Etnopsichiatria e migrazioni in un mondo creolo.* Milan: Franco Angeli, 2004.

Cingolani, Pietro. "Famiglie nigeriane in migrazione: Memorie, desideri e trasformazioni." *Narrare l'incontro con le culture dell'immigrazione: Memorie familiari, pratiche alimentari ed espressioni artistiche.* Turin: L'Harmattan, 2006. 21–56.

———. "L'imprevedibile familiarità della città: Luoghi e percorsi significativi dei migranti nigeriani a Torino." *Reti migranti.* Ed. Francesca Decimo and Giuseppe Sciortino. Bologna: Il Mulino, 2006. 59–87.

———. "Koming from Naija to Torino: Esperienze nigeriane di immigrazione e di fede." *Più di un Sud: Studi antropologici sull'immigrazione a Torino.* Ed. Paola Sacchi and Pier Paolo Viazzo. Milan: Franco Angeli, 2003. 120–54.

———. "Migranti nigeriani e associazionismo: Il caso di Torino." *Afriche e Orienti* 3 (2005): 68–91.

David. Personal interview. Strambino (Turin), June 14, 2009.

De Martino, Ernesto. *Il mondo magico: Prolegomeni a una storia del magismo.* Turin: Bollati Boringhieri, 1997.

Desiderato, Gisella. "Le migrazioni nigeriane." *Sedicesimo rapporto sulle migrazioni 2010.* Ed. Fondazione Ismu. Milan: Franco Angeli, 2011. 373–83.

Falola, Toyin, and Niyi Afolabi. "Introduction: Voluntarily Singing the Lord's Song . . . " *African Minorities in the New World.* Ed. Toyin Falola and Niyi Afolabi. New York: Routledge, 2008. 1–22.

Frances. Personal interview. Turin, November 5, 2008.

Hackett, Rosalind I. J. "Charismatic/Pentecostal Appropriation of Media Technologies in Nigeria and Ghana." *Journal of Religion in Africa* 28.3 (1998): 258–77.

Haynes, Jonathan. "Africans Abroad: A Theme in Film and Video." *Africa e Mediterraneo* 45 (December 2003): 22–29.

———. "Introduction." *Nigerian Video Films.* Ed. Jonathan Haynes. Athens: Ohio University Press, 2000. 1–36.

Haynes, Jonathan, and Onookome Okome. "Evolving Popular Media: Nigerian Video Films." *Nigerian Video Films.* Ed. Jonathan Haynes. Athens: Ohio University Press, 2000. 51–88.

Jane. Personal interview. Turin, March 9, 2009.

John. Personal interview. Turin, April 23, 2009.

Lydia. Personal interview. Luserna (Turin), February 28, 2009.

Mbembe, Achille. *Afriques indociles.* Paris: Karthala, 1988.

Meyer, Birgit. "Impossible Representations: Pentecostalism, Vision, and Video Technology in Ghana." *Religion, Media, and the Public Sphere.* Ed. Birgit Meyer and Annelies Moors. Bloomington: Indiana University Press, 2006. 290–312.

———. "'Praise the Lord': Popular Cinema and Pentecostalite Style in Ghana's New Public Sphere." *American Ethnologist* 31.1 (2004): 92–110.

Michael. Personal interview. Turin, July 25, 2009.

Oha, Obododimma. "The Rhetoric of Nigerian Christian Videos: The War Paradigm of the Great Mistake." *Nigerian Video Films.* Ed. Jonathan Haynes. Athens: Ohio University Press, 2000. 192–99.

Okome, Onookome. "'The Message Is Reaching a Lot of People': Proselytizing and Video Films of Helen Ukpabio." *Postcolonial Text* 3.2 (2007).

———. "Nollywood and Its Critics." *Viewing African Cinema in the Twenty-First Century: Art Films and the Nollywood Video Revolution.* Ed. Mahir Şaul and Ralph A. Austen. Athens: Ohio University Press, 2010. 26–41.

———. "Onome: Ethnicity, Class, Gender." *Nigerian Video Films.* Ed. Jonathan Haynes. Athens: Ohio University Press, 2000. 148–64.

———. "Writing the Anxious City: Images of Lagos in Nigerian Home Video Films." *Black Renaissance* 5.2 (2003): 65–75.

Okwori, Jenkeri Zakari. "A Dramatized Society: Representing Rituals of Human Sacrifice as Efficacious Action in Nigerian Home-Video Movies." *Journal of African Cultural Studies* 16.1 (2003): 7–23.

Peter. Personal interview. Turin, February 21, 2009.

Portes, Alejandro, and Rubén Rumbaut. *Immigrant America: A Portrait*. Berkeley and Los Angeles: University of California Press, 2006.

Sayad, Abdelmalek. *The Suffering of the Immigrant*. Cambridge: Polity Press, 2004.

Steve. Personal interviews. Turin, February 25 and May 18, 2009.

Ugor, Paul. "Censorship and the Content of Nigerian Home Video Films." *Postcolonial Text* 3.2 (2007): n. pag. Web.

Victoria. Personal interview. Strambino (Turin), April 25, 2009.

FILMOGRAPHY

Akpegi Boyz. Dir. Vincent Andrew Omoigui and Simone Sandretti. G.V.K. (Italy). 2009.

Blinded Devil. Dir. Vincent Andrew Omoigui and Simone Sandretti. G.V.K. (Italy). 2010. YouTube. Web.

Blood Billionaires. Dir. MacCollins Chidebe. Chez International (Nigeria). 2006.

Blood Money. Dir. Chico Ejiro. OJ Productions (Nigeria). 1997.

The Holocaust. Dir. Kalu Anya. Udodiri Mbagwu Productions (Nigeria). N.d.

Living in Bondage. Dir. Chris Obi Rapu. NEK Video Links (Nigeria). 1992.

The Master. Dir. Andy Amenechi. Kas-Vid (Nigeria). 2005.

The Native Son. Dir. Tchidi Chikere. Ocean Wave Movie (Nigeria). 2009.

Rituals. Dir. Andy Amenechi. NEK Video Links (Nigeria). 1997.

TWELVE

Nigerian Videos and Their Imagined Western Audiences: The Limits of Nollywood's Transnationality

BABSON AJIBADE

THE POPULARITY OF NOLLYWOOD VIDEO IS NOT NEW. ONE
reason for this is that it is able to read into the souls of its audience. This
popularity is also partly based on the narratives, which are easily recognized and held dear by ordinary Nigerians. It is popularity that has
sustained the industry thus far. What started out as a national visual
practice more than two decades ago has gained a transnational color-
ation brought on by an expanding diasporic spectatorship. In terms of
circulation, the video film does not just move from one African migrant
to another: video stores in Western cities and many Internet sites sell
them in virtual marketplaces. However, with the circulation of the Nollywood videos in global spaces, producers are beginning to rethink their
transnational audiences as part of the narrative and production equa-
tion. They are keenly contemplating the idea of generating a Western
audience for the video film. In my interviews and discussions with the
video filmmakers, they expressed hope that a Western audience would
yield more profits. However, given the divergence between the Western motion picture regime and Nollywood's video practice, this chapter
queries how a truly Western audience might be gained for the video
film. Using the experiment undertaken at Schlachthaus Theater in Bern,
Switzerland, in 2005, in which I recut Nigerian videos for a Western audience, the chapter explores one means by which Nollywood could address
non-African audiences.[1] While my recut made Nollywood video accessible to Western audiences, this is ambivalent because mainstreaming
Nollywood videos into a Western frame might prove futile. This process
is risky, as it could also disenfranchise African audiences without generating the imagined Western patronage. By recutting Nollywood to suit

the West, what remains of Nollywood, and can the resultant film still be called Nollywood?

In the late 1980s, when the video film began, it was difficult to say how far the medium would go. First, Nigerians conversant with cinema had come to know celluloid as *the* cinematic medium. People did not have a formal education in film, but from colonial times, celluloid has always been the medium to experience motion picture. Second, a nascent film culture was apparent by the 1970s when local producers made several celluloid features. These features, particularly those made by the Yoruba traveling theater troupes such as Hubert Ogunde's and Baba Sala's drew large audiences to the cinema.[2] Thus, with the rudimentary celluloid consciousness then, local film or literary critics did not take the advent of video films in the late 1980s seriously. As Ekwuazi notes, video films were then considered a "flash in the pan" – an aberration that would soon fade away. However, this has become a saturation of more than a thousand videos annually produced in Nigeria. This saturation has meant that an ever-increasing number of videos have had to compete for more or less the same audiences. To resolve the saturation, Nigerian video filmmakers have explored three avenues: instituting intermittent lulls, exploring audiences in other African states, and exploring imagined Western audiences.

Nigerian video filmmakers have tried to self-regulate the annual quantity of videos by agreeing on intermittent lulls during which everyone stops production. However, such lulls could not solve the problem, because as soon as they are lifted, producers make up for lost time and another level of video saturation is reenacted within a few days. The video filmmakers have also explored a broader African audience (Milon) on the continent by screening their films on satellite TV, making them available for sale via websites (Garritano), while also doing Nigerian-Ghanaian collaborative videos. This has resulted in a measure of success, as videos made by intra-African collaborators are being exposed to a broader African audience. But this expansion did not necessarily generate higher sales or increase video filmmakers' profits, as the majority of video audiences in Africa do not purchase the features. Many people watch videos for free at neighbors' homes, rent videos at a low price from a video store, or watch the video features in the store for a fee.[3] From 2005 the shelf price of videos was 400 naira/2000 CFA francs (US$3–4), while titles could be rented for 50 naira/200 CFA francs (US$0.40) in Nigeria and Cameroon, respectively. Today, titles are sold at even lower prices. Video filmmakers are no longer interested in single video releases but in sequels of two, three, or four simultaneously. This is driven by a renaissance among Nigerian audiences for cheaper and better visual quality films from Hollywood and India pirated from China. In fact, many video parlor operators now say they screen only Hollywood and Indian films because audiences are no longer patronizing the Nigerian videos. Chinese pirated Hollywood and Bollywood films on DVD sell for between 150 and 200 naira (US$1–1.30). At present, Nigerian video films on VCD sell for 200 naira (US$1.30) per title and 400 naira (US$2.60) for two combo-CDs with two sequels, meaning that the market value of the videos has been halved in Nigeria and in Cameroon. But in the video parlors, audiences can see videos at 50 naira/50 CFA francs (US$0.10–0.30) – a fraction of the purchase price. With the shelf price of videos now 200 naira (US$1.30), audiences are no longer flocking to video parlors to see Nigerian films, as many more can afford to buy them now. Video parlor operators say they now charge 50 naira (US$0.30) to see European and Spanish soccer leagues and pirated Hollywood and Bollywood films rather than Nigerian videos. Apparently, the cost of the video film now indicates socioeconomic change. This price restructuring underscores the fact that video filmmakers are making lower profits today, and the massive migration of videos from Nigeria into parts of Africa and beyond has generated more audiences than actual sales.

Crucially, Nigerian videos have moved from local spaces of production to global spaces as the features are circulated among Africans in the diaspora. Returning African migrants will often take back copies of videos for themselves and as gifts for other fellow Africans. Apart from Africans who sell videos in Western cities, many Internet sites sell the features. In 2005, Alfred, who sells videos in London, grossed more than one thousand features a month.[4] When I met Alfred in London in June 2007, his store was fuller and his clientele had not dwindled. Undoubtedly, Nigerian videos are selling to an audience in Europe and North America. And with the sale of Nigerian videos in the West, producers have begun to assume – without any form of substantiation – that Westerners are buying and consuming the features. First, producers know that satellite TV stations like Nollywood (Channel 329), AIT International (Channel 187), VOX Africa (Channel 218), and Africa (Channel 268) broadcast Nigerian videos to viewers in Britain. Second, in discussions with producers, they often alluded to Western video consumption, using pidgin English terms like "*oyinbo* self-de watch am" (meaning white people also see the videos) and "*oyinbo* self-de buy" (white people also buy). In Nigeria, the pidgin English word to refer to a Westerner is *oyinbo* – the Yoruba for "white man." This term refers mainly to a Caucasian of European or North American origin. As far as the video filmmakers are concerned, so long as an *oyinbo* buys a film, it means that *oyinbo* people are watching the videos. I am aware that some scholars of Africanist leaning do buy some Nigerian videos. In 2005, for instance, the Institute for Social Anthropology at the University of Basel bought more than a hundred Nigerian video titles through me for their library. Two years later, there was no indication in the library records that non-Africans were borrowing the videos. The question of whether *oyinbo* buyers of video films are buying for leisurely or academic consumption arises. When considering Western audiences, video film producers do not take into account whether satellite video beams in Britain are watched by African or indigenous populations. However, Nigerian producers hope to target Western audiences in a bid to resolve the oversaturation on the video market. But Nigerian video filmmakers do not distinguish between a "Western audience" and an "audience in the West." A *Western* audience means that the consumers are "Western," while an audience *in* the West refers to social actors living in Europe and North America who are not necessarily Westerners. In this case, video audiences in the West can be composed of African and other migrants whose cinematic menu includes both Nollywood videos and Hollywood features. But there are critical divergences between the laborious, big-budget Western motion picture regime and Nollywood's speedy and cheap video productions. This difference lies not only in the processes that each cinema employs to produce meaning, which also give direction to the nature of cinematic reading among the genres' audiences. In the Western cinematic regime, the camera rather than dialogue reveals the story, since the "beauty and visual sophistication of the images subvert" the story and the dialogue (Sontag 11). The case of avid Nollywood consumers such as Nigerian housewives illustrates this. These women are often busy in the kitchen, but playing a video in the living room with the volume turned up. They "see" the videos more through the actors' dialogue as they get fleeting glimpses of the TV only in between preparing food. They do not miss out on the story. When a Hollywood film is playing, the same audiences will pause the VCR/DVD when they need to leave the room. This different domestic mode of consuming Nollywood and Hollywood films subtly illustrates the audiovisual qualities punctuating the two genres. Thus, from the serious divergences that such practices suggest, is there a truly Western audience for the Nigerian video films? Are Westerners really accessing the world of the videos? And, if not, what factors deny "Western" access to the videos?

In terms of methodology, questionnaires were sent to Western persons who have seen the videos, and Nigerian producers and actors were interviewed. The latter two groups were crucial to the survey because they watch the videos to keep abreast of video sales and have an eye out for potential sellers. This gives them a direction for their next productions. Additionally, participant observation was undertaken, and a Western audience was shown a Nigerian video film – recut to make it more compatible with Western filmic regimes. One limitation of this study is that the majority of the Western respondents are linked to academia, which perhaps denies us the perspectives of ordinary Westerners. This limitation is unavoidable, as Nollywood videos have yet to spill over from academic circles into the general Western box office.

HOW NOLLYWOOD MAKES VIDEOS

The most remarkable aspect of Nollywood's video production processes is the time taken – from the start of shooting to the end of production – before its release on the market. Piracy mechanisms are swift, and there is serious competition among several daily video releases. Video marketers bankroll these productions. So, marketers exert pressure on the cast and crew as well as the producer-director to meet deadlines. Thus, the entire production circle is structured around serious improvisations that put videos on the market approximately a week after shooting begins. Whereas directors like Izu Ojukwu and Ifeanyi Onyeabor make videos in one or two weeks (Ayakoroma), the fastest directors in Nollywood are Chico Ejiro and Tchidi Chikere who shoot videos in three or four days (Williams). Chikere, for instance, has made more than three hundred video films under these circumstances. The budget for video films is just as tight and covers only the most basic things: cameras (DV cam, steady cam and tripods, and so forth), cast, and minimal crew, including improvised makeup and costumes. Post-production is done with a computer, and the videos are distributed on printed video CDs. Though producers are inclined to declare huge sums as production costs, Meyer's estimate of 5,000 to 15,000 US dollars for Ghanaian videos seems realistic. For instance, producers claim that the benchmark quantities sold for each video release is about ten thousand copies (as against two to five thousand copies by 2005), and the shelf price per CD is now 200 naira (about US$1.30). This means that the Nigerian videos average sales of 2 million naira (about US$17,000), which is comparable to what Meyer estimates for the Ghanaian video industry. Successful videos sell far above this benchmark. However, a crucial inference from this data is that the halving of shelf price counters the rise in benchmark sales. This means that producers are not necessarily making more profit from higher sales. In terms of fees, most actors' salaries are very low.

While the well-known faces of Nollywood's star system say they earn several hundred thousand dollars, some actors get as little as 10,000 naira, or about 83 US dollars (Okome, "The Message"). So far, there is no hard evidence that Nigerian videos can accommodate a huge budget: there is not much money to spend in the production process, and there are very clear limits about how many videos can be sold, as most African audiences do not actually purchase the videos. Even Jeta Amata's *The Amazing Grace* (2006), shot with a budget of 650,000 US dollars on 35mm, flopped on the Nollywood market. The film was not a Hollywood-Nollywood coproduction. Rather, it was a Nollywood production with enough cash to engage more "white" faces, and it was shot on celluloid. By the time Amata began shooting, Michael Apted's *Amazing Grace* (2006) was wrapping up in the United States.[5] Hollywood's business acumen will not shoot two films with the same theme and title simultaneously. The idea of producing the Nigerian version originated when Jeta Amata and British actor Nick Moran visited Donald Duke, the then governor of Nigeria's Cross River State (Cornel-Best). Moran was in Africa with Alicia Arce to film a documentary on Nollywood.

Amata's main concern was to make a 35mm film "with full Western production values" (Jury). But the film's production values may not have been "Western" enough. According to Ben Williams, the film's first assistant director, "Despite the white faces, it is still the Nollywood style of film shoot. It didn't even make it at the AMA Awards." The film did not make it to the Western box office and was unsuccessful with Nollywood audiences even when it was belatedly put on VCD. As Williams infers, "As compared to other successful films, I don't think it sold." The local people of Cross River and Akwa Ibom States, two states that share the cultural world of the film, complained about it because although the local language was spoken, it was translated in a very wishy-washy manner. Shot in one month, attention was not paid to actors learning the language in which they spoke their lines.[6] Thus, beyond the greater number of white faces and a few good shots in between, *The Amazing Grace* is very much a video film on celluloid. But for the fact that Donald Duke wholly bankrolled the film, it would have made a huge loss.

HOW DO WESTERN AUDIENCES REACT TO NOLLYWOOD VIDEOS?

Nollywood video filmmaking processes contrast very sharply with those of big-budget Hollywood movies with voluminous cast and crew and painstaking and lengthy production times. Not unmindful of the internal distinctions between Nollywood and Hollywood as well, table 12.1 highlights some of the contrasts. These differences, however, do not seem to be significant from the point of view of the Nigerian video filmmakers. Among those interviewed, actors tend to be more outspoken. They say Western people cannot understand the videos and are not buying them and that there is a need to improve the "quality" in order to appeal to a Western audience. However, producers and directors generally agree that Western audiences are buying and consuming the videos. This is understandable because producers and directors have higher stakes in the videos: they are the investors and are not about to speak negatively of their investments. They pretend that because the videos find their way into the West, Westerners are seeing them. The first reaction among the video filmmakers is to affirm that Western audiences are indeed consuming the features. But when one presses harder, the producers

Table 12.1. Some differences between Hollywood and Nollywood productions

Hollywood	Nollywood
Shot in several months/years	Shot in a few days
Script is very important	Script is unimportant
Storyboard is important	Storyboards are absent
Picture composition is important	Narrative is primarily based on dialogue
Assistant director prepares shooting schedules	Production manager prepares it
Casting is done by experts	Marketers often decide the cast
Track and crane shots are important	Track and crane shots are mostly absent
Rehearsals are given stringent attention	Rehearsals and dry runs overlap in the few days of shooting
Extensive attention to audiovisual quality	Little attention to picture and sound qualities
Strict attention to principles of visual design	No conscious attention paid to design principles
Rigorous postproduction over several months	Postproduction concluded in a few hours
Cuts are fast with less dialogue	Very slow cuts with a lot of dialogue

are not as convinced – leaving one to wonder whether it is just a case of imagined audiences. While Nollywood producers like to believe that Western people are consuming their videos, they fail to factor in two critical issues: that the quality of the videos differs vastly from Western filmic regimes and that together, these differences buffer Western viewers from the video films.

Table 12.1 highlights many factors that help understand Nollywood's transnational delimitations. An interesting aspect of this delimitation is the length of time it takes to shoot a film. From observations on locations, Nollywood videos can be on the market a week after shooting begins. This period includes postproduction and printing of the video jacket and posters. Unlike filmic traditions in Hollywood, the Nollywood process is fast-forward. Two examples might suffice. Ken Hughe's *Chitty Chitty Bang Bang* (1968) was shot in England, France, and Germany during 1967 and 1968. Hollywood could take two years to make a film, from start to finish. Another example is Michael Apted's *Amazing Grace* (2006), which has a Nollywood remake called *The Amazing Grace* by Jeta Amata (2006). Apted filmed in Gloucestershire, Wiltshire, Dorset, Hertfordshire, Oxfordshire, and Kent, and at Elstree Studios, London, and with celluloid, several cameras, cranes, dollies, and other lighting technologies. The makeup, costume design, set, and so forth were superbly done to replicate the historical period. On the other hand, Amata shot his version over a few days in Calabar, Nigeria. While Apted was still navigating his shoot through the many locations, Amata's remake was shot and distributed to audiences in Nigeria in 2006 – long before the original *Amazing Grace* premiered in London. During the shoot, Apted's team must have spent a great deal of time on production and postproduction details. And, of course, the preproduction schedules include scriptwriting, casting, and searching for locations and technical crew. To direct *Amazing Grace,* Apted would also have depended on storyboards made by a commissioned visual artist. Just as well, the entire production crew consists of carefully selected persons who are trained in the technologies and techniques of film production. There was also a team of historical consultants led by William Wilberforce's biographer, Kevin Belmonte. The film's credit line lists a four-hundred-member crew – minus the cast. Amata's remake had a mere forty-five-strong cast and crew.[7] The differences in production between Western filmic paradigms and Nollywood's affect the defining qualities of both film genres, as indicated in table 12.1.

From 2004 to 2006, I lived in a student hostel while I undertook my doctoral thesis at the University of Basel. Since my subject was Nigerian videos, several students soon found out that I had a collection of CDs. In the winter of 2004, six student friends asked me to screen a Nigerian video in the hostel's common room. I screened *My Command* (2004). I sat at the back to feed my own curiosity. My first European audience was challenged from the opening sequences of the movie onward. At practically every moment of the film, someone in the audience had a question. In the end, I ran commentaries throughout the screening. Some asked: "What is going on?" or "What are they saying?" or "Why are they doing that?" Nobody in the audience disagreed when one person ventured that the video has the same feel as a vacation video. There were similar reactions at several other screenings. One of my critical observations was that the audience wanted to see the video just as they would their usual Western film. However, unlike Western films that rely mainly on the visual narrative of the camera, the dialogue is far more important in Nigerian videos. Therefore, it is paramount for an audience to listen and *hear* rather than to sit and *see.* Among other issues with the Nigerian videos, "hearing" a film is not what Western audiences are used to. From these initial observations, my doubts about the possibilities of Western audiences for Nollywood films became even more pronounced and prompted the collection of data in the following years. My respondents consist of students at the University of Basel and other friends I met and made in Switzerland, Germany, Belgium, and Britain and include a larger circle of friends who filled out my questionnaire. In relation to students at the hostel in Basel, responses were elicited usually through focus groups at my video screenings. The total sample size was 112 persons.

The results of my findings from these interventions are quite revealing. For one thing, because of the simplistic subject of the videos, 81.8 percent of respondents can understand them (figure 12.1). Some respondents find the videos interesting – in an amusing way – because they are "new" and generate curiosity. A total of 53.8 percent of the respondents find the videos interesting, 38.5 percent find them amusing, and 7.7 percent find them uninteresting (figure 12.2). When it comes to *how* respondents learned of the videos, 16.7 percent bought them, 8.3 percent borrowed them, 85.3 percent saw them at a friend's, and 16.7 percent saw the video on satellite TV (figure 12.3). The data suggest that the interest of Western audiences in Nigerian videos is transient. They find the videos amusing, and as their interest is short-lived, Western audiences would not purchase any features. Data indicate that most Western audiences see the videos by chance at a friend's, outside their own homes. For some respondents (including all those who bought the videos), seeing the Nigerian feature was an academic necessity. As one respondent puts it: "It is rather because of professional reasons that I watch them." Interestingly, while 90 percent of the respondents want to see another video (figure 12.4), 100 percent of the respondents think that the Nigerian videos do not appeal to a Western audience (figure 12.5).

The most recurrent difficulty that Western respondents have with the Nigerian videos is not the video technology itself; it is the producers' inattentiveness to technical and production details. This is how one respondent puts it: "It is difficult as a Westerner that a Nigerian film can get into your head and become 'your' film. And then as a 'normal' Westerner you are used to Hollywood. So, you have some expectations, and if a film doesn't follow the rules of Hollywood, you are disappointed." Another respondent said, "The way they are shot seems

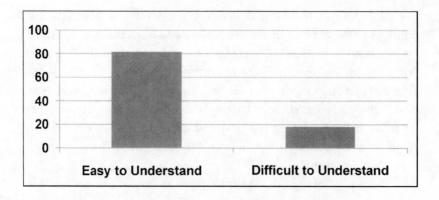

12.1. How Western audiences understand the videos.

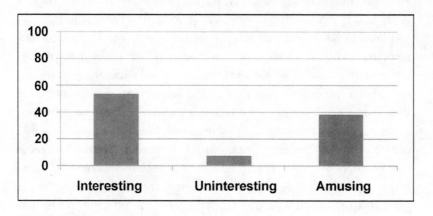

12.2. How Western audiences find the videos.

amateurish – in comparison to the kind of films Westerners are used to – which might already provoke a sense of ridicule rather than interest on the part of the audience." In this light also, another respondent says: "The story lines are uninteresting. The productions are very cheap. In some cases, you even see the shadow of the cameraman or part of the microphone." Many respondents also say that Westerners require a background knowledge in Nigeria's social culture to enable them understand the videos.

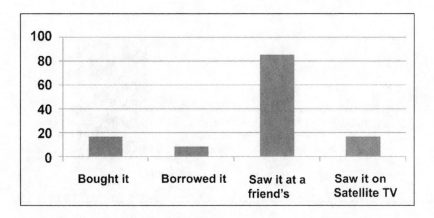

12.3. How Western audiences access the videos.

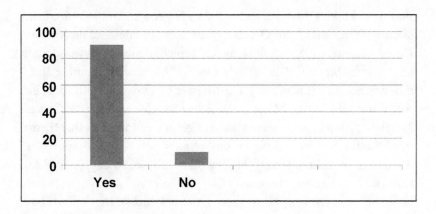

12.4. Will you want to see another video?

BRINGING NOLLYWOOD CLOSER
TO A WESTERN AUDIENCE

Several efforts have been made to bring Nollywood closer to the international community. While Nollywood videos have not yet made it to the Panafrican Film and Television Festival of Ouagadougou, Carthage Film Festival, or the Cannes Film Festival, producers have screened features at the Abuja International Film Festival. A joint Nollywood-

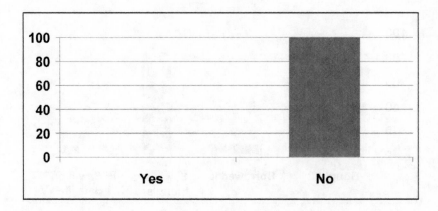

12.5. Can the videos appeal to a Western audience?

Bollywood Film Festival to be funded by Nigeria and India is also being planned (Onyedika). On October 13–19, 2005, the Festival du Nouveau Cinéma featured Genevieve Nnaji and screened four Nollywood films. Onookome Okome did the introduction for this special screening. In addition to documentaries like Jamie Meltzer's *Welcome to Nollywood,* Ben Addelman and Samier Mallal's *Nollywood Babylon,* and Saartje Geerts's *Nollywood Abroad,* there have also been several roundtables that thematized Nollywood from different disciplinary points and perspectives.[8] Also, there are the so-called Hollywood-Nollywood coproduced features, such as Lancelot Imasuen's *Close Enemies* and the United States–based Mildred Okwo's *30 Days* (Haynes, this volume). These efforts have yet to put Nollywood videos on the entertainment menu of Western audiences. However, together they draw attention to Nollywood's audiovisual potential. This is undeniably positive.

Critical Nigerian scholars have looked at ways of improving the narrative quality of video films. Ekwuazi, for instance, believes that the establishment of a Motion Picture Practitioners Council of Nigeria would "sanitize" the Nigerian video industry. He makes an analogy to what the Advertising Practitioners Council of Nigeria has done for Nigeria's advertising industry. Establishing a professional body to "sanitize" Nollywood may prove worthwhile even if it only prevents pirates from ripping off producers. However, there is also a critical difference between Nigerian advertisers and video filmmakers. The Advertising

Council includes trained professionals with diplomas, bachelors, master's, and Ph.D.s in mass communications, advertising, public relations, and visual arts. As members are trained in their industries' standards, they are able to produce global advertisements. It is global in the sense that advertisement producers in Nigeria employ standardized materials, techniques, and technologies to create products comparable to those from any part of the globe. Advertisements at Murtala Muhammed International Airport in Lagos illustrate this. Non-African passengers can identify with Nigerian advertisements because their message is global. The materials, techniques, finishing, and principles of advertising design are the same as those all over the world. But the same cannot be said of Nigerian video films.

Fosudo suggests that the provision of infrastructure for quality production will turn Nollywood around. The problem with this argument is that it assumes – almost naively – that once "quality infrastructure" is imported into the Nollywood production world, producers will make videos of good technical quality compatible with global principles and standards that Western consumers are used to. This assumption is naive, to say the least. Nollywood does not have enough trained manpower to set up such a "quality infrastructure." Unlike celluloid, the infrastructure required for video production is not as complicated. The infrastructure for video production in Nigeria is fully owned by private individuals. There is no government contribution. Several small-scale companies run camera and equipment rentals, including contractual postproduction and editing facilities. What is lacking is not so much "infrastructure" but technical expertise in making features that are compatible with global motion picture standards. Clearly, the lack of technical quality, which irritates Western audiences so much, indicates the absence of expertise in preproduction, production, and postproduction. Therefore, the fundamental question is: will Nollywood features fare better among Western audiences if they are restructured and live up to their expectations?

AN EXPERIMENT IN RECUTTING NOLLYWOOD VIDEOS

In 2005 I was contacted by Schlachthaus Theater in Bern, Switzerland, to include Nollywood films in the annual theater event called Afrique

Noire on November 3–13. I chose *Issakaba,* among other videos. Directed by Lancelot Imasuen, this video is the story of the Bakassi Boys, an ethnic militia in the Igbo states of Nigeria, notorious in the late 1990s for privatizing security where the state police had failed (Harnischfeger). As part of this project, I also chose *End of the Wicked,* made by Pastor Helen Ukpabio, as part of her church's evangelization project. The video dwells on localized Christian theology dealing with the wicked worlds of spirits and witchcraft that harm mankind. As the date for the event drew closer, I became apprehensive, as previous screenings of Nigerian videos to Western audiences had not been successful. I almost anticipated comments and reactions similar to those of respondents at my Basel hostel screenings, where audiences showed curiosity but had a lot of problems understanding the films. My methodology had always been to run rigorous commentaries at every video session to give Western audiences some understanding of the videos.

On the basis of my previous observations at the Basel hostel, recutting *Issakaba* was not a difficult exercise. I discovered that the essence of Nollywood's video sequences is not necessarily the problematic thing for Western audiences but the wordy (and often repetitive) nature of the story line. These repetitions are not only audible in the actors' lines and corresponding sound effects, but also very visible in their body language, such as bulging eyes, overstated gesticulations, and a lot of shouting. Another critical aspect of Nollywood's visuality is the camera's near-static point of view, which, rather than tell the story in images, merely offers a long look into the video drama, leaving much for the audience to fill in from actual social experiences. This is unlike the Western cinematic paradigm in which film is a visual medium where the camera tells the story from a very mobile and much faster perspective. Thus, my agenda with *Issakaba* was to recut and remove what might be redundant, to reduce it to its visual essence without losing the integrity of the story.

Issakaba is a four-part film on eight VCDs. It was not feasible to do any live commentaries for eight VCDs nor to expect my Western audiences in Schlachthaus Theater to endure a twelve-hour bombardment of Nigerian videos! The only option was to reedit the features with two clear objectives: to approximate the tempo of Western films by making fast cuts in the videos and to compress the videos by removing unnecessary material and shortening long sequences.

I removed scenes that dragged or where the dialogue was repeated as I noticed that Western audiences had difficulties understanding or accepting them. Take, for instance, the first part of *Issakaba*, which opens as we see the militia in a van approach and decapitate a young blind beggar sitting in the street. A protracted scene follows in which an irate bystander protests the violence, and Ebube, the unruffled militia leader, replies: "Issakaba has never shed innocent blood, and never will." After the lengthy dialogue, the militia then searches the dead man's belongings and finds several guns. It transpires that the scruffy man was merely pretending to be blind and was in reality a notorious armed robber and gun dealer masquerading as a beggar. In a manner that drives home the militia's populist victory over criminality, Ebube declares again: "Those who live by the gun shall die by the gun," and then, speaking into the camera, he tells the audience: "Justice has come to town." He then brings out his "medicine" gun and shoots the decapitated body. The corpse bursts into flames as the crowds cheer the militia's retributive justice, which seems more effective than the state's ineffective law and security agencies. Since the aim of this lengthy opening is to clear the air of any doubts about the militia's effectiveness and fairness, my recutting merely removed repetitive sequences and redundant moments in which nothing seemed to be happening. This shortened the film's length and sped up the sequences. In the end, the twelve-hour, four-part *Issakaba* became a one-hour story that was shown to the audience at Schlachthaus Theater. As usual, I was on hand to run commentaries. Audiences were told that they could ask questions, if they lost track of the story. Initially, I was surprised because nobody interrupted the screening to ask questions, and I was also amazed that no one in the audience got tired and walked out of the screening room. While my recut of *Issakaba* did not eliminate its poor technical quality, it did something that was not specifically Nollywood.[9] My recut eliminated profuse dialogue and unnecessary scenes, while also speeding up the video's tempo closer to what Western audiences are used to, as suggested in table 12.1. The reaction of the Western audience to the recut Nigerian video is very telling. It indicates one means by which Nollywood can reach its still imagined Western audiences by coming as close as possible to Westerners' technical expectations. The suggestion here is that if Nollywood producers truly wish to reach Western audiences, then they need to rethink how they make videos. They will have to imbibe and employ filmic principles recognized and acceptable to Western audiences, as we shall discuss shortly.

The data seem to suggest that Nigerian videos do not have a Western audience at present. And contrary to Nigerian producers, Western audiences are not buying the videos. For these audiences, the videos are what Okome terms "just another curiosity from Africa" ("It Is Difficult" 6). Nigerian videos are selling or circulating in the West but mainly among Africans and other migrants. It is clear from the data that Westerners who have seen the videos are most likely to have seen them by chance at a friend's, on satellite TV, or as part of an academic enterprise. There is no evidence to suggest that members of these audiences seek out and consume the videos for routine entertainment. Rather, what the data suggest is that, outside of academia, curiosity rather than entertainment is the primary motive for Western audiences to see Nigerian videos. Furthermore, the data also suggest that the major hindrance to the Nigerian videos is the technical quality of the products, which is the result of the producers' inattentiveness to established global principles and qualities accepted for film production and distribution. However, to be attentive to global standards in film production and distribution requires Nigerian video filmmakers to have the requisite training in all necessary aspects of film production. In Nollywood the vast majority of cast and crew are not trained in film production. Prospective actors and actresses merely improvise roles as directors and producers are eager to churn out hundreds of films. An improvised motion picture industry itself, Nollywood fails to meet the expectations of the Western audience it desperately seeks to count among its viewers. The videos could live up to Western expectations, if their producers wish. To meet these objectives, the issue of the social and cultural context of the videos need not be a serious problem. A film from any part of the world is equally a cultural product with its own social contexts. Competent producers can write sufficient social contexts and cultural backgrounds into their films. One should not require any elaborate thesis to understand a film from Europe, the United States, or elsewhere. *Slumdog Millionaire,* made in India, did not require any special knowledge of its social and cultural background for non-Indian audiences to understand. In other words, the limitations that

Nollywood films face in non-Nigerian filmic environments are inherent in the structure of Nollywood itself.

The analysis of data suggests that Nollywood could be more successful by overcoming the limitations that rob the videos of the quality and production standards expected by a Western audience. Mahmood Ali-Balogun, one of Nigeria's renowned filmmakers, believes that Nigerian producers are not doing "the right things" and that they should be more concerned with "quality" rather than "quantity." He insists that the videos are "half baked jobs," whereas they should meet what he calls "international standards" (Bumah). Ali-Balogun's gesture toward the international compares very much to Amata's dreams of "full Western production values." But then, is this inherent gesture toward sanitizing Nollywood and making its quality international or Western not negative in the sense that it is measured against what Ikheloa calls a "lily-white otherness"? And how much of the disapproval in Nigeria or the video filmmakers' aspiration to a Western audience is actually self-loathing – symptomatic of a colonial heritage that motivates the need to justify the self against an otherness? In the particular context of Nollywood films, if Nigerian critics insist on the West's qualities and producers want avid Western audiences, then the videos will have to be restructured to conform to their cinematic principles and expectations. Though my Nollywood recut in Bern was successful, the disadvantage in restructuring the video productions to fit a Western frame is that it may take the "Nolly" out of the "wood" – eliminating its essence and, thereby, excluding what might be important for African audiences while courting the elusive West. Besides, making Nollywood videos conform to Western principles and standards will bring it into direct and evidently into uneven competition with Hollywood or Western features. If video films are to hold their own, this competition may be as unnecessary as the elusive Western audience that Nollywood dreams of. That Nollywood producers dream up and aspire to Western audiences resonates with the uncanny migrations of young Africans, through devious routes, to European cities. It is only when they get to Europe that they find out that the streets are not paved with gold and life is not as good as they imagined, but is in fact rather demanding. In a keen sense, this beckoning for the West resonates with a defunct colonial notion of the noble savage – in which Africans loafed about in the jungle or on the beach waving in frenzy as Western steamers passed by. If Western cinema audiences are a global river of opportunities, Nollywood is now waving frantically at an unbothered steamer. Whether this steamer will one day take Nollywood on as its payload remains to be seen. At the moment, what is definite is that Western audiences for Nollywood videos do not exist and may be absent for the foreseeable future. And if Nollywood is to restructure and compel itself into a frame compatible with Western audiences, it will be at the risk of losing its African audiences yet being too inferior to films from Hollywood and the West. In the end, Nollywood producers may not gain much from trying to conform to Western audiences. Nollywood may in fact not need Western audiences to hold its own ground and remain a critical industry, just as Bollywood remains an important film industry without catering to the West.

NOTES

1. The videos were recut and presented to a Western audience at the festival Afrique Noire, organized by the Schlachthaus Theater, Bern, Switzerland, November 3–13, 2005.

2. These itinerant traditional theaters toured not only the Yoruba land but also the West African coast (Jeyifo; Kerr; Barber, Collins, and Ricard). Hubert Ogunde and Baba Sala ran two of the most popular Yoruba traveling theater troupes. In the 1970s and early 1980s, these troupes made celluloid features. They were also the first to move into video making – videoing their itinerant performances for much the same audiences.

3. Individuals may also see a feature free in a "found space" in front of a video store or through the opened door or window to a residence where a video is playing (Ajibade). The video parlor is a simple room fitted with benches, TV, and VCD/VCR, where audiences can pay to see video features.

4. Conversation with Alfred at his stand at Wentworth Street, Petticoat Lane market, London, June 30, 2005.

5. The film is based on the life of William Wilberforce, the antislavery pioneer.

6. The complaints are being made unofficially by people in the streets and everyday spaces. People have labeled it "The Amazing Disgrace," which indicates the level of popular disaffections.

7. See the Web sources for Chitty Chitty Bang Bang at http://www.chittygen11.com /movie.htm, Apted's Amazing Grace at http://www.amazinggracemovie.com /the_film.php, and Amata's The Amazing Grace at http://www.imdb.com/title/tto 804225/fullcredits#cast.

8. For example, "Nollywood: The Film Industry in Nigeria," featuring Nigerian producer Peace Anyiam-Fiberesima and American scholar Jonathan Haynes, held in June 2009 in Granada, Spain, and "Nollywood and Beyond," held in May 2009 in Mainz, Germany.

9. In the discussion session at the end of the screening, some of the audience speakers mentioned the poor technical quality of the video.

WORKS CITED

Ajibade, Babson. "From Lagos to Douala: The Video Film and Its Spaces of Seeing." *Postcolonial Text* 3.2 (2007): n. pag. Web.

Ayakoroma, Backlays. "An Evening with J. T. Tom-West." *Film Nigeria* 1.1 (2008): 44–46.

Barber, Karin, John Collins, and Alain Ricard. *West African Popular Theatre.* Bloomington: Indiana University Press, 1997.

Bumah, Julliet. "Nigerian Film Industry Needs Adequate Regulation, Institutional Support." *Sunday Punch,* July 19, 2009, 30.

Cornel-Best, Onyekaba. "I Lost My Lagos Home to Amazing Grace – Jeta Amata." *Modern Ghana News,* May 26, 2008. Web.

Ekwuazi, Hygenus. "Nollywood Is Like the Nigerian Economy: You Often Wonder Why It Has Not Collapsed." *Film Nigeria* 1.1 (2008): 36.

Fosudo, Sola. "The Infrastructure for Film Development Is Not Here." *Film Nigeria* 1.1 (2008): 43.

Garritano, Carmela. "Contesting Authenticities: The Emergence of Local Video Production in Ghana." *Critical Arts* 22.1 (2008): 21–48.

Harnischfeger, Johannes. "The Bakassi Boys: Fighting Crime in Nigeria." *Journal of Modern African Studies* 41.1 (2003): 23–49.

Ikheloa, Ikhide. "These Things around Our Necks." *Nextonsunday,* July 19, 2009, 36.

Jeyifo, Biodun. *The Yoruba Popular Travelling Theatre of Nigeria.* Lagos: Nigeria Magazine, 1984.

Jury, Louise. "Film Gives Nigeria's Side of the Slave Trade." *Evening Standard,* May 10, 2007. Web.

Kerr, David. *African Popular Theatre.* London: James Currey, 1995.

Meyer, Birgit. "'Praise the Lord': Popular Cinema and Pentecostalite Style in Ghana's New Public Sphere." *American Ethnologist* 31.1 (2004): 92–110.

Milon, T. *Audiovisual Production in Nigeria: Uniqueness and Strategies.* Lagos: Embassy of France, 2001.

Okome, Onookome. Interview. "It Is Difficult to Ignore Nollywood." *Film Nigeria* 1.1 (2008): 6–7.

——. "'The Message Is Reaching a Lot of People': Proselytizing and Video Films of Helen Ukpabio." *Postcolonial Text* 3.2 (2007): n. pag. Web.

Onyedika, Nkechi. "Nigeria, India Plan Joint Film Festival." *Naijarules,* June 23, 2009. Web.

Sontag, Susan. *Against Interpretation, and Other Essays.* New York: Picador, 2001.

Williams, Ben. Personal interview. Calabar, August 4, 2009.

FILMOGRAPHY

The Amazing Grace. Dir. Jeta Amata. Jeta Amata Concepts and Amazing Grace Films (Nigeria and UK). 2006.

Amazing Grace. Dir. Michael Apted. Four Boys Films et al. (UK and United States). 2006.

Chitty Chitty Bang Bang. Dir. Ken Hughes. Dramatic Features and Warfield (United States). 1968.

Close Enemies. Dir. Lancelot Oduwa Imasuen. Afro Media (United States and Nigeria). 2009.

End of the Wicked. Dir. Teco Benson. Liberty Films (Nigeria). 1999.

Issakaba 1–4. Dir. Lancelot Oduwa Imasuen. Kas-Vid and Mosco (Nigeria). 2000–2001.

My Command. Dir. Chinedum Nwoko. Dubem Holdings Productions (Nigeria). 2004.

Nollywood Abroad: A Nigerian Movie Maker in Europe. Dir. Saartje Geerts. Associate Directors (Belgium). 2008.

Nollywood Babylon. Dir. Ben Addelman and Samier Mallal. AM Pictures and National Film Board of Canada (Canada). 2008.

Osuofia in London, 1 and 2. Dir. Kingsley Ogoro. Kingsley Ogoro Productions (Nigeria). 2003, 2004.

Slum Dog Millionaire. Dir. Danny Boyle and Loveleen Tandan. Celador Films et al. (UK). 2008.

30 Days: Hell Hath No Fury. Dir. Mildred Okwo. Native Lingua Films and Temple Productions (United States and Nigeria). 2006.

Welcome to Nollywood. Dir. Jamie Meltzer. Walden Media (United States). 2007.

PART FOUR

Appropriations of Nollywood

Transgressing Boundaries: Reinterpretation of Nollywood Films in Muslim Northern Nigeria

ABDALLA UBA ADAMU

THE CULTURAL DIFFERENCES BETWEEN PREDOMINANTLY MUSLIM northern Nigeria and mostly Christian southern Nigeria reflect the different perceptions of the secular state. These differences are reflected not only in matters of state and policy, but also in how members of each region relate to the outside world. The differences are even more vivid in the popular culture industries. While they share common interfaces in terms of Western cultural products, the regional differences emerge when visually representative popular culture products are taken into consideration. In this way, and due to the British colonial precedent of encouraging mass translation of Middle Eastern folklore into the local Hausa language, the popular culture industries of northern Nigeria tends to have Middle Eastern and Asian "flavors." Consequently, northern Nigerians tend to make films the content of which is highly influenced by Indian (Hindi) films. The latter were imported by Lebanese merchants and shown in their own cinemas.

Films from other African countries are extremely rare on northern Nigerian television and in video stores. When the Nigerian film industry, Nollywood, became transnational, the Hausa were curious to see how it would develop, although Nollywood movies have never been as popular as Hindi films, particularly among the nonurban viewers of visual culture. However, with the increasing popularity of Nigerian films at home, elsewhere in Africa, and among Africans worldwide, more experimental Hausa filmmakers started toying with the idea of appropriating and reworking southern Nigerian films to make them more appealing to Muslim audiences in northern Nigeria. This was based on the fact that Nollywood films, which are referred to as Igbo films in the North, depict women in a more Westernized way. This applies to on-screen sexuality, social interaction, and dress.

In this chapter, I examine how Muslim Hausa video filmmakers in northern Nigeria overcome their cultural and religious prejudices and rework southern Nigerian video films for their Muslim audience. In particular, I examine the style of appropriation, which is marked by a selective choice of plot elements, and compare it to a similar style of appropriation practiced by the Indian film industry. As a case study, I analyze how a Muslim Hausa filmmaker, Baba Karami, appropriated and remade a Nollywood film, *Dangerous Twins,* as Hausa *Auduga* (Cotton). Based on interviews and discussions with the producer, who is considered the creative influence in the Hausa film industry instead of the director, as well as a close reading of *Auduga,* I examine his appropriation technique and how it reflects the religious and cultural divide between northern and southern Nigeria.

THE HAUSA VIDEO FILM INDUSTRY

Commercial Hausa video film production started in March 1990 with the production of *Turmin Danya* in Kano by a group of Hausa TV soap-opera stars. In 1997, the National Film and Video Censors Board (NFVCB) in Abuja began storing official records. By 2008, a total of 2,183 official Hausa video films had been censored for public release.

In 1998, a Hausa-language magazine, *Tauraruwa* (Star, modeled on the Bollywood magazine *Stardust*), was established in Kano city to report on emerging stars. In 1999, the third edition of the magazine (August 1998) created a column called "Kanywood," which discusses events in the Kano film industry (20). This created a label for an African film industry three years before Norimitsu Onishi coined the term *Nollywood* for the southern Nigerian film industry in his article in the *New York Times* on September 16, 2002. By 1998, a Hausa video film industry had been formed with its main creative and marketing nucleus in Kano – thus, Kanywood. However, nearby Kaduna and Jos were also centers of Hausa video film production, although the main market was in Kano.

Many Hausa video films follow three main story lines: *auren dole* (forced marriage, where a girl or boy is forced to marry someone not of their choice), love triangle (where two boys court the same girl or two wives fight over a single husband), and song and dance (more than 98 percent of Hausa video films have at least two to three song-and-dance routines; these song-and-dance routines are not part of the story line, but the filmmakers include them to boost the entertainment). All these elements were inspired by Hindi cinema, which Hausa had been exposed to via television stations in Kano, Kaduna, and Jos, as well as in Lebanese-owned cinemas. Films from Hollywood are rarely used as remake templates, because Hausa film producers perceive them as being the complete opposite of Islamic values. Nevertheless, a few American films served as templates, too, such as *Predator*, which was remade as *Tarzomar Shahada*; the T V series *Friend of the Family* inspired *Jalli*; the movie *What Lies Beneath* became *Salma Salma Duduf*; the Hausa video *Kauna* was adapted from the television series *Silent Witness*; and John Woo's made-for-T V film *Blackjack* was remade as *Tsaro*.

HAUSA FILM INDUSTRY AND NOLLYWOOD

From the start, it seems that debates about Nigerian films would center on English-, Yoruba-, and Igbo-language video films, but not Hausa video movies. The latter were not taken seriously, although Kanywood had become the second-largest indigenous-language video industry in Nigeria in 2002. This is reflected by the amount of column inches devoted to Nigerian films in Nigerian media, on the Internet, in books published, as well as at domestic and international conferences. More notable examples of such focus include foreign newspapers (for example, Jenkins; Kiefer), journals (Ebewo; Omoera), books (Haynes; Hugo; Barrot) and dissertations (Offord; Uchenna) and a foreign foundation, the Nollywood Foundation, in Los Angeles. To date, the only comprehensive study assessing the impact of Hausa video films in Nigeria is *Hausa Home Videos* by Adamu, Adamu, and Jibrin, while only two conferences were held on the Hausa video film (2003 in Kano and 2009 in Zaria). By 2007, the Hausa video film industry had undergone radical changes as a result of a new Islamic censorship regime that hampers the industry's development and ability to compete.

Yet the NFVCB approved 616 Hausa videos for screening in 2002, followed by Yoruba videos with 1,189 and far ahead of Igbo with 44 (166). As Krings pointed out: "At the moment, researchers in Nigerian video films seem to be stuck in regional compartments, and this state of affairs mirrors discourse within the respective industries in Nigeria itself, discourse that tends to ignore the interconnectedness of the regional industries" ("Conversion on Screen" 64). Of the various researchers (for example, Haynes and Okome; Adejunmobi; McCall) and journalists (for example, Steinglass; Onishi) who covered the early Nollywood phenomena, only Brian Larkin, Matthias Krings, and to some extent Johnson, Ekwuazi, Noy, and Behrend focused on the development of the video film industry in northern Nigeria. Indeed, Johnson added that between 1990 and 1997, "the Kano-Kaduna axis has produced a total of not more than fifty" (101) video films – contrary to the more than 300 unreleased, uncensored Hausa video films at the time.

By 2007, Onookome Okome had popularized the term *Nollywood* to refer to West African cinema in a special edition of *Postcolonial Text*, as well as selling the idea at the African Film Conference in November 2007 at the University of Illinois–Urbana-Champaign. Yet no debate on the development of popular culture in Nigeria can ignore Kanywood and how distinct it is from Nollywood. Kanywood films are gaining popularity in countries where there is a large concentration of either native Hausa speakers (for example, in Niger) or of second-language speakers (as in Ghana, Burkina Faso, Benin, Togo, and parts of Senegal). To these Hausa speakers abroad, Nigerian film is essentially Hausa, simply because many of them do not understand English and the cultural transmission of mainstream Nollywood. The term *Nollywood*, therefore, cannot be applied across the board to popular African cinema. A further attestation to this, for instance, is the increasing use of the term *Ghanawood* in reference to Ghana's video film industry.

From 1999 to 2001, Nollywood and Kanywood collaborated, and the National Film and Video Censors Board in Abuja officially recorded a total of 24 films from such collaborations – not including other productions. The few Hausa-speaking actors who appeared in Nollywood films were Hindatu Bashir, Ali Nuhu, Sani Danja, Ibrahim Mandawari, and Kabiru Mohammed Suleja. No notable Nollywood actor featured in any Hausa video film, although northern director Sani Mu'azu and cameraman Umar Gotip often worked with Nollywood producers.

Yet despite the mutual exclusivity of northern Nigerian Hausa-language video films and those in southern Nigeria, Hausa producers were inspired by Nigerian films, that is, English-language video films and Igbo and Yoruba videos. Indeed, some producers I talked to argued that violence in Hausa video film – for example, as depicted in *Takidi* and in *Mushkila* – was used to imitate southern Nigerian video film styles in which it is common. One of the southern Nigerian videos appropriated by Hausa video producers was *Dangerous Twins,* which was remade as the Hausa *Auduga.* Hereinafter, I will analyze how this film was remade and the passage of culture that this process entailed. Data for the analysis are from three sources: textual analysis of the *Auduga* video film; a review of *Dangerous Twins,* published online on IMDB.com (Sherazade); and a structured interview with the producer of *Auduga,* Baba Karami, who also doubled as the assistant director.

TAKES ON REMAKES

Imitation may be considered the sincerest form of flattery, but apparently not when it comes to artistic reinterpretation of creative works by others. The very practice of film remakes by major film production clusters around the world has caused ambivalence toward remakes as the production of "a new version of an older film that was commercially exhibited" (Forrest and Koos 3).

The very concept of the remake embeds two additional transpositional practices. These are *adaptation,* which is basically "cinematic versions of canonical plays and novels" (Sanders 23), and *appropriation,* a literary process that "frequently affects a more decisive journey away from the informing source into a wholly new cultural product and domain" (26). In all three strategies, an organic relationship with the original (source text) must exist. However, for the remake to achieve its artistic objectives, the audience must be aware of the original (source text) and its offspring, that is, the remake.

In his discussion of the remake, Thomas Leitch identifies "four possible stances a remake can adopt, each with its own characteristic means of resolving its contradictory intertextual claims" (142). These are the readaptation, update, homage, and the true remake. These stances actually refer to the intertextual relationship between the remake and the source text, rather than the general approach that motivates the *need* for the remake.

Readaptation is a twice-removed adaptation of a well-known literary work whose earlier cinematic adaptations the remake "ignores or treats as inconsequential" (ibid.). *Update* revises a well-known classic and relocates it to another setting, retaining its generic characteristics – in short, it is a more modernist interpretation of an earlier source text. The *homage* treats its cinematic precursor as a classic "in danger of being ignored or forgotten" (144). Finally, "*true remakes* depend on a triangular notion of intertextuality, since their rhetorical strategy depends on ascribing their value to a classic earlier text and protecting that value by invoking a second earlier text as betraying it" (147).

The remake itself is motivated by a series of factors that include technical, artistic, social, economic, and political reasons that warrant reworking the core messages of a particular film into a new one, either for the initial audiences or for another set of audiences. These factors actually provide a loose framework for generating models of remakes of which there are at least five: those based on technology, economic competition, genre switching, artistic, and cultural flows.

At what point does a remake become plagiarism? Forrest and Koos quote André Bazin, who speaks of plagiarism when the remake "has absolutely nothing to do with the updating of an old picture and everything to do with geography" (8). Thus, the fifth model of film remake, which deals with cultural flows, looks particularly at the inward and outward flows of filmic ideas between societies. Bazin's comments were made in the light of flows of filmic ideas mainly from European cinema to Hollywood, a direction he finds irritating. In Bazin's analysis, European films, particularly French, were considered more artistic than Hollywood movies. Remaking them in Hollywood constitutes crass cultural plagiarism. Bazin is not the only critic of the remake's cultural repercussions. Film critics such as Sharon Waxman, Vincent Canby, and Terence Rafferty see the remake, particularly when it crosses borders, as cultural piracy.

Culture plays a strong role in the remake process. An internal remake that amounts to circulating a new version of a film within the same cultural environment creates less tension than an external remake across cultural boundaries. Obviously, for transcultural remakes, the second version has to cater to the audience's sensibility. It is the remake producers' consideration for the target audience that has made French film critics such as Andre Bazin disdainful of American remakes of European films. Unlike Bazin, however, I am less interested in defending particular films against their alleged artistic degradation caused by the remaking process. Nor am I concerned with the violation of intellectual property so often at stake when films are remade. In my analysis of *Auduga*, a Muslim Hausa remake of the Nollywood video film *Dangerous Twins*, I focus on how its producer adapted the story line to cater to the cultural sensibilities of his northern Nigerian Muslim audience. Hence, I wish to highlight the very phenomenon Bazin and more recent film critics look down upon. As will become apparent, once cultural boundaries are crossed, the process is no longer a mere remaking; it becomes an appropriation. The translocated film *Dangerous Twins* is thus recast in a whole new "cultural product and domain" – to borrow a phrase from Sanders (26). Culturally, *Auduga* sells Islam, despite the absence of Christian iconography in its source text, *Dangerous Twins*. Islamic scholarship in *Auduga* (whose diegetic legal advice was even dispensed by an Islamic scholar) operates in a totally different domain than the high-octane urban lifestyle of *Dangerous Twins*.

BORN AGAIN: APPROPRIATION AND ISLAMIZATION OF NOLLYWOOD

Baba Karami is a video film producer in Kanywood. Although an indigene of Kano State, he was born and raised in Agege, a virtual Hausa community in Lagos. His nickname is "Dan OPC" ("Follower of Odu'a Peoples' Congress," a pan-Yoruba militant organization based in Lagos) because of his fluency in the Yoruba language and familiarity with Yoruba people and culture. He has been an avid fan of Nollywood films since the industry began in Lagos. By 2004, when Nollywood released *Dangerous Twins*, he had "become addicted to the industry." Indeed, he said that when watching a Nollywood film, he becomes carried away in the church rituals iconic to most of their story lines. As he is a Muslim, he felt uneasy about any affinity to Christian symbolism. He decided to join the Hausa film industry to give it a more Islamic slant. In effect, he was trying to rid Nollywood of Christian imagery by substituting it with Islamic symbolism in transcribed Hausa remakes. As he lived in Lagos, he had access to superior filming facilities, and he also knew some famous Nollywood stars. His favorite, Ramsey Nouah, starred in

Dangerous Twins. These combined factors gave him an edge over Kano-based Hausa video film producers.

Appropriation of films from Bollywood and Hollywood is common but by no means the norm among Kano-based video film producers. Karami decided to jump on the bandwagon by appropriating from a source he knows best – Nollywood. *Auduga,* the remake of *Dangerous Twins,* is his first film.

Dangerous Twins tells the story of twin brothers separated by distance and family problems. One is calm, levelheaded, progressive, and childless. He desperately wants children, is based in London, and is married to a British woman. The other is a pure rascal and lives in Lagos with his wife and children. Somehow the twins switch places – the Lagos twin goes to London and pretends to be the husband of the British wife so that they can have a child. The twins plot to return to their normal lives later (see Haynes, this volume, 93–94).

Baba Karami calls the remake *Auduga,* a Hausa word for "cotton." He used this term in reference to the London twin – weightless (childless) – as the attractions of his London lifestyle are crucial to the story. In *Dangerous Twins,* the story line revolves around the Lagos twin's efforts to impregnate the London twin's wife. *Auduga* highlights the same theme, but places the issue in the Islamic jurisprudence of inheritance rights of the child born from this sexual liaison.

Auduga narrates the story of twins (played in dual roles by Abba El-Mustapha, who is also codirector) separated by distance – one good, and the other evil to the core. However, the roles are reversed. In the Hausa remake, the London-based twin is bad and the Lagos-based twin is good. Their mother takes the London twin to Britain, where she raises him as a typical Briton. He is a lapsed Muslim. In Lagos, their wealthy father builds up a commercial enterprise with a first wife and their son Sheriff, the elder brother to the twins.

The London twin returns to Lagos when their father dies. But he is keen on drugs, liquor, and women. The family is puzzled by his conduct, but attribute it to living in a foreign land and mingling with abysmal cultures, as the London-based mother of the twins says in a remorseful scene.

The Lagos twin is a serious, devout person. The elder brother, Sheriff, played by Baba Karami, takes the reins when the London twin is out of control. Sheriff's wife has a pretty sister, Aisha, and the London twin desperately wants her, even though he has no shortage of female admirers. However, Sheriff does not approve, much to the annoyance of the London twin. In a spirit of fraternity, the twins demand that their share of their father's estate should be handed out to them. Sheriff agrees and calls their uncle to oversee the distribution of the wealth according to Islamic principles.

Basing his arguments on Islamic jurisprudence, the uncle insists that the London twin is a heretic, as he has forsaken Islam and its way of life. Therefore, he has no right to any part of his Muslim father's inheritance. In the middle of all this, a woman walks in and declares that more than twenty-two years previously, armed robbers had allowed her to be raped by a fellow traveler. It turns out that the traveler is Alhaji, the father of the twins and Sheriff. She became pregnant and eventually gave birth to a boy, Khalid, but unknown to Alhaji. Khalid's mother had no access to him due to his high position and wealth. Alhaji had tried unsuccessfully to trace her many times. Even before this revelation, Khalid has already made friends with the London twin and was trying to get him to slow down his excesses, but without knowing they are blood brothers.

The twins' London-based mother, who also pops up during the inheritance hearings and demands that her son's inheritance is handed out, blames herself for leading him astray. London's "abysmal culture" had corrupted him, and she asks him for forgiveness. The London twin accuses his mother of not teaching him Islamic ways and of rearing him as a godless person. The mother urges him to mend his ways, to effectively become a born-again Muslim. He forgives her, repents, and rediscovers Islam. But it is all a ploy to get his inheritance. In reality, he has no intention of becoming a proper Muslim.

Meanwhile, the Lagos twin has married, but his bride will not sleep with him. Apparently, she was having her period. Islam forbids women to have sexual intercourse until it is over. While ruminating over the issue, he is kidnapped by armed robbers hired by the London twin who intends to keep him locked up until his inheritance is handed over. When the Lagos twin asks about his marital responsibilities, the London twin offers to replace him as the husband – thus returning to the original plot of *Dangerous Twins*. Masquerading as the Lagos twin, the London twin sleeps with the bride and gets her pregnant. He also embezzles a lot of money from the elder brother's company. Sheriff has not noticed the switch.

Somehow the imprisoned Lagos twin escapes and confronts his wife. She is thunderstruck and informs her husband that she is pregnant with the London twin's baby. They wait for the London twin to return. Eventually, the Lagos twin shoots the London twin dead.

Auduga, as a remake of *Dangerous Twins,* appreciates the cinematic narrative of *Dangerous Twins* and pays homage to its plot elements of flashy cars, big houses, and an urban lifestyle. But its main technique is in the way two images of the same actor (Abba El-Mustapha) are juxtaposed in a dialogue like Ramsey Nouah's character in *Dangerous Twins.*

In a plot departure, however, the "abysmal culture" of London, the main cause of corrupting the London twin in *Auduga,* is transferred as the same abysmal culture of Lagos in *Dangerous Twins* – thus offering a devastating critique of Lagos as a chaotic den of immorality (perhaps Baba Karami, having been born and raised in Lagos, is trying to convey a particular message). This is because in *Dangerous Twins,* the London twin becomes trapped in Lagos and turns to the underground to sort out his problems. Thus, Lagos corrupts the neat and orderly life of the London twin. Again both video films end violently – with one twin killing the other.

HOLLYWOOD-BOLLYWOOD-KANYWOOD
APPROPRIATION STYLES

The producers of *Auduga* seem to follow the same appropriation strategies narrated by Tejaswini Ganti in her analysis of the "(H)Indianization" of the American movie *On the Waterfront* as *Ghulam.* Ganti argues that Indian filmmakers must identify with a film before they can appropriate it. Indian screenwriter Sutanu Gupta, who argues that adapting an American film to an Indian audience must be along Indian cultural norms, explains this. In his conversations with Ganti about the need to "Indianize" Hollywood, "Gupta uses a series of what may be regarded as social taboos and symbols of deviance to contrast what he sees as the lack of a moral universe in a Hollywood film with the implicitly moral one of the Hindi film, as well as to posit a metonymic association between cinema and society" (289).

In a similar way, *Auduga* seeks to Hausanize and Islamicize *Dangerous Twins* by using Islam to create the "metonymic" association between filmmaking and Islamic values. The central message of *Auduga* is parental responsibility and focuses on the role of the mother. The London twin is raised as a lapsed Muslim. It is not indicated that he is Christian – but it is suggested that merely living in London is enough to make him bad to the bone. His mother, a Muslim, played with great aplomb by the Hausa-Scottish actress Zainab Booth, did not bother to set him on the correct Islamic path. To emphasize the Islamicity of the plot element and to distinguish itself from the appropriated Nollywood film, *Auduga* introduces the laws of Islamic inheritance. Under sharia law, a non-Muslim (the London twin) cannot inherit property from a Muslim. In the plot of *Auduga,* the London twin refuses to accept this Islamic ruling. The plot then revolves around his attempt to wrest back what he feels is rightfully his by birth.

The producer Baba Karami had a special connection not with the plot elements of *Dangerous Twins,* but with the lead actor, Ramsey Nouah, "whom I admire greatly and watched all his films." Baba Karami, however, is uneasy with "too much Christianity in Nollywood films," and in a bid to diminish this, he decides to "Islamize" *Dangerous Twins* in the Hausa remake.

In Indian remakes of Hollywood originals, Indian filmmakers expand the original by adding emotions, extending the narrative, and including songs. They explain this with the need to meet audience expectations and in terms of artistic antecedents (Ganti 290). Subplots usually expand the narrative. This strategy was employed in *Auduga* with the subplot of Khalid's mother suddenly appearing during inheritance hearings to declare that her child is yet another son of the twin's father. Again in this expansion process, *Auduga* invokes Islamic jurisprudence to emphasize that illegitimate children have no right to inherit any of their father's property no matter the circumstances of their birth. Hence, in this case, adding the subplot is about "making narratives more moral" (ibid. 292) – and thus "educating the audience" (Karami) – the avowed main objective of Hausa video films for their Muslim audiences.

Furthermore, like Indian producers and directors who appropriate Hollywood films, Hausa video filmmakers feel the need to connect with their audience. In Tejaswini Ganti's study, Vikram Bhatt, *Ghulam*'s director, explains how he determines whether a film can be "Indianized" and what constitutes universal appeal: "A Hollywood film has to have its relevance with our audiences. For me the film has to be that of a universal appeal, by which I mean that a film needs to be centered around a human emotion more than a set of circumstances" (287). Similarly, producer Baba Karami, who also wrote the screenplay for *Auduga,* felt unable to translate *Dangerous Twins* as a Hausa story. He knew that his Muslim audience could not connect with un-Islamic plot elements in the Nollywood original, particularly when the Lagos twin sleeps with London twin's wife (Karami). Although Baba Karami loathed this scene, he kept it in *Auduga* – out of economic considerations. This process that I call selective inclusion is also typical of Indian filmic appropriations. As Ganti says about a similar process in India, "What must be stressed is that filmmakers' ideas about what constitutes acceptable representations are not fixed but fluid, and they are highly dependent upon commercial success or failure" (289). Thus, while *Auduga* uses Islam to address the issues of inheritance and promote Islam as a more desirable way of life (adroitly avoiding comparison with another religion), it fails to resolve the pregnancy of the Lagos twin's wife, who was made pregnant by the London twin. Clearly, there is a limit to the "Islamization" process of adapting a Nollywood film for Muslim Hausa audiences due to the selective-inclusion principle. If not for commercial reasons, the pregnancy scenes could have been removed and the core issue of maternal responsibility and Islamic inheritance maintained in *Auduga.*

Song-and-dance routines (*rawa da waka*) in Hausa video films serve the same purpose as in Hindi films. For instance: "The most common emotion expressed musically in Hindi films is love, and in films like *Ghulam* where a love story is not the main focus of the plot, a 'romantic track' is developed primarily through songs between the hero and the heroine" (Ganti 294). *Auduga* also pays homage to its Bollywood inspirations by including about four song-and-dance routines, none of which has any direct bearing on the story. As in Ganti's analysis of *Ghulam,* the love story is not central to *Auduga,* and the song-and-dance routines are used to embellish the story line. They introduce the love theme in the songs between the hero and heroines. Indeed, in one of the songs, two female actors who have nothing to do with the film suddenly appear briefly in a sitting room and start arguing about a male actor who does not star in the movie at all. In the next scene, all three are shown singing happily together. Baba Karami defends this as a means to attract bigger audiences, as a Hausa video film without song-and-dance routines is a sure recipe for commercial failure.

By emphasizing the role of religion in its reworked story line, *Auduga* acknowledges its audience and communicates a particular partisan perspective without insulting religious sensibilities. Its supportive argument of raising a child in an "abysmal culture" communicates a universal message of how cultural disjunctions can create culturally displaced individuals – regardless of their religion. Many religious doctrines would take exception to the London twin's conduct. After all, there are many strict, even fundamentalist, Muslims living in London who did not turn abysmal. But *Auduga* weaves around religious themes and does not blame the London twin's behavior on Christianity. It thus criticizes the Westernization of indigenous individuals originally without liberal Western values.

By 2002, the few collaborative efforts between Nollywood and Kanywood had dwindled, with only producers like Baba Karami attempting to generate interest in Nollywood by appropriating Nollywood films into Hausa. Two factors seem to have been responsible for stopping the collaborations.

The first was how Hausa video films were marketed in northern Nigeria. When a producer finishes a film, usually sponsored by a marketer, he sells a copy of the original master tape and a negotiated number of jackets (VHS cassette covers) to the marketer, who then makes duplicate copies and slots them in the jackets he has purchased. When the first batch is finished, he buys more jackets. Unsold tapes are removed from the jackets and returned to the producer. The tapes are then erased and overwritten with another film.

Nollywood marketers operate on a radically different principle. They usually bring their finished product to the markets to be sold. The Hausa distributors usually do not accept these, and as a result Nollywood-produced films are usually found only with southern Nigerian distributors, mainly Igbo merchants. This removes them from Hausa audiences, who go to Hausa merchants only for films. In any event, Hausa marketers rarely distribute films by producers who are not part of their marketing cartel – and Igbo merchants are rarely part of such a system.

In addition, to regulate the volume of video films being released, especially from 2000, the Hausa video film industry began lining up video releases on a weekly basis. As Nollywood producers are not part of this system, they felt frustrated (Baker). This led two of the strongest supporters of the Nollywood-Kanywood hybrid film strategy, Oskar Baker and Iyke Moore, to withdraw from further investments in Hausa video films.

Second, some of the early Nollywood-Kanywood hybrid video films attempted to create themes of national unity that were not well received by the Muslim Hausa. Some of the video films affected this way were *Almara, Dan Adam Butulu, Holy Law,* and *National Anthem.* They all deal with issues such as Islam, particularly sharia, and other cultural norms of northern Nigerian Muslim Hausa that are grafted into their story lines and local audiences felt unhappy with. This led to harsh criticism and angry reviews in local-language mass media (for example, Yahuza; Yahaya). Thus, Nollywood-Kanywood hybrid films that focused on Islam and cultural mediations often generated vitriol against southern Nigerian film producers, at least in northern Nigerian mass media (such as *Fim, Bidiyo, Duniyar,* and others). Consequently, many of the promoters of the hybrid strategies decided to cut their losses and quit the system. The hybridity continues on a limited scale, but controlled from Lagos, which saw, for instance, the involvement of northern Nigerian actor Ali Nuhu in *Sitanda.*

The cultural disjuncture between art and commercial film remakes, as reflected by French or general art films remade into Hollywood equivalents, provides a framework for understanding such disconnection between northern and southern Nigerian filmmaking. The remake of the southern Nigerian film *Dangerous Twins* as the northern Nigerian Islamic film *Auduga* exemplifies this. Yet *Auduga* is not, strictly speaking, a remake. As it has no literary antecedent, it is not a variation of adaptation. *Auduga* is an appropriation, for in its translocation of both text and context from the southern Nigerian *Dangerous Twins,* it recasts the original story line and its plot elements in a new cultural milieu – a similar cinematic strategy adopted by Hindi filmmakers appropriating Hollywood – and serves as a creative inspiration to Hausa filmmakers. This is similar to American remakes of French films, which tend to reveal differences "through film endings, with the former providing a comforting resolution altogether absent in their European counter-parts" (Forrester and Koos 8).

Thus, *Dangerous Twins* serves as a cosmopolitan tale of treachery and betrayal and targeted a general urban audience. Its remake, *Auduga*, is more didactic in its portrayal of Islamic values as guiding principles of Muslim life. This is because *Auduga* is not just a discourse about in-heritance rights, but also a reaffirmation of Islamic identity. The film portrays the man who leaves Islam as being without identity. In this respect, *Auduga* is almost evangelical – a subtle attempt to exorcize the Christian imagery of Nollywood films as perceived by Baba Karami. Clearly, Muslim producers, who have more clout than the director, could not simply remake a Nollywood film in northern Nigeria. Considering the differences in social, cultural, and religious mind-sets and beliefs that divide Muslim and Christian video film producers in Nigeria, a Nollywood film can only be *redirected* rather than remade by Muslim producers. That way, it is not just remade, but "born again" for a differ-ent audience.

While Hausa audiences perceive Hindi films as representing a "par-allel modernity, a way of imaginatively engaging with the changing so-cial basis of contemporary life that is an alternative to the pervasive influence of a secular West" (Larkin, "Indian Films" 16), both the audi-ence and the Hausa filmmakers do not see this parallel with southern Nigerian video films. Indeed, it is this identification with Hindi film ethos that seems to unite both the Hausa filmmakers and their audi-ence against Western influences in Hollywood films and, subsequently, Nollywood video films. Both Nollywood and Hollywood films are seen by the Muslim Hausa as decadent and un-Islamic. The colonial anteced-ent preference for Middle Eastern and Asian popular culture among the Hausa merely provided a ready template for this parallel modernity and subsequent condemnation of any Western filmic influence. As Krings discovered in his ethnographic study of Hausa filmmakers in the city of Kano: "Although Hausa videos share a great deal with their southern equivalents, and some may even be called transcripts of southern video films, northern filmmakers were reluctant to support my suggestion of commonalities between the regional video cultures of Nigeria. Against the overall discursive backdrop of cultural exclusion and critical debates

about the cultural authenticity of Hausa videos, it is only too comprehensible that my interlocutors had to argue in favor of sharp differences
between their own productions and those of their southern colleagues"
("Muslim Martyrs" 163).

The years of interethnic and interreligious conflicts between northern and southern Nigeria are further clear testimonies to cultural hos-
tilities that make it hard for domestic media to accept, unless, as done in
Nigeria, enforced by federal legislation.[1] Although National Television
Authority networks carry a dose of programs from all the regions, in
the North they are ignored increasingly in favor of ArabSat scheduling
that broadcasts a lot of American programs via free-to-air channels. Yet
worldwide Hindi films seem to be more acceptable. Despite religious
and linguistic divides, they have enough cultural motifs to approximate
the cultural spaces of Muslim northern Nigerians – for example, love
triangles and forced marriage issues. Essentially, they share similar cultural mind-sets.

As Krings concludes in his study of Hausa video filmmakers, "exploring the inter-connectedness of the regional video industries of Nigeria might be a fruitful direction for further research" ("Conversion
on Screen" 64). However, such interconnectedness would have to negotiate the myriad of cultural, ethnic, and religious barriers that have
characterized the Nigerian nation. Thus, cultural resonance and a shared
emotional grammar explain why young Hausa filmmakers, spoon-fed
Hindi film fare from birth, openly embrace the Hindi film motif, even if
aware that the cultural and religious realities of their society are totally
different from those of India and why they reject the much geographically closer southern Nigerian film influences.

NOTE

1. See Agi for a comprehensive   interreligious conflicts in
treatment of interethnic and   Nigeria.

WORKS CITED

Adamu, Abdalla Uba, Yusuf Adamu, and   ciety. Kano, Nigeria: Center for Hausa
    Umar Faruk Jibril, eds. *Hausa Home*   Cultural Studies, 2004.
    Videos: Technology, Economy, and So-   Adejunmobi, Moradewun. "English and

the Audience of an African Popular
Culture: The Case of Nigerian Video
Film." *Cultural Critique* 50 (Winter
2002): 74–103.

Agi, S. P. I. *Political History of Religious
Violence in Nigeria.* Calabar, Nigeria: Pi-
gasiann & Grace International, 1998.

Baker, Oscar. Interview. *Fim Magazine*
(July 2002): 28.

Barrot, Pierre, ed. *Nollywood: The Video
Phenomenon in Nigeria.* Bloomington:
Indiana University Press, 2008.

Behrend, Heike. "The Titanic in Northern
Nigeria: Transnational Image Flows
and Local Interventions." *Transmission
Image: Visual Translation and Cultural
Agency.* Ed. Birgit Mersmann and Al-
exandra Schneider. New Castle upon
Tyne: Cambridge Scholars Publishing,
2009. 224–39.

Canby, Vincent. "Movies Lost in Translation." *New York Times,* February 12,
1989, B1+.

Ebewo, Patrick J. "The Emerging Video
Film Industry in Nigeria: Challenges
and Prospects." *Journal of Film and
Video* 59.3 (2007): 46–57.

Ekwuazi, Hyginus. "The Hausa Video
Film: The Call of the Muezzin." *Film
International* 5.4 (2007): 64–70.

Forrest, Jennifer, and Leonard R. Koos.
"Reviewing Remakes: An Introduction." *Dead Ringers: The Remake in Theory and Practice.* Ed. Jennifer Forrest and
Leonard R. Koos. Albany: State University of New York Press, 2002. 1–36.

Ganti, Tejaswini. "'And Yet My Heart Is
Still Indian': The Bombay Film Indus-
try and the (H)Indianization of Hol-
lywood." *Media Worlds: Anthropology
on New Terrain.* Ed. Faye D. Ginsburg,
Lila Abu-Lughod, and Brian Larkin.
Berkeley and Los Angeles: University of
California Press, 2002. 281–300.

Haynes, Jonathan, ed. *Nigerian Video
Films.* Rev. ed. Athens: Ohio University
Press, 2000.

Haynes, Jonathan, and Onookome Okome.
"Evolving Popular Media: Nigerian
Video Films." *Research in African Litera-
tures* 29.3 (1998): 106–28.

Hugo, Pieter. *Nollywood.* Munich: Prestel,
2009.

Jenkins, Mark. "Hooray for Nollywood!
A Showcase of New Nigerian Video
Films." *Washington City Paper,* Febru-
ary 4, 2005. Web.

Johnson, Dul. "Culture and Art in Hausa
Video Film." *Nigerian Video Films.* Ed.
Jonathan Haynes. Jos: Nigerian Film
Corporation, 1997. 99–104.

Karami, Baba. Personal interview. Kano,
Nigeria, March 22, 2009.

Kiefer, Jonathan. "Hooked on Nollywood." *Utne Reader* 139 (January–February 2007): 32–34.

Krings, Matthias. "Conversion on Screen:
A Glimpse at Popular Islamic Imaginations in Northern Nigeria." *Africa Today*
54 (2008): 45–68.

———. "Muslim Martyrs and Pagan Vampires: Popular Video Films and the Propagation of Religion in Northern Nigeria."
Postscripts 1.2–3 (2005): 183–205.

Larkin, Brian. "Hausa Dramas and the Rise
of Video Culture in Nigeria." *Nigerian
Video Film.* Ed. Jonathan Haynes. Jos:
Nigerian Film Corporation, 1997. 105–25.

———. "Indian Films and Nigerian Lovers: Media and the Creation of Parallel
Modernities." *Africa* 67.3 (1997): 406–40.

Leitch, Thomas M. "Twice-Told Tales: The
Rhetoric of the Remake." *Literature/
Film Quarterly* 18.3 (1990): 138–49.

McCall, John C. "Nollywood Confidential: The Unlikely Rise of Nigerian
Video Film." *Transition Magazine* 13.1
(2004): 98–109.

National Film and Video Censors Board.
Film and Video Directory in Nigeria.
Abuja, Nigeria: National Film and
Video Censors Board, 2002.

Noy, Frederick. "Hausa Video & Sharia
Law." *Nollywood: The Video Phenomenon*

in Nigeria. Ed. Pierre Barrot. Bloomington: Indiana University Press, 2009. 78–89.

Offord, Lydia D. "Straight Outta Nigeria: Nollywood and the Emergence of Nigerian Video Film (Theory); Lost and Turned Out (Production)." Master's thesis, Long Island University, 2009.

Okome, Onookome. "Introducing the Special Issue on West African Cinema: Africa at the Movies." *Postcolonial Text* 3.2 (2007): n. pag. Web.

Omoera, Osakue Stevenson. "Video Film and African Social Reality: A Consideration of Nigeria-Ghana Block of West Africa." *Journal of Human Ecology* 25.3 (2009): 193–99.

Onishi, Norimitsu. "Step Aside, L.A. and Bombay, for Nollywood." *New York Times,* September 16, 2002. Web.

Rafferty, Terence. "Sisters and Brothers: 'Diabolique' Redux, and 'A Family Thing.'" *New Yorker,* April 1, 1996, 102–3.

Sanders, Julie. *Adaptation and Appropriation.* New York: Routledge, 2006.

Sherazade. "Excellent Nollywood Extravaganza by the Well Lauded Tade Ogidan." Review. *Internet Movie Database.* April 2006. Web.

Steinglass, Matt. "Film: When There's Too Much of a Not-Very-Good Thing." *New York Times,* May 26, 2002.

Uchenna, Onuzulike. "Nollywood: The Emergence of the Nigerian Video Film Industry and Its Representation of Nigerian Culture." Master's thesis, Clark University, 2007.

Waxman, Sharon. "A Matter of Deja View: French Cry Faux over U.S. Film Remakes." *Washington Post,* July 15, 1993, C1+.

Yahaya, Halima Adamu. "Jamila. Ba Al'adunmu Kenan Ba." *Fim Magazine* (May 2001): 41.

Yahuza, Bashir. "Holy Law: Da Dan Gari Kan Ci Gari!" *Fim Magazine* (May 2001): 40.

FILMOGRAPHY

Almara. Dir. I. Nwanko. Iyke More Investments (Nigeria). 2000.

Auduga. Dir. Abba El-Mustapha. Baba Karami Movies (Nigeria). 2004.

Blackjack. Dir. John Woo. WCG Entertainment Productions (United States). 1998.

Dan Adam Butulu I. Dir. Abdulkareem Mohammed. Iyke More Investments (Nigeria). 2001.

Dangerous Twins. Dir. Tade Ogidan. OGD Pictures (Nigeria). 2003.

Friend of the Family, 2. Dir. Fred Olen Ray. Andrew Stevens Entertainment and Royal Oaks Entertainment (United States). 1996.

Ghulam. Dir. Vikram Bhatt. Vishesh Films (India). 1998.

Holy Law. Dir. Ejike Asiegbu. Kingstream Productions (Nigeria). 2001.

Jalli. Dir. Hafizu Bello. Kainuwa Motion Image (Nigeria). 2002.

Kauna. Dir. M. Balarabe. Movie World (Nigeria). 2001.

Mushkila. Dir. Aminu Bala. Bright Star Entertainment (Nigeria). 2001.

National Anthem. Dir. Prince Emeka Ani. Great Movies (Nigeria). 2004.

On the Waterfront. Dir. Elia Kazan. Columbia Pictures Corporation (United States). 1954.

Predator. Dir. John McTiernan. 20th Century Fox (United States). 1987.

Salma Salma Duduf. Dir. Bala Anas Babinlata. Mazari Film Mirage (Nigeria). 2001.

Silent Witness. Dir. Mike Barker and Ben Bolt. BBC (UK). 1996.

Sitanda. Dir. Izu Ojukwu. Amstel Malta Box Office (Nigeria). 2006.

Takidi. Dir. A. A. Sheriff. Ibrahimawa Productions (Nigeria). 2001.

Tarzomar Shahada. Dir. A. Amge. Amge Video Treasury (Nigeria). 2002.

Tsaro. Dir. M. L. Jalingo. Kajal Productions (Nigeria). 2001.

Turmin Danya. Dir. Salisu Galadanci. Tumbin Giwa Film Productions (Nigeria). 1990.

What Lies Beneath. Dir. Robert Zemeckis. DreamWorks Pictures (United States). 2000.

FOURTEEN

Karishika with Kiswahili Flavor: A Nollywood Film Retold by a Tanzanian Video Narrator

MATTHIAS KRINGS

A NIGERIAN MISE-EN-SCÈNE OF HELL FILLS THE SCREEN. WHILE Satan sends his female assistant to the world of the living, the Kiswahili voice-over announces the background to the impending drama: "Karishika was sent into a world full of evil in order to afflict people and to win them over for the devil." A few seconds later the narrator continues: "She is called Becky Okorie, and she plays Karishika." Now her face becomes visible, she straightens up, and the invisible Kiswahili narrator switches to direct speech in the first person: "I am here at home in Nigeria, at Lagos. I am greeting all Tanzanians who are in Dar es Salaam. May God bless you!" Meanwhile, the screen is filled with a close-up of Karishika's face, her eyes beaming in electric blue rays symbolizing her otherworldly powers, and the narrator continues: "One day, I will come, and you will see me, King Rich, with your own eyes, and I will continue to narrate Nigerian films."

In Tanzanian video parlors, narrators are performing live translations of foreign films into Kiswahili so local audiences can follow the story. They are also ad-libbing, adding observations and personal commentary, and adapting the stories to a local hermeneutic framework. Pirated video copies of foreign films are thus subject to a profound practice of remediation. Recently, some video narrators also began selling their work as VHS cassettes and DVDs with Kiswahili voice-over. In this chapter, I will introduce one such video narrator, King Rich, who specializes in the interpretation of Nollywood films, and one of his works, the narration of *Karishika* – a Nigerian video film with strong Pentecostal imprint.

Video narrators do far more than simply translate or re-create preexisting filmic texts in a different language or medium. Their craft consists in creating new texts that speak to both the foreign film and its new local context. In the following, I will explore the art of video narration itself, as well as its concrete application to a single Nigerian film. After a brief exploration of the craft's trajectories in East and Central Africa and a sketch of its recent development in Dar es Salaam, I will place the phenomenon within a wider theoretical debate about the transnational circulation of media. Following Bouchard's explorations of orality and film spectatorship in Africa, I will argue that video narration may be understood as a reconfiguration of the video medium within a specific local media environment and that video narration domesticates a comparably new and foreign (audio)visual medium by amalgamating it with a much older local audio medium: the spoken word as used in a number of established speech genres, especially storytelling. Domestication, however, is not just a matter of reconfiguring the medium as such, but also a way of deriving meaning from its contents. If Nollywood films such as *Karishika* are subjected to this process of critical interrogation, the video narrator's remediation will serve (among other things) to reestablish the authenticity of their narratives, and thus provides repair. However, as the analysis of King Rich's version of *Karishika* will demonstrate, video narration does not only facilitate the communication of the film but, in several instances, also subverts its intended meaning, provides additional information – a who's who of Nollywood film, for example – or even distracts the audience's attention completely from the film by the narrator's self-marketing attempts. To a certain extent, then, video narration as currently practiced in Dar es Salaam addresses two different modes of film spectatorship – a contemplative-hermeneutical one and another that is keen on spectacle – and then conflates these categories within a single performance and its mediatized output, the dubbed v H S cassette.

TRAJECTORIES OF VIDEO NARRATION IN EAST AFRICA

Until recently, video narration in Tanzania was for many years associated with only a single name: Derek Gaspar Mukandala, a.k.a. Lufufu. When I first met him in 2007 in Dar es Salaam, he had stopped live interpretation of foreign films more than fifteen years earlier and had instead turned to a studio version of his craft, producing v H S cassettes of foreign films with Kiswahili voice-over. A retired fifty-seven-year-old naval officer, Lufufu claims to have translated more than one thousand films – mostly American and Chinese action movies, but also about ninety Nigerian films and a number of Indian movies. He told me that the initial idea came to him in 1971–72 while watching a Chinese live interpretation of a North Vietnamese propaganda movie while based in China for two years under a military training program. Back in Dar es Salaam in the early 1980s, he came across a 16mm film projector in his army barracks and started a mobile cinema show in his spare time. He toured the outskirts of the city with copies of old American westerns and action movies that he rented from Anglo-American (a distribution company that was still in Dar es Salaam at the time) and began live interpretation. In the 1990s, he started using VHS equipment, and later stopped performing live and switched to dubbing cassettes, a technology he came into contact with through a visit to his wife's relatives in Uganda. First, he ran the dubbed cassettes only in his own video parlor, and later he started selling them to video parlor and video store owners all over Tanzania (Mukandala). Lufufu became a role model for the new generation of Dar es Salaam's video narrators that has emerged over the past few years, and one of them, who was Lufufu's apprentice for some time, has even acquired the nickname of "Junior Lufufu."

Video narrators are cinematic go-betweens who speak along with or aside foreign films and thus mediate the filmic world for the audience. Precursors in the history of cinema may be found in the film narrator of the silent movie age (*bonimenteur* in France, *Kinoerzähler* in Germany, *benshi* in Japan) (Lacasse). One does not have to travel as far as China, as Lufufu did, to unravel the historical trajectories of video narration in East Africa. The forerunners of present Tanzanian video narrators may well be traced to the interpreters of colonial cinema who "translated" educational films into African languages during mobile cinema shows. The Bantu Educational Kinema Experiment, which ran from 1935 to 1937, based in Tanganyika, had running commentary in local languages to accompany their silent educational films (Notcutt and Latham). Mpungu Mulenda, who reports on film narrators in the cinema halls of Lubumbashi during the 1980s, considers evangelical film shows organized by missionaries to be at the root of this phenomenon. Local evangelists were recruited as commentators at such religious screenings. And well into the 1970s, live interpretation was an integral part of promotional mobile cinema shows that were organized by Kenyan operators who toured the Tanzanian countryside with American and Spaghetti westerns and Chaplin and Laurel and Hardy comedies to attract large crowds and promote consumer goods.[1]

Contemporary East African live interpretation of film may be traced back to the video parlors of Kampala, Uganda, where the art grew strong during the late 1980s. And to date, Uganda, with its three hundred plus video narrators, is certainly the East African country leading the way in this art form. The local term is *video jockey,* and Prince Nakibinge Joe, president of Uganda's Videojockeys Association, compares the VJ to the DJ, "who spices up music in a discotheque" and thus keeps dancers going until the early hours of the morning. "A VJ is also like that. He puts some jokes in the film, at the same time he translates it, at the same time he is also like an actor, because he is also acting.... VJs are the subtitles of the community, without us people cannot understand the movie" (qtd. in Joe 2). Compared to Uganda, where the profession has even gained some recognition beyond the video halls through VJ slams organized by the Amakula Kampala International Film Festival (Ondego), video narration in Tanzania is still in its infancy. In Dar es Salaam, it is labeled *tafsiri* (translation), and the one who performs is called a "DJ" rather than "VJ." Even in Dar es Salaam, Tanzania's economic and cultural capital, less than ten video narrators were operating in 2009 (Groß). Except for Lufufu, all of them started their careers after 2004. Most of them offer their services to video hall owners free of charge. Since they don't have their own equipment, this is the only way for them to record their performances on VHS tapes. These tapes are then sold for as little as 5.000 Tanzanian shillings (about US$3) as master tapes to Ajay Chavda, a local video store owner who reproduces them en masse.

Richard Jioni, alias King Rich, who calls himself "VC," video controller, or *mkurugenzi* (director general), used to sell his tapes to Ajay Chavda, too, before he managed to buy his own equipment (Jioni). He began live video narration in 2005 in Tarime, a northern Tanzanian town, close to the Kenyan border, after he had finished secondary school (O-level). The first film he mediated was *Above the Law,* an American action film, but he soon began to specialize in Nollywood films because he found Nigerian English much easier to understand. After leaving Tarime, he

14.1. King Rich performing in a video parlor, Dar es Salaam, 2008 (courtesy of Sandra Groß).

continued working as a video narrator in fishing camps on two islands of Lake Victoria before he stopped for about two years. His father had cautioned him to find a "real" job and suggested that he become a police officer. On his father's advice, he joined the police force. When he was posted to Dar es Salaam in 2007, he came across Mr. Kobla, the owner of a video parlor, who persuaded him to take up video narration again, and later on also introduced him to Ajay Chavda, who bought the recordings of his performances in Kobla's video parlor. Still working as a police officer, King Rich can only devote half of his time to video narration. Nevertheless, his oeuvre comprises about ninety Nollywood films so far. In about 2008, he set up his own recording equipment and stopped live interpretation, and since then he has been producing dubbed master tapes in his own "studio" instead. As he explained, narrating live is more demanding because the brouhaha in the video parlor sometimes makes it difficult to concentrate on the film, but at the same time it is more rewarding because of the immediate response the narrator gets from the audience. Performing live, however, does not generate much of an income because the audience would rather stay away than pay a higher entrance fee, which means that a live narrator has to depend on the token amount he gets from the owner of the video parlor who hires him to attract more customers. It is only consequential, therefore, to mediatize video narration and sell the tapes en masse to video parlors and video libraries across the country.

ORALITY AND SPECTATORSHIP

Video narration comprises two different aspects that, despite their heuristic separation, actually go hand in hand and inform one another in the East African video parlors: the appropriation and accommodation of the video medium itself and the appropriation of foreign films transmitted on video. "Technologies are unstable things," Brian Larkin reminds us, and "meanings attached to technologies, their technical functions, and the social uses to which they are put are not an inevitable consequence but something worked out over time in the context of considerable cultural debate" (2). The spectacular rise of the small medium video, which was used as recording technology in private households of the First World, to the cornerstone of African film industries such as Nollywood and its younger Tanzanian counterpart clearly speaks of the medium's enormous potential as well as the ingenuity of its African users – totally inconceivable to those who invented it. Less spectacular is the use of the video apparatus for the public projection of films. Thus, the invention of the video parlor (*vimkandala* in Kiswahili) allowed a cheap alternative to film theaters, and consequently allowed film viewing to spread to every nook and cranny of Africa – a pastime once by and large associated only with city life. The reconfiguration of the video medium through video narration connects well to that of the cinematographic medium, which was shaped decades earlier in East and Central Africa. In his essay "Commentary and Orality in African Film Reception," Vincent Bouchard concludes, "The practice of adding an oral commentary to popular film screenings is the result of a media reconfiguration born during the encounter between (non-modern) oral practices and the appropriation of a cinematographic apparatus born out of a foreign culture (in this case Western modernity)" (106). I propose to further this argument by paying closer attention to the nature of these "oral practices" that informed the reconfiguration of the apparatus and – in the current Tanzanian practice – have brought forth a new narrative genre that situates itself between the word and the screen.

Lufufu compares video narration with "the transformation of rice into *pilau*" (a delicious rice dish in Swahili cuisine). According to this metaphor, foreign films are like raw or unprocessed foodstuff, which has to be cooked and prepared according to certain principles of local cuisine in order to be turned into a palatable dish for the local audience. If we understand cooking as a culture-specific way of preparing food, where even new raw material is treated according to well-established principles, and transfer this back to our understanding of video narration as a relatively new speech genre, we may look out for those older speech genres that have informed video narration. During her fieldwork on storytelling in southern Tanzania, Uta Reuster-Jahn learned that performances of rural storytellers might be understood in terms of a "traditional village cinema" (*Erzählte Kultur* 177). Appropriating and expanding this metaphor, I suggest that what the urban video narrators do can be considered a kind of amalgamation of this "traditional village cinema" with "cassette cinema," that is, the local form of cinema, which takes place in the video parlor. As a tentative hypothesis, I propose to conceptualize video narration as a practice of domestication of foreign films in terms of media. This would imply that in Tanzania, such films are made digestible – to apply Lufufu's metaphor once again – through the use of another medium, the spoken word, and that their exhibition in video parlors is reconfigured in terms of the classical live performance of oral storytelling. I hasten to caution against misinterpreting this argument as reproducing a much-criticized tendency of anthropologists to look for explanations that associate Africans with a traditional past rather than a modern present. Video narration is indeed a very modern phenomenon, and commentators who mediate between the standardizing industrial nature of cinema and local spectators have been a feature of cinema right from its beginning. As will become apparent below, video narration is more than just adding commentary and observations, which may well be understood as an effect of cinema in general (Hansen); it is also different from lip-synching dialogues, a form of translation that is practiced in some European countries and helps to foster the spectator's immersion in the film. Tanzanian video narrators do both, but most of the time they actually perform as *narrators* who "translate" moving images into words and thus literally *retell* film. It is thus safe to say that the emerging genre of video narration casts oral genres of different origin – film commentary, radio and television soccer commentary, and oral storytelling – into something new and entirely modern.

In his essay, Bouchard sketches a continuum of film commentary practices in Africa, which corresponds with two distinct modes of spectatorship. On one end, we find what I would call the contemplative-hermeneutical mode characterized by silent spectators who attempt to understand the original meaning of a film and a commentator whose essential task is to make sure that the meaning is transmitted. In colonial Africa, this mode of spectatorship was established during mobile cinema shows that featured religious and governmental propaganda films. This mode corresponds with a conceptualization of cinema as a tool of communicating messages. At the opposite end of the continuum, cinema is conceptualized as spectacle, as an entertaining attraction that addresses the spectators' senses and allows for an emotional engagement. Here commentators become an integral part of the attraction and their "objective is not to transmit the original meaning to the spectators, but to bring to light whatever elements can make the show most entertaining" (96).

The act of Tanzanian video narration is somewhere in between these two distinct modes. On the one hand, it is characterized by the narrator's attempt to transmit the original meaning of a film, by "repairing" the communication of the film through his commentary, and on the other hand by the narrator's disturbance of the film's communication by subverting its meaning, or by simply drawing attention to his own project, in order to foster his career and distinguish himself from his professional colleagues.

VIDEO NARRATION AS REPAIR

Karishika is most typical of a Nigerian film genre Okome has dubbed the "Hallelujah film." An important feature of this genre is the Pentecostal coloring of its content.[2] *Karishika* displays how Satan eats his way into the souls of the living. To recruit new followers for his kingdom of darkness, he sends out Karishika, queen of the demons, to the world of the living. Once in the physical world, she misguides and seduces a number of people, all of whom fall prey to her because of their own shortcomings.

The last, a pastor, resists all temptations and is saved from hell through divine intervention in a final showdown between a Pentecostal congregation and Karishika and her helpers.[3]

Video narrators reenact filmic dialogues, narrate the story, and add commentary or explanation to the original film text. When King Rich translates dialogues, he speaks in direct speech and changes his voice more or less according to the gender and age of the screen characters (though other film narrators, Lufufu, for example, pay far more attention to this). He thus mimics women and men, old and young. Technically speaking, he oscillates between first-person voice-over dialogue and third-person narration and commentary, using an audio mixer to add his soundtrack to the original video, whereby he constantly fades in and out (sometimes after every sentence) to preserve as much of the original sound track as possible.

King Rich opens his version of *Karishika* by introducing himself as the one who translates the film into Kiswahili and an advertisement of where in Dar es Salaam it can be ordered on cassette, including the cell phone number of the "Kobla Video Store" – all of these activities going on while the opening credits are still running. As soon as the first images appear, which depict a Nollywood mise-en-scène of hell, he begins to comment as if reporting on a live event. He even pretends to be in Nigeria himself:

> As usual I am telling you I am in Nigeria, there in West Africa. I am sending you my missiles [here: "blockbusters," that is, films], and they are sold by Mr. Ajay Chavda, who is based in the Nyamwezi lane. The Nigerians are greeting all of you. May God bless Tanzania! (*Karishika* 0:02:20–34).[4]

Situating himself in Nigeria adds credibility to his commentary and in fact serves to authorize him. Similar phrases occur throughout the film. King Rich explained this to me as originating early in his career when his ability to interpret Nigerian films caused some among his audiences to wonder if he was a Nigerian. Later on, while narrating, he developed this identity of a Tanzanian based in Lagos who sends his commentary directly from Nigeria. This obviously addresses an imagined audience not present at the recording venue and highlights the fact that even though the recording was made during a live show, the narrator has a wider audience in mind.

King Rich continues his narration of *Karishika* by elaborating on the meaning of the Christian concept of Satan. The camera pans across hell, a gruesome location dimly lit by fires and full of captured souls, half naked, hands and feet in chains. Following his opening sentence, the original voice of Lucifer becomes partially audible in English, but King Rich, still somewhat attached to the modus of commenting on a live event, refrains from translating what Lucifer says, and instead introduces the actor who plays Lucifer, and then is at pains to translate the meaning of "Lucifer" into Kiswahili:

> We are now formally beginning with our film. Today, we are having someone here who is called Obi Madurugwu who plays Lucifer. Who is Lucifer? Lucifer is the Satan [*shetani*]. One can call him "devil" [English in Kiswahili version] or Satan (0:02:36–03:02).

King Rich combines actors' names with the characters they are playing, and sometimes uses them interchangeably. This is a typical feature of video narration. Using the actors' names, which are well known to Tanzanian followers of Nigerian films, avoids ambiguity and makes it easier for both the narrator and the audience to follow the story. Translating "Lucifer" or the Christian concept of "devil" to a local audience heterogeneous in religious terms turns out to be quite complex, especially since in Kiswahili the Arabic loan word *shetani* is also used to denote any kind of spirit. After this, he sets out with the even more complex task of explaining the concept of "hell"–within just a few words, lest he lose track of the film:

> Direct speech: "I am the king of the whole world."
>
> Narration: This is the one whose name is Obi Madurugwu and who plays Lucifer.
>
> Direct speech: "I am the ruler over this world. Who dares to challenge me?"
>
> Narration: Now we return to the camp of the *shetani,* where there was Satan who ruled over the world of the spirits. And all the people who once had committed sins had been thrown into the world of the spirits. Those who are there are people who have pretended to be followers of God, but in fact have used Satan instead. They were thrown into the world of the spirits, to the devil. Europeans call this "hell" [English in Kiswahili version] (0:03:03–46).

While the narrator's commentary on sequences such as the above is quite lucid, the commentary of many others seems to be full of redundancy.

What astonished me most when I first saw Lufufu "dubbing" foreign films in his studio was that in several instances he seemed to duplicate images through his words, as if he were afraid that images alone could not move on or carry the narrative in between dialogues that he translated in direct speech. A similar duplication of images occurs in King Rich's version of *Karishika,* where literally almost every sequence that has no dialogue in the original version is literally *retold* or commented upon. Asked why, King Rich explained that he finds moving images without commentary inadequate and that he considers filling such gaps with meaningful information part of his job. Interestingly, he cited the screening of the film *Jesus,* which he experienced many times during his youth, as an authoritative example for a running commentary over otherwise "silent" images.[5] A closer analysis, however, reveals that a "literal" transcription of images through voice-over rarely occurs and that the narrators' commentary on otherwise "silent" sequences, in fact, serves many different purposes – summarizing for those who have arrived late, forecasting to ease the shift from one sequence to the next, establishing the authenticity or truthfulness of certain images. Thus, the explanation of images is by far not the only function of the video narrators' commentary. However, these different forms of commentary have the same general effect, for they cause the (foreign) images to lose their governing function in telling the story. The added voice-over takes the upper hand over the preexisting moving images, which are transformed by the video narrator into mere illustrations of the verbal narrative. The hierarchy of original and copy is thus reversed, something that is also neatly reflected in King Rich's self-ascriptions as "video controller" and "director general." In this regard, the video narrator takes over control of the narrative order for the benefit of his local audience.

The analysis of another "silent" sequence of *Karishika* may help to highlight some more functions of the voice-over, which is inserted by the video narrator. In this sequence, Karishika arrives outside Bianca's house in a car and miraculously takes on the appearance of Bianca's friend before going through the gate. King Rich opens the sequence as narrator. While the car is still moving, he provides information about setting and personnel, and since this is not yet known to the spectator, his commentary turns into a forecast: "Today the girl Karishika, Becky Okorie, came to Sandra Achums's house, because she knew about her problem of not getting a child" (0:23:24–34). Again King Rich combines actors' names with character names and even substitutes the latter with the former. The car stops, and he continues by recalling earlier sequences of the film. This enables the audience to recapitulate Karishika's motives and also makes it easy for those who entered the video parlor while the show is already running to pick up the story:

> At the same time she was sent by someone who pretends to be Satan, Obi Madurugwu – Lucifer. He had shown her that some people have difficulties to beget children. Now, how should she go about to lead her [Bianca] astray from her faith [in God] so that she will instead turn to the devil? (0:23:36–50).

Although he adds information that the uncommented original sequence of the film does not contain, King Rich stays faithful to the overall pedagogical purpose of the film, which is the revelation of Satan's many wily ways to lead faithful Christians astray. In two other sequences, King Rich makes this quite explicit: for instance, he tells the audience, "These are the evil things that take place around us every day. That's why I like Nigerian films, because they talk about everyday life" (0:09:30–39). Such commentary in fact serves to authorize Nigerian films as depicting authentic images of the battle between good and evil, despite their being foreign and fictitious. Their moral lessons might therefore as well be transferred to local everyday realities.

In the case of a Pentecostal film like *Karishika,* the video narrator's performance must in fact be considered as "re-mediation" (Bolter and Grusin), which adds one more layer to the multilayered mediations observable in Nollywood films. Birgit Meyer has argued that Pentecostal Ghanaian (and by extension Nigerian) video films may be considered as remediations of older, already existing forms of mediation of the divine and the demonic, previously "tied to specific media such as the biblical text, sermons, and services" (160). According to Meyer, Ghanaian and Nigerian video films with Pentecostal content are constructed in such a way as to allow for an "authentic" and seemingly immediate experience of the divine and the demonic. The notions of authenticity and immediacy cannot be reduced to an effect of media alone. However, equally important, she claims, are the practices and discourses that authorize authenticity and immediacy of certain media in particular social fields (ibid.). Following Meyer's argument, it is obvious that such films risk losing their notion of immediacy and "truth" if watched outside the discursive realm that helps to establish their "authenticity." In order to produce an effect of immediacy again, they need to be remediated and situated within a new discursive realm that serves to reauthorize their authenticity – a task that is fulfilled by the video narrator.

Sometimes, King Rich, himself a born-again Christian and regular attendant of Tanzanian Assemblies of God, one of Tanzania's most prominent Pentecostal churches, asks his spectators to reflect upon a particular religious issue raised in the film. Thus, the sequence quoted above continues with Karishika getting out of her car. She then opens her arms as if to receive a spiritual force from above, and through a morphing effect she changes her appearance into that of Bianca's friend. While this happens, King Rich remains silent, as if to accord this astonishing special effect its due right of undivided audience attention. Only afterward does he explain what has just happened and combines this again with a statement about Karishika's plans (yet unknown to the audience):

> She has changed herself and taken on the appearance of the friend of Bianca, Sandra Achums. Then she entered into her house in order to persuade her to consult a traditional healer, hehehe [laughs]! (0:24:18–31).

And while we see her entering a gate and the camera pans across the outer walls of the house before a jump cut takes us inside, King Rich poses a rhetorical question directly to his audience:

> Is it possible for a faithful believer in God to engage with traditional [magical] methods? The answer is up to you! May God bless you, you who are following my Nigerian films! (0:24:32–44).

Through this direct address, the narrator initiates the active participation and critical inquiry of his audience. Each spectator may thus pause for a couple of seconds and think about his or her own previous experiences comparable to those of "Sandra Achums." King Rich believes his audience is interested in Nigerian films because unlike American or Indian films, Nollywood focuses on contemporary African realities where witchcraft, "a setback to development" (Jioni, alias King Rich), really exists. During an interview, he left no doubt that he shares these beliefs and cited a couple of examples of witchcraft from his hometown Kigoma. In his opinion, Nigerian films teach powerful lessons that are also applicable to Tanzanian realities. "After watching these films for quite a while, I have discovered that most of the big guys in Nigeria get their money through witchcraft and I believe the same may also happen here in Dar es Salaam."

Through his commentary and translation, King Rich actually provides "repair." In linguistic conversation theory, repair describes a phenomenon in which a hearer helps a speaker to clarify an utterance, the meaning of which otherwise would have been ambiguous or totally incomprehensible. To a certain extent, then, the video narrator as facilitator of the film-audience relationship engages in permanent repair in the real time that the film runs. The video film is thus constructed as communicating only partially meaningful messages that need the video narrator's repair to be comprehensible. A somewhat similar constellation can also be found in performances of oral storytelling, which may involve not only a narrator and an audience but also an equally important third part. Uta Reuster-Jahn, who has studied storytelling among the Mwera of southern Tanzania, reports on the "co-operative style" of Mwera oral performances, which apart from narrator and audience always involve a "respondent" ("Interaction in Narration"). The respondent serves a couple of functions. One purpose is to encourage the narrator through utterances of approval; another is to step in and help the narrator out if he misses a word, gets stuck, or produces ambiguous meaning. This intervention supplies repair to the performance of the oral artist. In such instances, he may turn into a conarrator (168–70). Based on this model, a video narrator may be considered a permanent respondent who has to assume the task of conarratorship not only temporarily but also permanently because foreign films continuously produce ambiguous meaning.

VIDEO NARRATION AS DISTRACTION

So far I have only highlighted moments of King Rich's performance that seem to aid or facilitate the relationship between the film and its audience. Video narration, however, is based on a paradox, for the video narrator's translation and commentary not only supply repair but *at the same time* may also distract. In certain instances, he may even divert the spectators' attention away from the screen, like a respondent-turned-wild, who starts telling his own story, and in so doing turns against his narrator. In such instances, the video narrator seizes the audience's attention and troubles both the preferred meaning of the film and the medium's illusion of immediacy. Most remarkable in this sense are moments of King Rich's performance in which he directly addresses the audience in the first person. Such addresses clearly have a self-advertising character but also serve to negotiate the art of video narration itself, which has yet to be firmly established as a cultural practice.

One example of such a direct address to the audience and a meta-commentary on the art of interpretation occurs during a rather dramatic sequence of *Karishika* (1:12:30–14:22) in which Bianca, who is somehow troubled by the pregnancy she has developed through Karishika's satanic intervention, is comforted by her Pentecostal husband. The sequence opens with a medium close shot of the couple lying in bed, Bianca telling her husband that she is not sure "if she is carrying a baby or a stone." The husband comforts her and tells her that she should have faith "in the work of God Almighty." This dialogue is only partially audible in King Rich's version, neither in the original English nor in Kiswahili translation, for he enters the sequence by situating himself again in Nigeria, reiterating that he is actually based in Lagos, Nigeria, from which he sends "this missile" to the owner of "Kobla Video Store, in Nyamwezi Street, Kariakoo quarters" (where the cassette can be bought). He then catches up on the last part of the dialogue, switching to the direct speech of the husband (whose part he does not translate literally). Next he uses the lack of dialogue in the original to deliver background information on the actor playing Bianca, which he considers part of his job, as he makes clear in a direct address to his audience:

She is called Sandra Achums, and she is well established in the film business. I have promised you to interpret [this film] good . . . (1:13:06–10).

A sudden outbreak of action on screen forces him to redirect his attention and that of the audience back to the film. Bianca is haunted by the image of Karishika as a mermaid – a satanic reaction to the husband who has mentioned God Almighty as the source of her pregnancy – and jumps up screaming. King Rich picks up on this, imitates Bianca's screaming, and translates what she shouts in direct speech, "I have seen this woman who took me to that healer, I have seen her," and then switches back to the commentary, explaining that "Karishika appeared to her." After that, and while Bianca and her husband are still jumping and screaming on the bed, the video narrator is quiet for a couple of seconds and leaves the original sound untouched, before he picks up the loose thread of his self-advertisement and metacommentary, which he dropped earlier on:

> I have promised you, my beloved spectator, that I will start to explain the pictures and the lives of the actors. In the pictures that will follow, I will tell you who each actor is, where he lives in Nigeria – there, where I am living – how many children he has, how many wives he has, to which school he went. Apart from this I will tell you many other things regarding the art [of filmmaking] itself. I am begging you to sit down and listen, so that I can do my work properly. I wish to thank all of those who are sending me their commentaries, which enable me to do my job even better. I have promised you to begin introducing the actors to you one by one, and all pictures, by commenting upon two to three people, if I have the time [to do so] (1:13:28–14:15).

By redirecting the spectators' attention to his own project, King Rich in fact minimizes the importance of this sequence and symbolically tells his audience to ignore the film for a second because he has something important to tell them. Though this is distracting, King Rich considers such intervention behind the scene an important aspect of his work. As he told me, he gathers the required background information on the Internet and through Tanzanian magazines that sometimes report on Nollywood stars. An important side effect of such interventions is that they expose the medium as medium and call attention to the context in which the film is watched.

Through certain comments King Rich exposes cultural differences between those acting on-screen and those looking at the screen. He may even subvert the film's intended meaning by ridiculing certain images. Such instances, again, create a distance between film and audience and trouble the viewers' identification with screen characters. King Rich's version of *Karishika* contains some hilarious examples of such subversions. When Lucifer is about to send his female agent, Karishika, to the world of the living, we see a close-up of his face, and Obi Madurugwu, who plays Lucifer, declaims in a very theatrical style: "Karishika . . . Karishika . . . shika . . . shika . . . shika!" (0:07:00–16). King Rich picks up on this and continues by saying in similar intonation: *"shika, shika, kamata, chukua!"* thus giving Lucifer's acting an ironic, almost absurd twist: *ku-shika* means "to hold" in Kiswahili, its imperative form being *shika; kamata* and *chukua* are imperative forms of verbs with similar semantic content. In a similar manner, King Rich also ridicules Satan's former antagonists, the two pastors, who fell for Karishika. Praying aloud in the typical declamatory style of Pentecostal churches, he mocks this mode of praying by the pastors, imitating the sound and using meaningless syllables like "Holy baba shanta baba kunta baba shantra babababa!" (1:15:00–07). As he explained to me, he reserves this mockery only for "fake" pastors who have already fallen for the devil. When Pastor James is seduced by Karishika and thus transformed into her "spiritual husband," King Rich not only mocks his prayers, but imitates the sound of kissing lips and puts additional words into Karishika's mouth using a high-pitched voice, advising the pastor "to keep away from that fruit!" (1:15:48–51).

Clearly, the act of video narration serves to bridge cultural gaps between foreign films and local audiences and at the same time contains moments of subversion. It thus fosters a contemplative-hermeneutical mode of spectatorship interspersed with instances of spectacle. Applied to Nigerian films such as *Karishika*, the narrator's mediation also serves to reestablish the film's claim of authenticity. On another level, video narration underpins the agency of local audiences vis-à-vis transnational media. Far from being victims of an alleged cultural imperialism – be it American, Indian, Chinese, or in our case Nigerian – Tanzanian spectators of foreign films pirated on video have developed a modus operandi to domesticate the content of such films. In the sense of subjecting something alien to the conditions of "home," the invention of the video parlor may well be read as a domestication of the cinema theater. Video narration, then, reconfigures the domesticated medium and domesticates the foreign audiovisual material. The video narrator's voice-over channels the foreign content, or – to call up another connotation of domestication – *tames* it through his verbal commentary, which is given the upper hand over the filmic images and sounds.

The infrastructure of the video parlor – hard wooden benches, small TV screen, bad video copies, and bad sound – already restricts the power of illusion and make-believe that the cinema hall gives, which causes people "to forget the film, forget the screen, and even forget themselves"

(Hansen 44). Live video narration pushes this effect of the video parlor a step further, for it, too, creates an awareness of the viewing situation, which is different from that of traditional cinema but nonetheless has some affiliation to it. Perhaps what is even more telling is the presence of the narrator, who adds excitement to the filmic world into which the audience is invited. In other words, the mediatory power of the narrator is at once felt in the alteration of the content of the filmic world as well as in the redefinition of the viewing space.

Looking at video narration from a historical perspective of global cinema, the current practice in Tanzania inverts a process that began early on in the history of cinema in the 1900s, with the shift from the cinema of attractions that fostered a mode of spectatorship informed by spectacle and vaudeville to narrative cinema with its power of absorption that fosters silent spectatorship and surrender to the medium. According to Miriam Hansen, this early notion of cinema, which allowed nonfilmic acts and activities within the theater space such as live sound and live commentary, underwent negation early in the evolution of cinema, especially after the invention of sound in 1927. Hansen argues that "this process of negation involved representational strategies aimed at suppressing awareness of the theatre space and absorbing the spectator into the illusionist space on screen" (44). Video narration reverses this process, for it creates an awareness of the medium through the presence of the narrator and the addition of live sound because comments that lead away from or add meaning to the film, such as the filmographies of Nollywood actors provided by King Rich, reveal the film as film and raise an awareness of the viewing situation as well as a critical distance between spectator and video film.

In the past two years, after Nigerian video films had almost disappeared from Tanzanian shops, rentals, and video parlors, video narration also seems to have generated new interest in Nollywood productions. Their rise and fall in popularity are certainly connected to the emergence of the Tanzanian local video industry, which gained momentum in about 2005. Tanzanian video filmmakers, who initially took Nollywood as their model and source of inspiration, eventually came up with local films that more or less looked just like Nigerian video films, but had the advantage of being shot in Kiswahili.[6] As a result, Nollywood films, once hailed for their "Africanness" and for being much closer to local everyday realities than the average Hollywood, Bollywood, or Hong Kong movie, became more or less obsolete. Four years later, in 2009, however, the excitement over Kiswahili video films somewhat cooled again. Limitations to economic growth due to piracy, and a growing competition among rising numbers of producers, have affected the quality of local video production. Filmmakers feel the need to slash their budgets in every possible way, and this leads to a repetition of story lines, smaller casts, limited sets, and a reduction of average film length to forty minutes – something that is discussed very critically among Tanzanian audiences.[7] This setback seems to work in favor of Nollywood films, which are becoming more attractive again, especially if dubbed by Dar es Salaam's video narrators. When the Tanzanian Copyright Society (CO-SOTA) arrested the major distributor of dubbed foreign films on DVD and VHS during a campaign against video piracy conducted in Dar es Salaam in September 2009, rumor had it that COSOTA was tipped off by some of this distributor's jealous competitors dealing in Kiswahili films who attributed a decline in their sales to the competition from dubbed foreign films. Whether this is true must remain unknown. What remains a fact, however, is that the interpretation of foreign films through video narrators is in great demand. King Rich sells his voice-over cassettes to customers throughout Tanzania, and wherever his Kiswahili-flavored versions of Nigerian films are screened, his brandlike last words may be heard: "The Kiswahili words of this movie have been inserted by King Rich–on–the–microphone. If you like you can also call me 'VC,' 'Video controller,' or 'The director.' . . . May God bless you, good-bye!"

NOTES

1. I gained this information in Tanzania in August 2009 through interviews with a number of people who attended such screenings during their youth.

2. In neighboring Congo, *Karishika* has even turned into a generic name for Pentecostal Nollywood films (see Pype, this volume).

3. My analysis of King Rich's version of *Karishika* is based on a voice-over VHS copy as sold in Dar es Salaam. The cassette initially reached me in 2008 with Sandra Gross's and Andres Carvajal's help. Both of them also shared information about Dar es Salaam's video narrators other than Lufufu and King Rich with me, something I greatly appreciate. According to King Rich, the master of this VHS copy was produced during a live performance, most likely in 2008. I also wish to thank Claudia Böhme and Uta Reuster-Jahn for their tremendous support in translating sequences

of King Rich's work for me and their comments on earlier versions of this essay.

4. This voice-over passage is original in Kiswahili and like all others that follow has been transcribed from V HS tape and translated with the aid of Claudia Böhme, Deograce Komba, and Uta Reuster-Jahn.

5. This film is a major evangelical tool, which has been dubbed into more than a thousand languages. The Kiswahili version can be accessed at http://www

.jesusfilm.org/film-and-media/watch -the-film. The film features a running commentary based on the Gospel according to Luke.

6. See also Claudia Böhme's essay in this volume and my essay "Nollywood Goes East."

7. For this information I depend on Claudia Böhme, who has conducted extensive fieldwork on the local video industry.

WORKS CITED

Bolter, Jay, and Richard Grusin. *Remediation: Understanding New Media*. Cambridge, Mass.: MIT Press, 1999.

Bouchard, Vincent. "Commentary and Orality in African Film Reception." *Viewing African Cinema in the Twenty-First Century: Art Films and the Nollywood Video Revolution*. Ed. Ralph Austen and Mahir Şaul. Athens: Ohio University Press, 2010. 95–107.

Groß, Sandra Katarina. "Die Kunst afrikanischer Kinoerzähler: Video Jockeys in Dar es Salaam." Master's thesis, University of Mainz, 2010.

Hansen, Miriam. *Babel and Babylon: Spectatorship in American Silent Film*. Cambridge, Mass.: Harvard University Press, 1991.

Jioni, Richard. Personal interview with the assistance of Claudia Böhme and Uta Reuster-Jahn. Dar es Salaam, August 22, 2009.

Joe, Nakibinge. "Vee-jay Translators in Uganda." Interview by Didac P. Lagarriga. Oozebap, February 2007. Web.

Krings, Matthias. "Nollywood Goes East: The Localization of Nigerian Video Films in Tanzania." *Viewing African Cinema in the Twenty-First Century: Art Films and the Nollywood Video Revolution*. Ed. Ralph Austen and Mahir Şaul. Athens: Ohio University Press, 2010. 74–91.

Lacasse, Germain. *Le bonimenteur de vues animées. Le cinéma 'muet' entre tradition et modernité*. Quebec and Paris: Éditions Nota Bene and Méridiens Klincksieck, 2000.

Larkin, Brian. *Signal and Noise: Media, Infrastructure, and Urban Culture in Nigeria*. Durham, N.C.: Duke University Press, 2008.

Manuels, Peter. *Cassette Culture: Popular Music and Technology in North India*. Chicago: University of Chicago Press, 1993.

Meyer, Birgit. "Religious Remediations: Pentecostal Views in Ghanaian Video Movies." *Postscripts* 1.2–3 (2005): 155–81.

Mpungu Mulenda, Saidi. "Un regard en marge. Le public populaire du cinema au Zaire." Ph.D. diss., Université Catholique de Louvain, 1987.

Mukandala, Gaspar Derek. Personal interview. Dar es Salaam, September 10, 2007.

Notcutt, L. A., and G. C. Latham. *The African and the Cinema: An Account of the Work of the Bantu Educational Cinema Experiment during the Period of March 1935 to May 1937*. London: Edinburgh House Press, 1937.

Okome, Onookome. "Introducing the Special Issue on West African Cinema: Africa at the Movies." *Postcolonial Text* 3.2 (2007): n. pag. Web.

Ondego, Ogova. "Uganda: A New Cinema-Going Culture." *New People* 116 (2008). Web.

Reuster-Jahn, Uta. *Erzählte Kultur und Erzählkultur bei den Mwera in Südost-Tansania.* Cologne: Köppe, 2002.

————. "Interaction in Narration: The Cooperative Style of Mwera Storytelling." *Oralité africaine et creation.* Ed. Anne-Marie Dauphin-Tinturier and Jean Derive. Paris: Karthala, 2005. 161–79.

FILMOGRAPHY

Above the Law. Dir. Andrew Davis. Warner Bros. Entertainment (United States). 1988.

Jesus. Dir. John Krish and Peter Sykes. Warner Bros. Entertainment (United States). 1979.

Karishika. Dir. Chika Onu. Tony Jickson (Nigeria). 1998.

FIFTEEN

Bloody Bricolages:
Traces of Nollywood in
Tanzanian Video Films

CLAUDIA BÖHME

DURING THE SHOOTING OF *POPOBAWA*, A TANZANIAN HORROR
movie, the actors were preparing a ritual scene about three witch doctors
(*waganga*) who would call upon and kill an evil spirit named Popobawa.
While the actors changed into red and white costumes and painted their
faces black, the rest of the crew prepared the props for the waganga. The
director was concerned about the authenticity of his movie and wanted
it to seem Tanzanian. When he saw cowrie shells and a small bottle of
medicine arranged on a mat, he picked them up, shouting angrily, "We
don't copy the Nigerians!"[1]

Popobawa, a myth about a batlike ghost, is one of the many orally
transmitted horror stories circulating in Tanzania. These stories were,
from the indigenization of media in the 1970s, turned into novels, comics, and to a lesser extent popular theater. With the liberalization of
the Tanzanian economy in the 1980s, transnational flows of video film
horror reached Tanzania. If seen as traveling aesthetics, the horror film
started in Germany, where early horror film classics were produced, then
traveled to America with the establishment of the Hollywood horror
movie, and later to the African video industries, which appropriated
the genre. Starting in Ghana, video horror film was established by Nollywood and eventually adapted by filmmakers on the East African coast.

In this chapter, which is based on sixteen months of fieldwork for
my Ph.D. thesis carried out in 2006, 2007, and 2008, I use the Tanzanian
video industry as an example of Nollywood's traveling aesthetics. The
release of *Nsyuka – filamu ya kwanza ya kutisha ya Tanzania*, "the first
Tanzanian horror movie" – in 2004 marks the appropriation of the genre
and the beginning of the Tanzanian video film industry. As *Nsyuka* was

one of the first locally produced video films to be commercially distributed, the genre is closely connected to the development of the Tanzanian
video film industry as a whole. As in *Nsyuka*, one of the bricks used to
build the narrative is local mythology and folklore. By giving a close-
up perspective of Tanzanian mythological figures, I will investigate the
transformation of these creatures into monsters for the screen through
the filter of Hollywood and Nollywood aesthetics. On the basis of several
horror film examples, I argue that Tanzanian horror movies are much
more than mere copies of Nollywood, as their Tanzanian critics often
claim. They stand for a local genre with its own aesthetics and language
through which filmmakers, in the longer tradition of Tanzanian horror
myth and literature, prompt a public debate on issues in Tanzanian society. They are in fact the products of a very complex and creative artistic
process, which I will refer to as bricolage. By looking at the narratives
of these movies, I will also explore the elements that give them their
specific Tanzanian character.

FROM LAGOS TO DAR TO *DAR 2 LAGOS*

The roots of the Tanzanian video industry are in fact comedy skits from
King Majuto and Mzee Small, two famous comedians, who started recording their performances on video in the late 1990s and sold them to
Indian businessmen for distribution.[2] When Nigerian movies entered
the country around 2000, they functioned as a *changa moto,* an "initial
spark," and inspired many young Tanzanian artists to make movies with
their own stories, in the national language of Swahili. "When the Nigerian films entered the country some time ago and we watched these
movies, they gave us the idea and motivated us to produce our own work.
Because we didn't have a cinema and people watched the Nigerian films,
we were anxious to produce movies (Banzi)." Indian-owned companies,
which dealt originally with local music and pirated movies from outside
the country, sensed big business in the creation of a local movie industry.
The hub of the industry is in Dar es Salaam, with the main distribution
network in the market area of Kariakoo.[3] In its formative year, 2003,
the industry consisted of only three distribution companies: Wananchi,
GMC, and Game 1st Quality. The latter was the only African distributor
and distributed its own movies. A couple of directors and their crew of

artists, camera staff, and editors produced one movie a month. Their Tanzanian audiences, accustomed to seeing foreign films, criticized the poor quality of the movies and compared them not only with Hollywood and Bollywood movies but especially with Nollywood productions. Five years later, at least five movies per week were being produced, and the change from VHS to VCD and DVD had been completed, as more and more people in Dar es Salaam owned a DVD player.[4] Two more distribution companies, Kapico and Steps, have appeared, and meanwhile the latter has established itself as the most popular producer and distributor in Tanzania.

Directors like Haji Dilunga would try to prevent their productions from copying the Nigerians, as described in the introduction, because of the ambivalent discourse about Nollywood in Tanzania. Like the country itself – held in high esteem by Tanzanians for the entrepreneurship and creativity of its people, but feared for its tribalism and political unrest – Nigerian films are received very ambiguously. On the one hand, they are defined as mere horror films and condemned for showing witchcraft and ritual murder; on the other, they are praised for their quality, expertise, and authenticity, while the local films are considered unsuccessful attempts to copy them. Among filmmakers, the discourse essentially became a struggle for authenticity and authorship. Some filmmakers allegedly copy Nigerian films, while others claim to work creatively. A battle between two critics broke out over the value of local film productions in 2007. Whereas Mapunda Selles, who has spent some time in Nigeria and claims to be an expert on Nollywood films, has criticized Tanzanian productions as being poor-quality copies of foreign "originals," Sultan Tamba wrote in defense of local movie production and called for a revolution in Tanzanian film.

The example shows how the debate about Nigerian movies became a platform to discuss the localization of film production in Tanzania. While Nollywood remained a reference point for film critics and viewers, Tanzanian movie productions grew rapidly and became far more popular than their Nollywood counterparts. Although at the beginning of my research in 2006 one would say "*wanaiga Wanigeria*" (they imitate/copy the Nigerians), just two years later "*wanajitahidi*" (they make an effort) stood for the increasing popularity of local movies. Today the popularity of Tanzanian movies can be measured by the level of displacement

of their Nigerian counterparts in shops, libraries, and video shows, as
their contents have been appropriated and reproduced (see also Krings,
"Nollywood Goes East" 74). Mtitu Game, the only legal distributor of
Nigerian movies in Tanzania, said that business with Nigerian movies
is no longer profitable. When he began his own movie production in
2006, he wanted to merge the two movie industries and initiated a coproduction of several Tanzanian-Nigerian stories. The first movie was
symbolically titled *Dar 2 Lagos – 4 Re-union,* and is about a young man
sent to Nigeria to find his friend's lost son. *Dar 2 Lagos* was enthusiastically embraced by the audience as the biggest success of the Tanzanian
film industry. If the Tanzanian video film industry was initiated by the
traveling aesthetics from Lagos to Dar es Salaam, *Dar 2 Lagos* can also
be considered the "return journey" of Tanzanian filmmakers, who have
since gained a firmer footing.

THE EVOLUTION OF *FILAMU YA KUTISHA*

Mussa Banzi, a cartoonist and fan of Western and Nigerian horror movies, founded Tamba Arts Group in 2001 to make his own movies.[5] When
his first film, *Nsyuka,* was completed in 2003, Mussa Banzi asked Farhad
Mohammed Shivji, the Indian owner of Wananchi Video Production,
which at the time only distributed local music, if he would agree to buy
and distribute the movie. Farhad loved the film and was excited by the
idea of entering the movie business. Wananchi soon outdid the rival
company, GMC, which in early 2003 had kicked off with the hip-hop
video film *Girlfriend,* but Banzi also established the genre of horror movies in Tanzania.

Robin Wood offers a very simple, basic formula for the horror film,
namely: "Normality is threatened by the monster," with three variables,
normality, the monster, and the relationship between the two. Wood
defines normality as "the heterosexual monogamous couple, the family,
and the social institutions (police, church, armed forces) that support
and defend them," the monster as "society's basic fears," and continues, "It is the third variable, the relationship between normality and the
Monster, that constitutes the essential subject of the horror film. It, too,
changes and develops, the development taking the form of a long process
of clarification or revelation" (79). Tanzanian horror movies are defined

by the element of fear, as *filamu ya kutisha* means "frightening film." When buying or borrowing a horror movie, Tanzanian fans ask whether it is scary (*Inatisha?*). But as elsewhere, movie genres in Tanzania help viewers discuss certain types of films. The genres have blurred boundaries, and what could be classified as horror is sometimes described as *filamu ya kutisha* or *filamu ya kusisimua,* as "thrilling film" or "suspenseful film," on the cover of a movie. *Filamu ya kichawi,* referring to the subgenre of "witchcraft film," is also often used in discussions about movies. Not only are *filamu za kutisha* very popular, but since they almost always guarantee financial success, they also function as entry tickets for new aspirants to the industry. So far around 90 out of roughly 450 movies produced in Tanzania can be classified as *filamu za kutisha.*

Tanzanian horror filmmakers can be categorized as either *wakongwe,* "old and wise," or *wageni,* "newcomers." The *wakongwe* include Mussa Banzi and Sultan Tamba, who started working together in 2003 mainly on horror movies, though they would later split and take different directions. Whereas Banzi's horror movies are set in cities with more visual horror effects, Sultan Tamba's films are set in villages and focus on ghost or witchcraft stories, using an element of suspense, and are better suited to the *filamu ya kusisimua* category. The newcomers include Haji Dilunga and Shariff Jumbe, who began making films in 2006. They were obviously influenced by their predecessors, but also developed their own style of horror movie. Haji Dilunga started with stories about witches and circles of witches who turn relatives into zombies when it comes to inheritance disputes. Sharriff Jumbe, more influenced by Hollywood, mixes foreign narrative patterns with local ghost stories. What both filmmakers have in common is an underlying narrative of killing off protagonists. This decimation of protagonists in what can be called Tanzanian Splatter is called the "body count" principle in the classical horror film.[6]

As Wood argues, the monster changes "from period to period as society's basic fears clothe themselves in fashionable or immediately accessible garments" just like "dreams use material from recent memory to express conflicts or desires that may go back to early childhood" (79). Horror video filmmakers highlight social taboos by visualizing the suppressed. Their viewers are forced to look at a distorted mirror of society in a bid to process such topics. When I asked the filmmakers about their reasons for making horror movies, their approach was very educative and moralistic, which differs from the Western horror film. As postulated in the catharsis theory, they are trying to persuade their audiences to give up sorcery practices and to return to their faith, be it Islam or Christianity. But crucially and unlike Western horror filmmakers, many of them believe in the supernatural.

TANZANIAN HORROR MOVIES AS BRICOLAGES

As Linda Badley stresses, of all the popular genres, horror is the best example of a transmedia phenomenon and can be best described by what Edgar Allan Poe called "the philosophy of composition." This means that the text or film is a "technological apparatus" used to produce an intense reaction in the audience (Badley 2, 9). I argue that while this composition is always subject to global and transnational stylistic currents, the Tanzanian horror video films differ in their aesthetic and stylistic work from Western horror movies. They are the product of a very creative process, which I will refer to as bricolage. When building the narrative, Tanzanian moviemakers draw on a set of ideas, including global and local media flows, motives, and iconographies from Hollywood, Bollywood, and Nollywood and local sources such as folklore, literature, and theater. All of these are used to create something new. This process of creation or composition can be both conscious and unconscious. When asking a filmmaker why he used a certain kind of mise-en-scène, he would say, "*Nimeitunga tu!*" (I have just composed it). Banzi has what Lévi-Strauss called the *bricoleur*'s "treasury" (18). In this case, his "treasury" is several plastic bags full of notes, scripts, storyboards, comic sketches, and newspaper articles that serve as inspiration for a new movie. Bricolage is also the governing principle for the mise-en-scène of the monster and its antagonist, the healer. The "heterogeneous objects" (ibid.) and materials employed not only comprise a certain repertoire of objects such as costumes, makeup, and so forth, but also sound, speech, gesture, and production design. During editing, the monsters' supernatural powers are made visible and audible using special effects from Nigerian and Hollywood movies. These effects allow the monsters to vanish, to walk through walls, or to use lightning weapons to destroy their opponents. In his description of Ghanaian and Nigerian horror movies, Tobias Wendl compares this process to musical "sampling," which results in "a highly original, hybrid cocktail; and in this respect the current video production can aptly be conceived as a 'local address' for reconfiguring and rearticulating the global flow of images for new local audiences" (266).

THE ELEMENTS OF HORROR BRICOLAGE

One of the most important elements for video filmmakers is myth, which Lévi-Strauss referred to as an "intellectual bricolage" (17). No other film genre draws so heavily on myths as horror films do, and at the same time horror writers or filmmakers are often described as creators of myths. However, unlike their Western counterparts, the Tanzanian filmmakers use both global and local myths from their respective ethnic groups. As in Ghana and Nigeria, the horror filmmakers draw heavily on myths and folklore, as reflected in the story line (see also Wendl 275). In the Tanzanian case, this applies to the myth and folklore of the Zaramo people on the coast near Dar es Salaam, the Nyakyusa from the South, and the Waluguru from the Morogoro region. Incidentally, many horror filmmakers belong to the Zaramo ethnic group. Just like the Ewe area in Ghana (ibid.), the towns of Sumbawanga and Mbeya in Tanzania are notorious for witchcraft. A very important figure in this context is the *mganga,* traditional healer, who appears in 90 percent of all movies and makes use of local Tanzanian languages in ritual performances.

By using ethnic folklore, the filmmakers achieve what can be called a "Tanzanization" of horror, similar to what Jigal Beez describes in terms of Swahili comics with the genre of *katuni za miujuza,* or "miracle comics" (153). Like the Tanzanian miracle comic designers, the moviemakers draw on a cultural repertoire of fear to frighten or shock their audiences.

The first global flows of horror film to be circulated in Tanzania were the movies shown in local cinemas and from the 1980s onward circulated as VHS copies. At the turn of the century, Nigerian movies entered the country and were embraced for their Africanness. Among them were Nollywood classics such as *Living in Bondage, Suicide Mission,* and *Karishika.* They exemplified what an African horror film could look like and had a great influence on early filmmakers' productions. Elements of Nollywood horror, like narrative threats and characters such as the mganga and the witch, were adopted because they were well known in Tanzania.

Today movies from Nollywood, Hollywood, and elsewhere are sold in the markets as pirated copies from China in so-called collections. Such collections may contain up to thirty movies in one DVD, and they are divided into genre, topic, and actor collections. This also applies to horror movies, and there are many "horror collections." These are subdivided into all kinds of genres or subtopics of horror. They have titles such as: *Terrorist Dismembered Killing, Vampire Zombie Brutal War, Hollywood Vampire Zombie, Vampire and Corpse,* or *Terrorist Ghost Killing,* to name but a few.

Nigerian movies are available in so-called *Nigerian Box Office* or *Africa Movie* collections, and their horror classics are labeled *The Hottest and Most Wanted.* These collections are very popular with Tanzanians in general, but with directors and editors in particular. When I visited filmmakers at home or in the editing studios, these collections were often watched and the subject of heated debate. Obviously, movies from such collections create a wealth of ideas and serve as a means of comparison for their own work. Furthermore, these collections function as a frame of reference and perception to create genres and concepts.

These aesthetic elements that the Tanzanian video film bricoleur uses in his artistic work, what he selects and excludes, will be analyzed in the following examples. To identify their "Tanzanianness," I want to point to the stylistic parallels and differences to horror films from Hollywood and Nollywood.

VAMPIRIC MONSTERS

Mussa Banzi started shooting his first movie, *Nsyuka,* with his favorite actors from the Tamba Arts Group and a Rasta musician from Mwanza in the role of the monster. The idea for the movie came from his friend Askofu, who told him about the ancestral mythology of his ethnic group, the Wanyakyusa. They live in southern Tanzania's Mbeya Region and in northern Malawi on the shores of Lake Nyasa. They believe that the dead enter the underworld (*ubusyuka*) through a banana tree trunk and live there as *abasyuka.* From the recordings of Joseph Busse, a German missionary who worked with the Wanyakyusa in the 1930s, the abasyuka are described as either having kept their appearance at the time of their death or having received "a wonderful body" and white skin (11). Sometimes during the night, the abasyuka come up to the surface and gather at graves, near fires. If their descendants stop praying for them, the abasyuka can change into snakes, frogs, or insects, and if the Wanyakyusa misbehave, the abasyuka get angry and punish them (8, 9), as the movie shows.

Following stylistic currents of Western horror movies, in the opening sequence of *Nsyuka* the camera takes the viewer through a nighttime cemetery to the sound track of Hollywood's psycho-slasher classic *Friday the 13th*. After one cut, we get a first glimpse of the monster Nsyuka, who is digging his way out of a grave. When he finally emerges, the camera follows his feet as he walks slowly through the cemetery. The story begins with the heroine, Dorin, who has a nightmare about Nsyuka entering her house and killing her housemaid and dog. When she wakes up, she finds that it was only a nightmare, but it leaves her restless, as she still hasn't managed to have a child with her fiancé, Sanjo. One of Dorin's friends advises her to visit a mganga, who tells her that while her mother was pregnant with her, she went to collect water and made the mistake of taking a forbidden trail near Nsyuka's homestead. The only way to break this spell is to have intercourse with the mganga while possessed by Nsyuka. Then Dorin decides to visit a female mganga, who manages to bring Nsyuka into her fiancé's body. Dorin finally gets pregnant, marries, and gives birth to her baby. However, the doctor in the hospital removes a guiding charm, given to her by the mganga, and her baby soon shows all the signs of a monster's son. Throughout the movie, Nysuka appears to Dorin with raised arms and laughing loudly before he disappears through the wall.

As Lévi-Strauss has already pointed out, the elements that the bricoleur collects and uses are like units of "preconstrained" myths, and their combination is restricted by the fact that they are drawn from the language in which they already possess a meaning, which sets a limit to their freedom of maneuver (19). "*Nimeongeza*" (I have added some things), said Banzi when talking about the outward appearance of Nsyuka. As opposed to the standard description of the abasyuka, Nsyuka instead has long dreadlocks, a dirty gown, and long teeth and nails. Nsyuka is portrayed as bloodthirsty, with plastic vampire teeth, and long nails, allowing us to draw parallels with other vampire figures in film history. The lead actor, Bob Kijiti, refers to *Nsyuka* as Tanzania's first Dracula movie, which brings us to an important element of horror movies: the vampire, with Dracula as the most depicted figure in films around the globe (Vossen 61). Created by Bram Stoker in his Victorian Gothic novel, *Dracula* was first adapted in 1922 in Germany with the horror film classic *Nosferatu – Symphony of Horror –* by Friedrich Wilhelm Murnau, who thus established the subgenre of vampire film (Vossen 40–49). Could Nsyuka be one of the descendants of Graf Orlok in *Nosferatu*?[7] However, unlike classical vampires who appear as tall noblemen in elegant dress, Nsyuka is the opposite. Nsyuka's behavior also represents the bricolagian artwork. Despite his thirst for blood, raised arms, and diabolic laughter, neither is he out for romantic love like Dracula, nor does he behave like a typical abasyuka. As with other figures of Tanzanian mythology, whose behavior is rather ambivalent, the abasyuka are said to keep their human behavior. Nsyuka, influenced by the Hollywood horror genre, turned into an evil monster for the purposes of the movie and frightens, punishes, and kills its victims (see also Krings, "Video-Vampire").

In 2004, Mussa Banzi separated from Dr. Tamba and the Tamba Arts Group because of disputes over financing during the production of *Nsyuka*. He took half of the actors with him and founded his own group called White Elephant. In *Shumileta,* his first movie with this new group, Banzi used the vampiric element again at the beginning of the film, this time, however, a vampiress. Like the Nigerian *Karishika* from 1998 (see also Krings, this volume), *Shumileta* is the story of a female spirit. Whereas Karishika is sent to earth by Lucifer to recruit sinners for his kingdom, Shumileta is sent to earth by her parents from an underwater world, looking for her husband-to-be.

While roaming the streets at night, she gets to know Mack, a young man who gives her a ride home. Mack's fiancée, Monte, gets jealous. Together with Mack, she traces her origins and finds out that she died many years earlier. By that point Shumileta has begun pursuing Mack as a future husband. When Monte asks a mganga for help, Shumileta turns her into a chicken, kidnaps Mack, and flies with him to the underwater world, where she lives with her parents – the king and queen – and her sister.

At the beginning of the film, the viewer sees an object flying toward the earth, and in the next scene a white goat on the beach is turned into Shumileta – dressed as a bride, complete with a white wedding dress.

Offstage, we hear a sinister voice saying, "Nenda katafute mchumba un-ayotaka!" (Now go and look for the fiancé you want). As the bride gazes at the sky, blue lightning comes out of her eyes to illustrate her lunar connection. In the following scene, we see her walking along Tunisia Road in Dar es Salaam, a place notorious for prostitutes. As in *Nsyuka,* the next setting is a cemetery, to which she leads her first victim. The viewer then witnesses a dispute about money and safe sex, which finally results in the man's death when he is bitten by the vampiress for refusing to use a condom. Like many vampire narratives, whose stories are linked to the fear of epidemic plagues, as in *Nosferatu*'s pest (Vossen 45–46), Banzi wanted to educate his viewers about the dangers of HIV/AIDS. The final "kiss of death" is presented in a very long, slow sequence, in which she bites him in the neck with blue lightning in her eyes. This type of violence is not usually attributed to local amorous spirits, who alleg-edly force their victims to love them. But they do not kill or bite them to death. Like Nsyuka, Shumileta has turned into an evil monster, raising her arms and laughing diabolically after a torturing and killing spree.

The fact that Shumileta is a woman puts this story in the long but for-gotten tradition of female vampire tales. "We added a little bit teeth and fingernails," said Banzi about the creation of Shumileta, and continued: "Since we don't know what the ghosts or their bodies look like, we added a little bit, so what we did, we created something which could be enjoyable for the viewers, but we are not sure if ghosts have long teeth like that." According to Flocke's interpretation, the female vampire can be consid-ered a figure created by men to demonize femininity through her obvious eroticism. Like Shumileta, female vampires symbolize the alliance of femininity and death. As such, she has a subversive potential concerning female identity; she does not fit completely into the model of femininity attributed to women by their respective societies (Flocke 7–8). Read in such a way, *Shumileta* stands for a mediation and negotiation of a chang-ing understanding of gender relations in Tanzanian society.

Vampiric figures such as Nsyuka or Shumileta can also be traced back to older East African tales of vampirism described by Luise White. According to White, vampire myths in East Africa occurred during co-lonialism in the early twentieth century when rumors surfaced of blood-sucking firefighters called *wazimamoto* in Kenya and Tanganyika. In White's collected stories, these firemen allegedly caught their victims in their fire engine and drained their blood ("Cars Out of Place" 31). In colonial Tanganyika, the rumors were about Dar es Salaam's firefighters, who allegedly sucked the blood of innocent African men, making them impotent and lazy. However, as Shumileta is a prostitute and not a fire-woman, the stories about wazimamoto in housing settlements managed by women in Nairobi in the 1920s and 1930s is an interesting connection. As White describes, single women and prostitutes were victims of the wazimamoto. Not only were the prostitutes victims of bloodsucking fire-men, but they were also hired by the wazimamoto to get access to more male victims (*Speaking with Vampires* 151–59).

As James Brennan shows, a more recent discourse on vampirism can be found in the Swahili term *unyonyaji,* or "exploitation," derived from the verb *kunyonya,* which means "to suck(le)." This was used in political discourse during the *Ujamaa* or Tanzanian socialist era. The Marxist picture of the bloodsucking capitalist has been projected onto Indian, Arab, and European but also African businessmen as the main enemies of the socialist project (398). In the context of the video indus-try, directors and actors often used the phrase "Sisi tunanyonywa na Wahindi" (We are exhausted by the Indians), which is the same vampiric metaphor reflecting the division of labor along racial lines, as the Indian producers are always accused of cheating and exploiting the African artists.

Another local myth that echoes the vampire tale is *Popobawa,* "Bat Wing," a name for the shadow of an evil spirit. Stories about Popobawa surfaced initially in 1965 on Pemba Island (Parkin 114). An angry sheikh is said to have conjured up the ghost to take revenge on his neighbors, with whom he was embroiled in a love affair.[8] Some sources claim the man was a Makonde from Mozambique because he had to divorce his estranged Pemban wife (Walsh 7). Popobawa is described as a black, batlike creature with big wings, one eye, pointy ears, and long claws. Like its animal relatives, it is said to live in mango or jackfruit trees. At night, it haunts and sodomizes its victims – usually men, rarely women, children, and dogs. The victims have to report the attack in public to keep Popobawa at bay. Popobawa's link to a vampire-type figure be-comes obvious in various descriptions of it as a shape-shifter. It pos-sesses a human being's body during the day and turns into a batlike creature at night.

15.1. At the shooting of *Popobawa* in the outskirts of Dar es Salaam.

Interpretations of the Popobawa myth range from the incubus legends resulting from sleep paralysis (Walsh 14) to the memory of the horrors of slavery (Parkin 115) and to the memory of political restive and transformative eras, as the first rumors of the myth are said to have appeared the year after Zanzibar's 1964 revolution (Walsh 19). During my fieldwork in 2007 and 2008, I also heard rumors that Popobawa had been coming to Temeke, a suburb of Dar es Salaam, which was the subject of heated debate on radio and in the local newspapers. As Katrina Daly Thompson (13–14) has shown, this occult sex with Popobawa creates an important conversational resource used by young women in Zanzibar to talk about sex.

Walsh makes an interesting point in connecting the myth to cinematic influences by referring to the collection *Zanzibar Ghost Stories*, by
Amir A. Mohammed, in which Popobawa is called Dracula. As Zanzibar
hosted Africa's first color television broadcasting station and was one of
the main centers of cinema business in East Africa, we might think of
Popobawa as a reflection of horror film memories from movies such as
Dracula (Walsh 16), *The Bat*, or *Batman*. Popobawa was the subject of
diverse newspaper and Internet articles and blogs and also became part
of pop cultural products such as novels and video films. In 2007, John P.
Oscar, a young cartoonist from Dar es Salaam, published the "Gothic
novel" *Usiku wa Machungu: Mikononi mwa Popobawa* (Night of bitter-
ness: In the hands of Popobawa).[9] In 2008, Popobawa was first adapted
for the screen by Haji Dilunga.

During the shooting, I asked Haji Dilunga why he chose Popobawa.
He replied that he wanted to make a movie based on a real story (as
the opening credits would later state). The movie was a great success
precisely for this realism, as most of the audience had heard rumors of
Popobawa in their neighborhoods.[10] But Dilunga made several changes
to the actual myth when developing the script. The male sheikh was
turned into the female witch Mamakibibi who calls Popobawa to punish
her relatives. In Tanzanian witchcraft discourses, witches are believed
to be women. Finally, as in a splatter movie, he starts to kill everybody,
including the witch who originally called him into existence. His appearance is humanlike; he has dreadlocks and wears a red gown with a
hood and a plastic horror mask. Dilunga justified the change by stating
that "red is the color of danger." He also decided that Popobawa, as a
shape-shifter, would only wear the mask while killing and would have
a simple appearance when sodomizing his victims. Popobawa's sodomizing character, displayed and articulated in several scenes where the
viewer sees Popobawa raping his victims, shows its connection to discourses on male and female homosexuality (see also Walsh 16–17). We
also see the first depiction of homosexuality in Tanzanian movies when,
during a party scene, we see an older lesbian woman trying to seduce a
much younger girl.

While I was on the set of *Popobawa*, Dilunga asked me to play a
doctor in the movie, a role often given to guest actors from abroad. In
the scene set in a small HIV-testing dispensary, I read the results of a

medical examination to a couple who alleged to be Popobawa's victims. The results show that they have been neither raped nor infected with the HIV virus. During the rehearsal with my fellow thespians, I advised them to consult a psychiatrist, and this was included in the dialogue. On completion, the director decided to add an extra scene in which Popobawa would follow me at night to shatter my rational explanation of the case. This idea led to a scene in a hotel room where Popobawa climbs onto me while I am sleeping. Upon waking up the next morning with the feeling of having been raped, the rational European doctor comes to the conclusion that a being such as Popobawa could actually exist.

TRACES OF NOLLYWOOD

While Tanzanian filmmakers seem to have developed their own stylistic identity, the parallels with Nollywood are nonetheless visible, especially in the horror film genre. African video filmmakers share common visual aesthetics and horrific narratives to shock their audiences. These narratives can be best described by what Larkin calls the "aesthetics of outrage, a narrative based on continual shocks that transgress religious and social norms and are designed to provoke and affront the audience" (184). These shocks are created by Tanzanian filmmakers through the adaptation of different aesthetics of horror from Nigerian horror films.

One example is the scene in which Shumileta kills her second victim, a taxi driver. After biting him to death, she tears out his heart and eats it with zest. This street scene shows strong parallels with *Karishika*. Like her Tanzanian counterpart, she bites a taxi driver to death after emerging from a grave. In contrast to the Nigerian version, its slow pace and the obvious physical horror characterize the Tanzanian scene. Another difference between the two video industries is the visualization of religion in horror movies. As most of the Tanzanian horror filmmakers are Muslims, Nollywood narratives are taken out of their dualistic context of Satan versus the Christian God. They are presented neutrally, which means that humans battle ghosts who are considered to be created by God, too. As the filmmakers cannot show Islamic practices, the fight against evil is led not by a Muslim cleric, who would have been the equivalent of the Christian priest in Nollywood films, but often by a traditional healer.

One of the figures that is said to be most often borrowed from Nollywood is the witch doctor with his equivalent, the mganga. While the mganga figure could be found in Swahili literature and theater before the arrival of Nigerian films, it has certainly been influenced by the depiction of Nigerian witch doctors. Similar costumes, colors, and paraphernalia are used to portray the witch doctor, and he has the same narrative function. As in Nollywood films, mganga scenes are often given a comical treatment and thus serve to ridicule such traditional practices.

As a very important narrative element in 90 percent of all Tanzanian movies, the mganga is a fundamental element of horror films. As Wendl points out, the healer, witch doctor, or jujuman can be compared to the mad scientist in Western horror films:

> What, from a structuralist point of view, makes the jujumen resemble the 'mad scientist' (like Victor Frankenstein, Dr. Jekyll or Dr. Moreau) is that both attempt to transgress normality and manipulate the natural reproductive cycle. The jujuman operates in his shrine, the mad scientist in his laboratory. Generally they both overestimate their powers and their creations (or transformative acts) go out of control. In the end, both become tragic figures and are destroyed. This is usually due to fate, (or to "God") who restores the rules of reproduction. A significant difference between the two is that the mad scientist is largely inspired and motivated by his own mad dreams, whereas the jujuman does not act out his own dreams, but those of his clients. (275–76)

While watching *Shumileta*, a friend's mother remembered a neighbor who was haunted by a love spirit and had to consult a mganga to get rid of the unwanted lover. In the movie, Mack's mother-in-law does exactly the same: while Mack lives under water and his fiancée, Monte, is transformed into a chicken by Shumileta, Monte's mother visits Mganga Ndele, a powerful mganga to ask for help. As with the witch doctor in the Nigerian movies, the mganga uses an "African television" called *TV asilia*, "traditional television," to show the mother how her daughter was transformed into a chicken and where her son-in-law can be found. "African television," which Behrend discusses using the case of South African witch hunts in the 1980s, seems to be a pan-African phenomenon whereby new media forms are combined with older divination techniques that would traditionally have projected pictures onto the surface of water (195). In Tanzania, healers used a *kibuyu*, that is, a prepared calabash, a mirror, or a traditional clay pot, in which the client sees his enemies on the water's surface. If the mganga is the equivalent of the mad scientist in Western horror films, the video filmmakers themselves are like "mad scientists" bringing the monsters to life.

Contrary to the Nigerian monsters, Shumileta does not appear in a Christian or Pentecostal context of hell or Satan, nor is there any obvious religious presentation in the movie. But as the quote in the credits of Shumileta shows, ghosts are equally perceived God's creatures: "Mungu ametuumba binadamu na majini ili tumwabudu" (God has created us as humans and spirits to adore him).

From the beginning of the Tanzanian video industry to the present day, *filamu za kutisha* are discussed in relation to Nollywood more than any other genre. But as I have argued in this chapter with the examples of *Nsyuka, Shumileta,* and *Popobawa,* Tanzanian horror movies are quite a complex bricolage of ethnic myth and Hollywood and Nollywood aesthetics. Different sources of global and local horror genre are brought together using the technique of bricolage. In this respect, both Nollywood and Hollywood serve as important sources of reference and ideas. Nollywood styles and aesthetics are used either as a frame or as pieces inserted into the movies. Just as Lévi-Strauss placed the artist somewhere between the bricoleur and the scientist, the African video filmmaker, as an artist, can be viewed as an intellectual bricoleur. The new medium video film enables the filmmakers for the first time to actually visualize narratives about the occult and their main protagonists like ghosts and ancestor spirits. In looking at the construction of these ghosts, I have argued that while these creatures of mythical folklore have been rather ambiguous in their character, neither solely good nor bad, they have turned into evil and bloodthirsty monsters in the movies. This transformation of characters into monstrous shape-shifters is itself the main subject of horror film, as the classic example of Frankenstein shows. But while Tanzanian filmmakers obviously use horrific elements in their movies, these movies do not completely fit into Western genre categories. Not only do they believe in the monsters they have created, but they consider their horrific movies educational.

The cemetery setting in *Shumileta,* for example, which could be classified as a typical element of the Western horror genre, is in fact related to a real-life experience. Banzi said he wanted to show people that prostitutes actually do take their suitors to cemeteries. Apart from the depiction of events viewers consider realistic, the horror film is also used to discuss changes in society and its taboos. This is especially true for gender relations. In *Nsyuka,* the social order is disrupted by Dorin's barrenness, an often articulated theme in Tanzanian movies. In *Shumileta,* a monster threatens to disrupt the relationship between Mack and Monte. But while Monte's mother repeatedly implores her to forget about Mack, Monte stands by him and fights for her love. When Shumileta is banned, the lovers are reunited.

As the comparison of the street scene in *Karishika* and *Shumileta* has shown, Nollywood, which functioned as a role model for Tanzanian artists, has left visible traces. Obviously, Nigerian and Tanzanian horror filmmakers draw on similar figures to frighten their audiences: for example, vampires, mermaids (*mami wata*), or witch doctors. These similarities are articulated by filmmakers such as Mussa Banzi as the common "African culture" of the two countries. In spite of the similarities between these two African video industries, the examples have shown that Tanzanian filmmakers have developed their own type of horror film aesthetics.

NOTES

1. Participant observation during the shooting of *Popobawa,* Buguruni, Dar es Salaam, September 30, 2008.

2. I am using "Indian," *Wahindi,* here as a local category that does not distinguish between Tanzanians of Indian origin and Indian nationals.

3. Some movies have also been produced in Tanga, Arusha, Mbeya, and Kigoma. A small but growing scene can be found in Mwanza, where a number of very popular movies have been produced and distributed by the African distributor B. M. Capital.

4. The price of DVDs and VCDs was reduced from 8,000 Tanzanian shillings (US$5) to 2,500 Tanzanian shillings (US$1.60) to combat the street vendors

(*machinga*), who sell pirated copies for a third of the original price.

5. Mussa Banzi, born as Mussa Iddy Kibwana Bwaduke in 1978 in Dar es Salaam, was working as a cartoonist for several Tanzanian newspapers. When he left Bagamoyo High School, he joined the Kaole Sanaa Group, where he became a cameraman and director for television serials on ITV (Independent Television).

6. Splatter: subgenre that is defined by tearing and chopping bodies into pieces (like a butcher or cannibal). The perpetrators are serial killers, normally reduced to their weapon and a mask (Seeßlen and Jung 800). The body-count principle is based on the idea of counting rhymes, like (the very racist) "ten little niggers" or "ten

little Indians," as well as on older traditions of macabre folktales. In the modern
horror film, post-1974, it refers to the killings during the war in Vietnam (personal
communication with Marcus Stiglegger,
February 2, 2009).

7. I would like to thank Julian Schro-
eder for helping me to compare the characters of both films.

8. He is also known under the Arabic
name *Imram* (father of Mary in the Quran)
and is categorized as a *shetani* or *jini*, "spirit."

9. The cover of the book is a col-
lage of *Star Wars'* Master Yoda with bat
wings, one yellow cat eye, vampire teeth,
and claws. He is flying beside a beautiful
Afro-American model with an American
skyline in the background. On the back
cover, several Yoda-Popobawas are flying with a dragon in front of a medieval
castle.

10. Personal communication with
Bashir Rajabu, owner of a video library in
Magomeni, Dar es Salaam.

WORKS CITED

Badley, Linda. *Film, Horror, and the Body
    Fantastic.* Westport, Conn.: Greenwood
    Press, 1995.
Banzi, Mussa. Personal interview. Dar es
    Salaam, September 26, 2006.
Beez, Jigal. "Großstadtfieber und Hexen-
    meister. Horror- und Fantasycomics aus
    Tansania." *Africa Screams. Das Böse in
    Kino, Kunst und Kult.* Ed. Tobias Wendl.
    Wuppertal: Peter Hammer Verlag,
    2004. 153–63.
Behrend, Heike. "'Call and Kill.' Zur Ver-
    zauberung und Entzauberung westli-
    cher technischer Medien in Afrika." *Sig-
    nale der Störung.* Ed. Erhard Schüttpelz
    and Albert Kümmel. Munich: Wilhelm
    Fink Verlag, 2003. 287–300.
Brennan, James. "Blood Enemies: Exploi-
    tation and Urban Citizenship in the Na-
    tionalist Political Thought of Tanzania,
    1958–75." *Journal of African History* 47
    (2006): 389–413.
Busse, Joseph. *Die Nyakyusa. Religion und
    Magie.* Bonn: Holos-Verlag, 1998.
Flocke, Petra. *Vampirinnen: "Ich schaue in
    den Spiegel und sehe nichts." Die kulturel-
    len Inszenierungen der Vampirin.* Tübin-
    gen: Konkursbuchverlag, 1999.
Krings, Matthias. "Afrikanische Video-
    Vampire – Wiedergänger zwischen den
    Kulturen." *All about Evil. Das Böse.* Ed.

Silke Seybold. Mainz: Verlag Phillip
    von Zabern, 2007. 120–27.
———. "Nollywood Goes East: The Lo-
    calization of Nigerian Video Films in
    Tanzania." *Viewing African Cinema in
    the Twenty-First Century: Art Films
    and the "Nollywood" Video Revolution.*
    Ed. Ralph Austen and Mahir Şaul.
    Athens: Ohio University Press, 2010.
    74–91.
Larkin, Brian. *Signal and Noise: Media,
    Infrastructure, and Urban Culture in Ni-
    geria.* Durham, N.C.: Duke University
    Press, 2008.
Lévi-Strauss, Claude. *The Savage Mind.*
    Chicago: University of Chicago Press,
    1966.
Mohammed, Amir A. *Zanzibar Ghost-
    Stories.* Zanzibar: Good Luck Publish-
    ers, 2000.
Parkin, David. "In the Nature of the Hu-
    man Landscape: Provenances in the
    Making of Zanzibar Politics." *Figured
    Worlds: Ontological Obstacles in Inter-
    cultural Relations.* Ed. John Clammer,
    Sylvie Poirier, and Eric Schwimmer.
    Toronto: University of Toronto Press,
    2004. 113–31.
Seeßlen, Georg, and Fernand Jung. *Hor-
    ror: Geschichte und Mythologie des Hor-
    rorfilms.* Marburg: Schüren, 2006.

Thompson, Katrina Daly. "Zanzibari Women's Discursive and Sexual Agency: Violating Gendered Speech Prohibitions through Talk about Supernatural Sex. " *Discourse & Society* 22 (2011): 3–20.

Vossen, Ursula. *Filmgenres: Horrorfilm.* Stuttgart: Reclam, 2004.

Walsh, Martin T. "Diabolical Delusions and Hysterical Narratives in a Postmodern State." Paper presented at the Department of Social Anthropology, University of Cambridge, 2005.

Wendl, Tobias. "Wicked Villagers and the Mysteries of Reproduction: An Exploration of Horror Movies from Ghana and Nigeria." *African Media Cultures.* Ed. Frank Wittmann and Rosemarie Beck. Cologne: Köppe, 2004. 263–85.

White, Luise. "Cars Out of Place: Vampires, Technology, and Labor in East and Central Africa." *Representations* 43 (1993): 27–50.

———. *Speaking with Vampires: Rumor and History in Colonial Africa.* Berkeley and Los Angeles: University of California Press, 2000.

Wood, Robin. *Hollywood from Vietnam to Reagan.* New York: Columbia University Press, 1986.

FILMOGRAPHY

The Bat. Dir. Crane Wilbur. Liberty Pictures (United States). 1959.

Batman. Dir. Tim Burton. Warner Bros. Entertainment et al. (United States and UK). 1989.

Dar 2 Lagos – 4 Re-union. Dir. Femi Ogedegbe. Game 1st Quality (Tanzania). 2006.

Dracula. Dir. Terence Fisher. Hammer Productions (UK). 1958.

Friday the 13th. Dir. Sean S. Cunningham. Paramount Pictures et al. (United States). 1980.

Girlfriend – Filamu ya maisha na muziki. Dir. George Tyson. LeteMambo Productions and GMC (Tanzania). 2003.

Karishika. Dir. Chika Onu. Tony Jickson (Nigeria). 1998.

Living in Bondage. Dir. Chris Obi Rapu. NEK Video Links (Nigeria). 1992.

Nosferatu – Eine Symphonie des Grauens. Dir. Friedrich Wilhem Murnau. Prana Film (Germany). 1922.

Nsyuka. Dir. Mussa Banzi. Wananchi Video Production (Tanzania). 2003.

Nsyuka, II. Dir. Mussa Banzi. Wananchi Video Production (Tanzania). 2005.

Popobawa. Dir. Haji Dilunga. Wananchi Wote (Tanzania). 2009.

Shumileta – The Queen of Devil. Dir. Mussa Banzi. Wananchi Video Production (Tanzania). 2005.

Shumileta – The Queen of Devil, II. Dir. Mussa Banzi. Wananchi Video Production (Tanzania). 2006.

Suicide Mission. Dir. Fred Amata. Great Movies (Nigeria). 1998.

Contributors

Abdalla Uba Adamu is Professor of Science Education as well as Media and Cultural Communication at Bayero University, Kano, Nigeria. His most recent publications include "Transnational Flows and Local Identities in Muslim Northern Nigerian Films: From Dead Poets Society through Mohabbatein to So . . ." (2010) and "The Muse's Journey: Transcultural Translators and Domestication of Transnational Music in Hausa Popular Culture" (2010). His current research focus includes Muslim Hausa urban youth tribes and Hausa online youth cultures. He was a European Union Visiting Professor for the project "The Modern University" at the University of Warsaw, Poland, in 2012, where he taught courses on transnational popular cultures.

Babson Ajibade is Reader and Dean, Faculty of Environmental Sciences, Cross River University of Technology, Calabar, Nigeria. He specializes in African visual culture in the Department of Visual Arts and Technology. He is editor of *Global Journal of Humanities*. His research articles have been published in academic journals, including *Journal of Media and Communication; Asian Journal of Information Technology; Mediterranean Journal of Social Sciences; Postcolonial Text; Review of Education, Pedagogy, and Cultural Studies;* and *Visual Studies.*

Heike Becker is Professor of Anthropology at the University of the Western Cape, where she lectures on social identity, popular culture, visual culture, multiculturalism, and anthropological theory. She currently conducts research on cultural performance, belonging, and citizenship in contemporary South Africa. Her earlier work on gender, culture, politics, and memory in Namibia has appeared in *Namibian Women's Movement, 1980 to 1992: From Anti-colonial Resistance to Reconstruction* (1995) and in numerous journal articles and book chapters.

Claudia Böhme is Lecturer in the Department of African Studies at the University of Leipzig. Her research interests include media and popular culture in Africa. She has received her Ph.D. in anthropology from the University of Mainz. Her doctoral thesis is an ethnography of video film production in Dar es Salaam. She has acted in several Tanzanian video films and TV series. Her work will appear in forthcoming chapters in the edited volumes *Trance Media and New Media* (Fordham University Press) and *Listening to Africa: Anglophone Literatures and Cultures* (Winter).

Jane Bryce is Professor of African Literature and Cinema at the University of the West Indies, Cave Hill. Born and brought up in Tanzania, she was educated there, in the UK, and in Nigeria. She publishes in the areas of contemporary African and Caribbean fiction, film and visual culture, popular fiction, life writing and memoir, women's writing, journalism, and her own creative writing. She initiated and ran the Barbados Festival of African and Caribbean Film (2002–2004) and is now co-curator of the annual Africa World Documentary Film Festival at Cave Hill.

Jordache A. Ellapen has graduate degrees from both Wits University and New York University. He is currently a Ph.D. candidate at Indiana University's Department of American Studies. His research interests include South African and African cinemas, diaspora studies, and visual culture. In 2011 *cane/cain,* his first short film, which explores the intersections of migration, desire, and sexuality, premiered at the Durban International Film Festival.

Jonathan Haynes is Professor of English at the Brooklyn Campus of Long Island University. He is the coauthor, with Onookome Okome, of *Cinema and Social Change in West Africa* (1995) and edited *Nigerian Video Films* (1997, 2000) and a special Nollywood issue of *Journal of African Cinemas* (2012). His articles on Nigerian and Ghanaian videos have appeared in a number of edited volumes and journals, including *Research in African Literatures, Africa, African Affairs, Africa Today, Film International,*

Journal of African Cultural Studies, and *Situations.* In 2011 he received a Guggenheim Fellowship and, in 2012, a Lifetime Achievement Award from the Nigerian Film Corporation.

Claudia Hoffmann is Assistant Professor of English at the University of Toronto–Scarborough. Her publications engage with diasporic Nollywood filmmaking in the United States and questions of identity, transnational discourse, and the significance of the cinematic city. She is currently working on a book-length study on the cinematic representation of clandestine migration in international cinema.

Alessandro Jedlowski is Lecturer in African History and Popular Culture at the University of Rome "La Sapienza" and holds a Ph.D. in African studies at the University of Naples (L'Orientale). He previously studied at the University of Paris VIII–St. Denis and at the School of Oriental and African Studies in London. His main publications include the book *Teatro, violenza e resistenza in Congo Brazzaville. Il percorso di Dieudonné Niangouna* (2007) and the essays "Small Screen Cinema: Informality and Remediation in Nollywood" (2012) and "Nigerian Videos in the Global Arena: The Postcolonial Exotic Revisited" (2012).

Matthias Krings is Professor of Anthropology and African Popular Culture at Johannes Gutenberg University in Mainz, Germany. He has specialized in the study of popular culture in Africa, particularly Nigeria and Tanzania; the anthropology of migration and diaspora; and the anthropology of religion. His most recent articles include "A Prequel to Nollywood: South African Photo Novels and Their Pan-African Consumption in the Late 1960s" (2010) and "Nollywood Goes East: The Localization of Nigerian Video Films in Tanzania" (2010). He is currently working on a book titled *Contact and Copy: Mediations of Cultural Difference in Africa.*

Jyoti Mistry is a filmmaker and Associate Professor at the University of the Witwatersrand–Johannesburg in the Wits School of Arts. She has taught at New York University, the University of Vienna, and Arcada University of Applied Science Polytechnic in Helsinki. Her research areas include cultural policy, questions of identity, visual culture practices, and representations of multiculturalism. Mistry's publications include numerous book chapters and journal articles on a range of issues dealing with cinema and contemporary South Africa art practice. Her critically acclaimed films have been screened at numerous festivals internationally.

Onookome Okome is Professor of African Literature and Film Studies at the University of Alberta, in Edmonton, Canada. His academic publications include the coauthored book *Cinema and Social Change in Nigeria* (with Jonathan Haynes) and the edited volumes *Before I Am Hanged: Ken Saro-Wiwa, Literature, Politics, and Dissent* (2000), *Ogun's Children: The Literature and Politics of Wole Soyinka since the Nobel Prize* (2004), and *Writing the Homeland: The Poetry and Politics of Tanure Ojaide* (2002). He has published numerous essays on the video film phenomenon in West Africa. He is currently an Alexander von Humboldt Fellow.

Katrien Pype is Postdoctoral Researcher (Marie Curie IOF) at the Massachusetts Institute of Technology (United States) and Katholieke Universiteit Leuven (Belgium). She is an anthropologist, studying media and popular culture in Kinshasa. Her previous projects dealt with TV fiction, religion, and evangelization and with memory, TV journalism, and politics. Currently, she examines the intersections of information and communication technologies, old age, and social and religious life worlds in Kinshasa. An ethnography on the production of Kinshasa's evangelizing TV serials, *The Making of the Pentecostal Melodrama: Religion, Media, and Gender in Kinshasa,* was published in 2012. Articles have appeared in *Africa, Journal of Southern African Studies, Journal of Modern African Studies, Journal of African Media Studies, Visual Anthropology,* and *Journal of Religion in Africa.*

Sophie Samyn studied media and theater studies at the University of Ghent, Belgium. During her studies she specialized in African cinema, in particular the Nigerian video film industry. She completed her master's degree with the thesis "Nollywood Made in Europe: An Exploratory Study on Transnational Aesthetics." For this thesis she collaborated with Nigerian filmmakers in Europe.

Giovanna Santanera studied cultural anthropology at the University of Turin (Università degli Studi di Torino), where she submitted her master's thesis titled "Nollywood in Turin: A Research Project among Nigerian Immigrants." She is an anthropology Ph.D. student at the University of Milan (Università degli Studi di Milano–Bicocca) and at the School for Advanced Studies in the Social Sciences (École des Hautes Études en Sciences Social), in Paris. She is currently conducting research on urban cinema practices in Douala, Cameroon. Her research interests include migration, visual culture, and popular culture in Nigeria and Cameroon.

Paul Ugor is currently a Newton Postdoctoral Fellow at the Centre for West African Studies, University of Birmingham, UK. He locates his work at the intersection of three fields of study: postcolonialism, cultural studies, and the sociology of youth. His current research examines the identity politics of youth in three cities in Nigeria, especially as a response to difficult social, economic, and political conditions in their everyday lives. Ugor is also working on a book manuscript titled "Nollywood: African Popular Culture and New Narratives of Marginalized Youth."

General Index

182; piracy and, 31–34, 40; urban settings and, 131
transportability, 47, 58, 65–67
travel narratives, 141
Treasure Islands (Shaxon), 238
Trinidad, 224, 231, 239, 242n3
Turin, city of, 245–47, 248–52; absurd lives
of immigrants in, 252–55; Nollywood
video films watched in, 247–48; Pen-
tecostalistic videos in, 248–52; settled
immigrants in, 255–60; video stores in,
247–48, 249. *See also* Italy, diasporic
Nigerians in
TV Zion (Togolese station), 8

Uganda, 1, 3, 32, 189, 309
Ukadike, Frank N., 18
Ukpabio, Pastor Helen, 15, 278
Unachukwu, Dolly, 160, 167
underdevelopment, 9
unemployment, 81, 86, 253–54
United African Artists Incorporated, 130
United Arab Emirates, 32
United Kingdom. *See* Britain
United States, 26, 30, 81, 280; African im-
migrants in, 2; African video distribu-
tion based in, 34–35; Caribbean migra-
tion to, 232; Congolese migrants to,
209; diasporic audience in, 32; Nigerian
films shot in, 75–76, 121–23
University of the West Indies (UWI), 224,
225, 226, 233
Usiku wa Machungu (Oscar), 340, 345n9
Utietiang, Bekeh, 13, 145

Van Dijk, Rijk A., 207
VCDS (video compact discs), 26, 42n5,
219n5; in Italy, 248, 260n5; in Kinshasa,
202; live commentaries for, 278; number
of copies and, 28–29; in Tanzania, 329
Vee's Video (chain store), 188
VHS (Video Home System), 26, 306; illegal copies of American/Western films,
205; switch to VCD and DVD, 28, 329;
with voice-over translations, 307–308
Video Censors Board of Nigeria. *See* Censors Board

video film, 1, 11, 12, 96; "city video films,"
125, 127; epic video film, 139; history of,
265, 282n2; map of experience and, 259;
poor technical quality of, 277, 282n9;
religious ("hallelujah films"), 139, 156n1,
313; rentals of, 188, 265–66; sales figures
for, 269; street vendors of, 188, 202, 206,
219n6; success of, 65
video jockeys, 309
video narration, in Tanzania, 306–307,
322–24; as distraction, 319–22; history
of, 307–11; orality and spectatorship in
relation to, 311–13; as repair, 313–19
video parlors, 19, 266, 282n3, 310–11; "cassette cinema" in, 312; as cheap alternative to movie theaters, 311; in East Africa, 309; infrastructure of, 322–23
video stores, 264, 265
Video Zone, 188
village life, 5, 6, 183–84
villains, depiction of, 16–17
Virgo Foundation, 43n10
voice-over narration, 7, 8, 20n5, 82, 135; as
uncommon feature in Nollywood films,
153; warning of dangers abroad, 95. *See
also* video narration, in Tanzania
Vollywood, 55, 56, 68n5
voodoo (Vodun), 231, 233, 239, 241, 249
VOX Africa (satellite TV station), 267

Wananchi Video Production, 328, 330
Wanyakyusa people, 334–35
Waxman, Sharon, 292
wazimamoto (blood-sucking firefighters),
337–38
Wendl, Tobias, 332–33, 342
Werrason, 219n6
Western world, 5, 301; Africans in beliefs
of, 13; beauty standards of, 4; cultural
domination by, 184; Westernization,
191–93, 194
White, Luise, 337–38
White Elephant, 336
whiteness, 145, 157n6
Wilberforce, William, 272, 282n5
Willemen, Paul, 49, 66
Williams, Ben, 270

Film Title Index

Page numbers in *italics* represent
illustrations.

Above the Law (1988), 309
Akpegi Boyz (2009), 260n6
Almara (2000), 300
Amazing Grace (2006), 269, 271, 272
Amazing Grace, The (2006), 19, 37–38, 269,
    271
Amazing World (2010), 102
Anchor Baby (2010), 39
Aristotle's Plot (1996), 15
Auduga (2004), 288, 291, 293, 294–96, 297,
    298, 300, 301

Baara (1978), 50
Back to Africa (1997), 34, 78
Bat, The (1959), 340
Batman (1989), 340
Battle of Musanga, The (1996), 9, 139–40
Black Gold (2011), 38
Black Hawk Down (2001), 226
Blackjack (1998), 289
Black Night in South America (2007), 78, 81,
    83, 88, 89, 95
Blinded Devil (2010), 261n6
Blood Billionaires (2006), 253
Blood Diamond (2006), 96n6, 226
Blood Money (1997), 254, 261n10
Blood on the Altar (2006), 241
Blood Sisters (2004), 235–36
Bold and the Beautiful, The (TV serial,
    1987–), 185, 232

Boys from Holland (2006), 75, 78, 81
Boyz n the Hood (1991), 189
Broken Pitcher, The (2008), 78, 81, 87, 89, 95
Broken Promises (2004), 51, 55, 56–57
Broken Promises, 2 (2007), 55, 56, 59
Bursting Out (2010), 36

Camp de Thiaroye (1987), 50
Cartas de Alou, Las (1990), 137n2
Champion Sportsman, The (2010), 103, 106,
    108, 110; audience for, 112; financing of,
    111; self-reflexivity in, 116–17, 118; tech-
    nological complexity of, 114; telephone
    conversations in, 115, *116*
Chitty Chitty Bang Bang (1968), 271
Close Enemies (2009), 74, 76, 276
Columbia Connection (2004), 77
Coming to South Africa (2004), 78, 82, 88, 89
Coming to South Africa, 2 (2005), 78
Crazy Like a Fox (2008), 77, 78, 81, 84, 89
Crossing Paths (2008), 78, 81, 84, 85, 87

Dan Adam Butulu (2001), 300
Dangerous Twins (2003), 9, 77, 80, 97n7;
    Auduga as remake of, 288, 293, 294–96,
    297, 300–301; betrayal-by-intimates
    theme, 89; Nigerian national character
    in, 93–94; online review of, 291; success
    of, 73; themes in, 78
Dapo Junior (2000), 78, 101, 102, 104;
    betrayal-by-intimates theme, 89, 90;
    Dutch subtitles in, 109; financing of,
    111; secondary plot in, 107